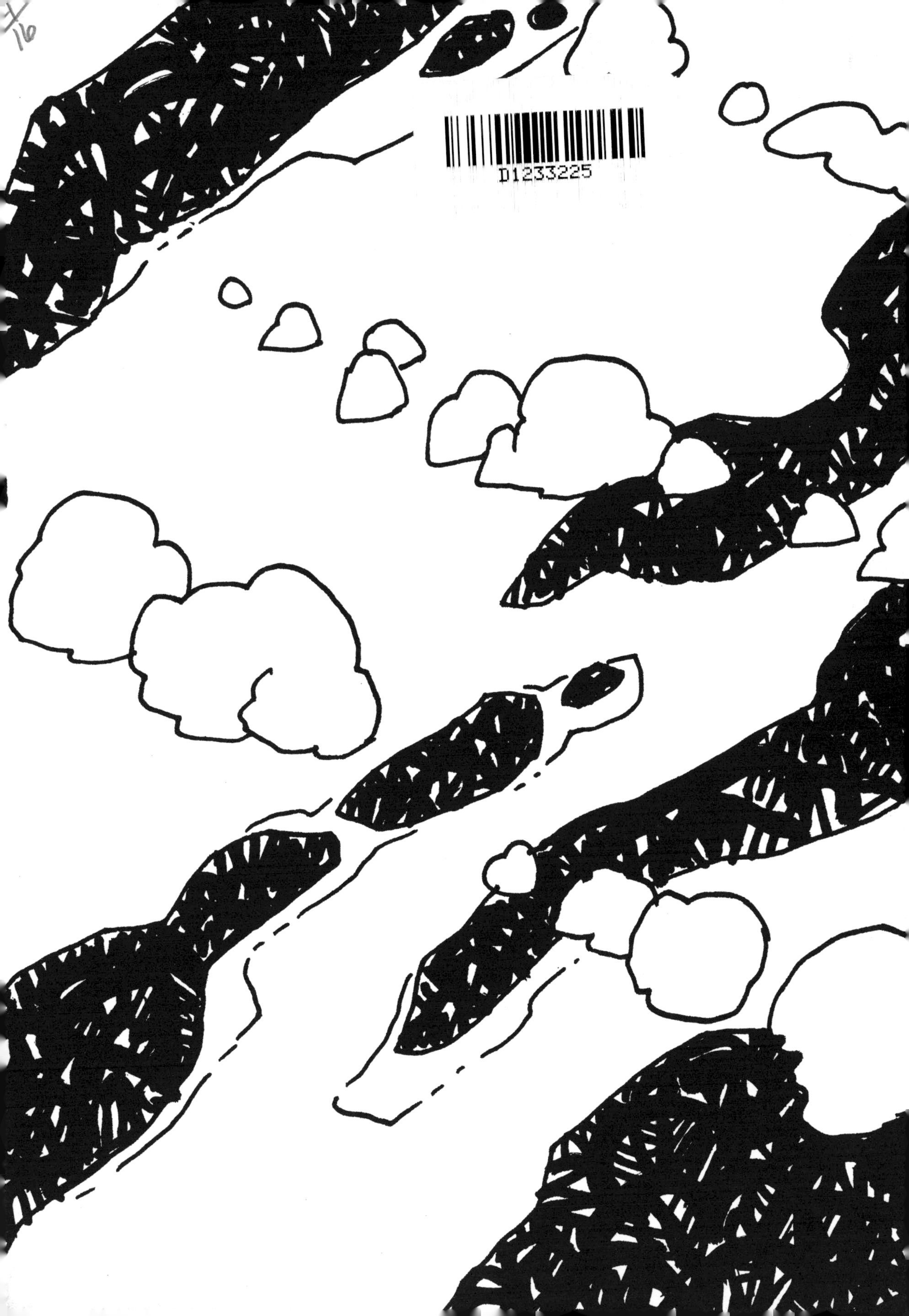

TWO BROTHERS

DARK HORSE BOOKS

President & Publisher MIKE RICHARDSON

Editor SIERRA HAHN

Assistant Editor SPENCER CUSHING

Collection Designers GABRIEL BÁ and AMY ARENDTS

Digital Art Technician ALLYSON HALLER

NEIL HANKERSON Executive Vice President • TOM WEDDLE Chief Financial Officer • RANDY STRADLEY Vice President of Publishing • MICHAEL MARTENS Vice President of Book Trade Sales • SCOTT ALLIE Editor in Chief • MATT PARKINSON Vice President of Marketing • DAVID SCROGGY Vice President of Product Development • DALE LAFOUNTAIN Vice President of Information Technology • DARLENE VOGEL Senior Director of Print, Design, and Production • KEN LIZZI General Counsel • DAVEY ESTRADA Editorial Director • CHRIS WARNER Senior Books Editor • CARY GRAZZINI Director of Print and Development • LIA RIBACCHI Art Director • CARA NIECE Director of Scheduling • MARK BERNARDI Director of Digital Publishing

PUBLISHED BY DARK HORSE BOOKS
A DIVISION OF DARK HORSE COMICS, INC.
10956 SE MAIN STREET
MILWAUKIE, OR 97222

FIRST EDITION: OCTOBER 2015
ISBN 978-1-61655-856-7

10 9 8 7 6 5 4 3 2 1
PRINTED IN CHINA

INTERNATIONAL LICENSING: (503) 905-2377
COMIC SHOP LOCATOR SERVICE: (888) 266-4226

LIBRARY OF CONGRESS CATALOGING-IN-PUBLICATION DATA

MOON, FÁBIO.
    [DOIS IRMÃOS. ENGLISH]
TWO BROTHERS / FÁBIO MOON, GABRIEL BÁ. -- FIRST EDITION.
       PAGES CM
 SUMMARY: "TRANSLATED FROM ITS BRAZILIAN EDITION TWO BROTHERS IS A GRAPHIC NOVEL ADAPTATION OF MILTON HATOUM'S THE BROTHERS. COMICS SUPERSTARS GABRIEL BÁ AND FÁBIO MOON BRING THE BRILLIANT NOVEL TO A WHOLE NEW MEDIUM"-- PROVIDED BY PUBLISHER.
 ISBN 978-1-61655-856-7 (HARDBACK)
1. BROTHERS--COMIC BOOKS, STRIPS, ETC. 2. FAMILY SECRETS--COMIC BOOKS, STRIPS, ETC. 3. BRAZIL--COMIC BOOKS, STRIPS, ETC.
4. GRAPHIC NOVELS. I. BÁ, GABRIEL. II. HATOUM, MILTON, 1952- III. TITLE.

 PN6790.B73M6813 2015
 741.5'981--DC23
                              2015018060

Based on the work of Milton Hatoum

TWO BROTHERS

Fábio Moon
Gabriel Bá

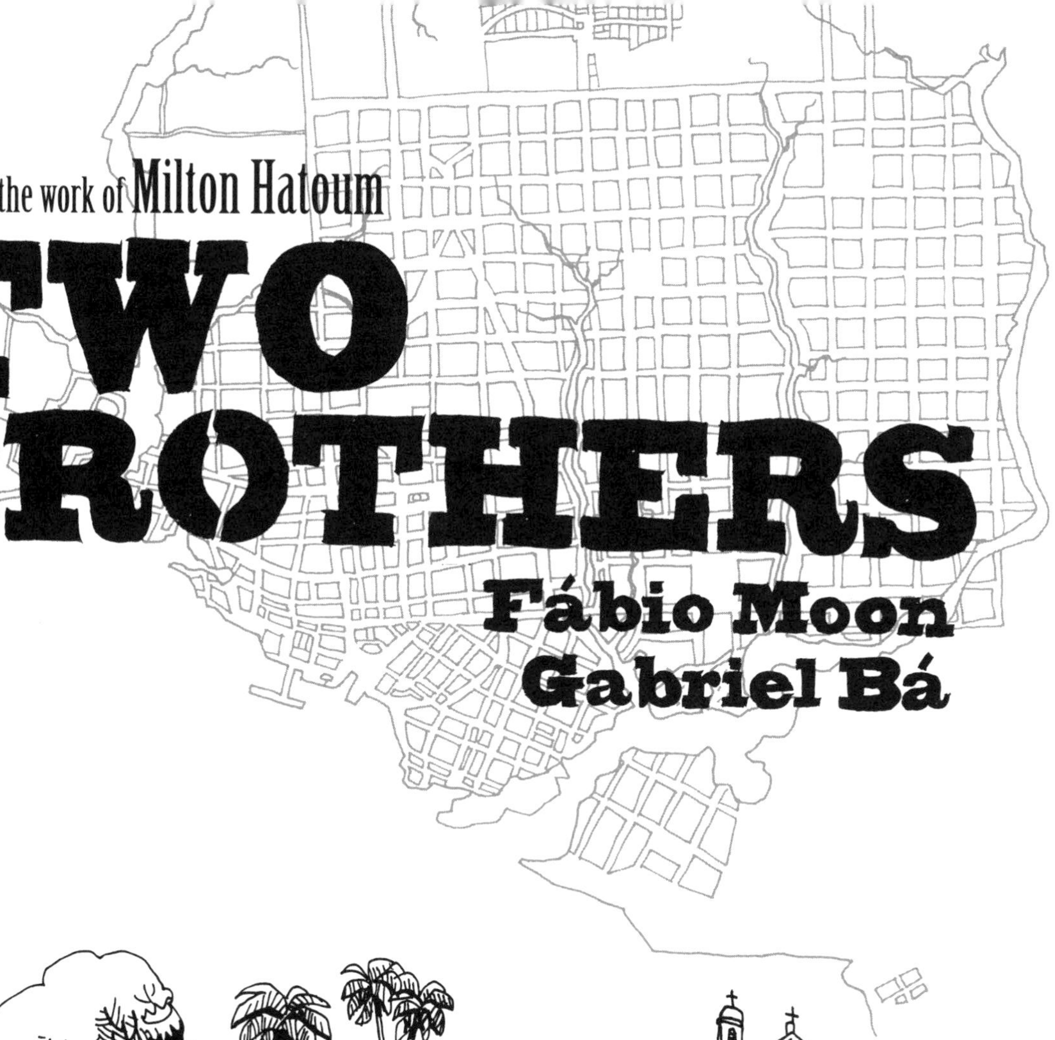

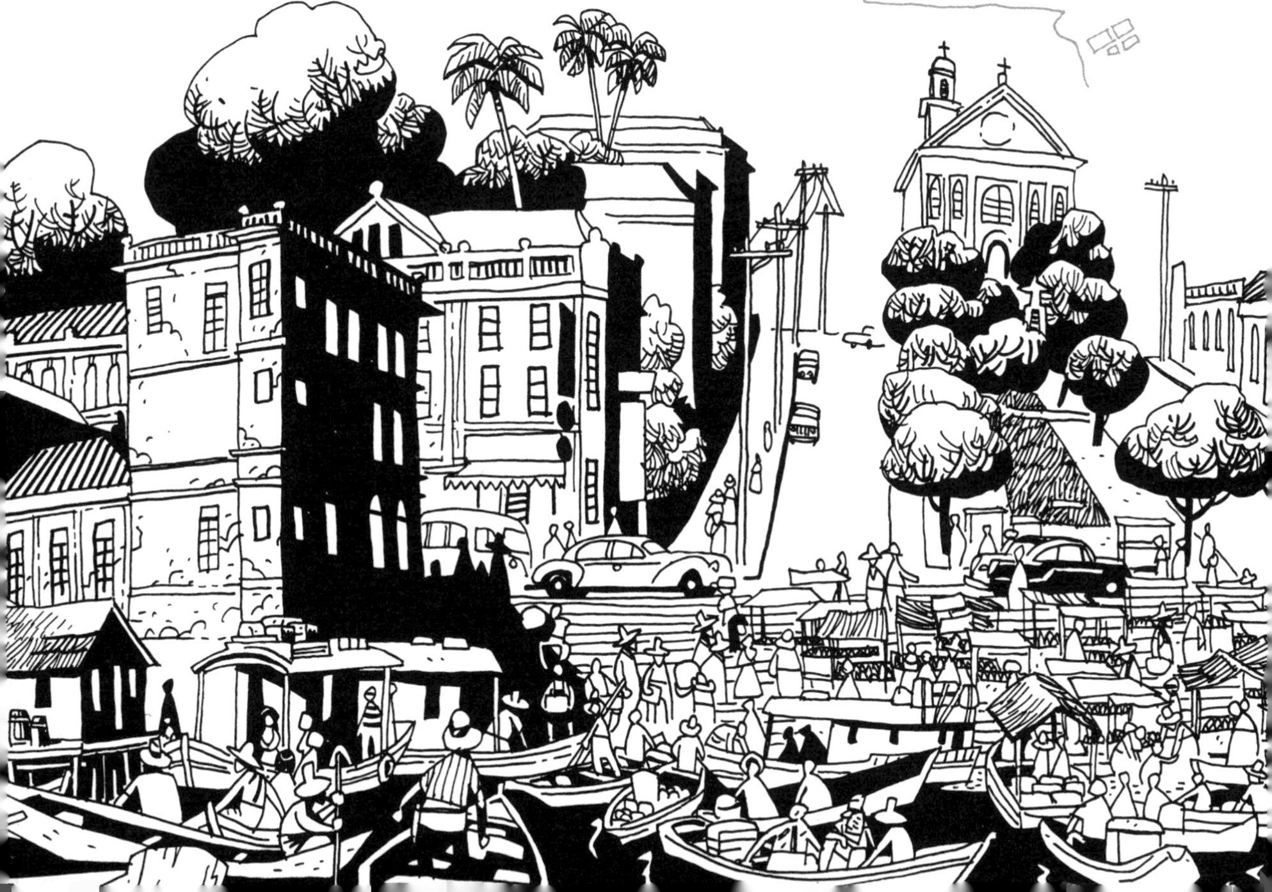

to Dulcinea Carvalho Araújo,
Ms. Duda, our Zana.

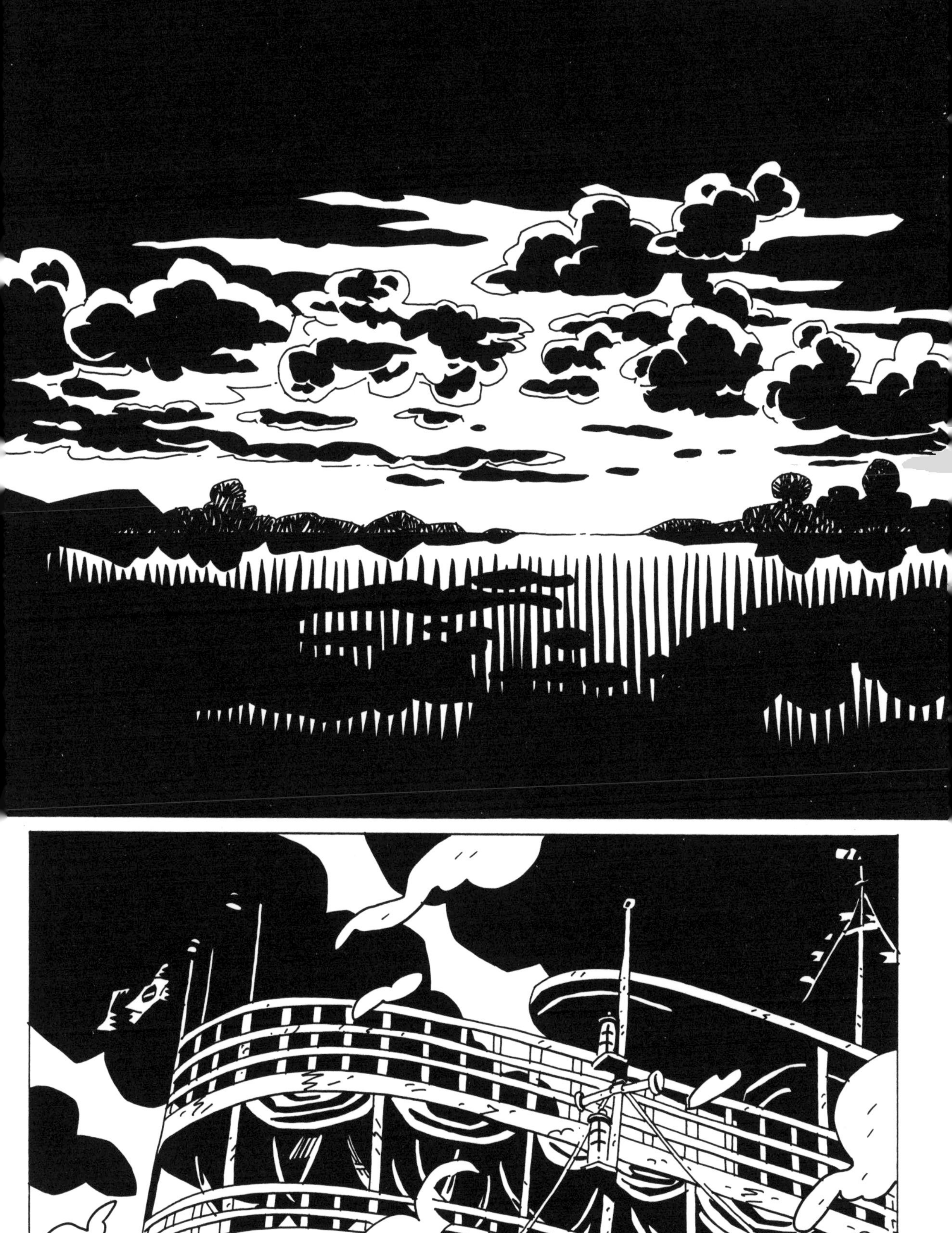

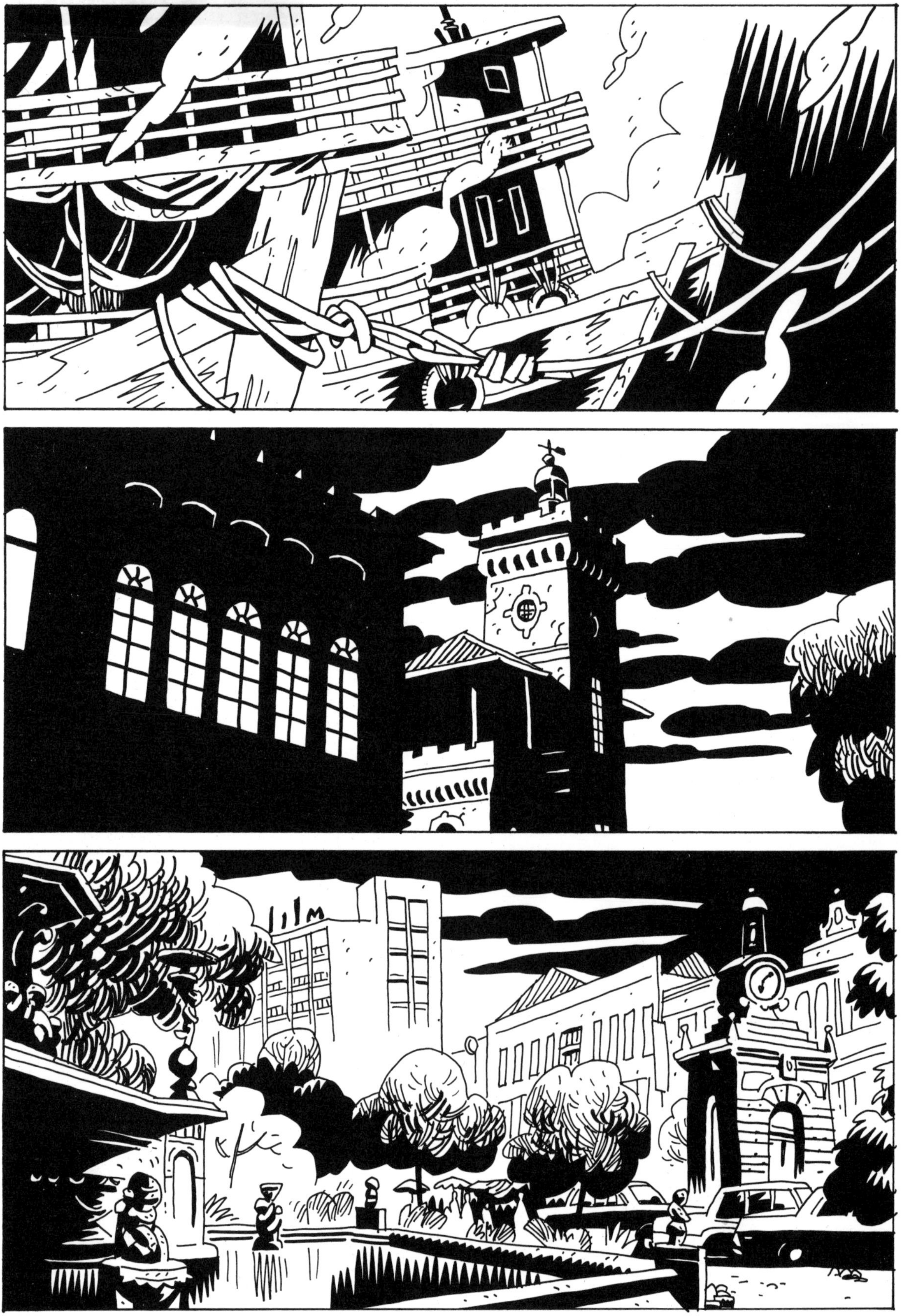

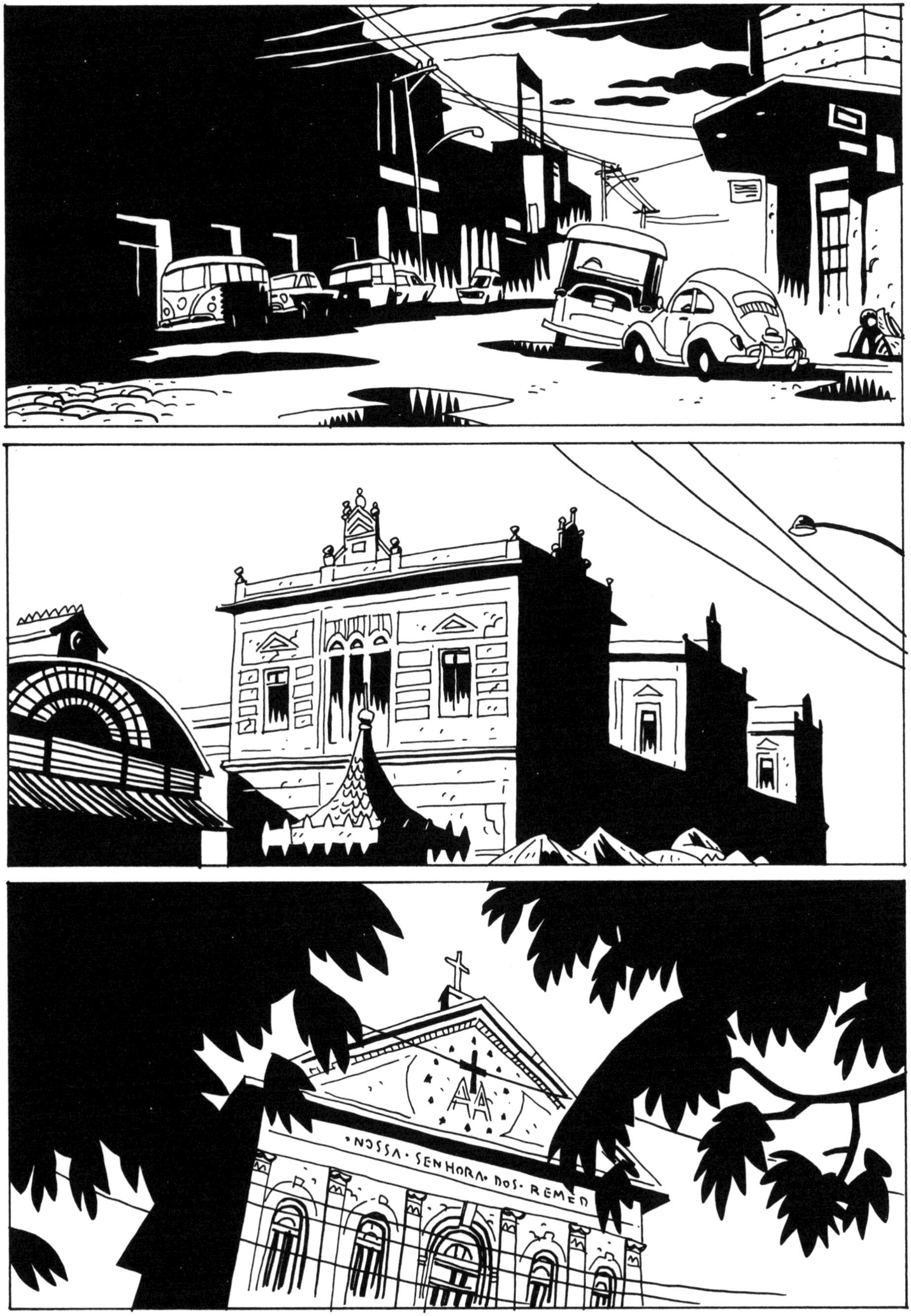
AA
NOSSA · SENHORA · DOS · REMED

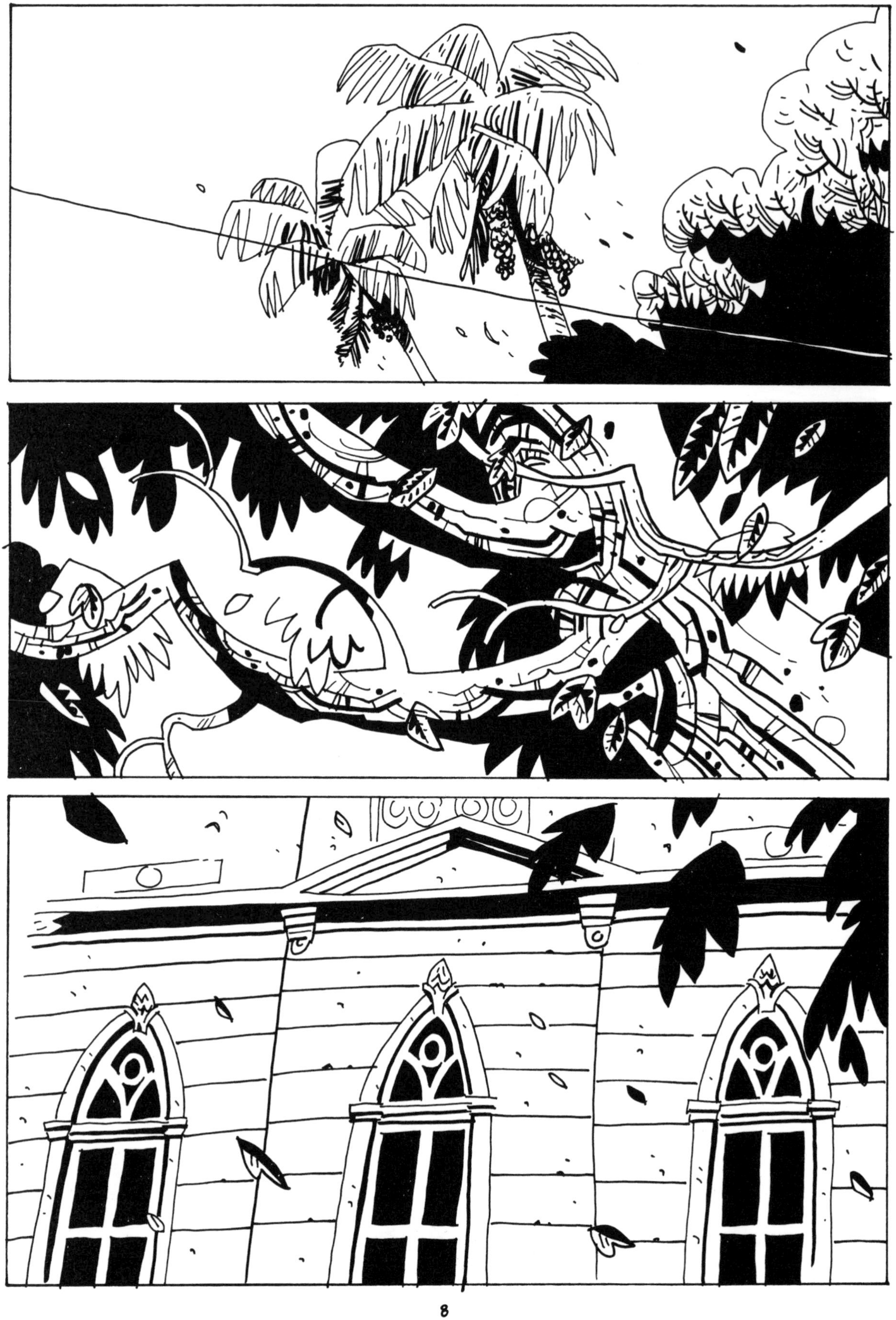

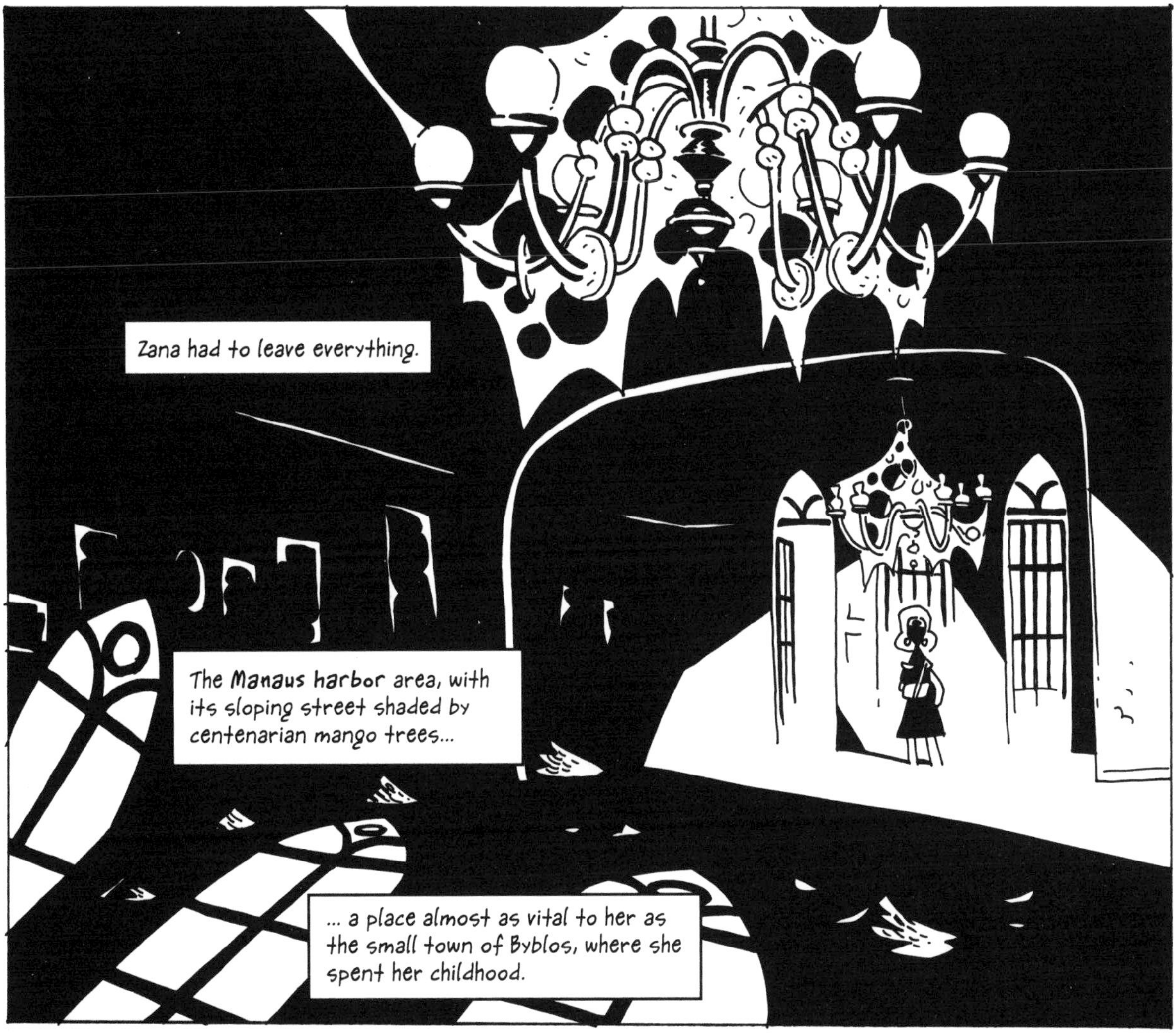
Zana had to leave everything.
The **Manaus harbor** area, with its sloping street shaded by centenarian mango trees...
... a place almost as vital to her as the small town of Byblos, where she spent her childhood.

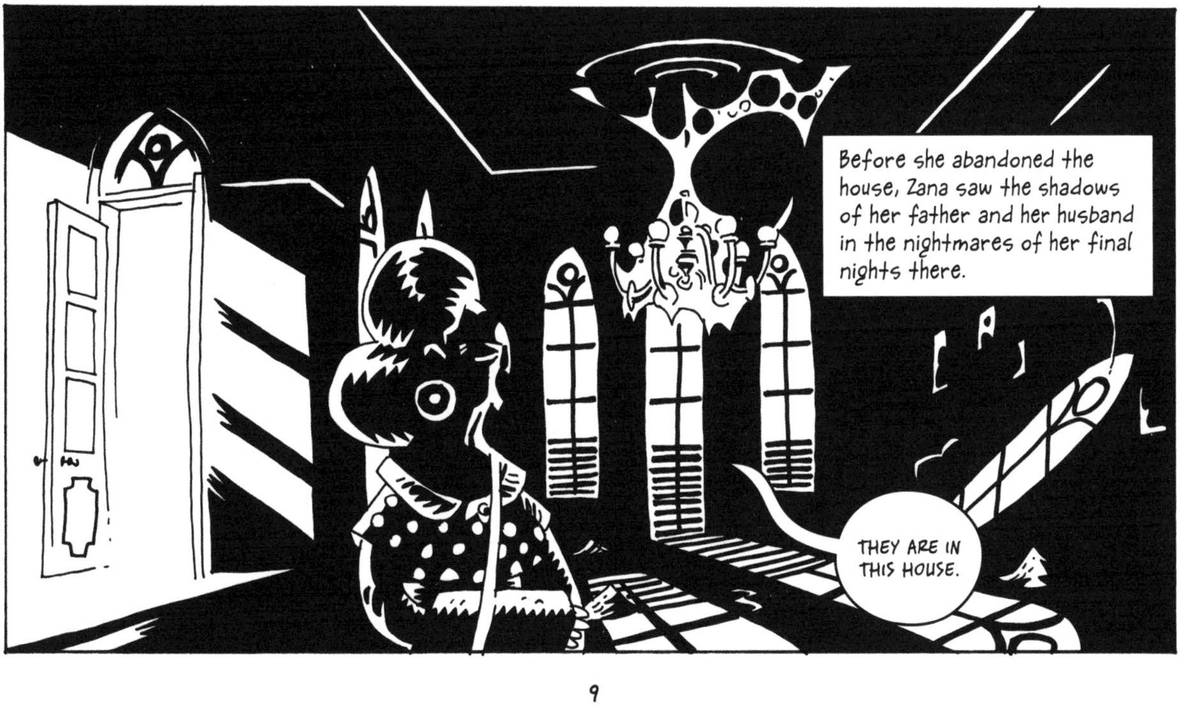
Before she abandoned the house, Zana saw the shadows of her father and her husband in the nightmares of her final nights there.
THEY ARE IN THIS HOUSE.

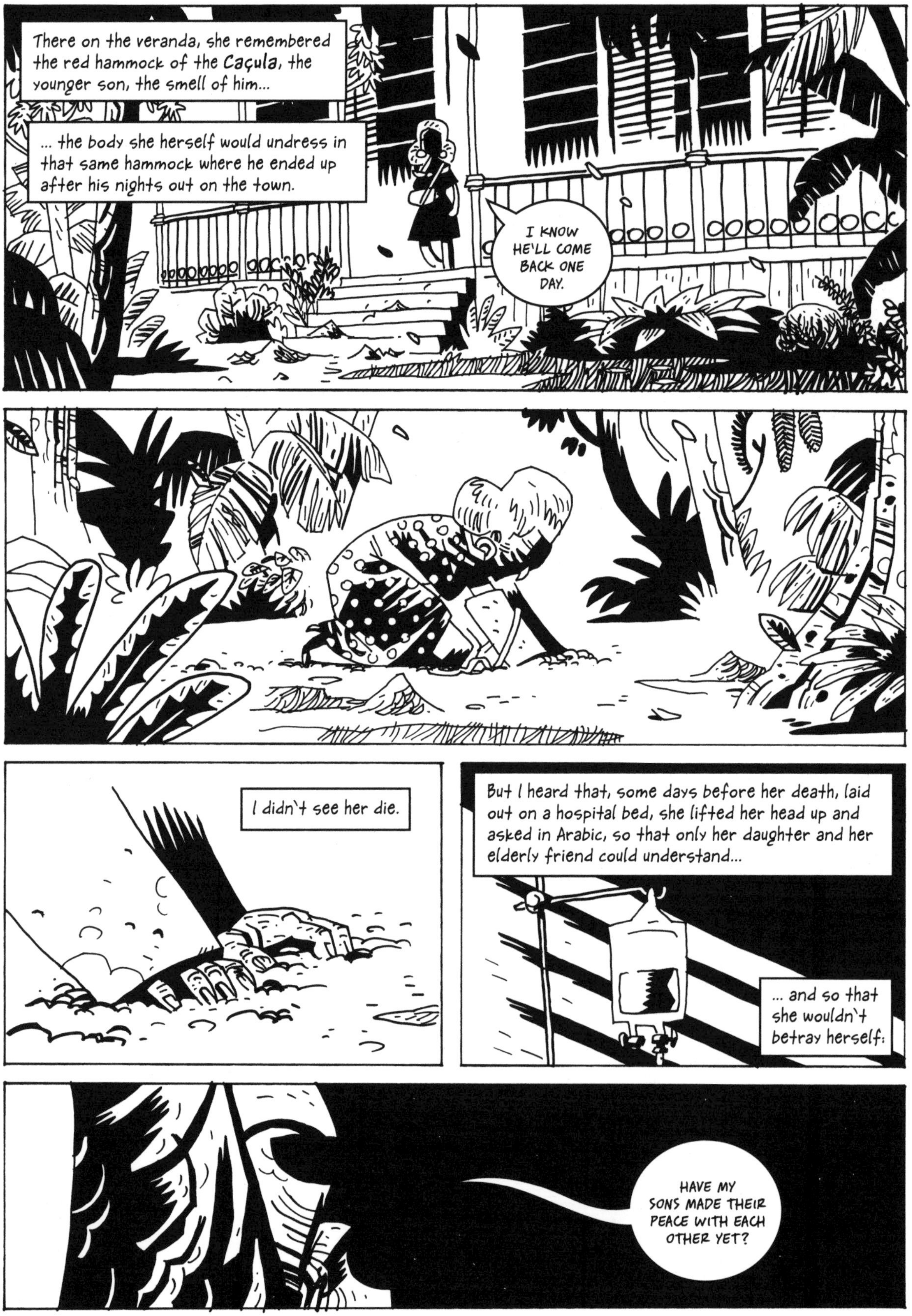
There on the veranda, she remembered the red hammock of the Caçula, the younger son, the smell of him...
... the body she herself would undress in that same hammock where he ended up after his nights out on the town.
I KNOW HE'LL COME BACK ONE DAY.
I didn't see her die.
But I heard that, some days before her death, laid out on a hospital bed, she lifted her head up and asked in Arabic, so that only her daughter and her elderly friend could understand...
... and so that she wouldn't betray herself:
HAVE MY SONS MADE THEIR PEACE WITH EACH OTHER YET?

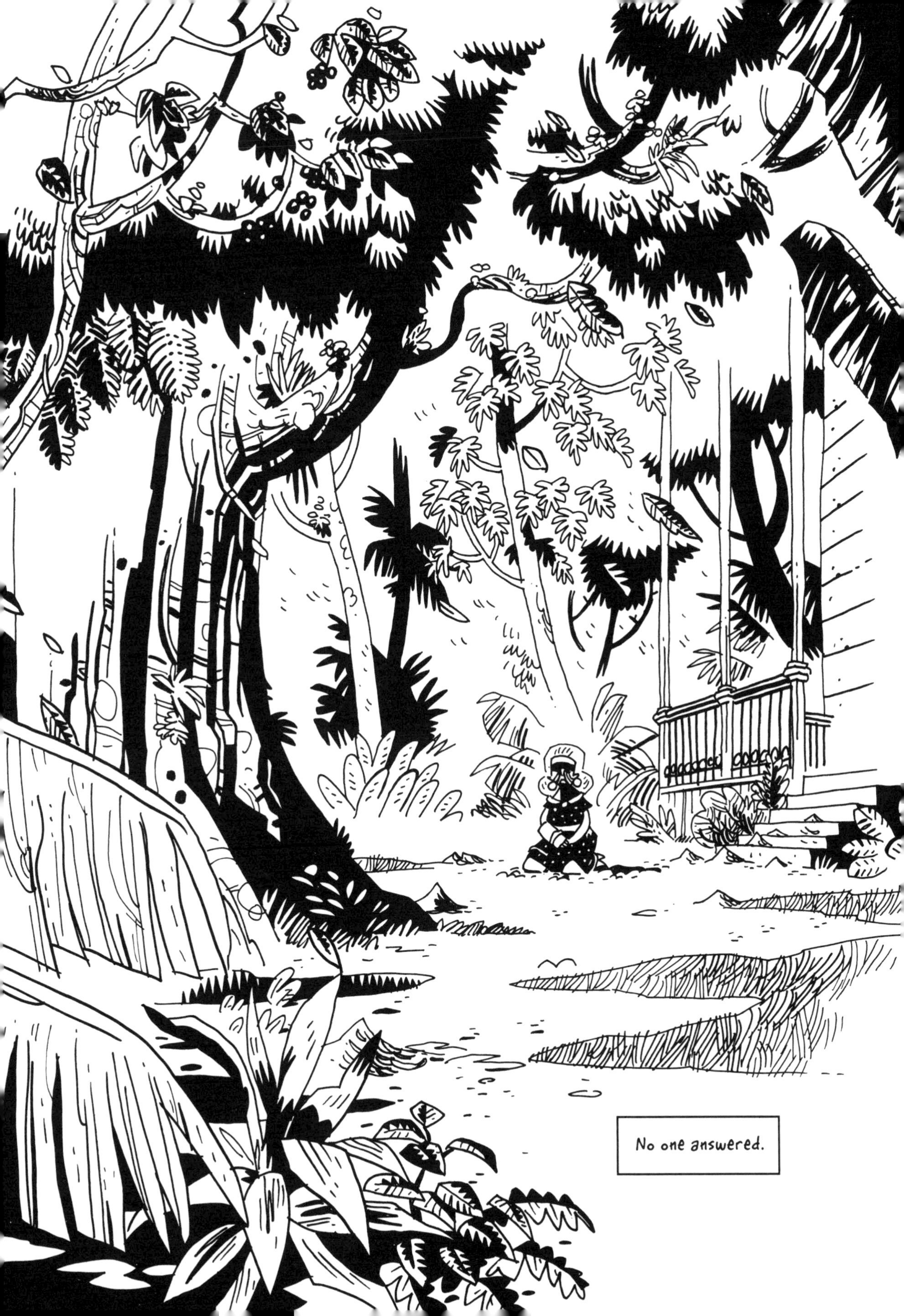
No one answered.

Chapter 1

When Yaqub arrived from Lebanon, his father went to Rio de Janeiro to fetch him.

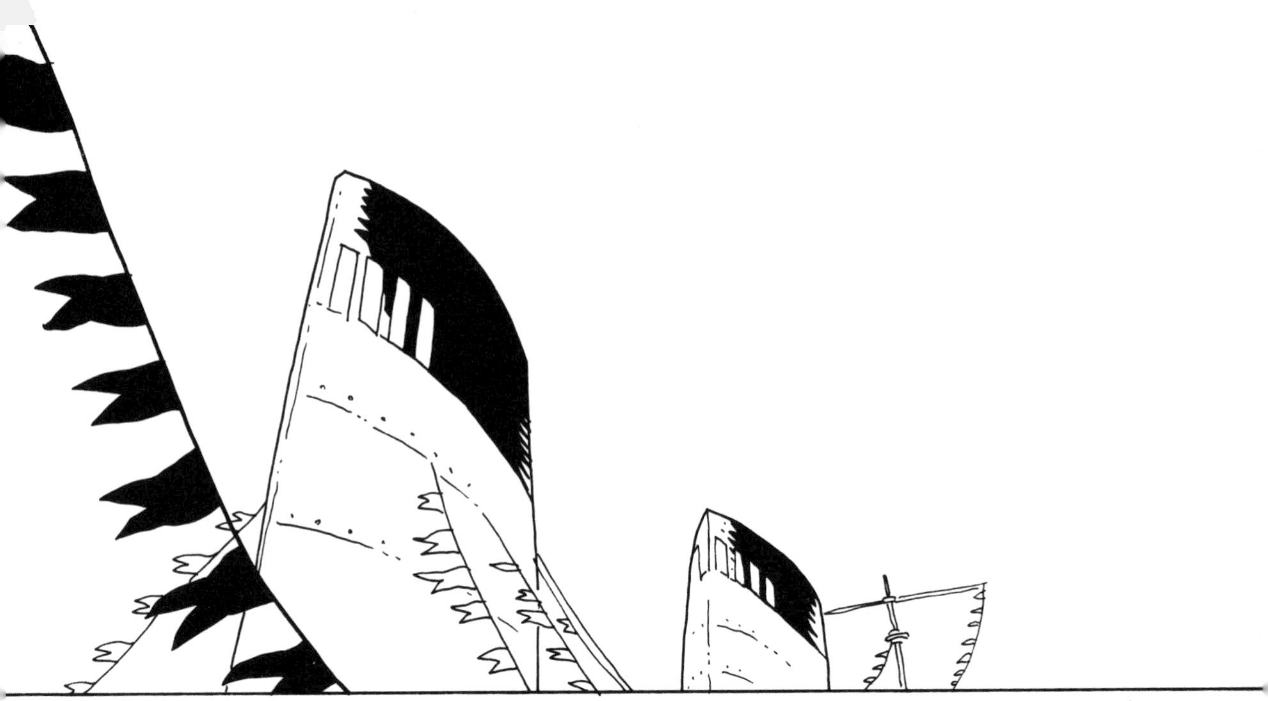

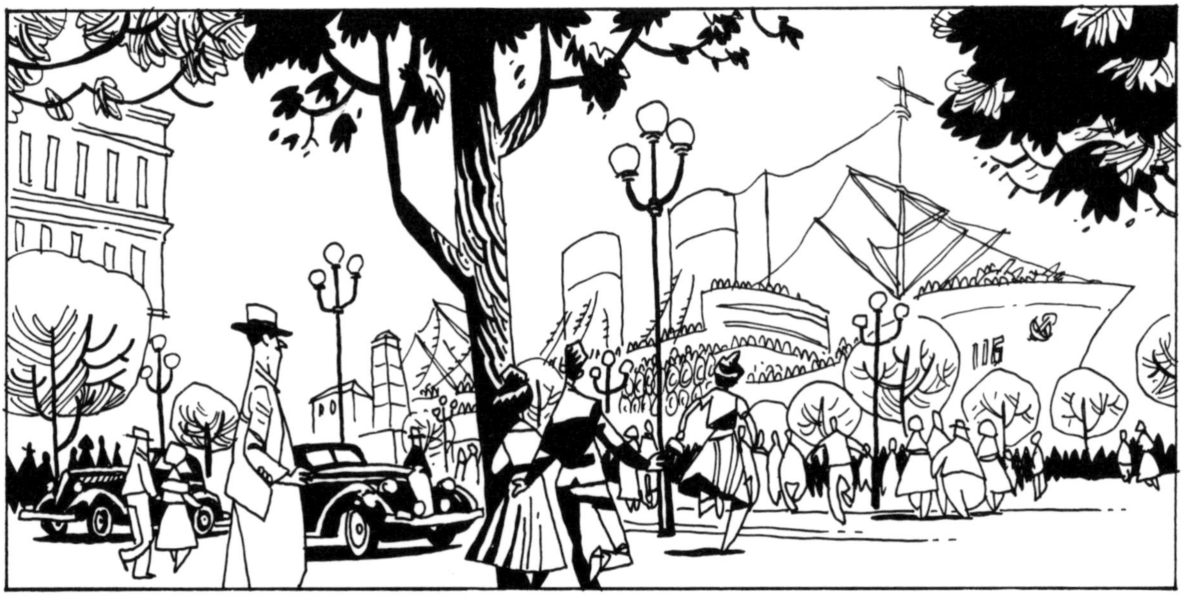
116

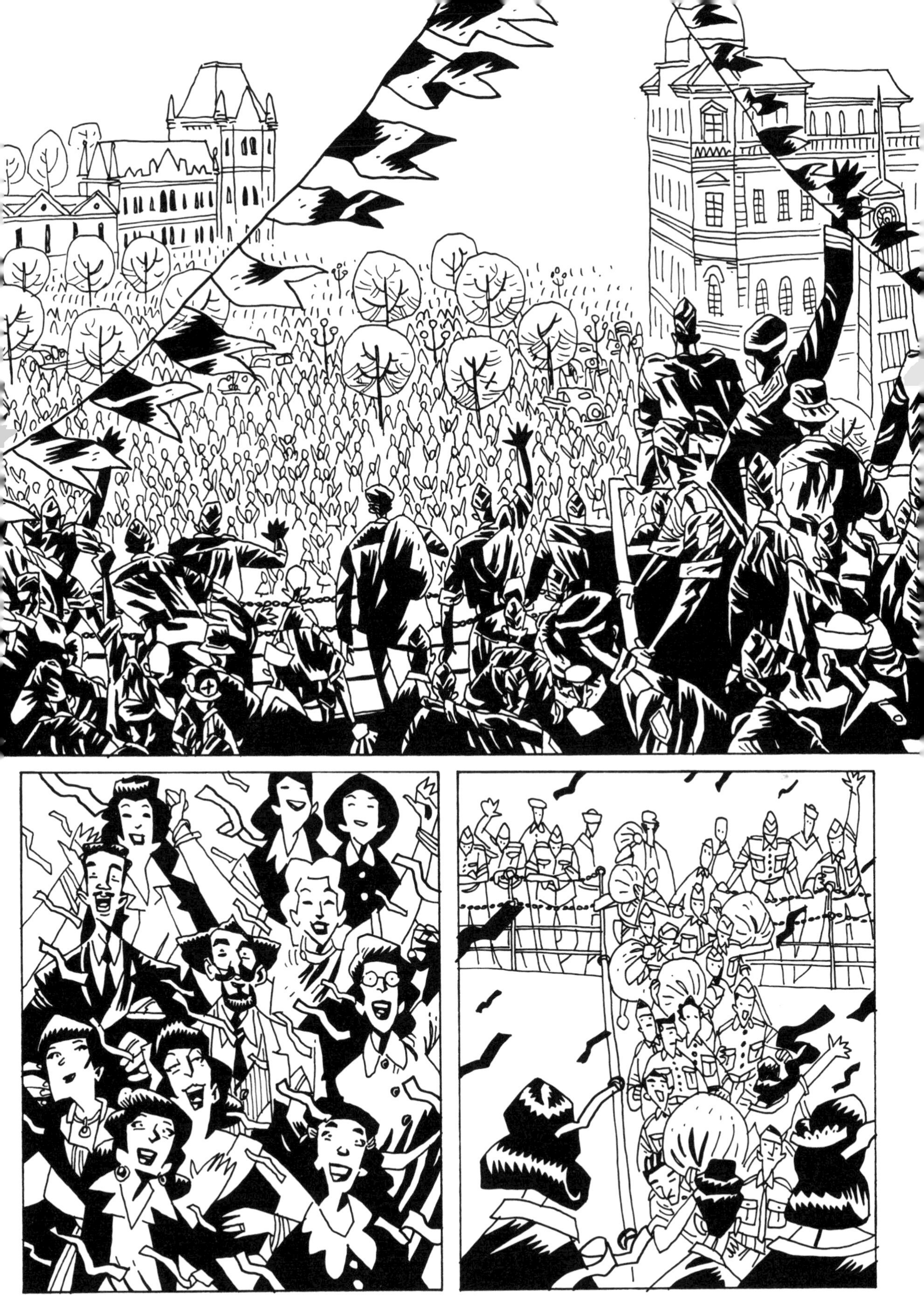

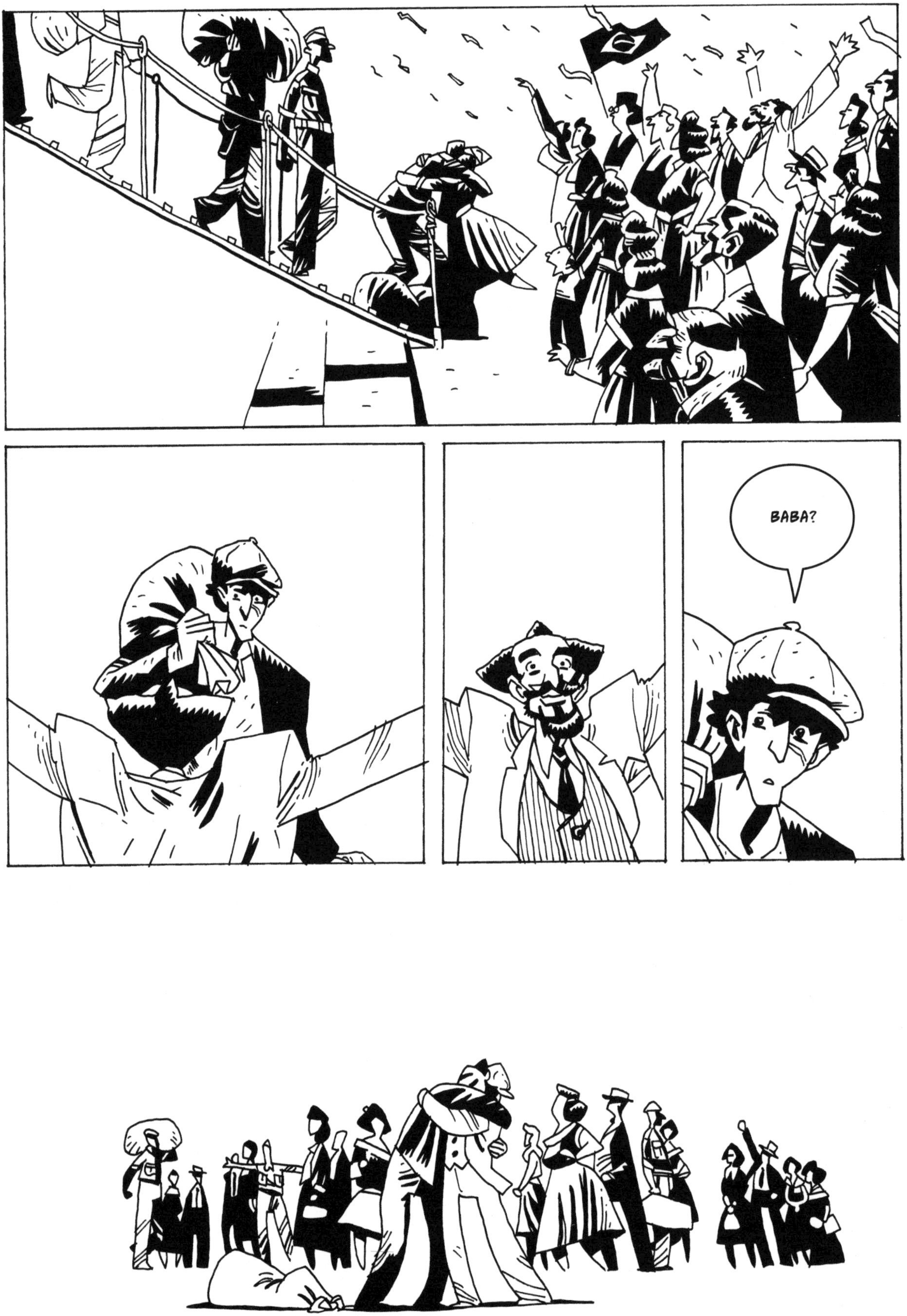
BABA?

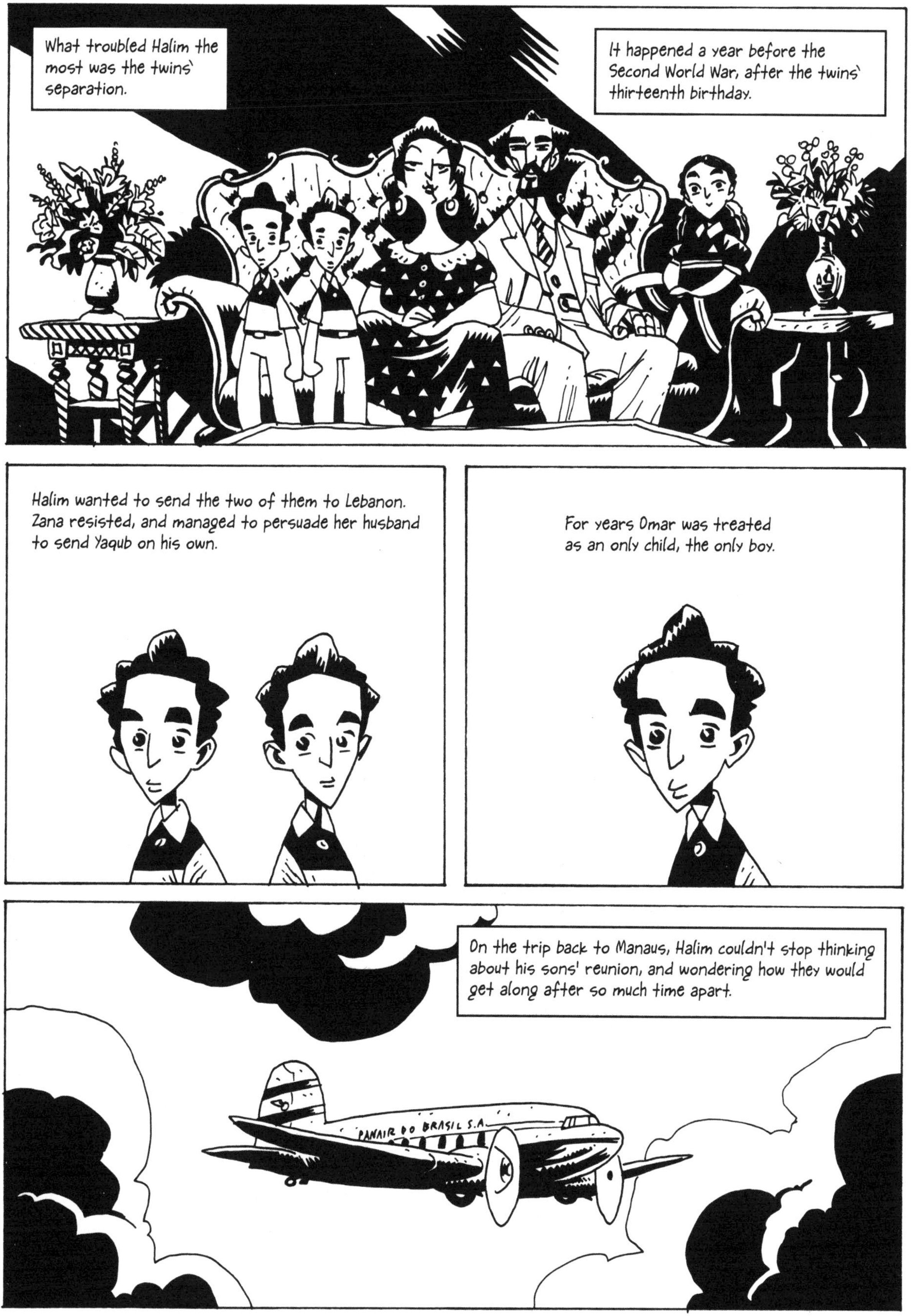
What troubled Halim the most was the twins' separation.
It happened a year before the Second World War, after the twins' thirteenth birthday.
Halim wanted to send the two of them to Lebanon. Zana resisted, and managed to persuade her husband to send Yaqub on his own.
For years Omar was treated as an only child, the only boy.
On the trip back to Manaus, Halim couldn't stop thinking about his sons' reunion, and wondering how they would get along after so much time apart.
PANAIR DO BRASIL S.A.

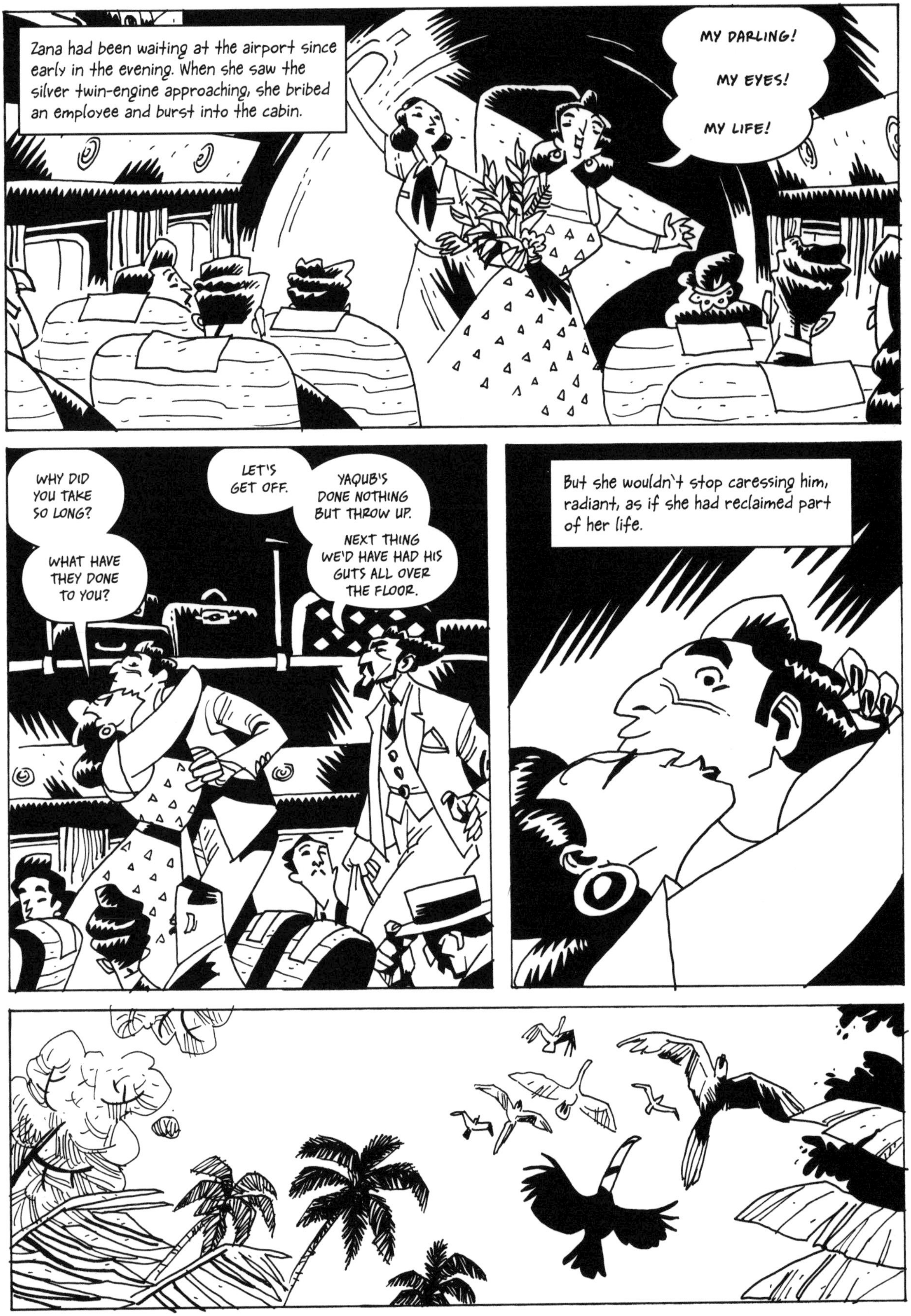
Zana had been waiting at the airport since early in the evening. When she saw the silver twin-engine approaching, she bribed an employee and burst into the cabin.
MY DARLING!
MY EYES!
MY LIFE!
WHY DID YOU TAKE SO LONG?
WHAT HAVE THEY DONE TO YOU?
LET'S GET OFF.
YAQUB'S DONE NOTHING BUT THROW UP.
NEXT THING WE'D HAVE HAD HIS GUTS ALL OVER THE FLOOR.
But she wouldn't stop caressing him, radiant, as if she had reclaimed part of her life.

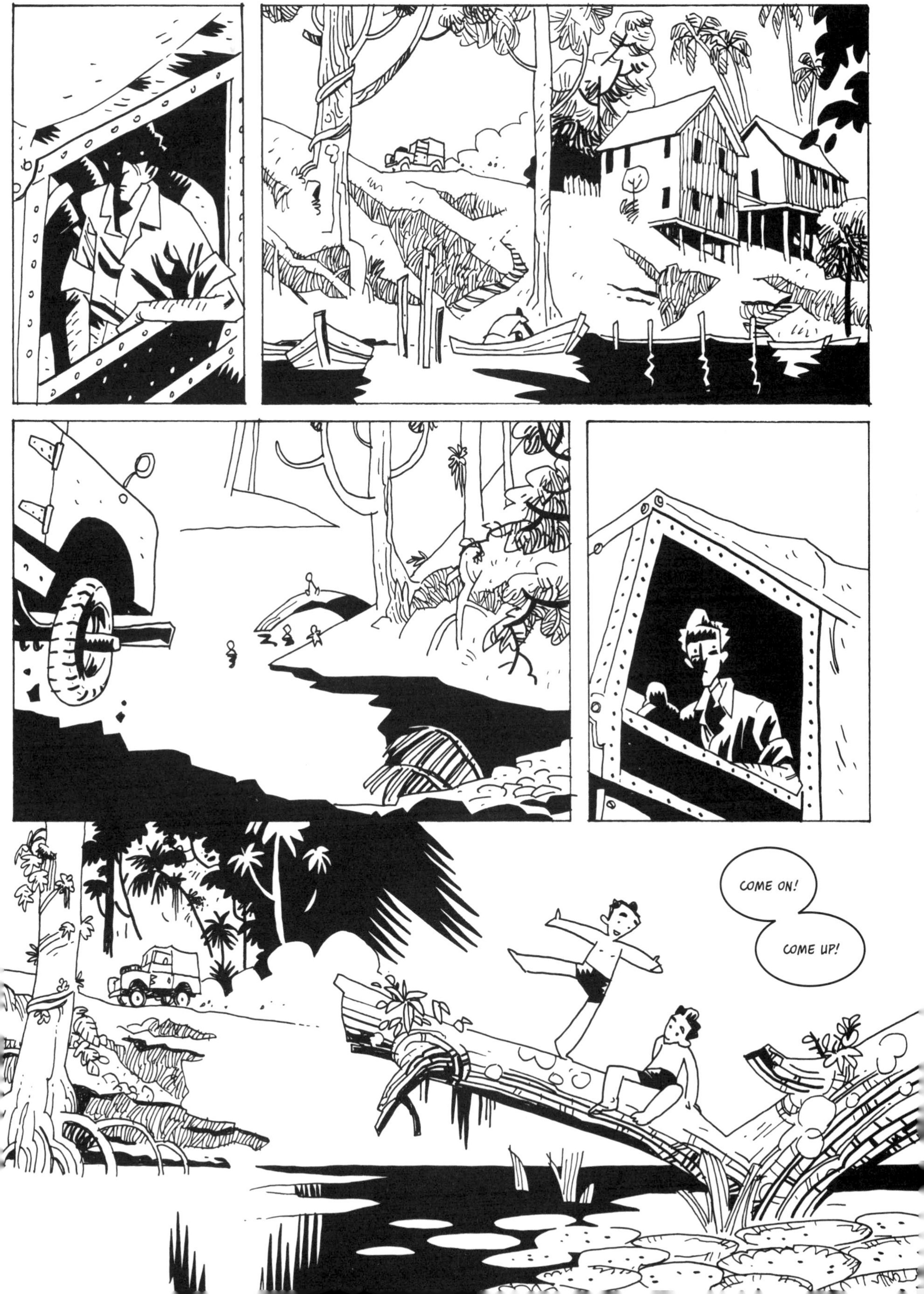
COME ON!
COME UP!

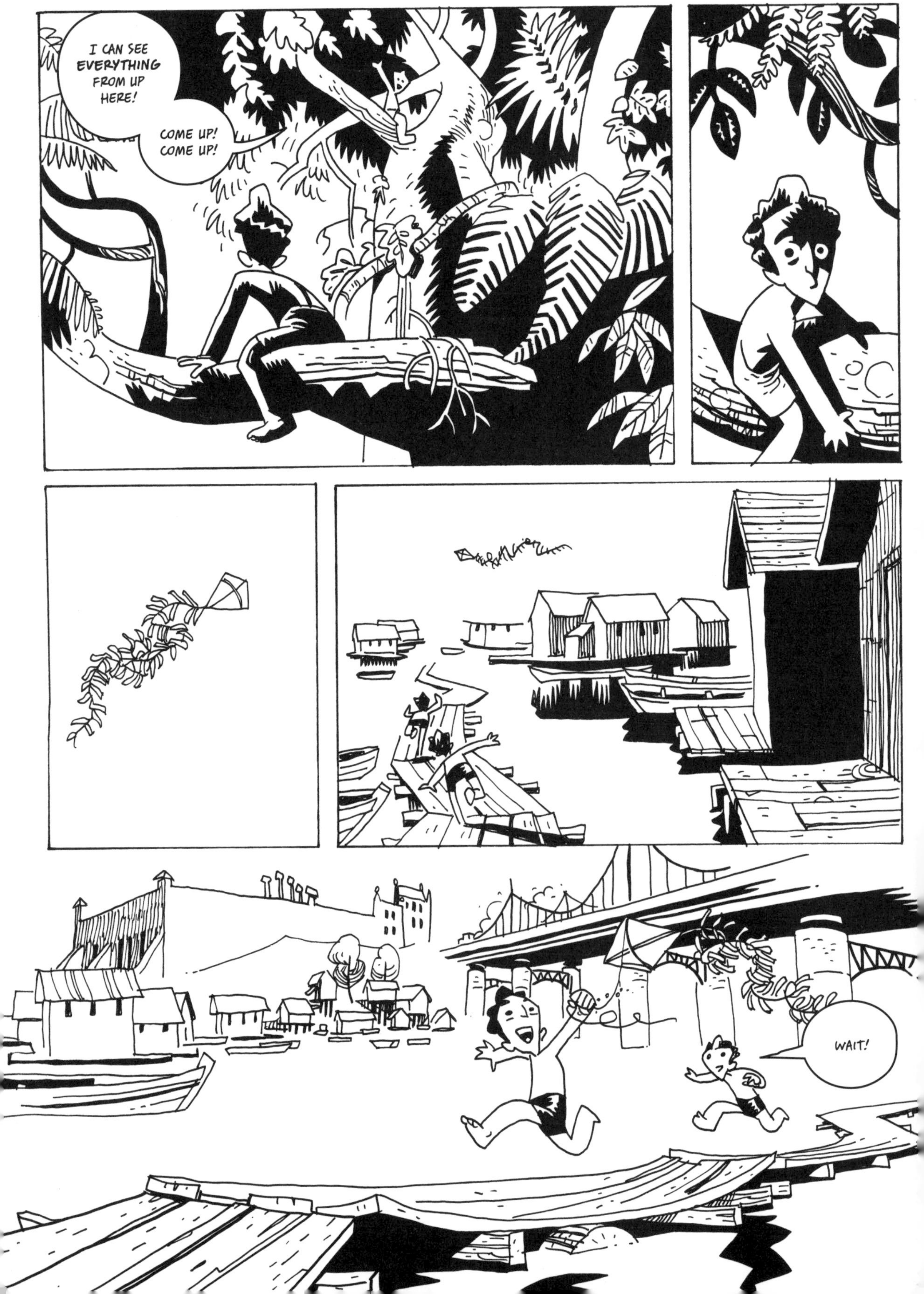
I CAN SEE EVERYTHING FROM UP HERE!
COME UP! COME UP!
WAIT!

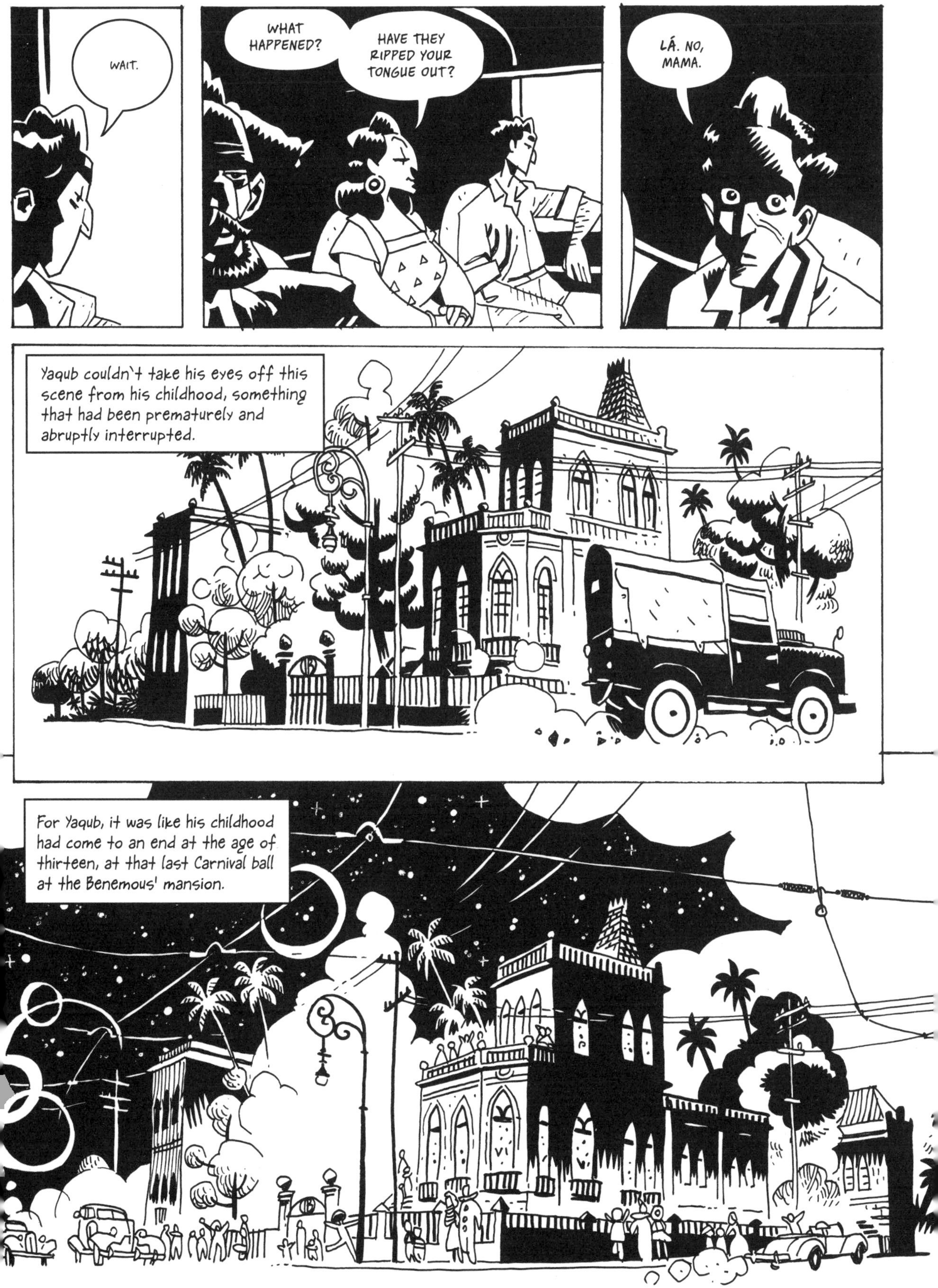
WAIT.
WHAT HAPPENED?
HAVE THEY RIPPED YOUR TONGUE OUT?
LÁ. NO, MAMA.
Yaqub couldn't take his eyes off this scene from his childhood, something that had been prematurely and abruptly interrupted.
For Yaqub, it was like his childhood had come to an end at the age of thirteen, at that last Carnival ball at the Benemous' mansion.

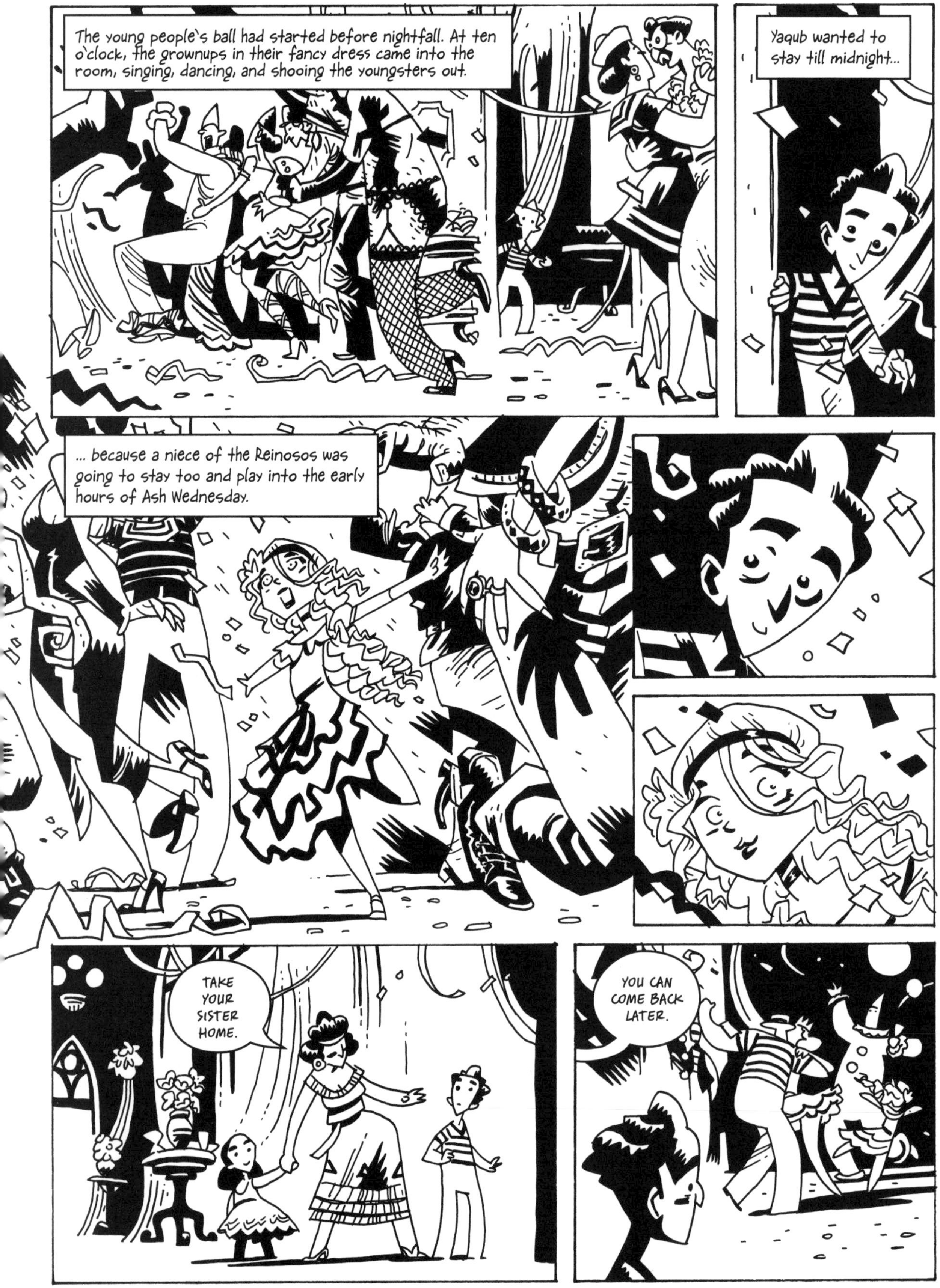
The young people's ball had started before nightfall. At ten o'clock, the grownups in their fancy dress came into the room, singing, dancing, and shooing the youngsters out.
Yaqub wanted to stay till midnight...
... because a niece of the Reinosos was going to stay too and play into the early hours of Ash Wednesday.
TAKE YOUR SISTER HOME.
YOU CAN COME BACK LATER.

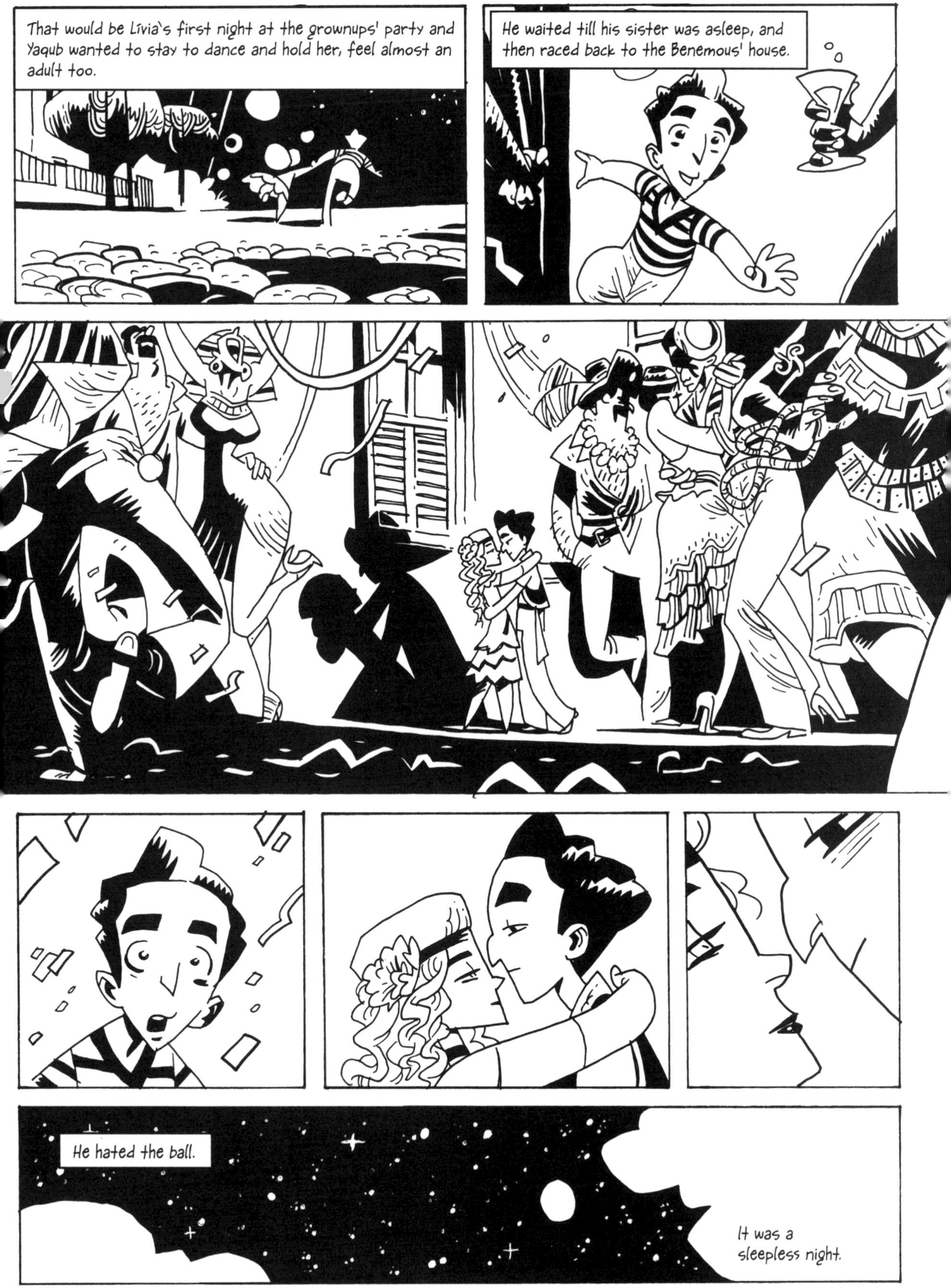
That would be Lívia's first night at the grownups' party and Yaqub wanted to stay to dance and hold her, feel almost an adult too.
He waited till his sister was asleep, and then raced back to the Benemous' house.
He hated the ball.
It was a sleepless night.

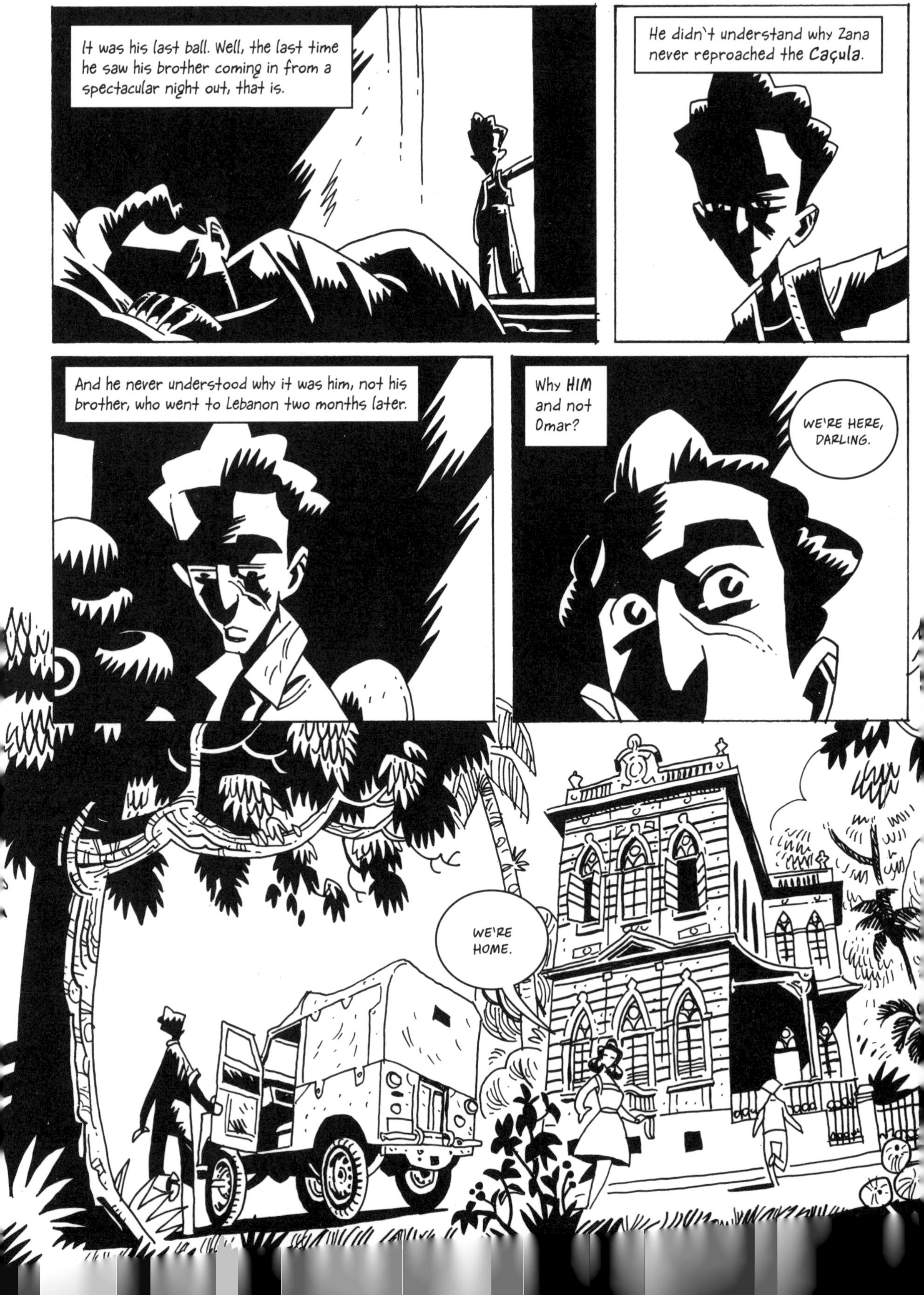
It was his last ball. Well, the last time he saw his brother coming in from a spectacular night out, that is.
He didn't understand why Zana never reproached the Caçula.
And he never understood why it was him, not his brother, who went to Lebanon two months later.
Why HIM and not Omar?
WE'RE HERE, DARLING.
WE'RE HOME.

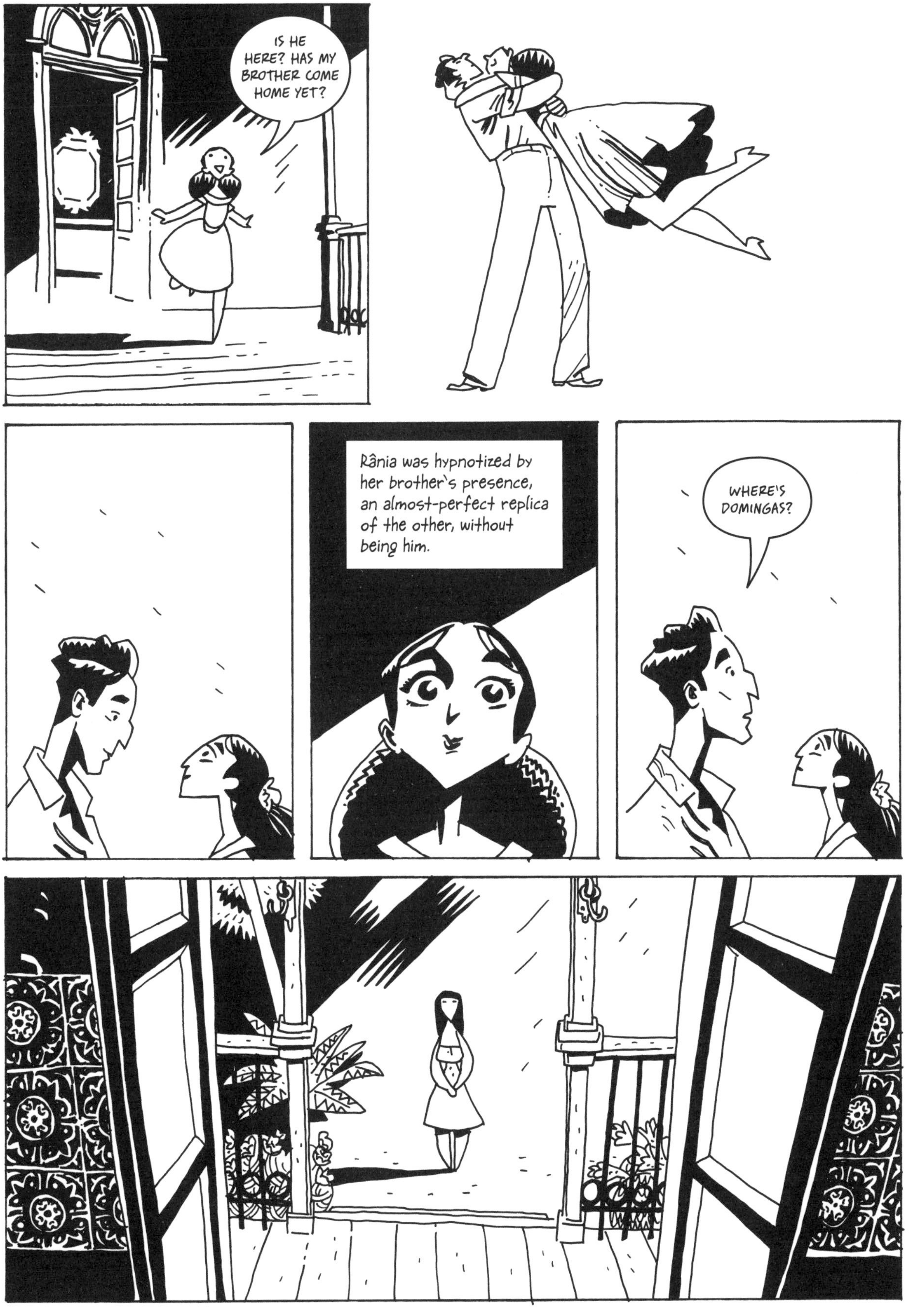
IS HE HERE? HAS MY BROTHER COME HOME YET?
Rânia was hypnotized by her brother's presence, an almost-perfect replica of the other, without being him.
WHERE'S DOMINGAS?

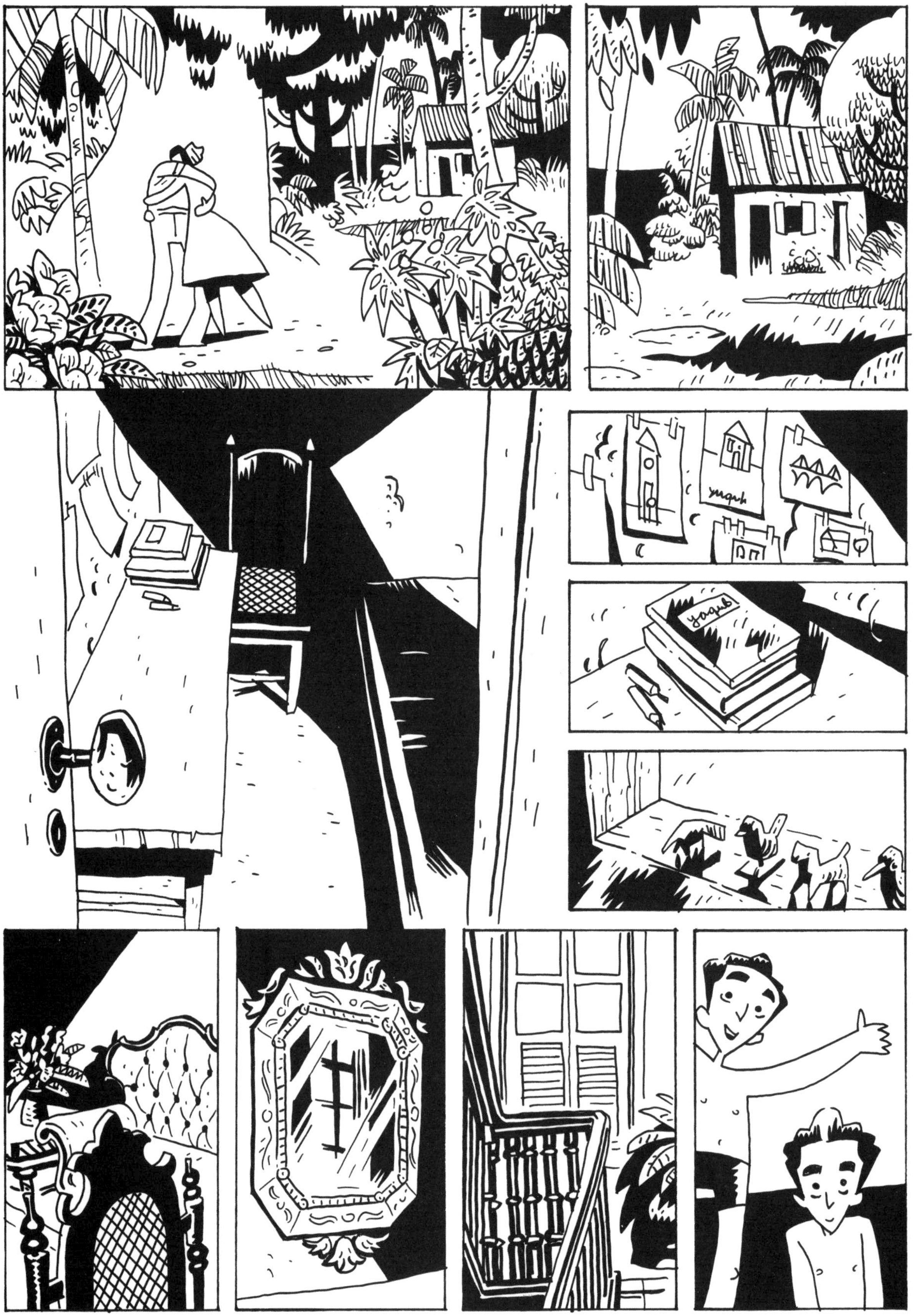

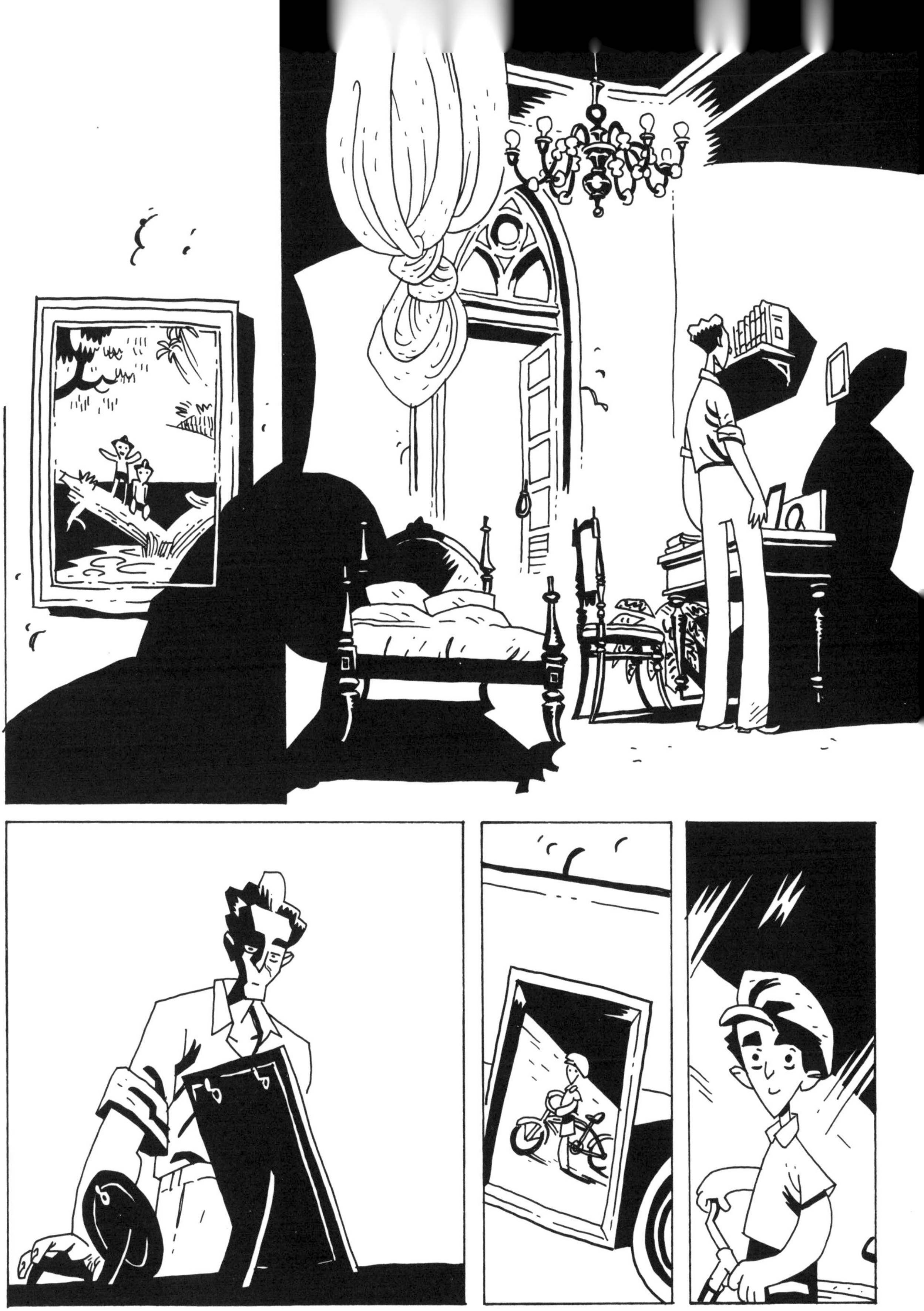

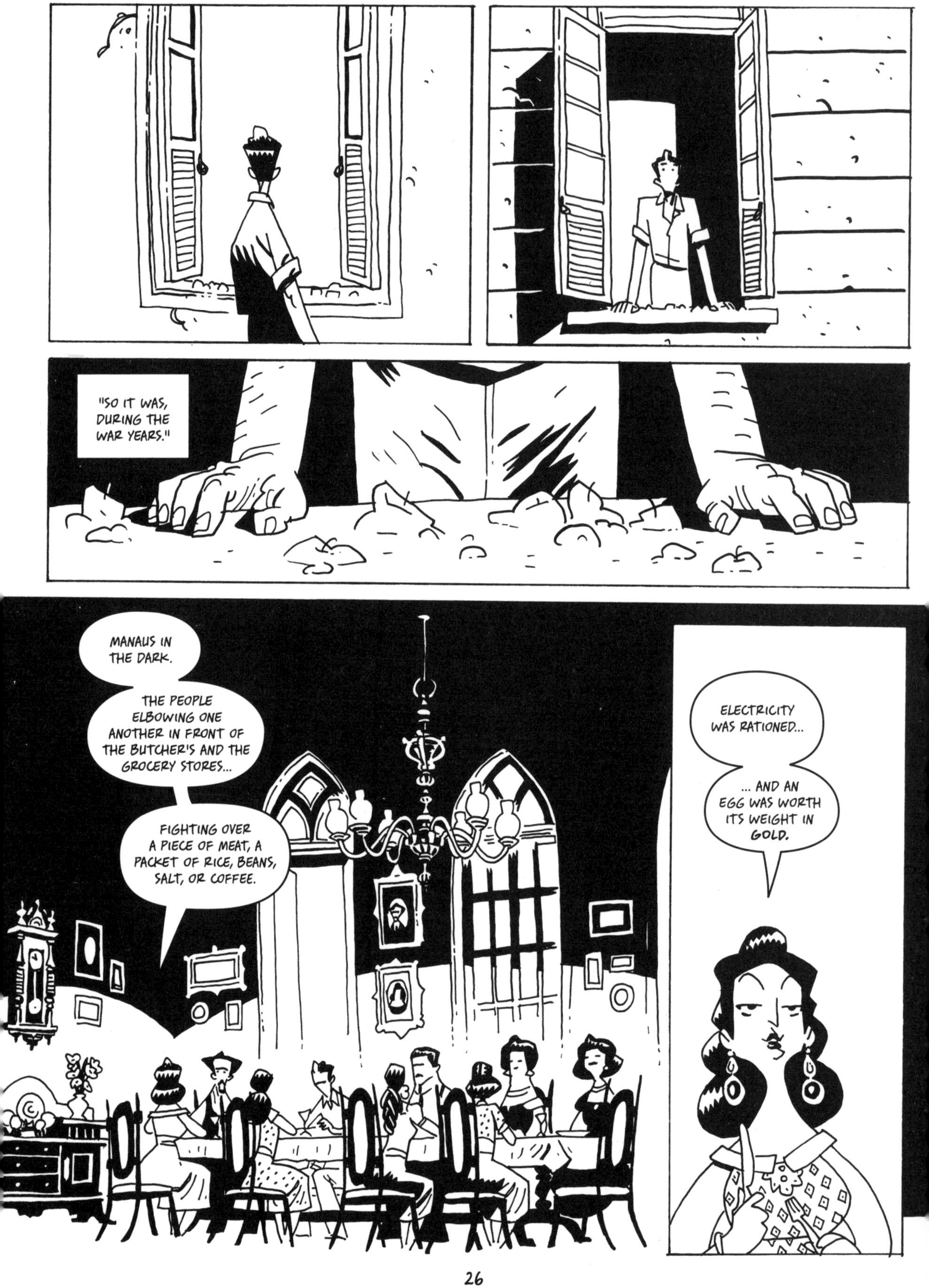
"SO IT WAS, DURING THE WAR YEARS."
MANAUS IN THE DARK.
THE PEOPLE ELBOWING ONE ANOTHER IN FRONT OF THE BUTCHER'S AND THE GROCERY STORES...
FIGHTING OVER A PIECE OF MEAT, A PACKET OF RICE, BEANS, SALT, OR COFFEE.
ELECTRICITY WAS RATIONED...
... AND AN EGG WAS WORTH ITS WEIGHT IN GOLD.

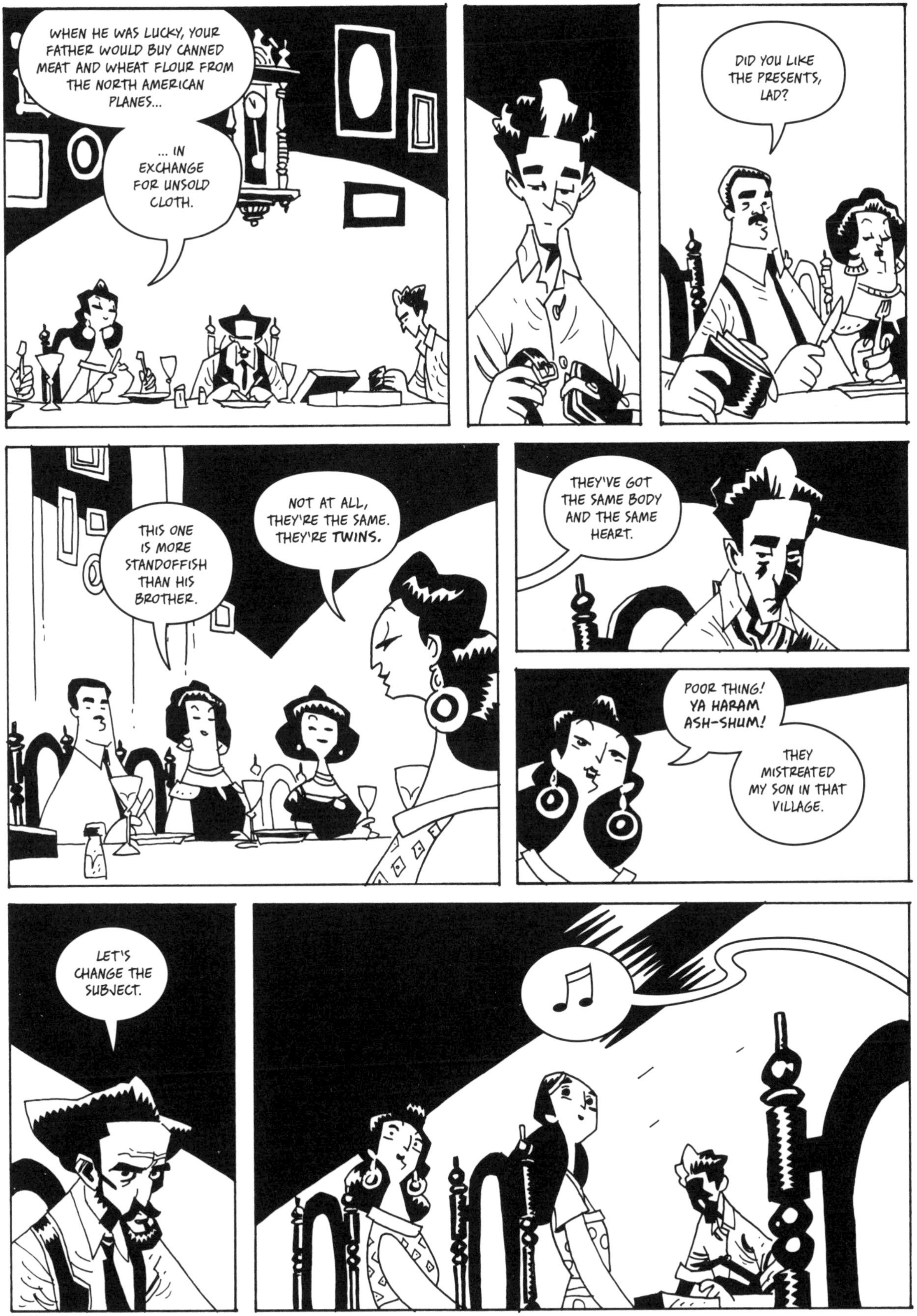
WHEN HE WAS LUCKY, YOUR FATHER WOULD BUY CANNED MEAT AND WHEAT FLOUR FROM THE NORTH AMERICAN PLANES...
... IN EXCHANGE FOR UNSOLD CLOTH.
DID YOU LIKE THE PRESENTS, LAD?
THIS ONE IS MORE STANDOFFISH THAN HIS BROTHER.
NOT AT ALL, THEY'RE THE SAME. THEY'RE TWINS.
THEY'VE GOT THE SAME BODY AND THE SAME HEART.
POOR THING! YA HARAM ASH-SHUM!
THEY MISTREATED MY SON IN THAT VILLAGE.
LET'S CHANGE THE SUBJECT.
♫

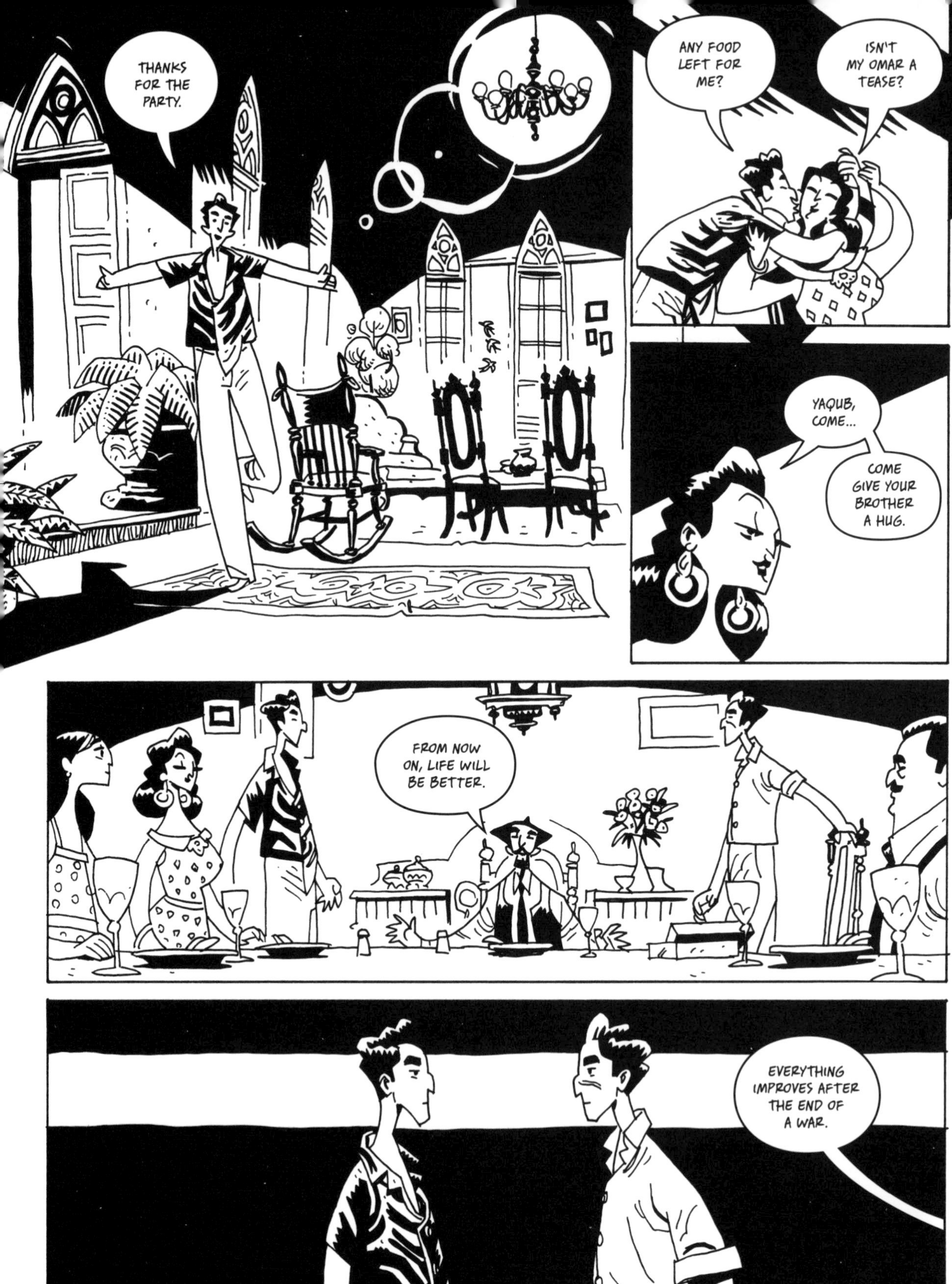
THANKS FOR THE PARTY.
ANY FOOD LEFT FOR ME?
ISN'T MY OMAR A TEASE?
YAQUB, COME...
COME GIVE YOUR BROTHER A HUG.
FROM NOW ON, LIFE WILL BE BETTER.
EVERYTHING IMPROVES AFTER THE END OF A WAR.

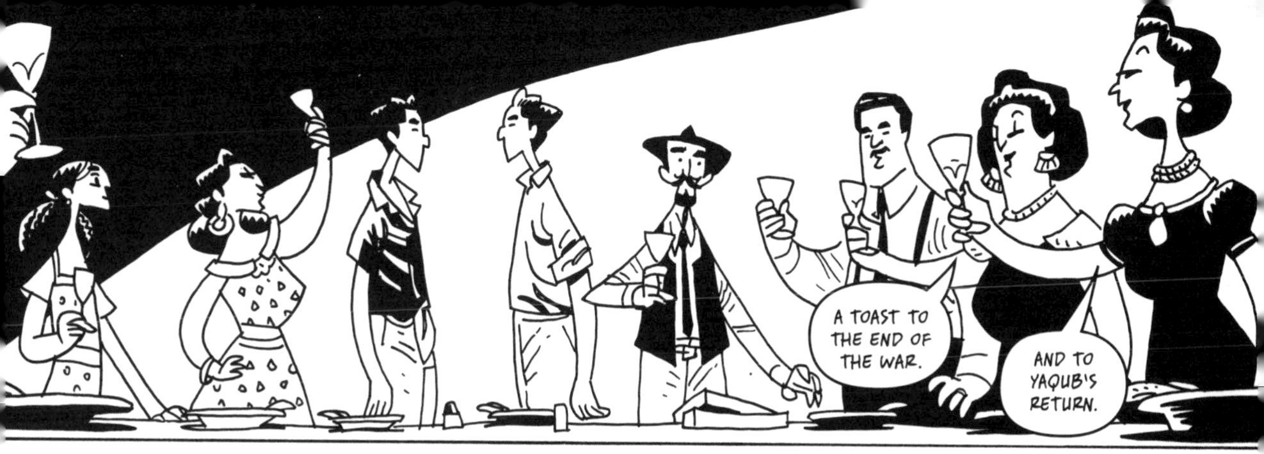
A TOAST TO THE END OF THE WAR.
AND TO YAQUB'S RETURN.

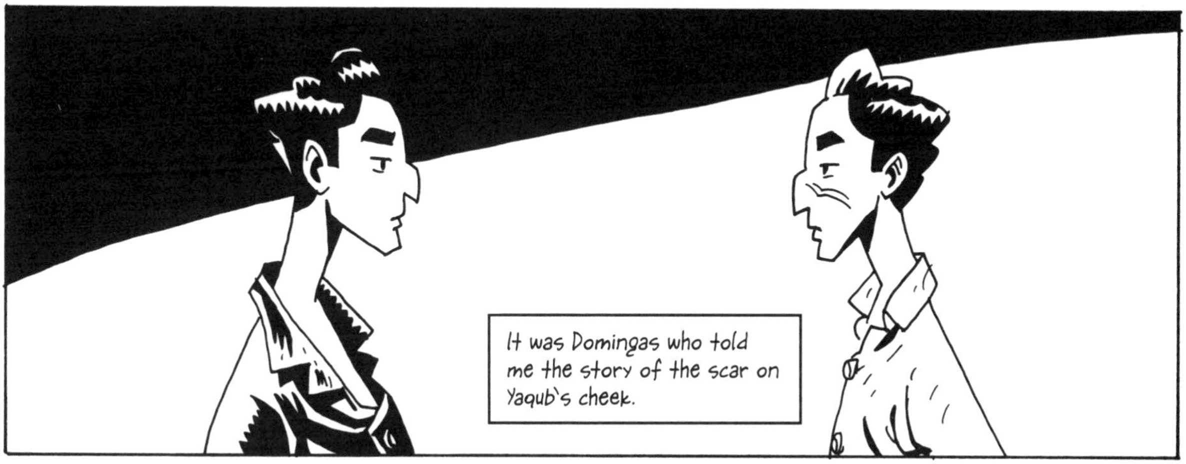
It was Domingas who told me the story of the scar on Yaqub's cheek.

She was always alert to the twins' smallest movements, listened to conversations, spying on everyone's privacy.

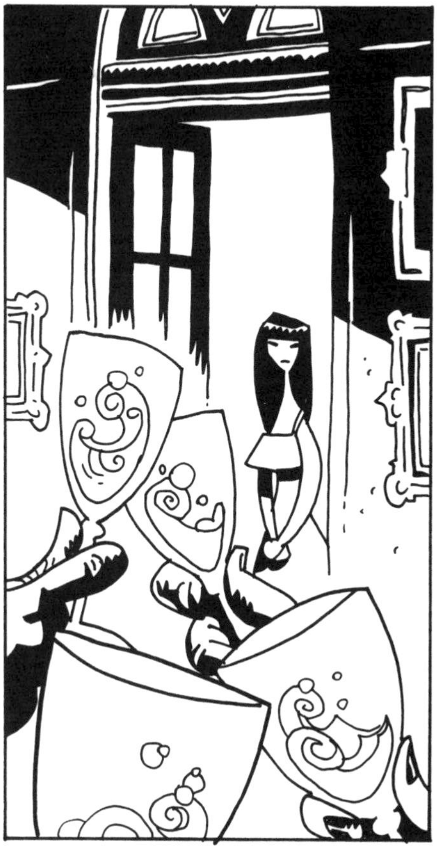

She was able to do this because the family's meals, and the shine on the furniture, were under her care.

My story, too, depends on her, on Domingas.

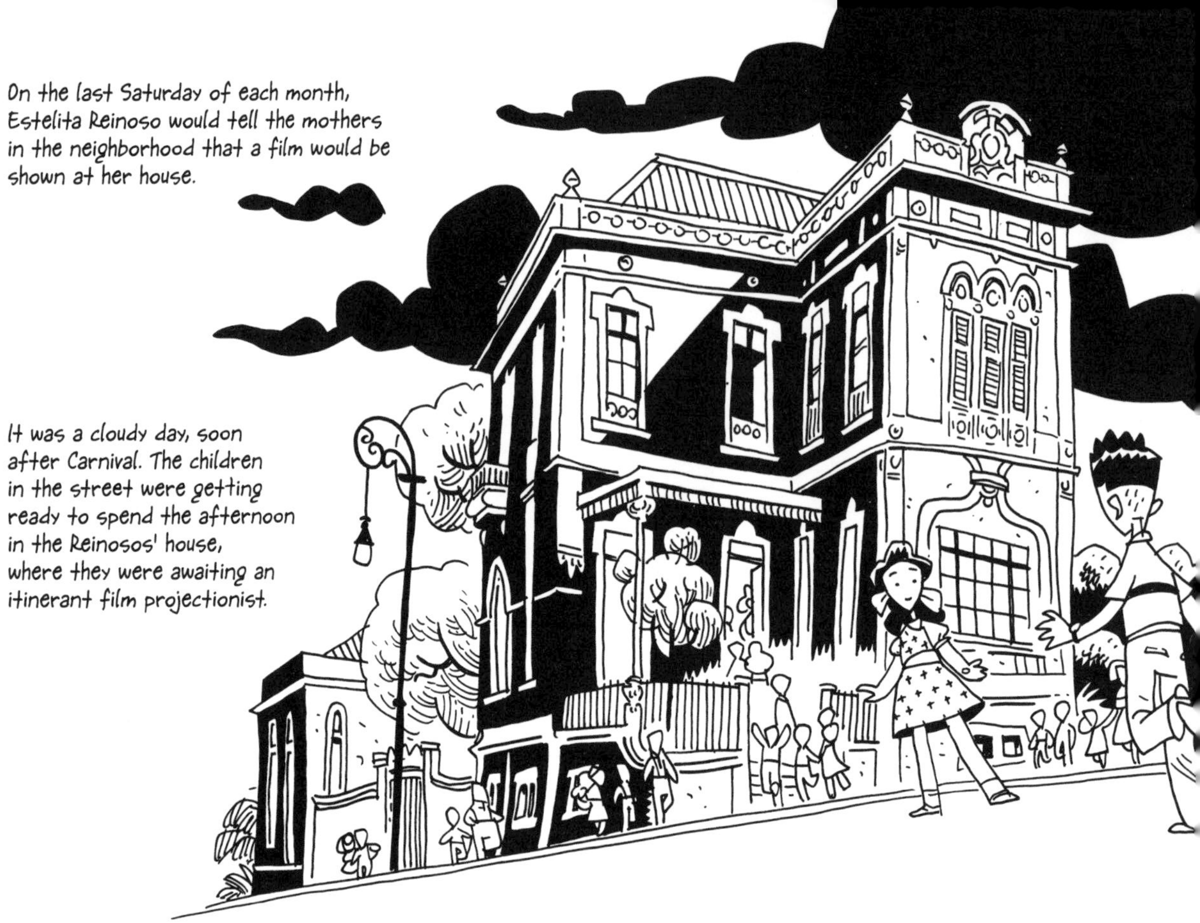
On the last Saturday of each month, Estelita Reinoso would tell the mothers in the neighborhood that a film would be shown at her house.
It was a cloudy day, soon after Carnival. The children in the street were getting ready to spend the afternoon in the Reinosos' house, where they were awaiting an itinerant film projectionist.

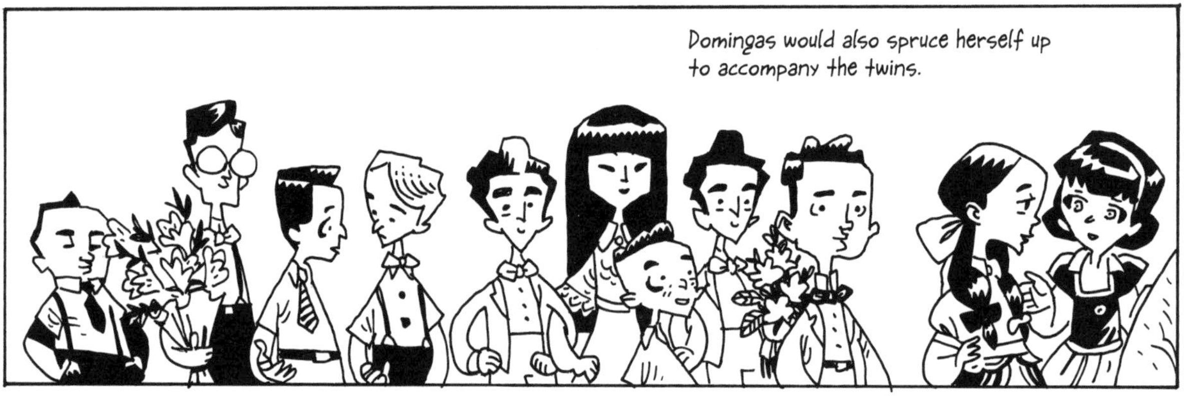
Domingas would also spruce herself up to accompany the twins.

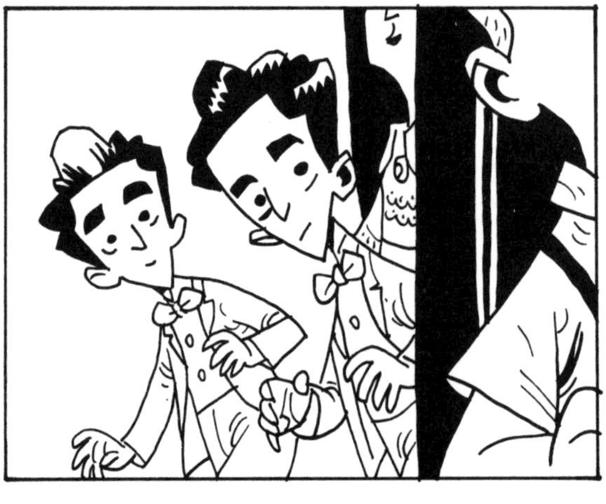

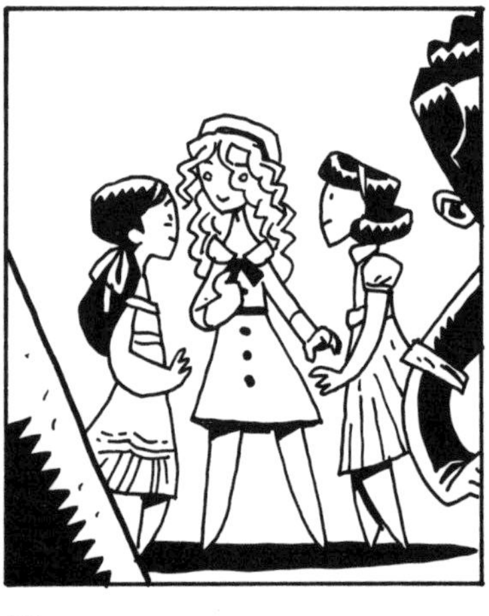

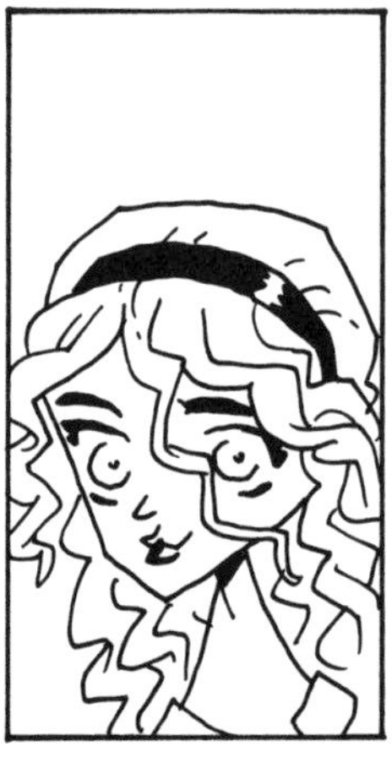

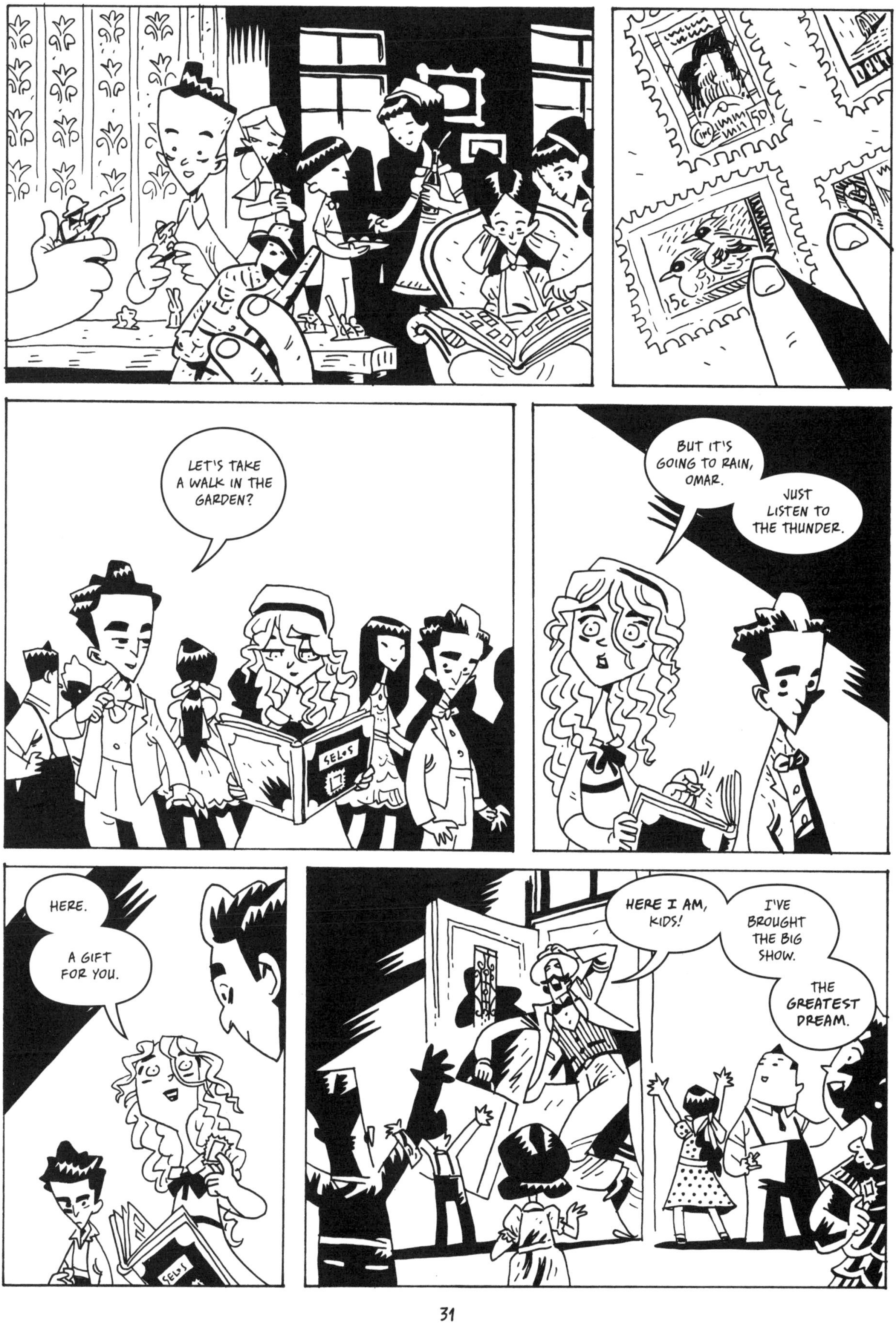
LET'S TAKE A WALK IN THE GARDEN?
SELOS
BUT IT'S GOING TO RAIN, OMAR.
JUST LISTEN TO THE THUNDER.
HERE.
A GIFT FOR YOU.
SELOS
HERE I AM, KIDS!
I'VE BROUGHT THE BIG SHOW.
THE GREATEST DREAM.

LÍVIA!

I SAVED A SEAT FOR YOU.

The magic of the dark basement lasted some twenty minutes.

KRAKA-BOOM

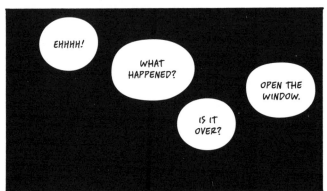

EHHHH!

WHAT HAPPENED?

OPEN THE WINDOW.

IS IT OVER?

SCRICH SCRICH SCRICH

CRAASH!

SHHHIKK

AAAAAAHHAAAAA

WHAT'S WITH ALL THIS NOISE?

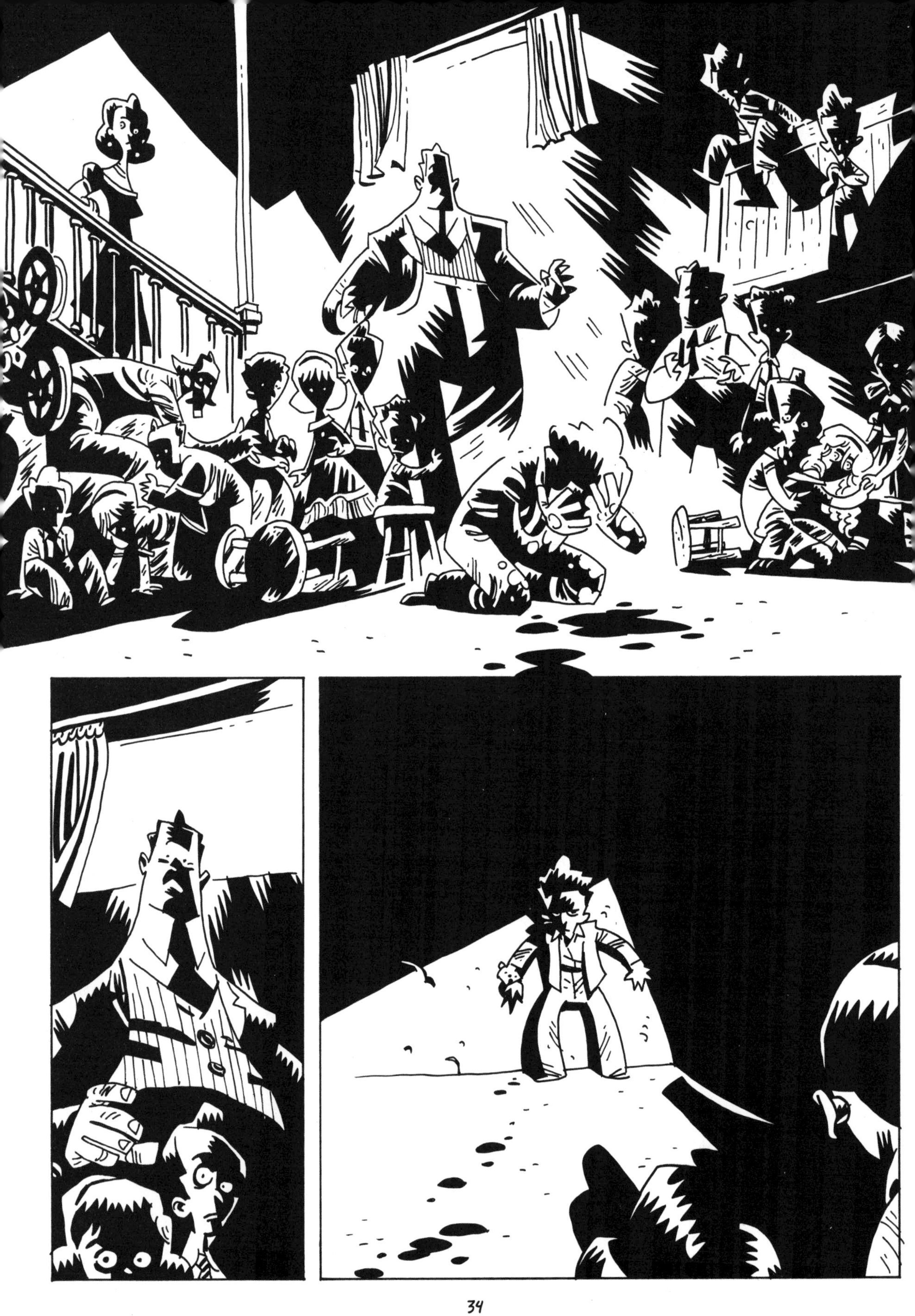

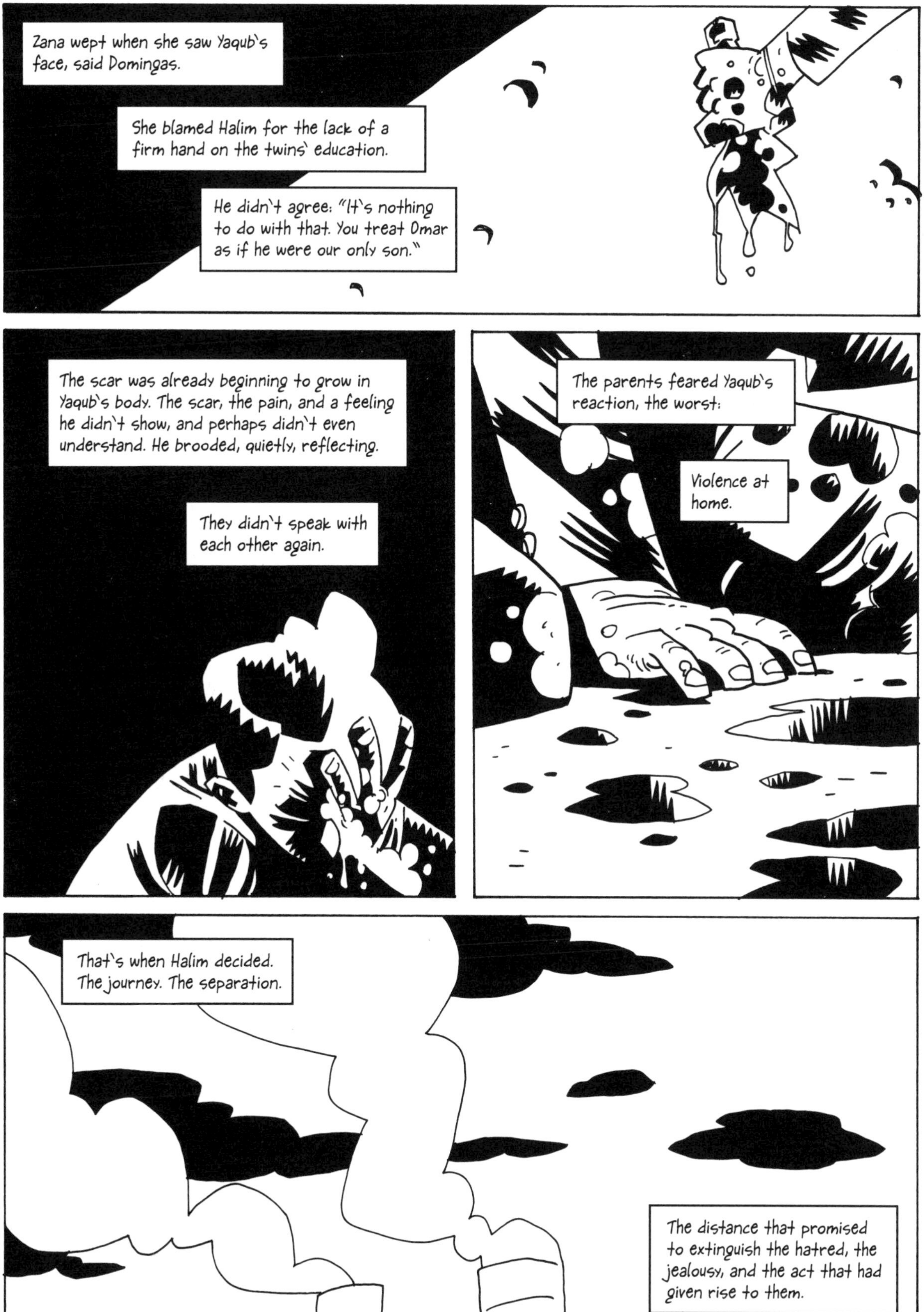
Zana wept when she saw Yaqub's face, said Domingas.
She blamed Halim for the lack of a firm hand on the twins' education.
He didn't agree: "It's nothing to do with that. You treat Omar as if he were our only son."
The scar was already beginning to grow in Yaqub's body. The scar, the pain, and a feeling he didn't show, and perhaps didn't even understand. He brooded, quietly, reflecting.
They didn't speak with each other again.
The parents feared Yaqub's reaction, the worst:
Violence at home.
That's when Halim decided. The journey. The separation.
The distance that promised to extinguish the hatred, the jealousy, and the act that had given rise to them.

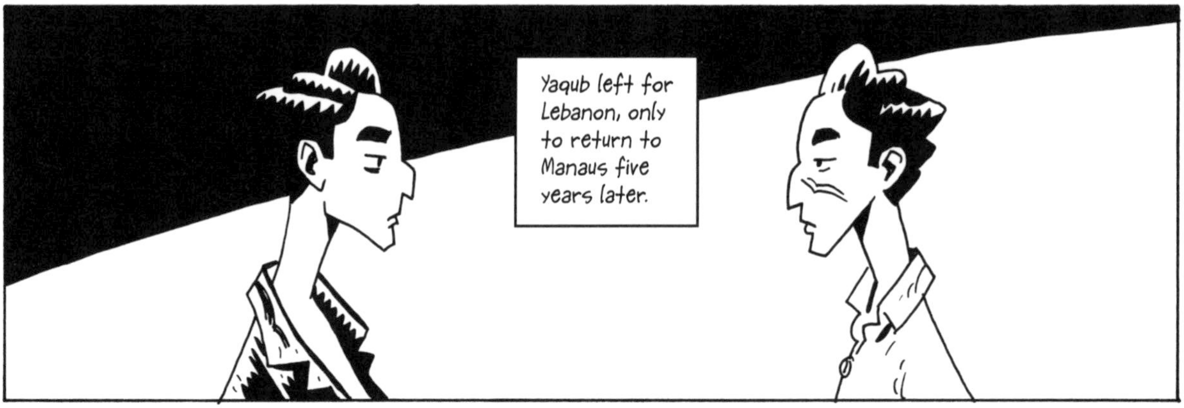
Yaqub left for Lebanon, only to return to Manaus five years later.

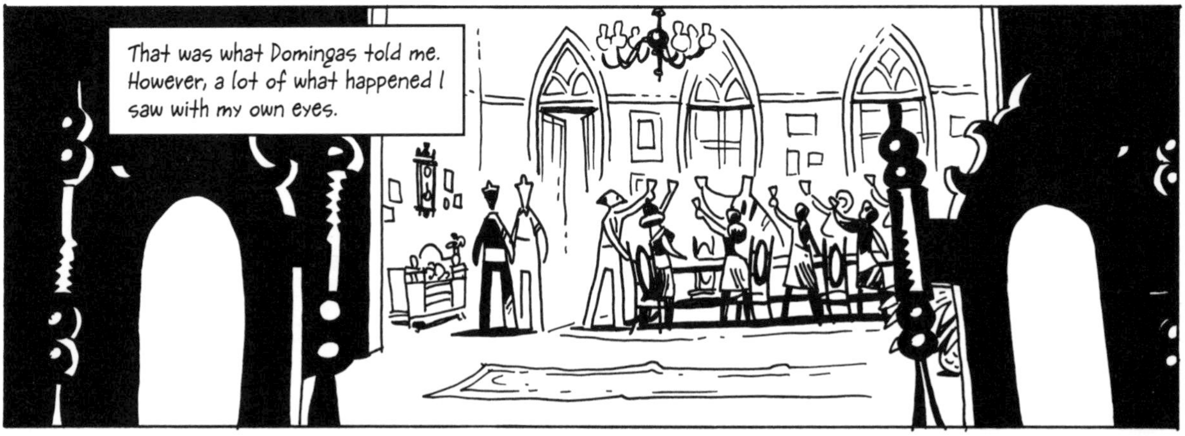
That was what Domingas told me. However, a lot of what happened I saw with my own eyes.

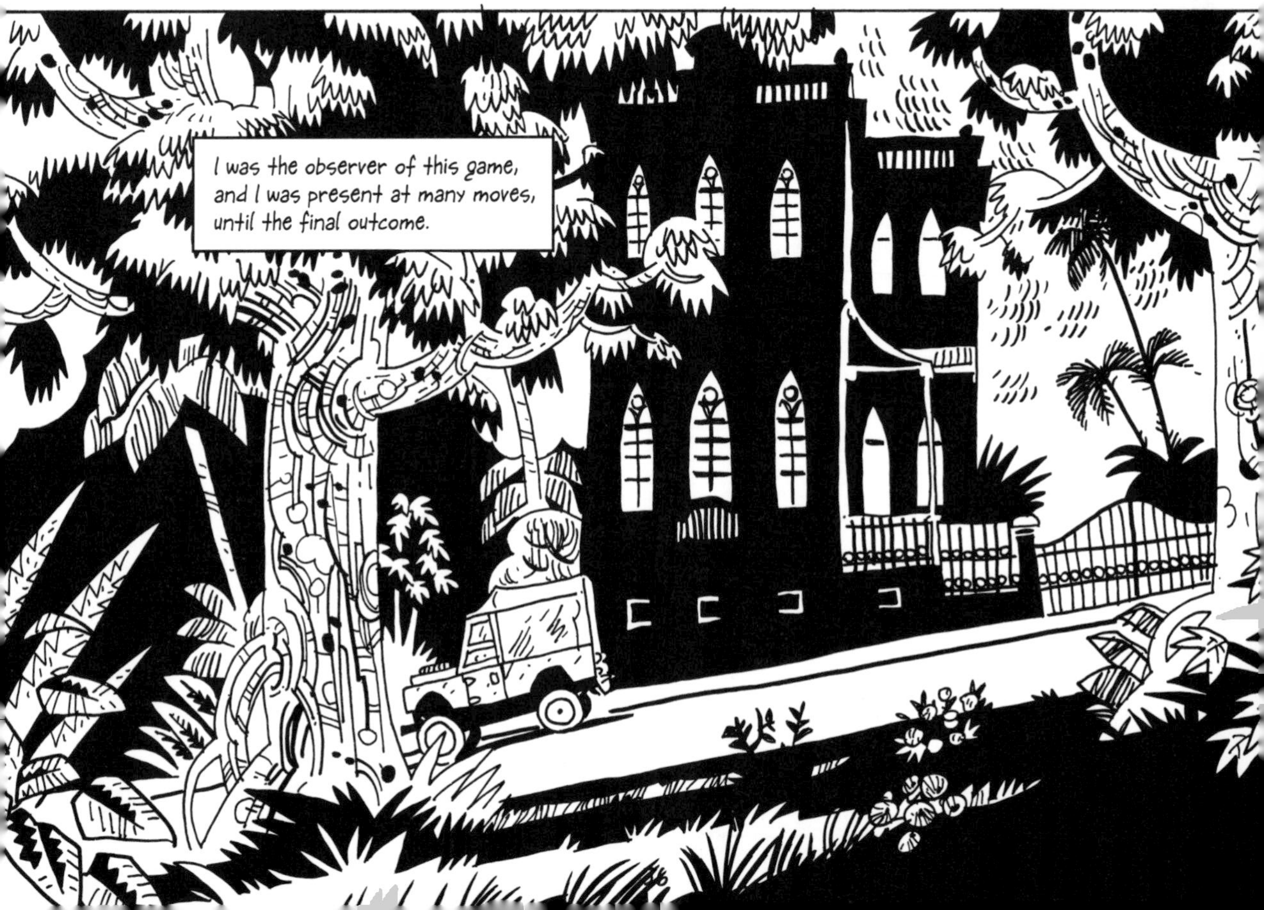
I was the observer of this game, and I was present at many moves, until the final outcome.

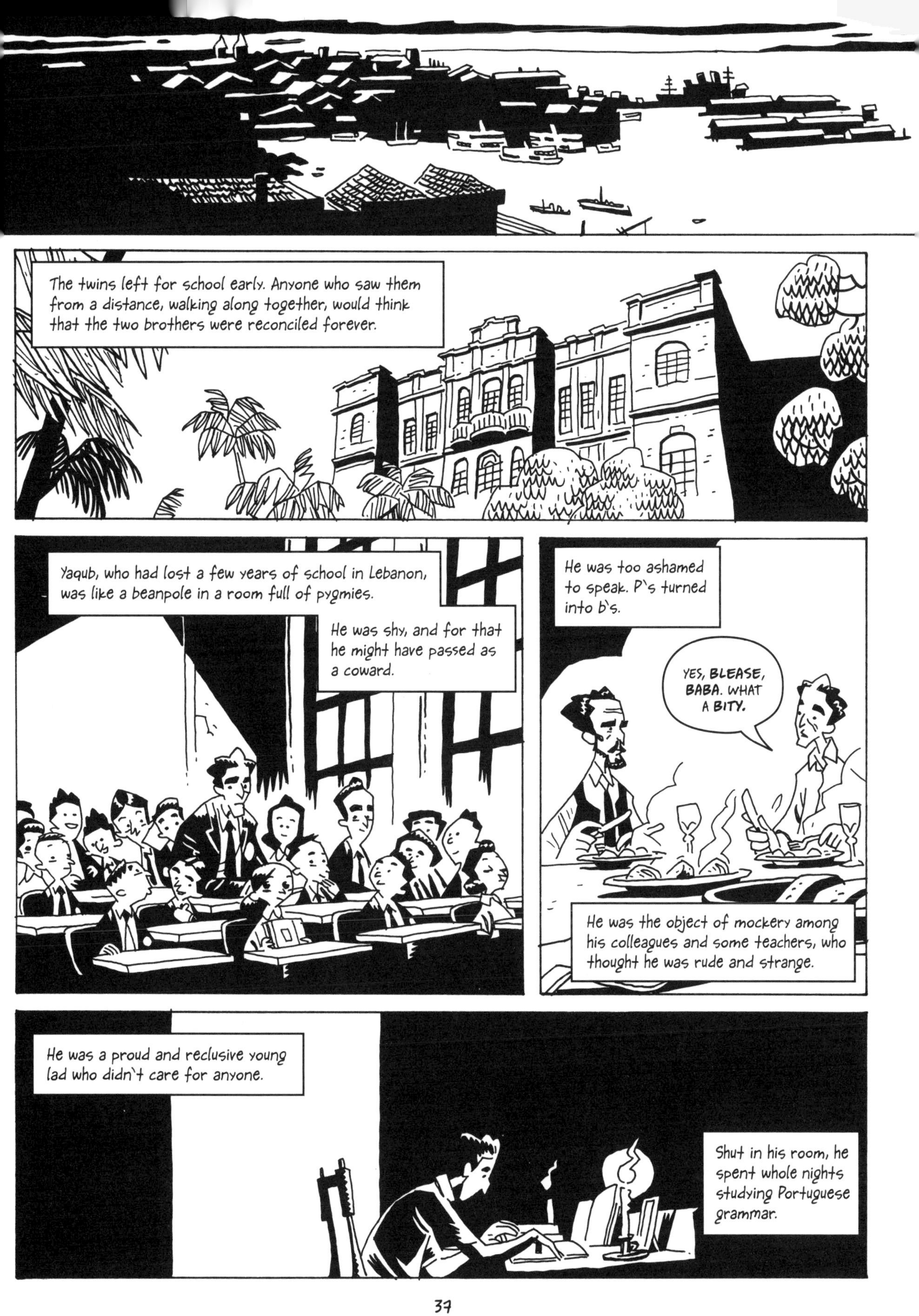

The twins left for school early. Anyone who saw them from a distance, walking along together, would think that the two brothers were reconciled forever.
Yaqub, who had lost a few years of school in Lebanon, was like a beanpole in a room full of pygmies.
He was shy, and for that he might have passed as a coward.
He was too ashamed to speak. P's turned into b's.
YES, BLEASE, BABA. WHAT A BITY.
He was the object of mockery among his colleagues and some teachers, who thought he was rude and strange.
He was a proud and reclusive young lad who didn't care for anyone.
Shut in his room, he spent whole nights studying Portuguese grammar.

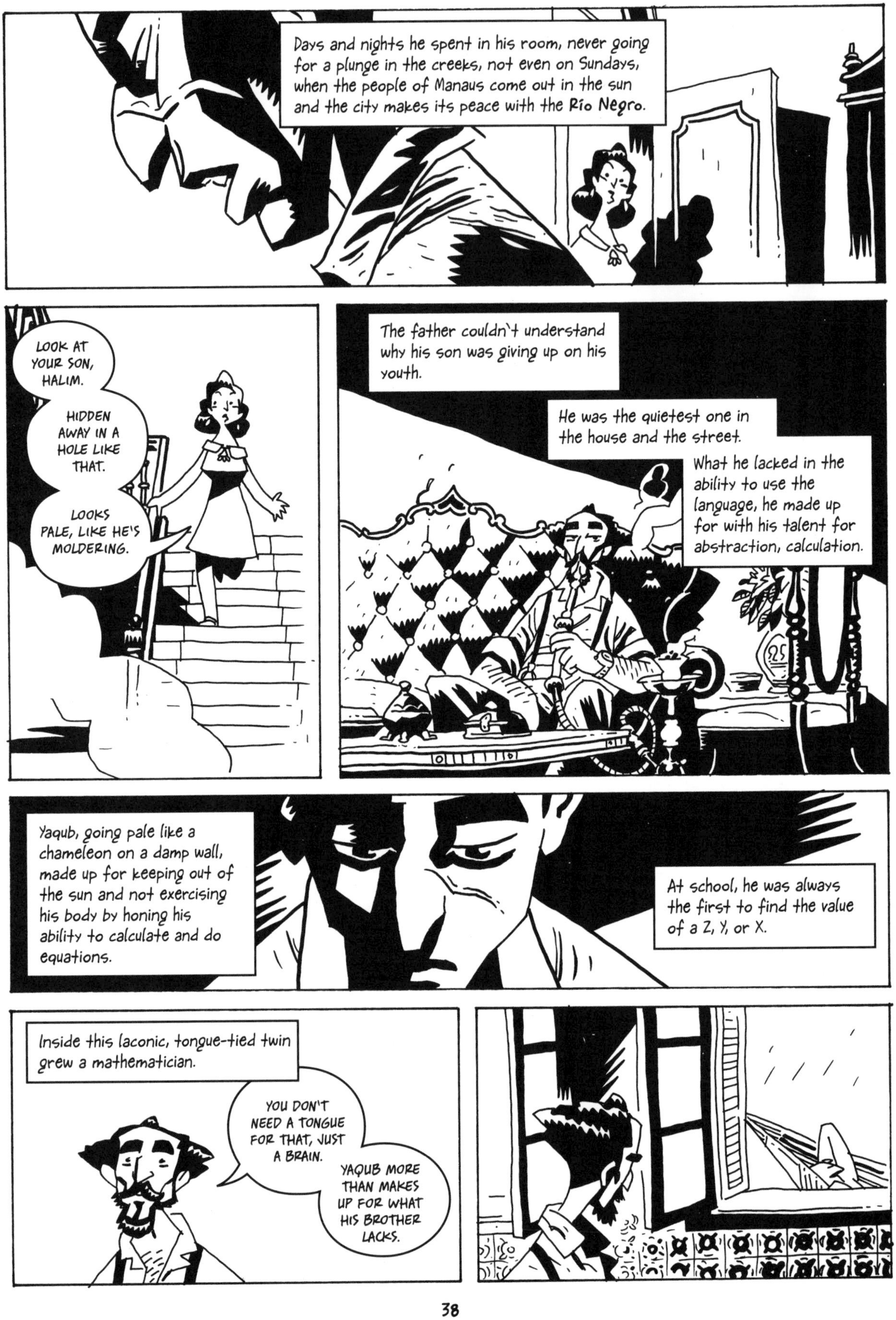
Days and nights he spent in his room, never going for a plunge in the creeks, not even on Sundays, when the people of Manaus come out in the sun and the city makes its peace with the Río Negro.
LOOK AT YOUR SON, HALIM.
HIDDEN AWAY IN A HOLE LIKE THAT.
LOOKS PALE, LIKE HE'S MOLDERING.
The father couldn't understand why his son was giving up on his youth.
He was the quietest one in the house and the street.
What he lacked in the ability to use the language, he made up for with his talent for abstraction, calculation.
Yaqub, going pale like a chameleon on a damp wall, made up for keeping out of the sun and not exercising his body by honing his ability to calculate and do equations.
At school, he was always the first to find the value of a Z, Y, or X.
Inside this laconic, tongue-tied twin grew a mathematician.
YOU DON'T NEED A TONGUE FOR THAT, JUST A BRAIN.
YAQUB MORE THAN MAKES UP FOR WHAT HIS BROTHER LACKS.

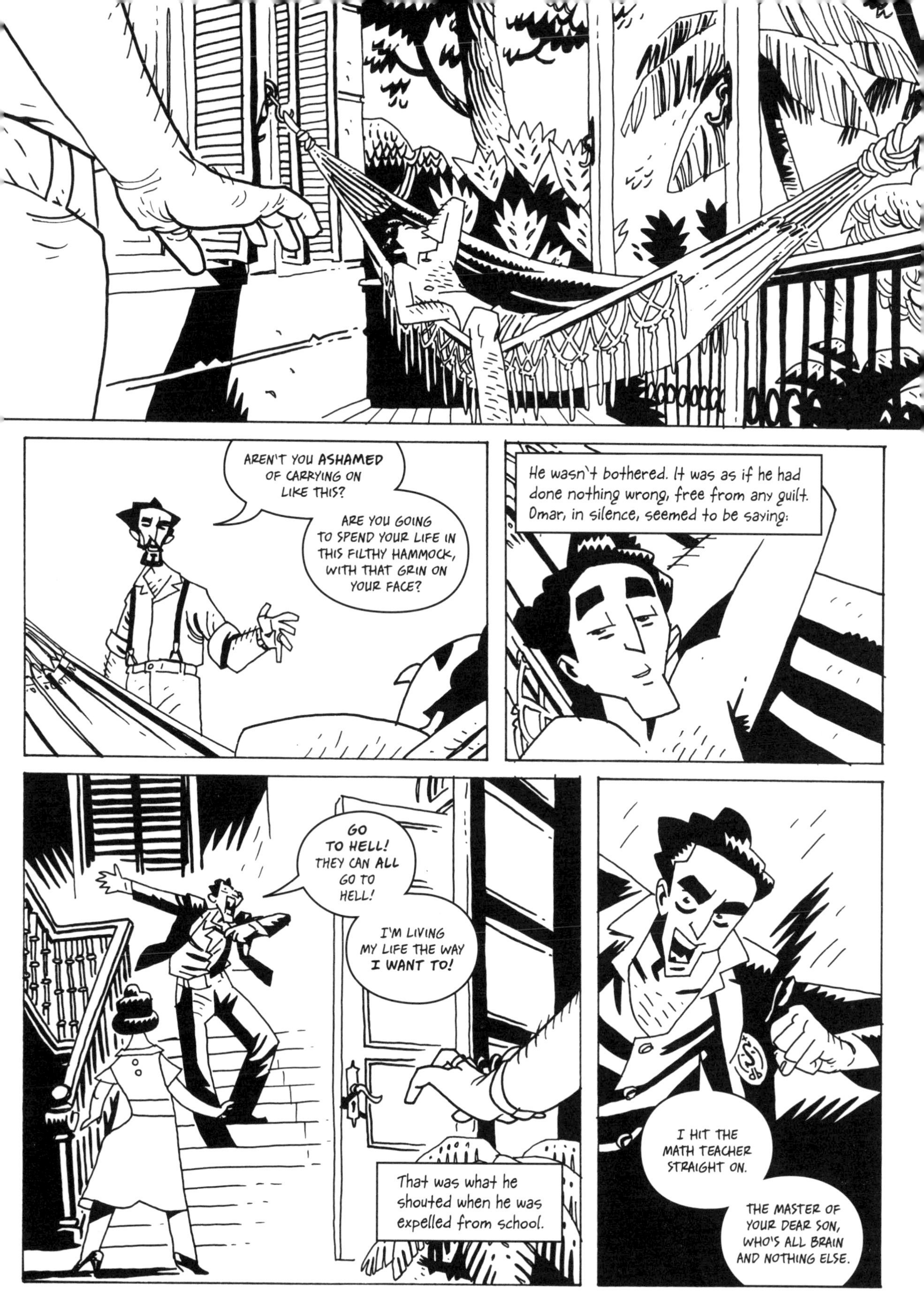
AREN'T YOU ASHAMED OF CARRYING ON LIKE THIS?
ARE YOU GOING TO SPEND YOUR LIFE IN THIS FILTHY HAMMOCK, WITH THAT GRIN ON YOUR FACE?
He wasn't bothered. It was as if he had done nothing wrong, free from any guilt. Omar, in silence, seemed to be saying:
GO TO HELL! THEY CAN ALL GO TO HELL!
I'M LIVING MY LIFE THE WAY I WANT TO!
That was what he shouted when he was expelled from school.
I HIT THE MATH TEACHER STRAIGHT ON.
THE MASTER OF YOUR DEAR SON, WHO'S ALL BRAIN AND NOTHING ELSE.

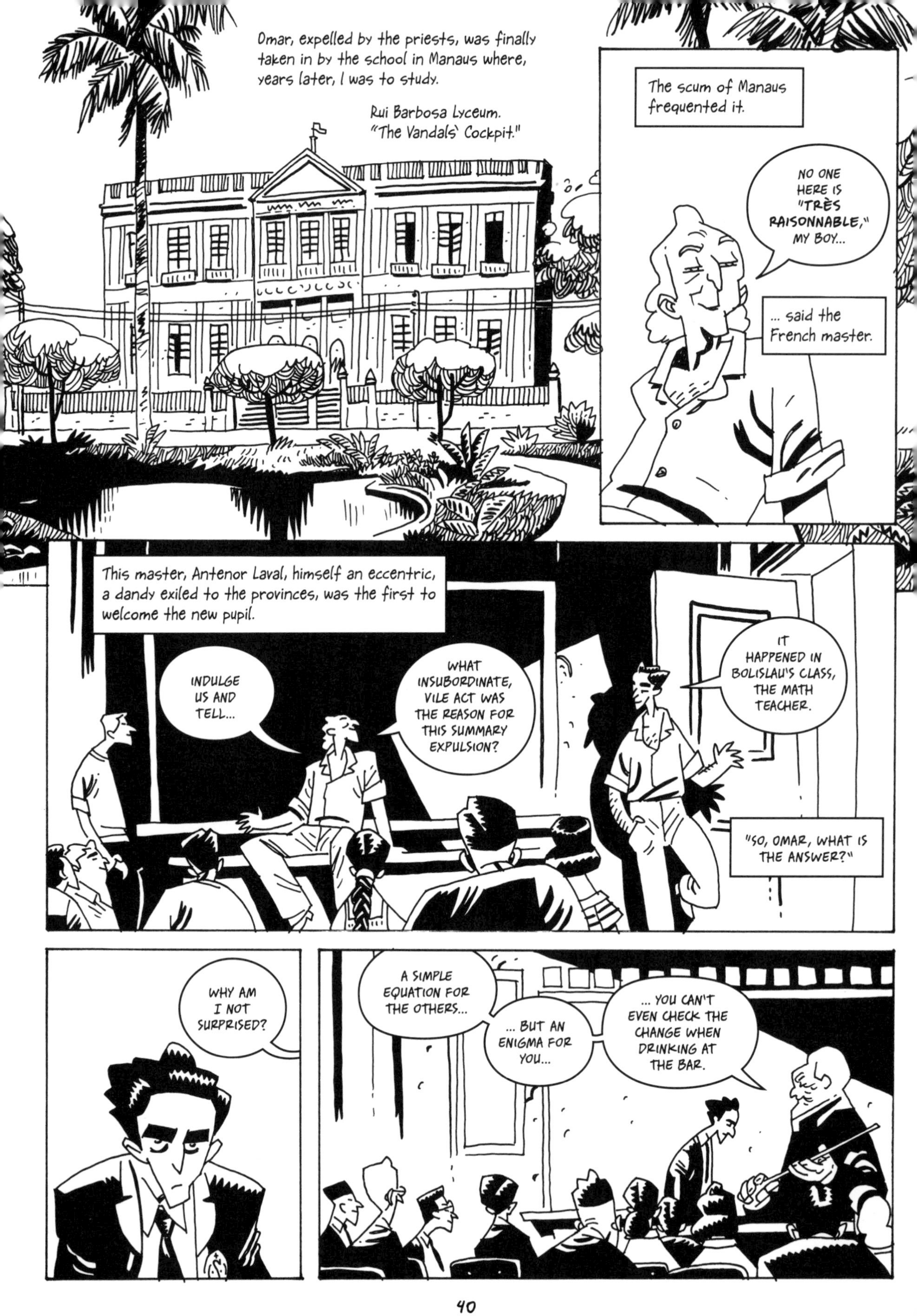

Omar, expelled by the priests, was finally taken in by the school in Manaus where, years later, I was to study.
Rui Barbosa Lyceum. "The Vandals' Cockpit."
The scum of Manaus frequented it.
NO ONE HERE IS "**TRÈS RAISONNABLE,**" MY BOY...
... said the French master.
This master, Antenor Laval, himself an eccentric, a dandy exiled to the provinces, was the first to welcome the new pupil.
INDULGE US AND TELL...
WHAT INSUBORDINATE, VILE ACT WAS THE REASON FOR THIS SUMMARY EXPULSION?
IT HAPPENED IN BOLISLAU'S CLASS, THE MATH TEACHER.
"SO, OMAR, WHAT IS THE ANSWER?"
WHY AM I NOT SURPRISED?
A SIMPLE EQUATION FOR THE OTHERS...
... BUT AN ENIGMA FOR YOU...
... YOU CAN'T EVEN CHECK THE CHANGE WHEN DRINKING AT THE BAR.

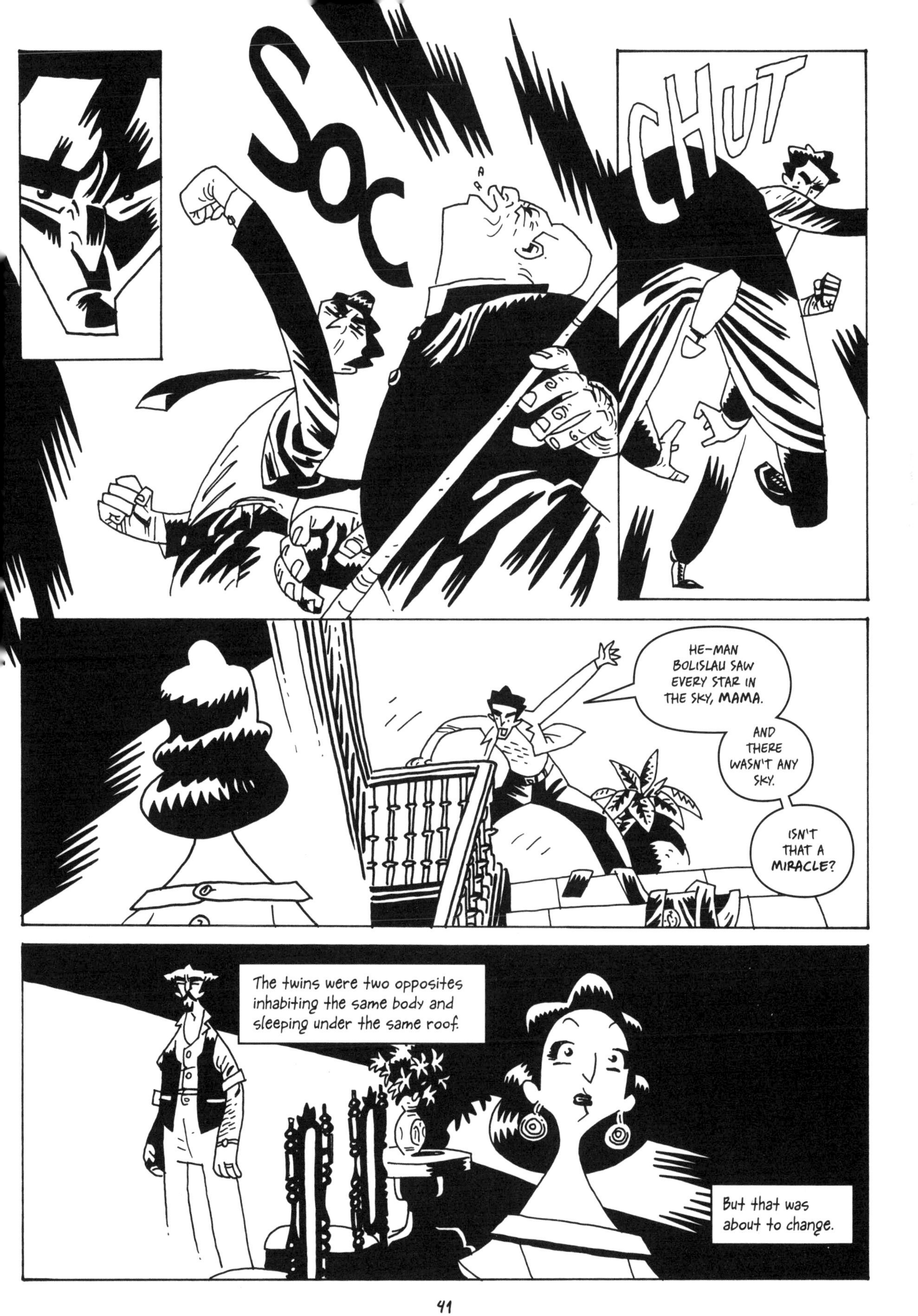
SOC
A
A
CHUT
HE-MAN BOLISLAU SAW EVERY STAR IN THE SKY, MAMA.
AND THERE WASN'T ANY SKY.
ISN'T THAT A MIRACLE?
The twins were two opposites inhabiting the same body and sleeping under the same roof.
But that was about to change.

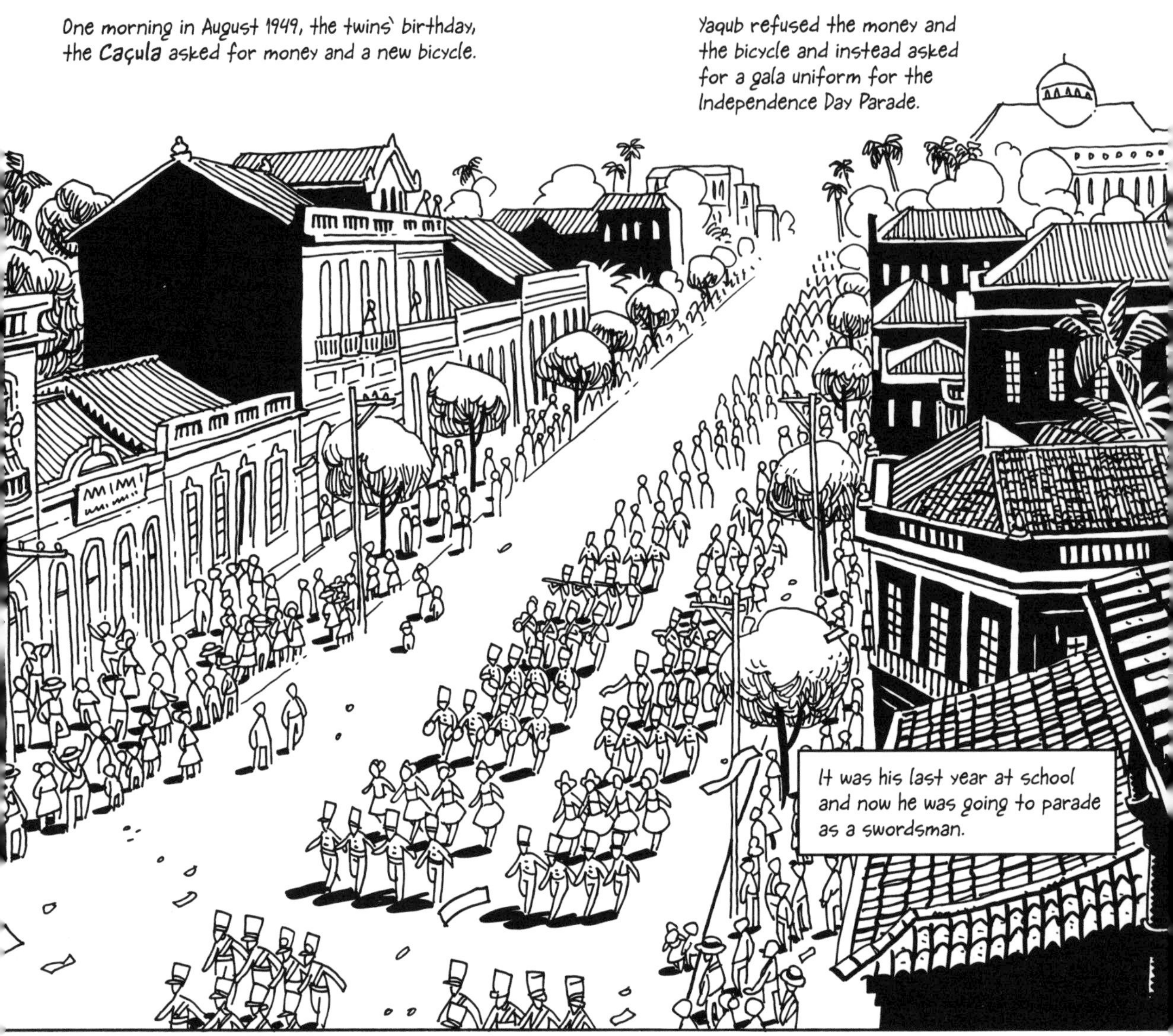
One morning in August 1949, the twins' birthday, the **Caçula** asked for money and a new bicycle.
Yaqub refused the money and the bicycle and instead asked for a gala uniform for the Independence Day Parade.
It was his last year at school and now he was going to parade as a swordsman.

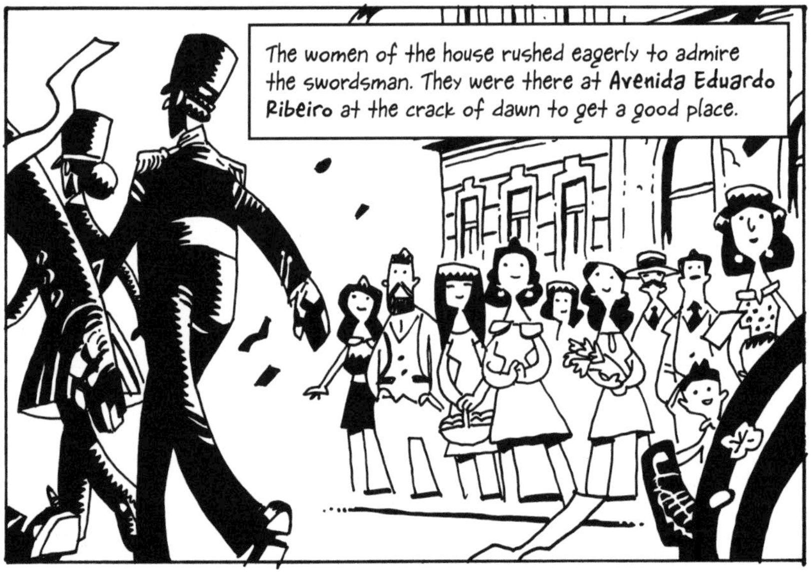
The women of the house rushed eagerly to admire the swordsman. They were there at **Avenida Eduardo Ribeiro** at the crack of dawn to get a good place.

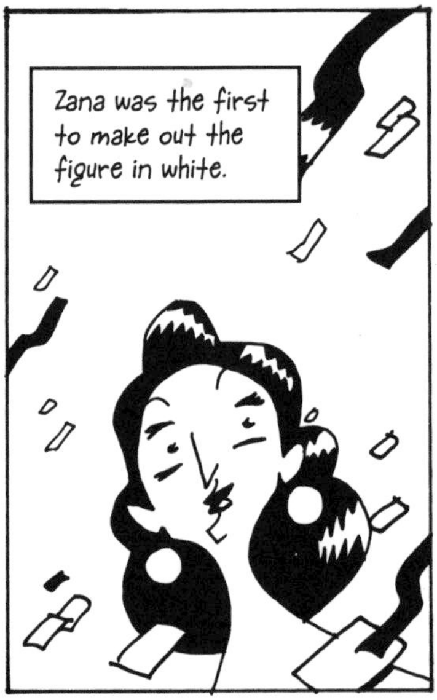
Zana was the first to make out the figure in white.

The parade in his gala uniform had been Yaqub's farewell.

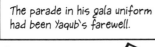

In the Salesian school they had a ceremony in his honor. He got two medals and ten minutes of speeches.

Yaqub -- and Brazil itself -- seemed to have a promising future.

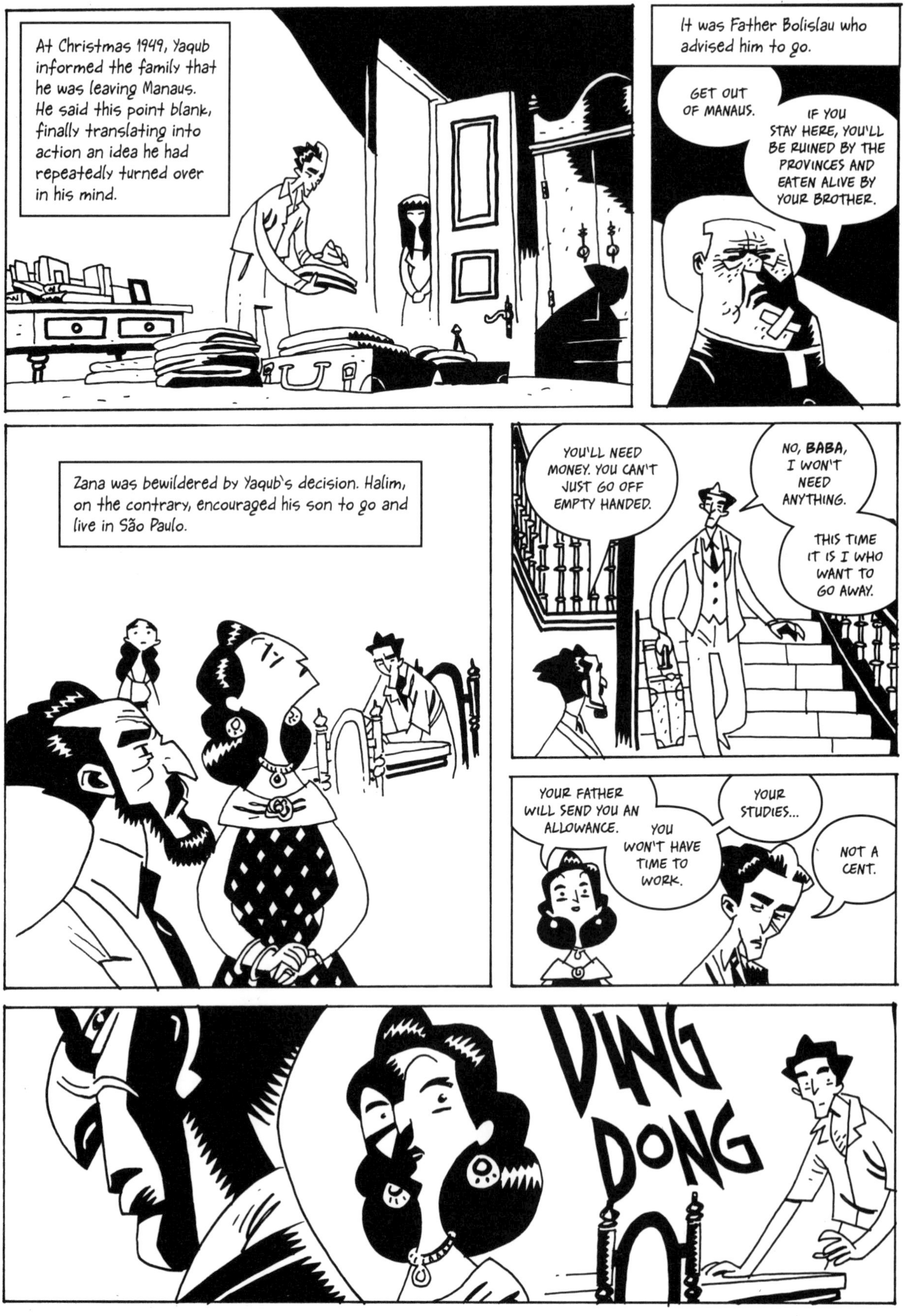

At Christmas 1949, Yaqub informed the family that he was leaving Manaus. He said this point blank, finally translating into action an idea he had repeatedly turned over in his mind.
It was Father Bolislau who advised him to go.
GET OUT OF MANAUS.
IF YOU STAY HERE, YOU'LL BE RUINED BY THE PROVINCES AND EATEN ALIVE BY YOUR BROTHER.
Zana was bewildered by Yaqub's decision. Halim, on the contrary, encouraged his son to go and live in São Paulo.
YOU'LL NEED MONEY. YOU CAN'T JUST GO OFF EMPTY HANDED.
NO, **BABA**, I WON'T NEED ANYTHING.
THIS TIME IT IS I WHO WANT TO GO AWAY.
YOUR FATHER WILL SEND YOU AN ALLOWANCE.
YOU WON'T HAVE TIME TO WORK.
YOUR STUDIES...
NOT A CENT.
DING DONG

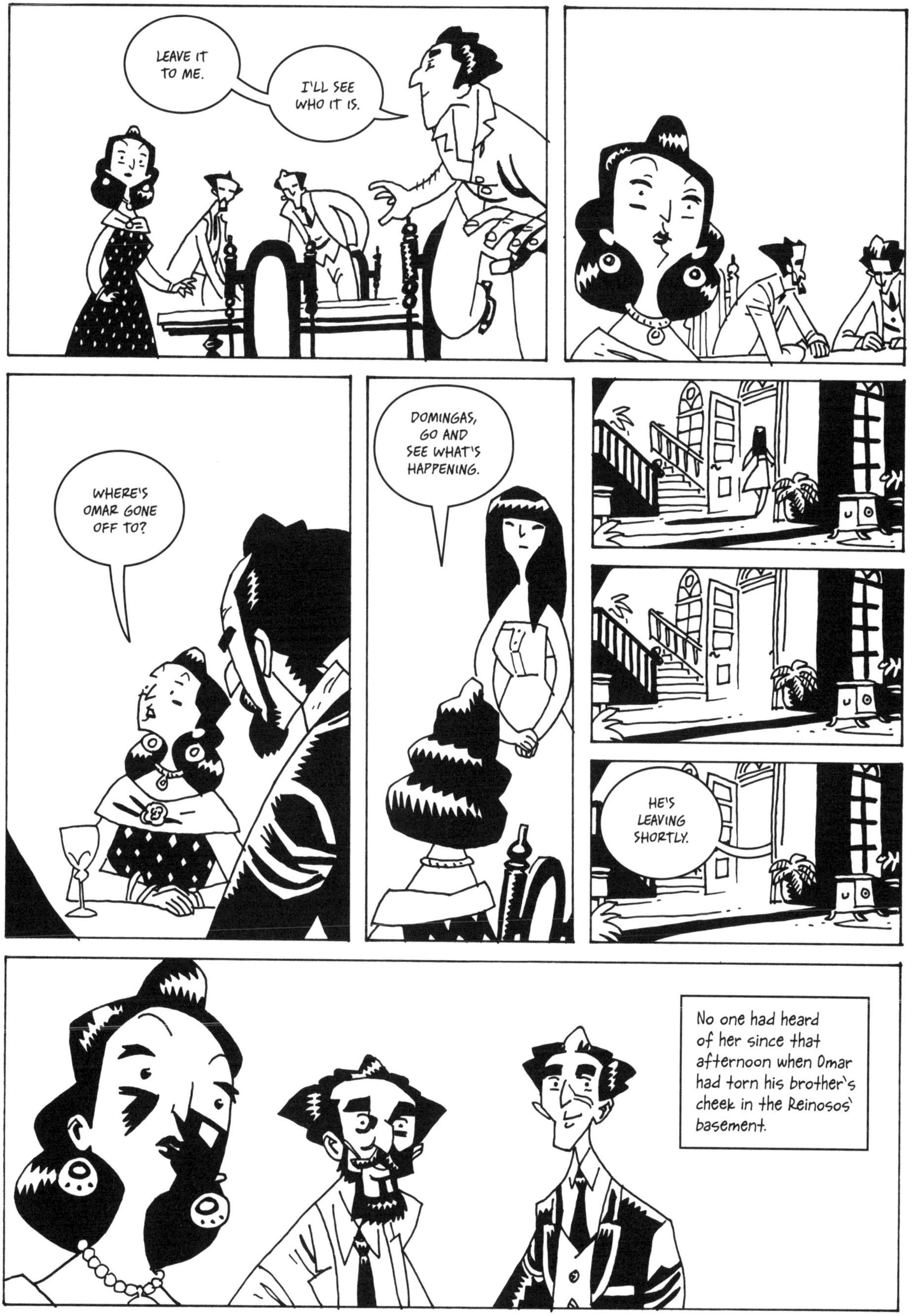
LEAVE IT TO ME.
I'LL SEE WHO IT IS.
WHERE'S OMAR GONE OFF TO?
DOMINGAS, GO AND SEE WHAT'S HAPPENING.
HE'S LEAVING SHORTLY.
No one had heard of her since that afternoon when Omar had torn his brother's cheek in the Reinosos' basement.

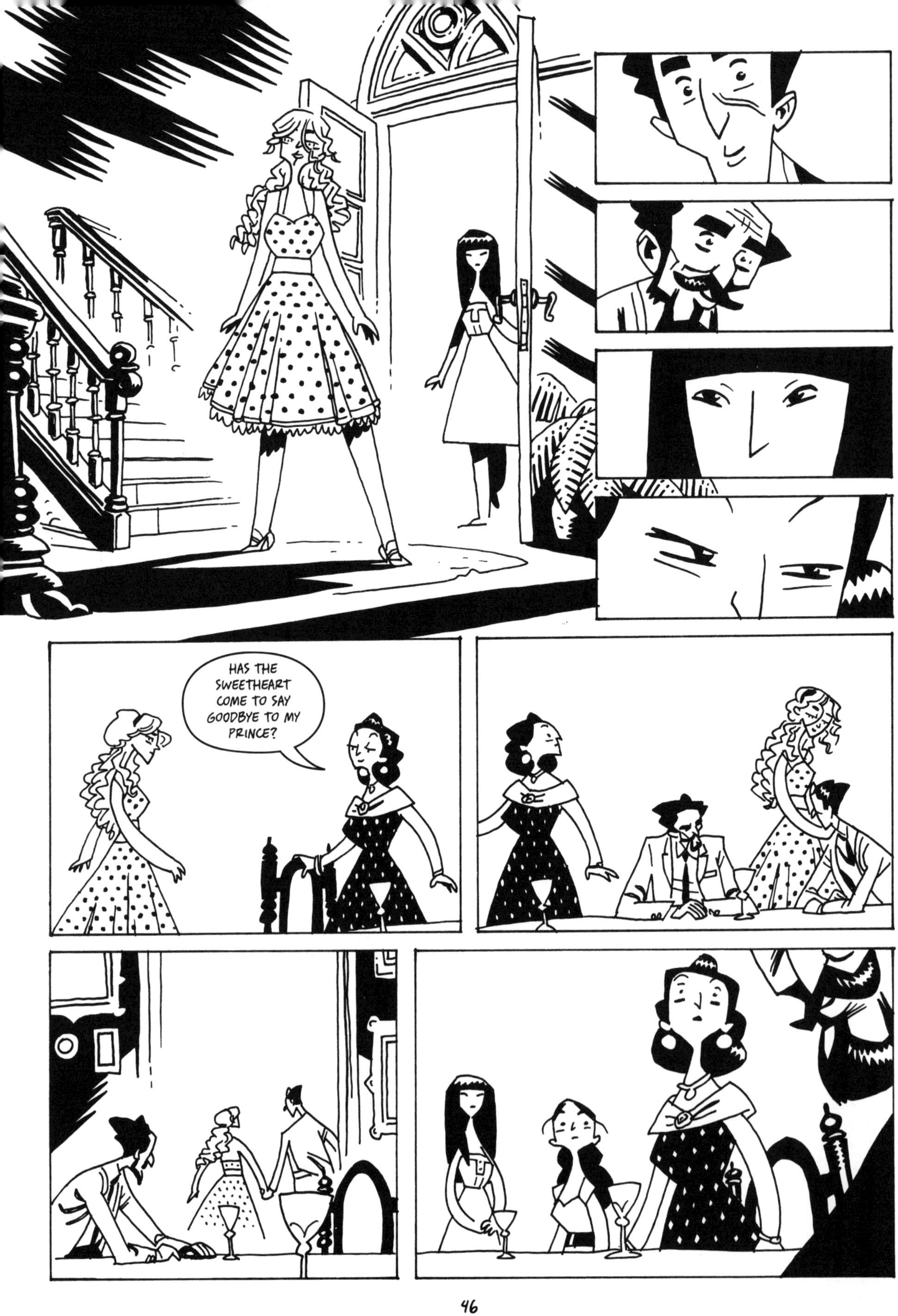
HAS THE SWEETHEART COME TO SAY GOODBYE TO MY PRINCE?

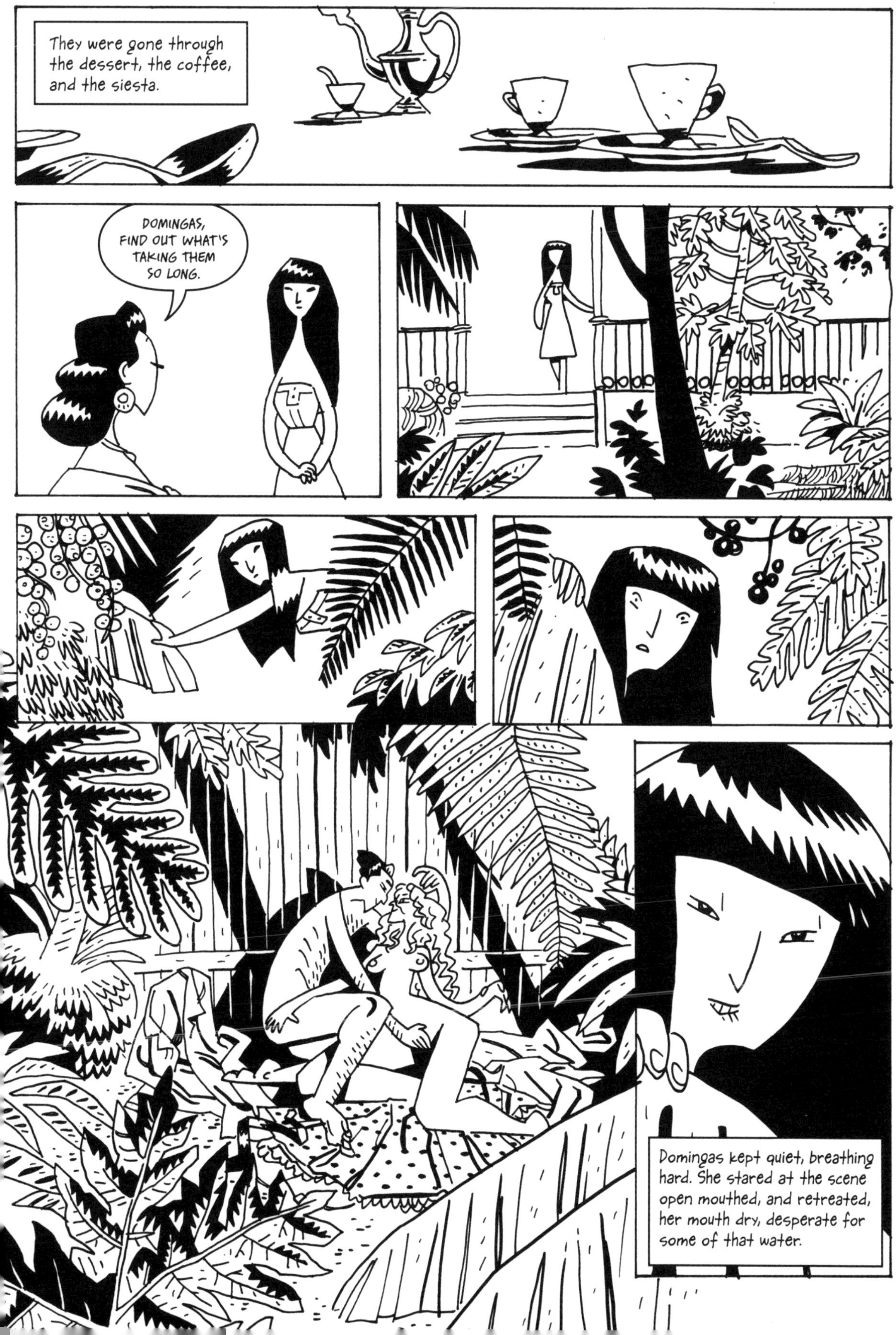
They were gone through the dessert, the coffee, and the siesta.
DOMINGAS, FIND OUT WHAT'S TAKING THEM SO LONG.
Domingas kept quiet, breathing hard. She stared at the scene open mouthed, and retreated, her mouth dry, desperate for some of that water.

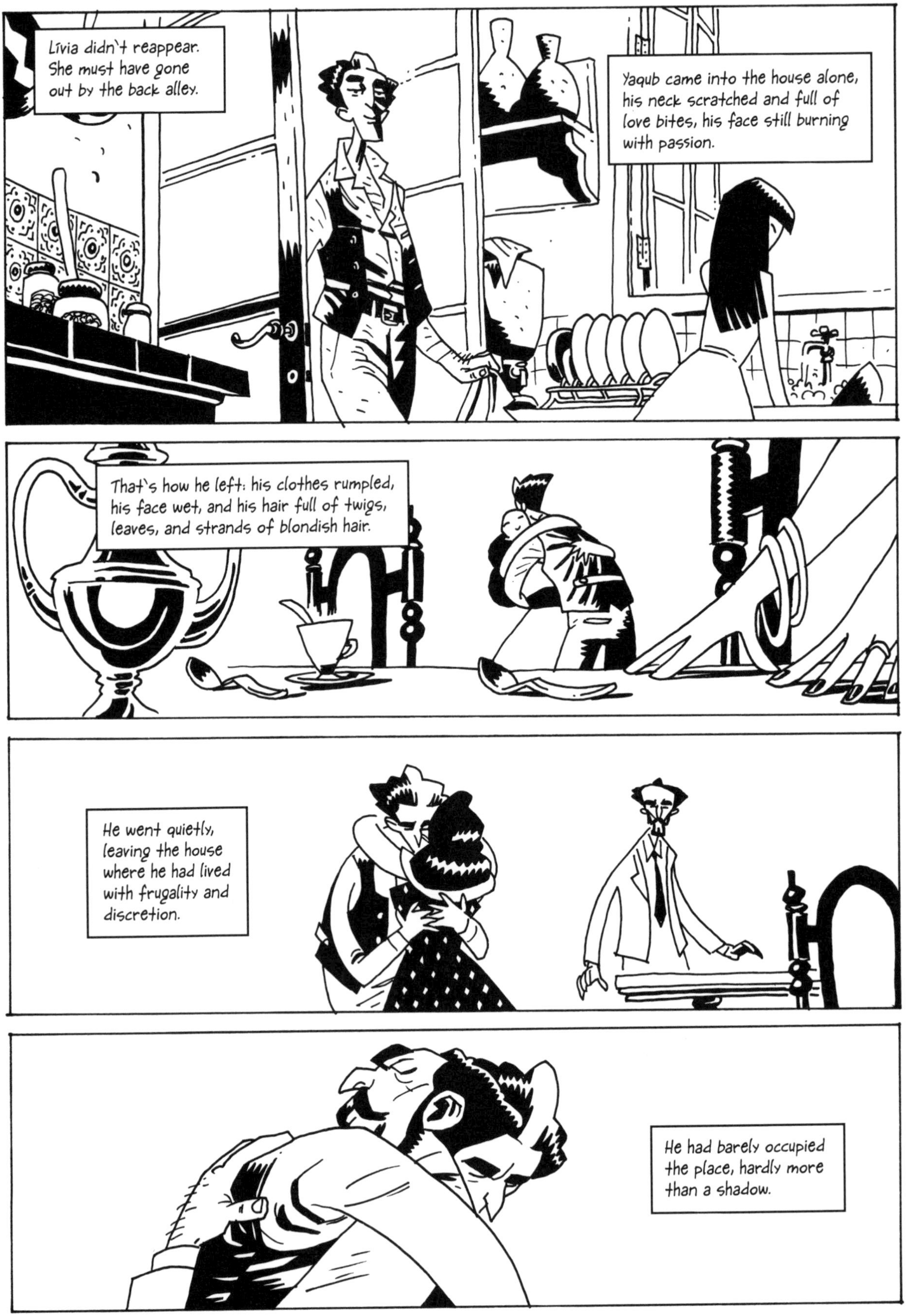
Lívia didn't reappear. She must have gone out by the back alley.
Yaqub came into the house alone, his neck scratched and full of love bites, his face still burning with passion.
That's how he left: his clothes rumpled, his face wet, and his hair full of twigs, leaves, and strands of blondish hair.
He went quietly, leaving the house where he had lived with frugality and discretion.
He had barely occupied the place, hardly more than a shadow.

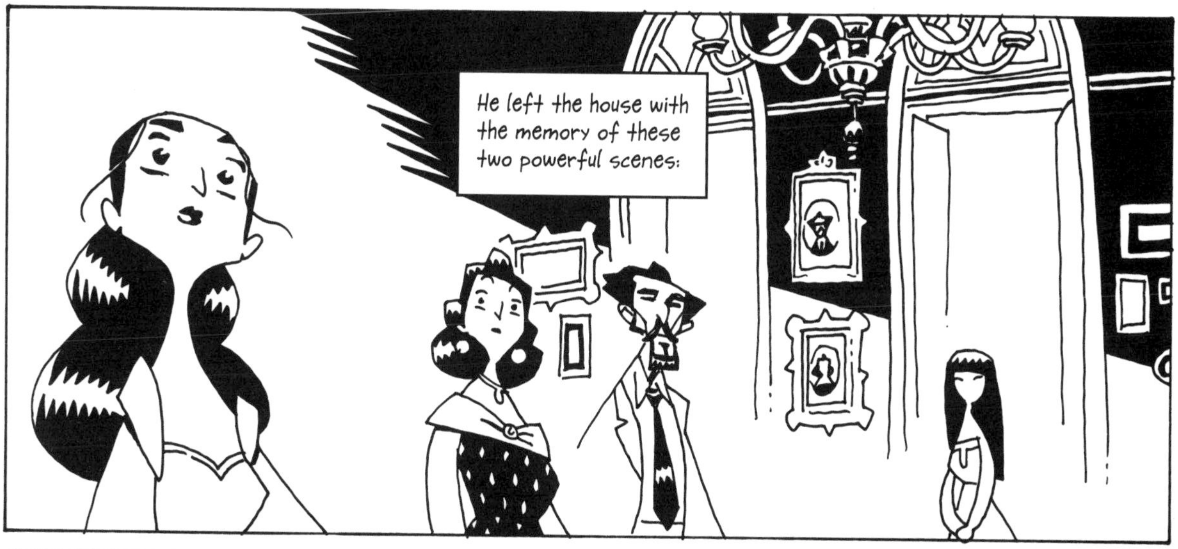
He left the house with the memory of these two powerful scenes:

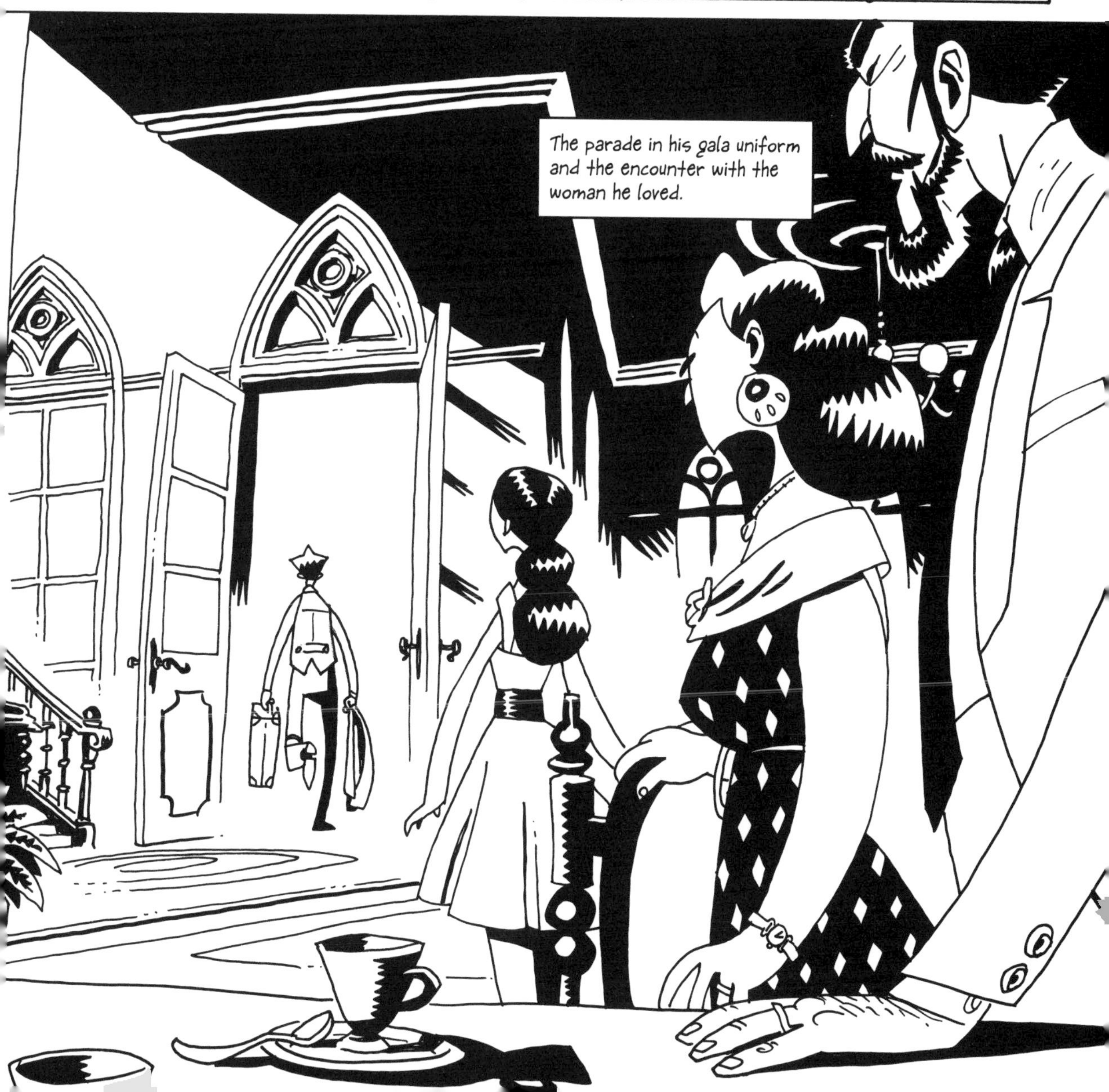
The parade in his gala uniform and the encounter with the woman he loved.

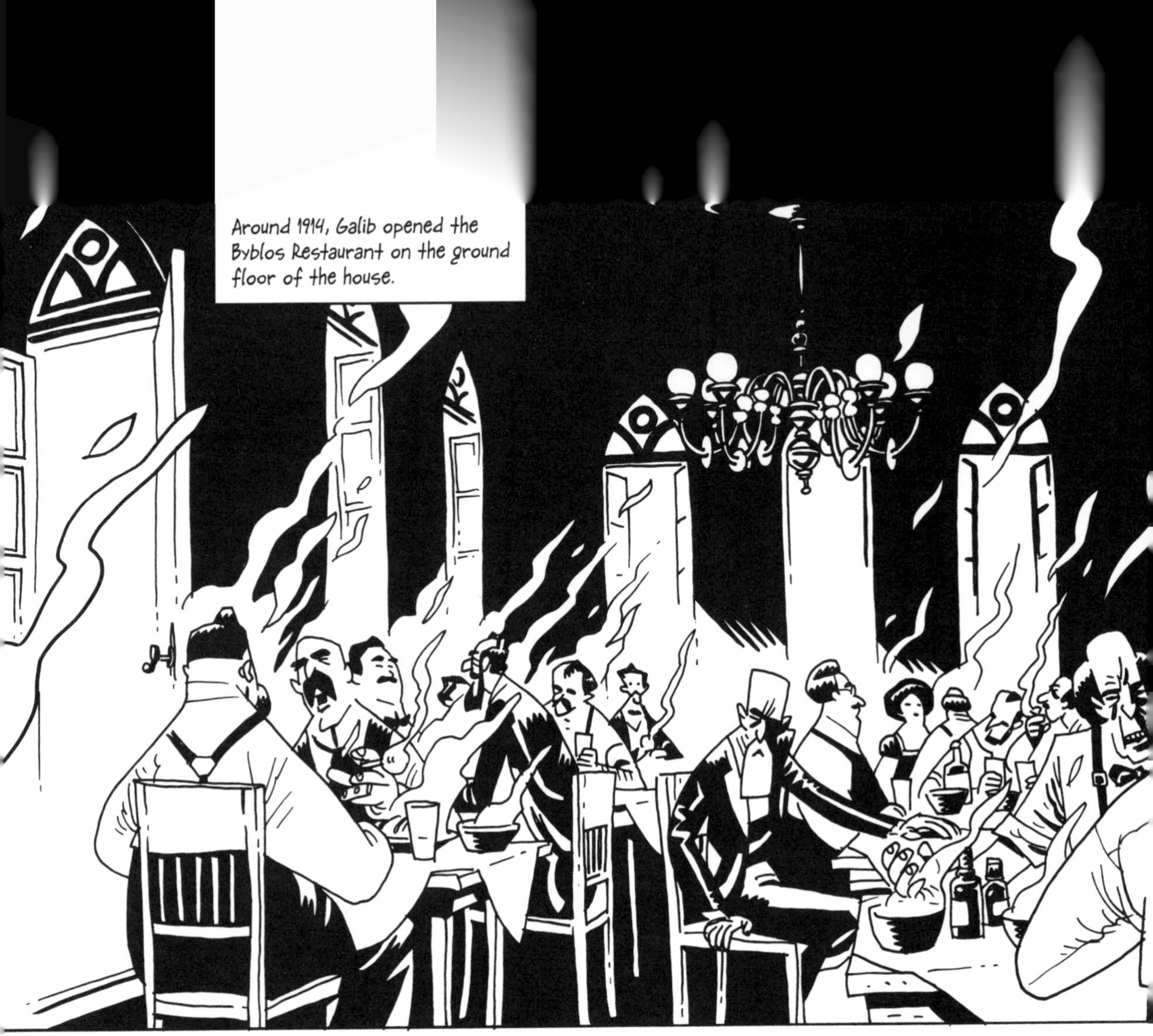
Around 1914, Galib opened the Byblos Restaurant on the ground floor of the house.

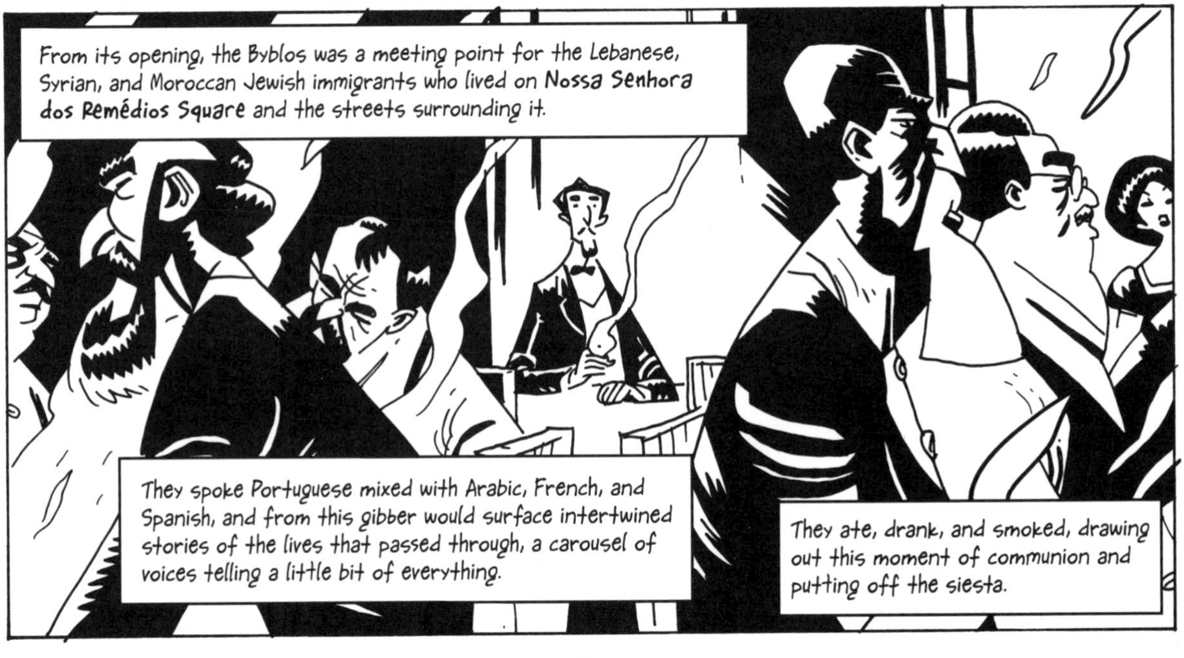
From its opening, the Byblos was a meeting point for the Lebanese, Syrian, and Moroccan Jewish immigrants who lived on **Nossa Senhora dos Remédios Square** and the streets surrounding it.
They spoke Portuguese mixed with Arabic, French, and Spanish, and from this gibber would surface intertwined stories of the lives that passed through, a carousel of voices telling a little bit of everything.
They ate, drank, and smoked, drawing out this moment of communion and putting off the siesta.

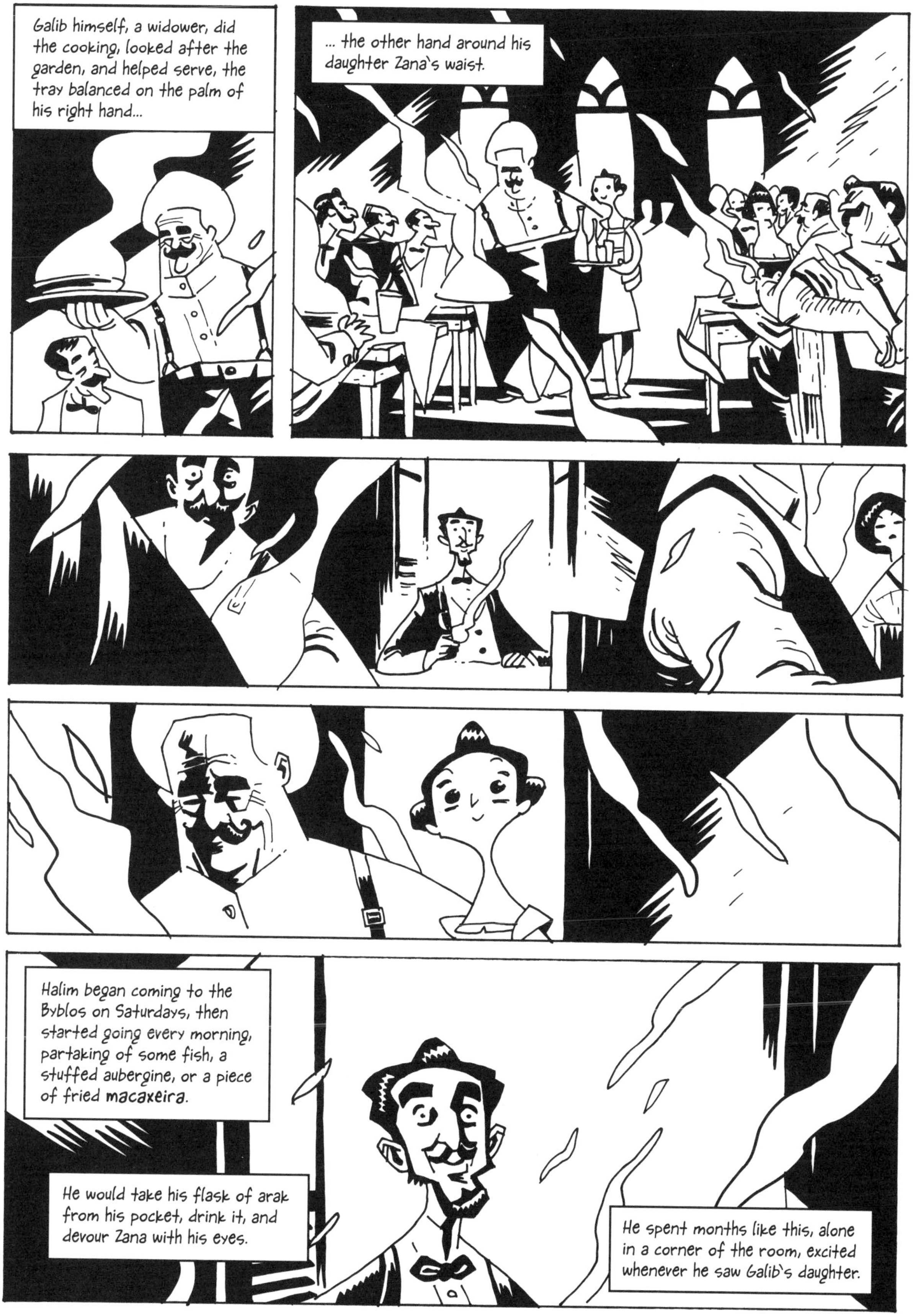
Galib himself, a widower, did the cooking, looked after the garden, and helped serve, the tray balanced on the palm of his right hand...
... the other hand around his daughter Zana's waist.
Halim began coming to the Byblos on Saturdays, then started going every morning, partaking of some fish, a stuffed aubergine, or a piece of fried macaxeira.
He would take his flask of arak from his pocket, drink it, and devour Zana with his eyes.
He spent months like this, alone in a corner of the room, excited whenever he saw Galib's daughter.

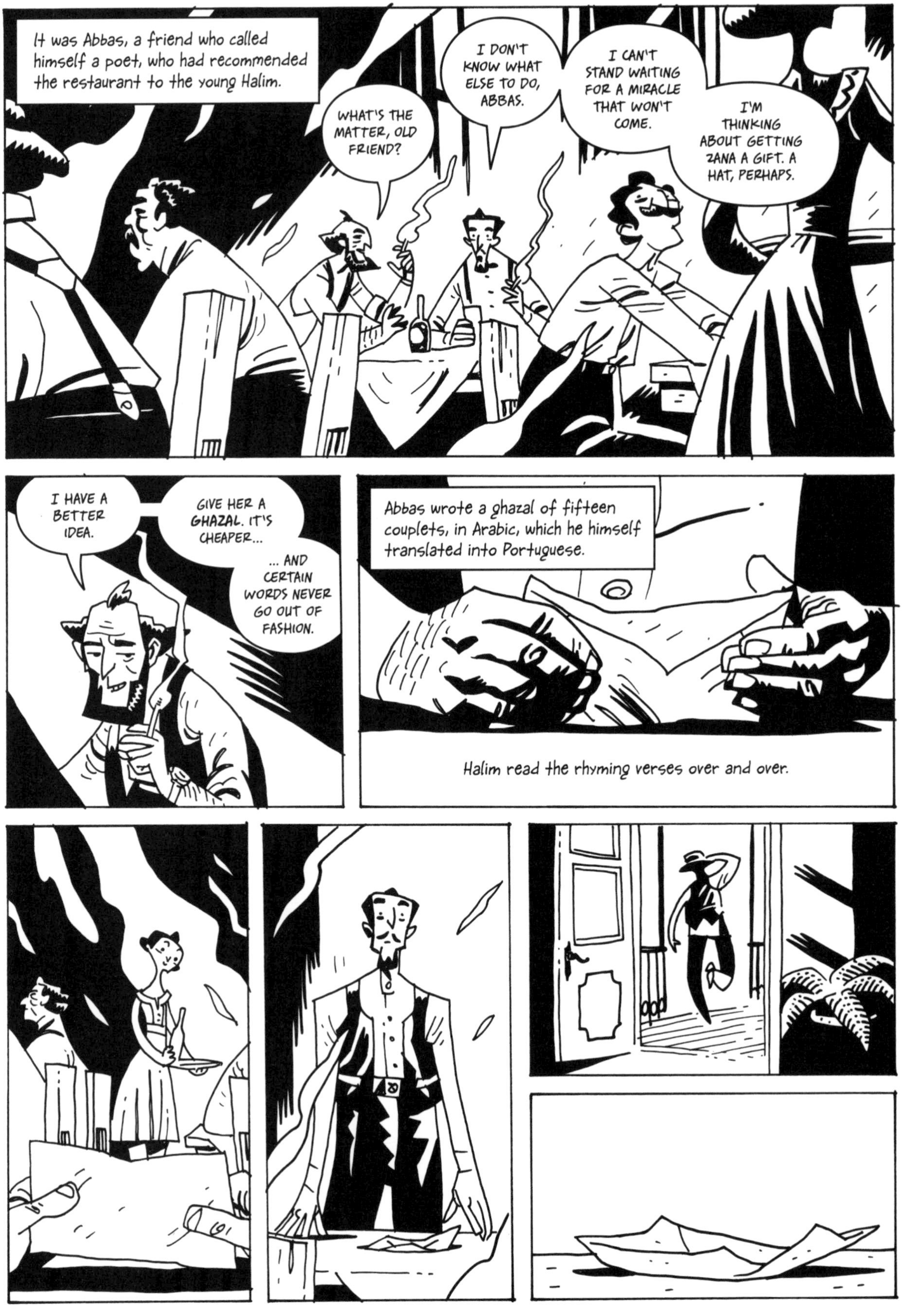
It was Abbas, a friend who called himself a poet, who had recommended the restaurant to the young Halim.
WHAT'S THE MATTER, OLD FRIEND?
I DON'T KNOW WHAT ELSE TO DO, ABBAS.
I CAN'T STAND WAITING FOR A MIRACLE THAT WON'T COME.
I'M THINKING ABOUT GETTING ZANA A GIFT. A HAT, PERHAPS.
I HAVE A BETTER IDEA.
GIVE HER A GHAZAL. IT'S CHEAPER...
... AND CERTAIN WORDS NEVER GO OUT OF FASHION.
Abbas wrote a ghazal of fifteen couplets, in Arabic, which he himself translated into Portuguese.
Halim read the rhyming verses over and over.

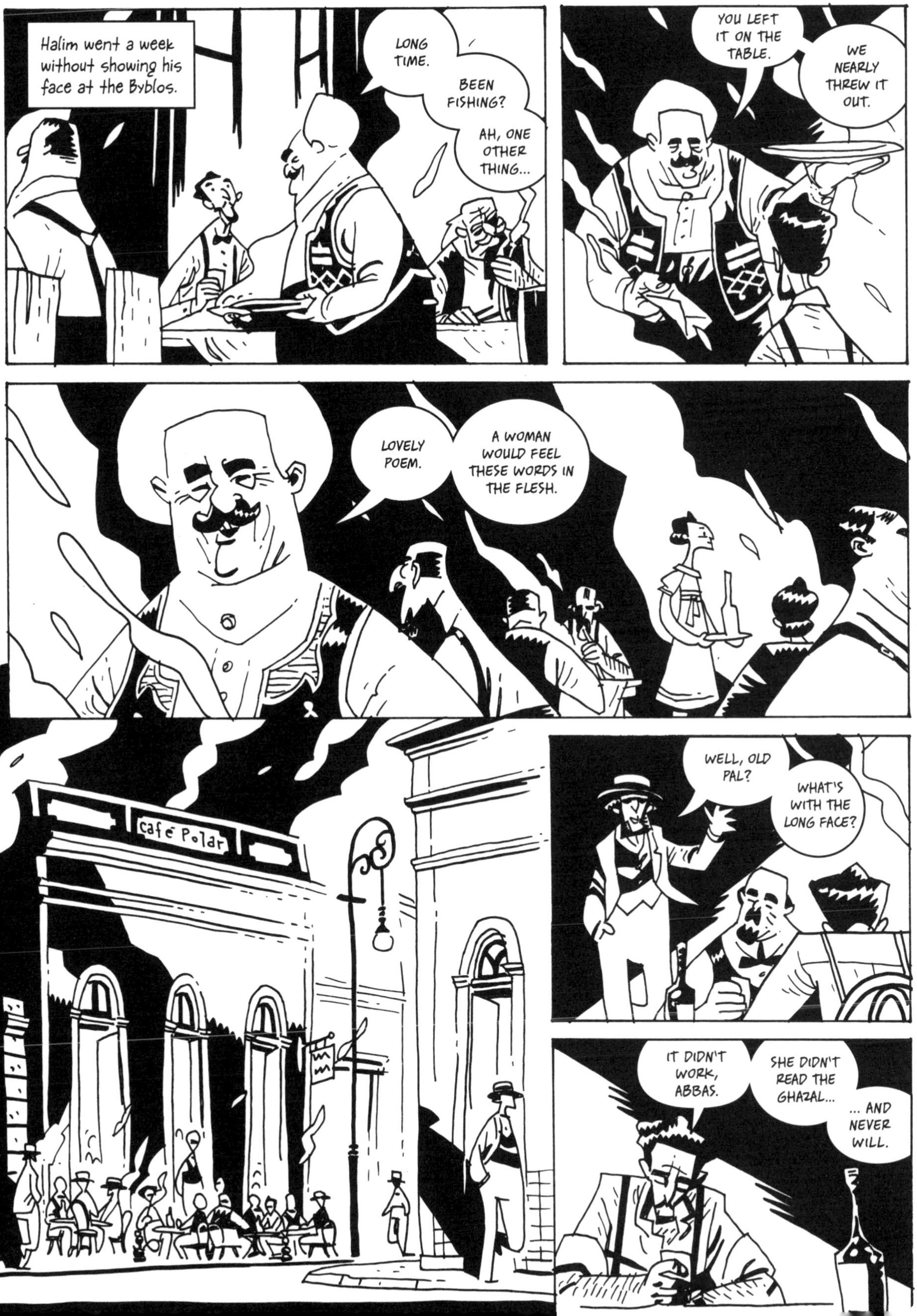
Halim went a week without showing his face at the Byblos.
LONG TIME.
BEEN FISHING?
AH, ONE OTHER THING...
YOU LEFT IT ON THE TABLE.
WE NEARLY THREW IT OUT.
LOVELY POEM.
A WOMAN WOULD FEEL THESE WORDS IN THE FLESH.
café Polar
WELL, OLD PAL?
WHAT'S WITH THE LONG FACE?
IT DIDN'T WORK, ABBAS.
SHE DIDN'T READ THE GHAZAL...
... AND NEVER WILL.

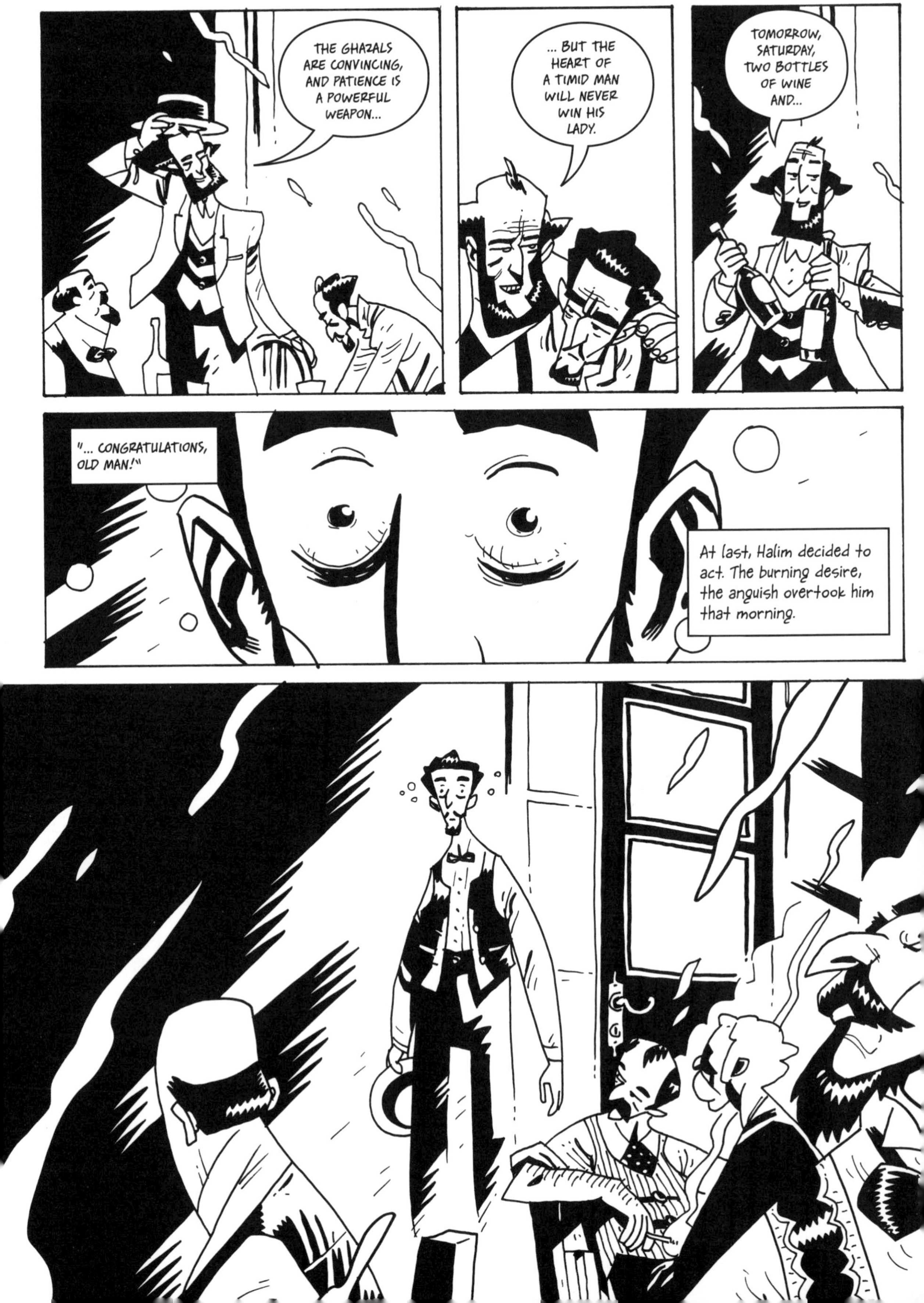
THE GHAZALS ARE CONVINCING, AND PATIENCE IS A POWERFUL WEAPON...
... BUT THE HEART OF A TIMID MAN WILL NEVER WIN HIS LADY.
TOMORROW, SATURDAY, TWO BOTTLES OF WINE AND...
"... CONGRATULATIONS, OLD MAN!"
At last, Halim decided to act. The burning desire, the anguish overtook him that morning.

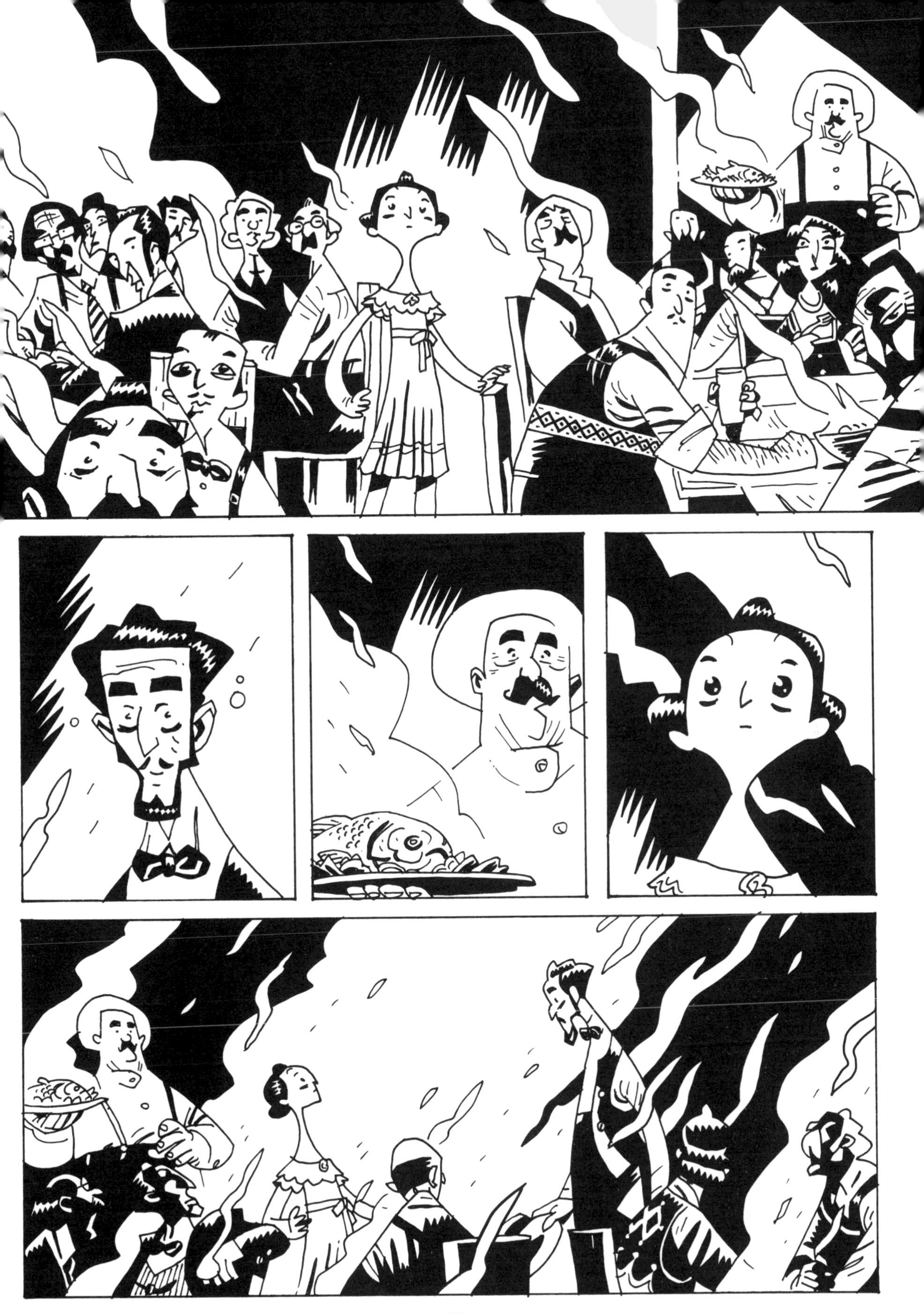

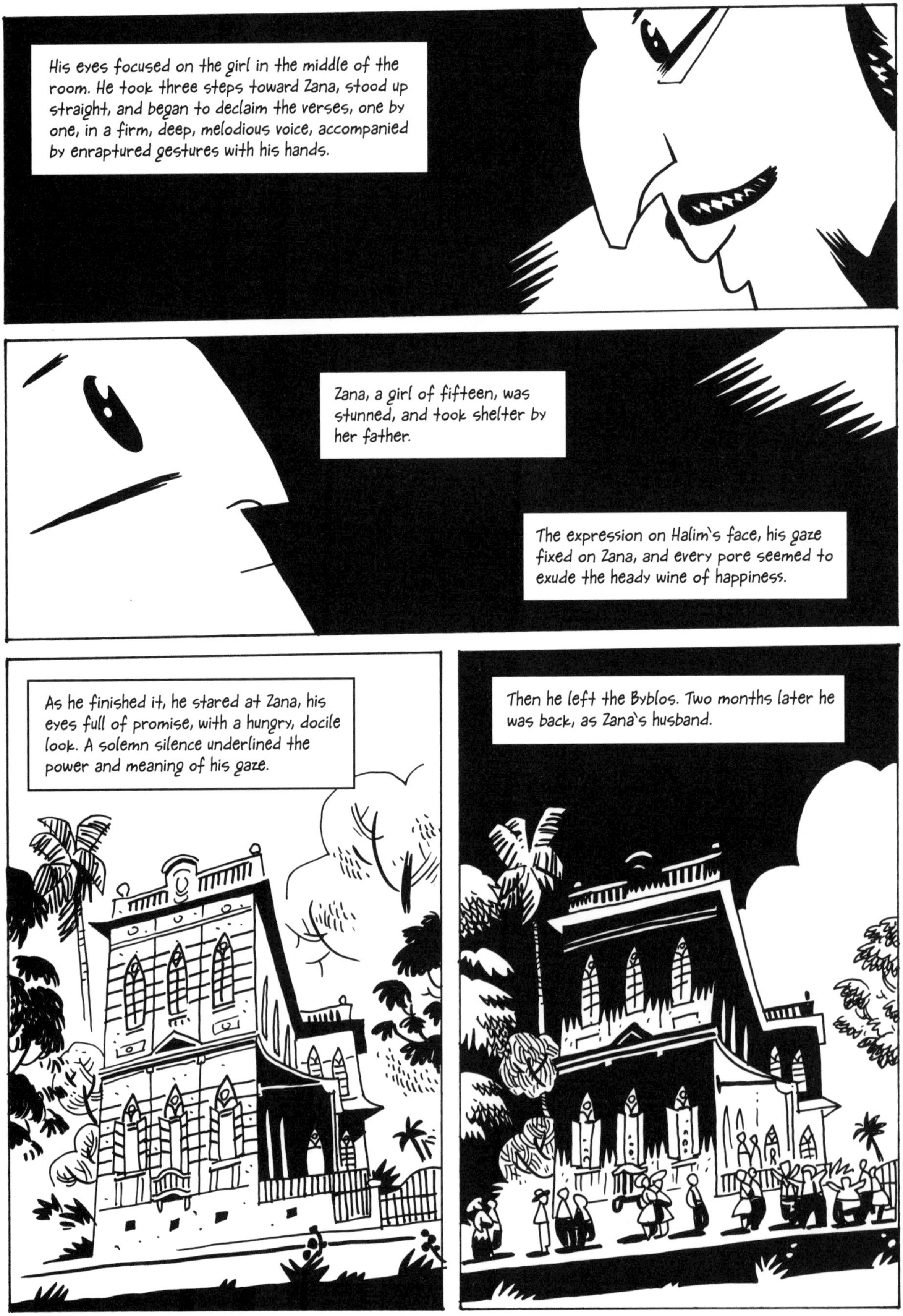
His eyes focused on the girl in the middle of the room. He took three steps toward Zana, stood up straight, and began to declaim the verses, one by one, in a firm, deep, melodious voice, accompanied by enraptured gestures with his hands.
Zana, a girl of fifteen, was stunned, and took shelter by her father.
The expression on Halim's face, his gaze fixed on Zana, and every pore seemed to exude the heady wine of happiness.
As he finished it, he stared at Zana, his eyes full of promise, with a hungry, docile look. A solemn silence underlined the power and meaning of his gaze.
Then he left the Byblos. Two months later he was back, as Zana's husband.

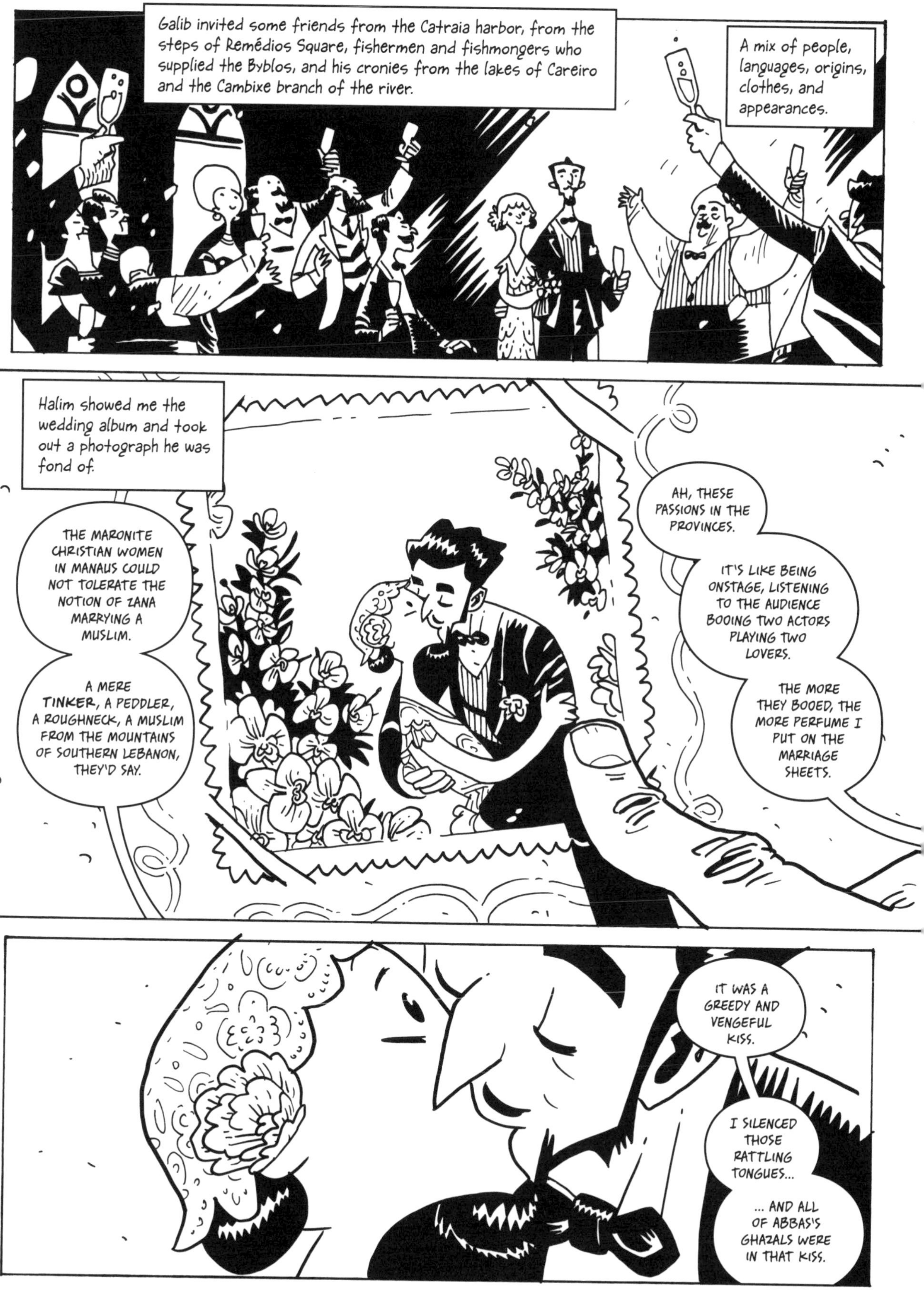

Galib invited some friends from the Catraia harbor, from the steps of Remédios Square, fishermen and fishmongers who supplied the Byblos, and his cronies from the lakes of Careiro and the Cambixe branch of the river.
A mix of people, languages, origins, clothes, and appearances.
Halim showed me the wedding album and took out a photograph he was fond of.
THE MARONITE CHRISTIAN WOMEN IN MANAUS COULD NOT TOLERATE THE NOTION OF ZANA MARRYING A MUSLIM.
A MERE TINKER, A PEDDLER, A ROUGHNECK, A MUSLIM FROM THE MOUNTAINS OF SOUTHERN LEBANON, THEY'D SAY.
AH, THESE PASSIONS IN THE PROVINCES.
IT'S LIKE BEING ONSTAGE, LISTENING TO THE AUDIENCE BOOING TWO ACTORS PLAYING TWO LOVERS.
THE MORE THEY BOOED, THE MORE PERFUME I PUT ON THE MARRIAGE SHEETS.
IT WAS A GREEDY AND VENGEFUL KISS.
I SILENCED THOSE RATTLING TONGUES...
... AND ALL OF ABBAS'S GHAZALS WERE IN THAT KISS.

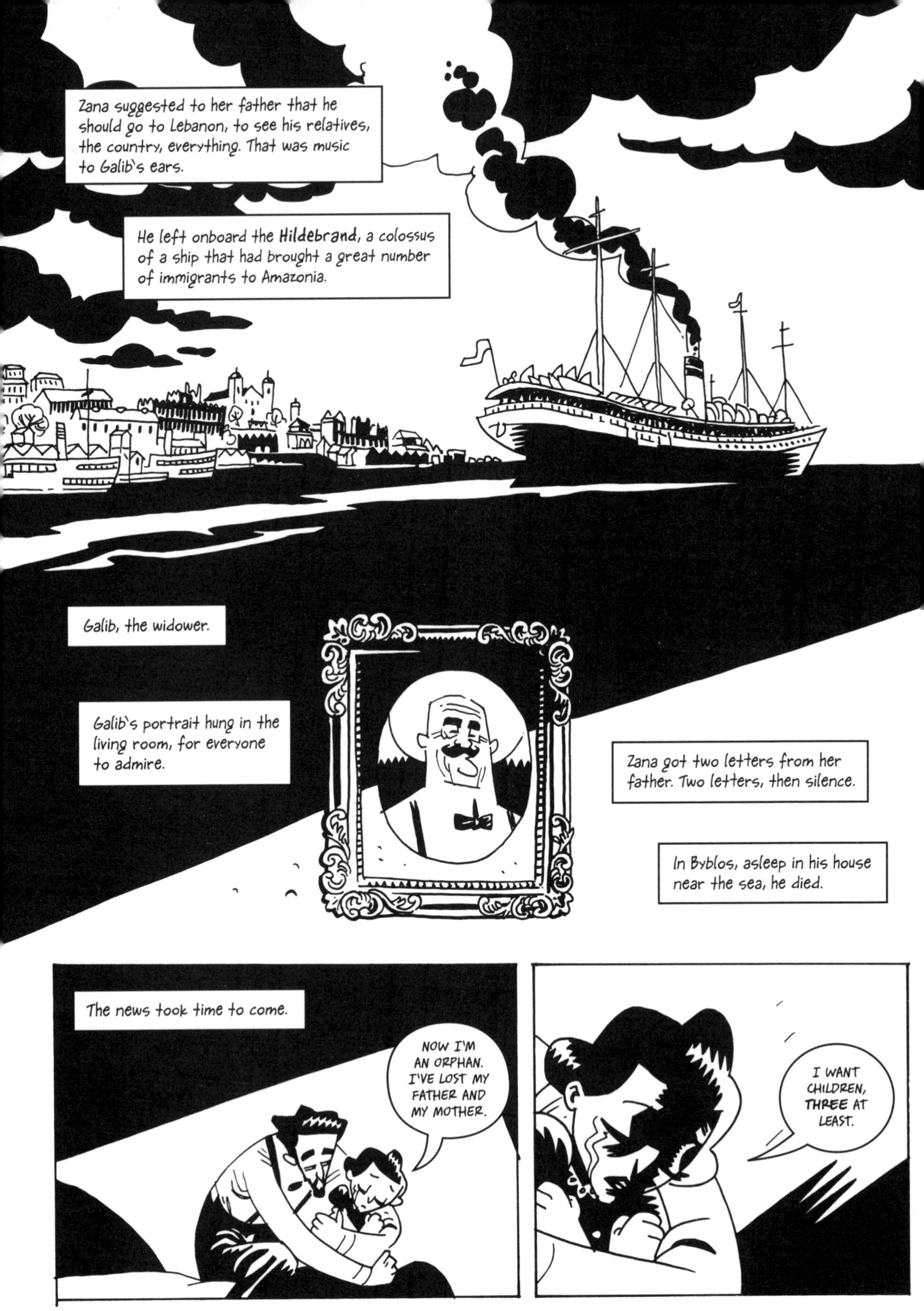
Zana suggested to her father that he should go to Lebanon, to see his relatives, the country, everything. That was music to Galib's ears.
He left onboard the **Hildebrand**, a colossus of a ship that had brought a great number of immigrants to Amazonia.
Galib, the widower.
Galib's portrait hung in the living room, for everyone to admire.
Zana got two letters from her father. Two letters, then silence.
In Byblos, asleep in his house near the sea, he died.
The news took time to come.
NOW I'M AN ORPHAN. I'VE LOST MY FATHER AND MY MOTHER.
I WANT CHILDREN, **THREE** AT LEAST.

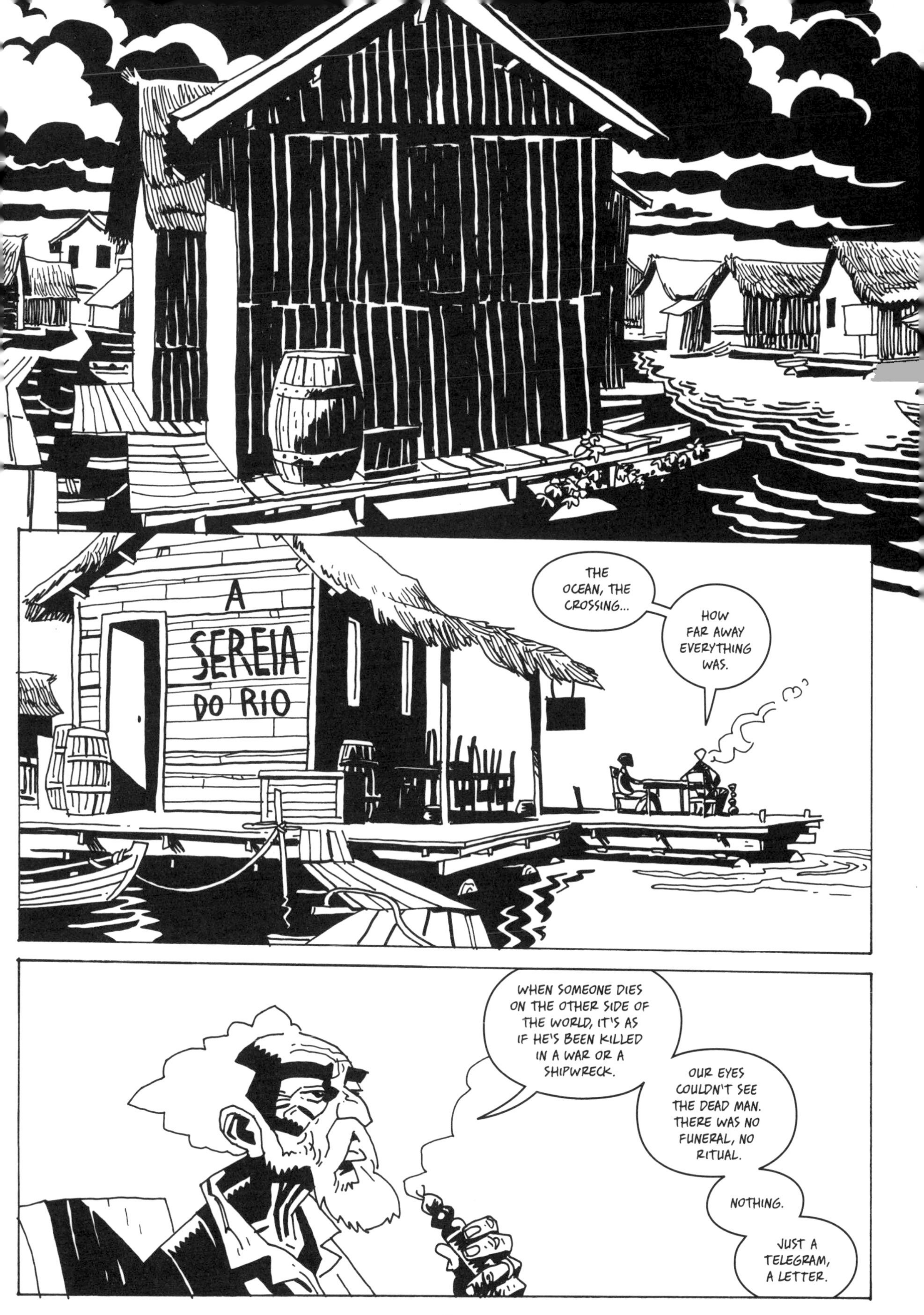
A SEREIA DO RIO
THE OCEAN, THE CROSSING...
HOW FAR AWAY EVERYTHING WAS.
WHEN SOMEONE DIES ON THE OTHER SIDE OF THE WORLD, IT'S AS IF HE'S BEEN KILLED IN A WAR OR A SHIPWRECK.
OUR EYES COULDN'T SEE THE DEAD MAN. THERE WAS NO FUNERAL, NO RITUAL.
NOTHING.
JUST A TELEGRAM, A LETTER.

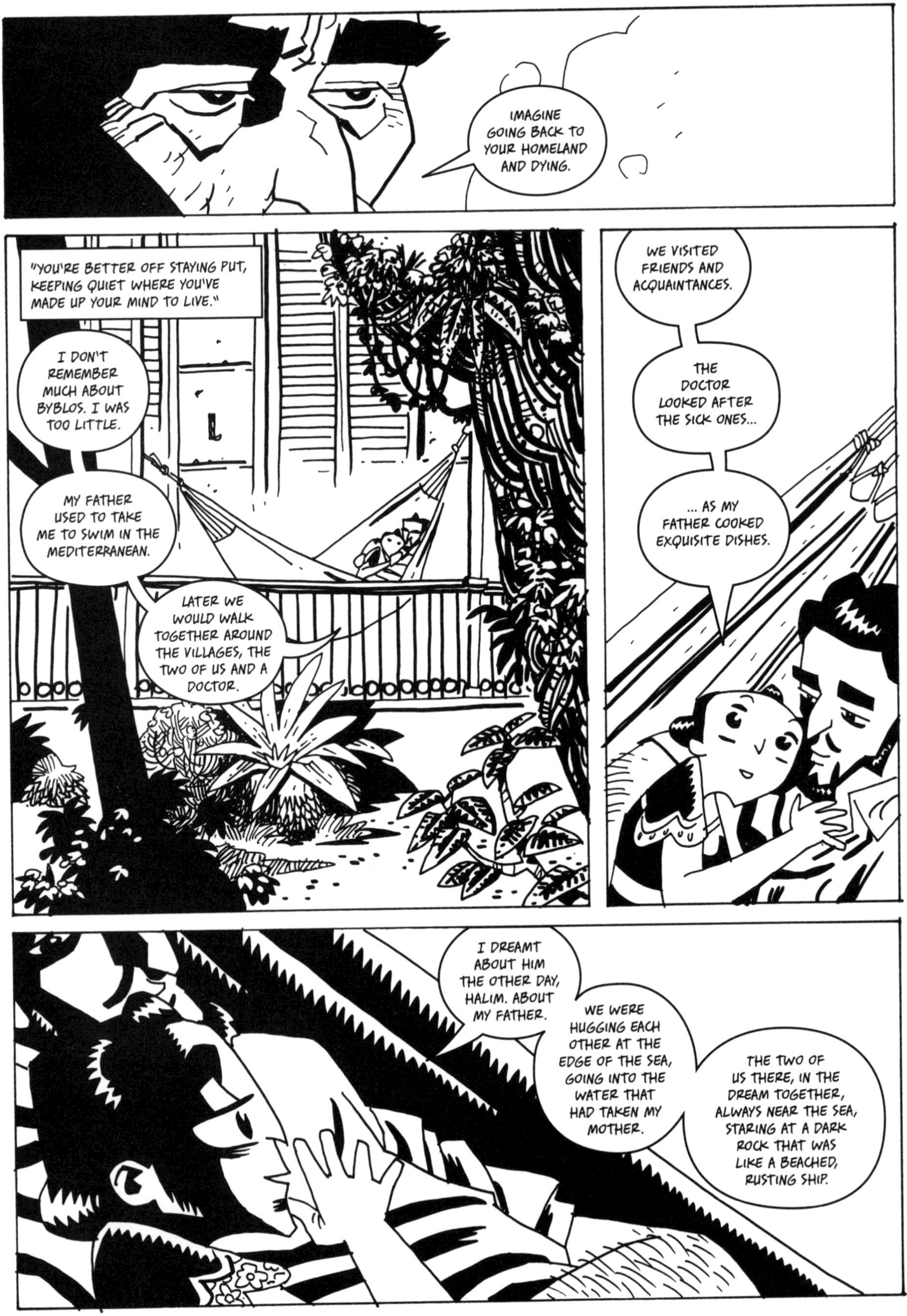
IMAGINE GOING BACK TO YOUR HOMELAND AND DYING.
"YOU'RE BETTER OFF STAYING PUT, KEEPING QUIET WHERE YOU'VE MADE UP YOUR MIND TO LIVE."
I DON'T REMEMBER MUCH ABOUT BYBLOS. I WAS TOO LITTLE.
MY FATHER USED TO TAKE ME TO SWIM IN THE MEDITERRANEAN.
LATER WE WOULD WALK TOGETHER AROUND THE VILLAGES, THE TWO OF US AND A DOCTOR.
WE VISITED FRIENDS AND ACQUAINTANCES.
THE DOCTOR LOOKED AFTER THE SICK ONES...
... AS MY FATHER COOKED EXQUISITE DISHES.
I DREAMT ABOUT HIM THE OTHER DAY, HALIM. ABOUT MY FATHER.
WE WERE HUGGING EACH OTHER AT THE EDGE OF THE SEA, GOING INTO THE WATER THAT HAD TAKEN MY MOTHER.
THE TWO OF US THERE, IN THE DREAM TOGETHER, ALWAYS NEAR THE SEA, STARING AT A DARK ROCK THAT WAS LIKE A BEACHED, RUSTING SHIP.

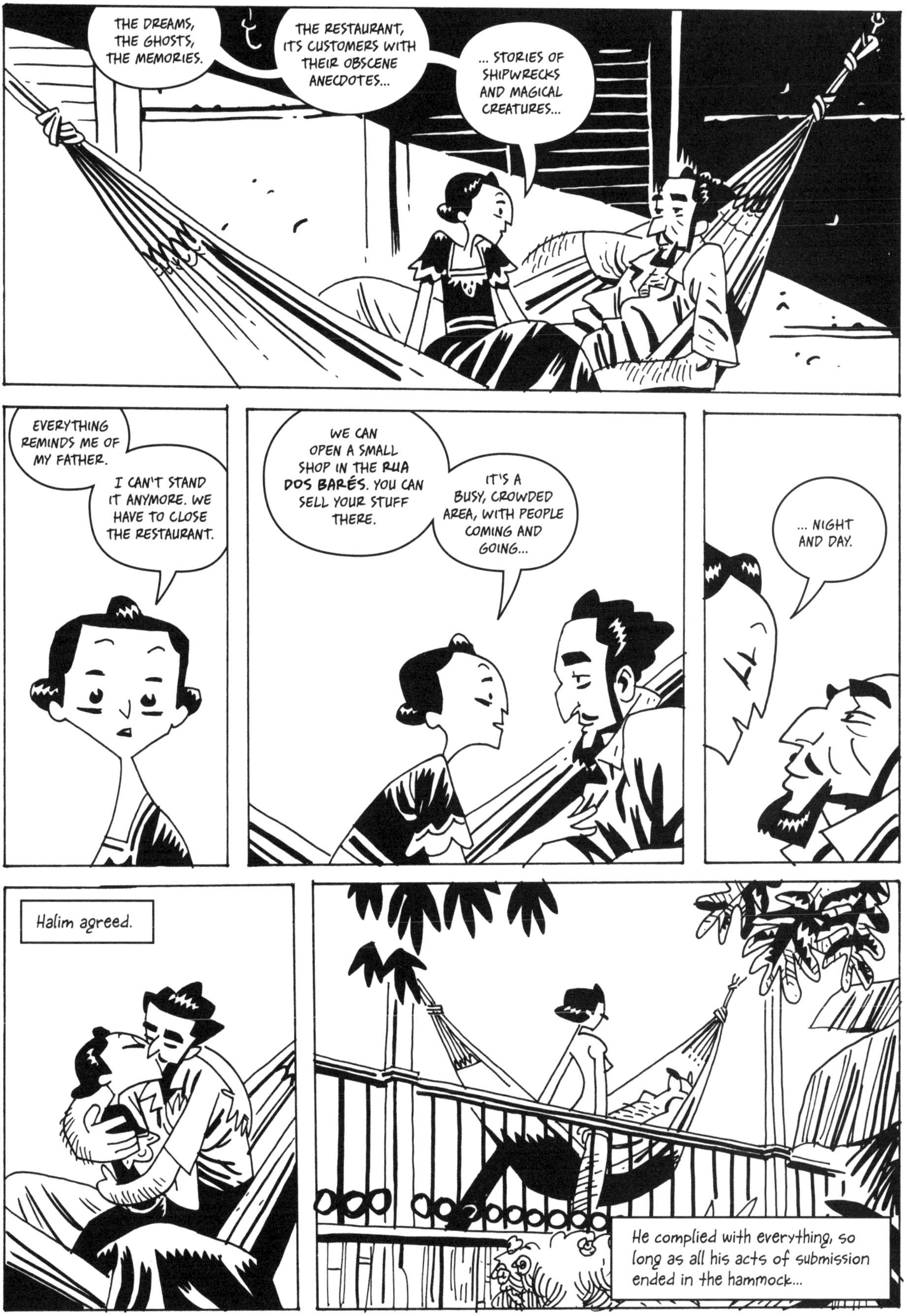
THE DREAMS, THE GHOSTS, THE MEMORIES.
THE RESTAURANT, ITS CUSTOMERS WITH THEIR OBSCENE ANECDOTES...
... STORIES OF SHIPWRECKS AND MAGICAL CREATURES...
EVERYTHING REMINDS ME OF MY FATHER.
I CAN'T STAND IT ANYMORE. WE HAVE TO CLOSE THE RESTAURANT.
WE CAN OPEN A SMALL SHOP IN THE RUA DOS BARÉS. YOU CAN SELL YOUR STUFF THERE.
IT'S A BUSY, CROWDED AREA, WITH PEOPLE COMING AND GOING...
... NIGHT AND DAY.
Halim agreed.
He complied with everything, so long as all his acts of submission ended in the hammock...

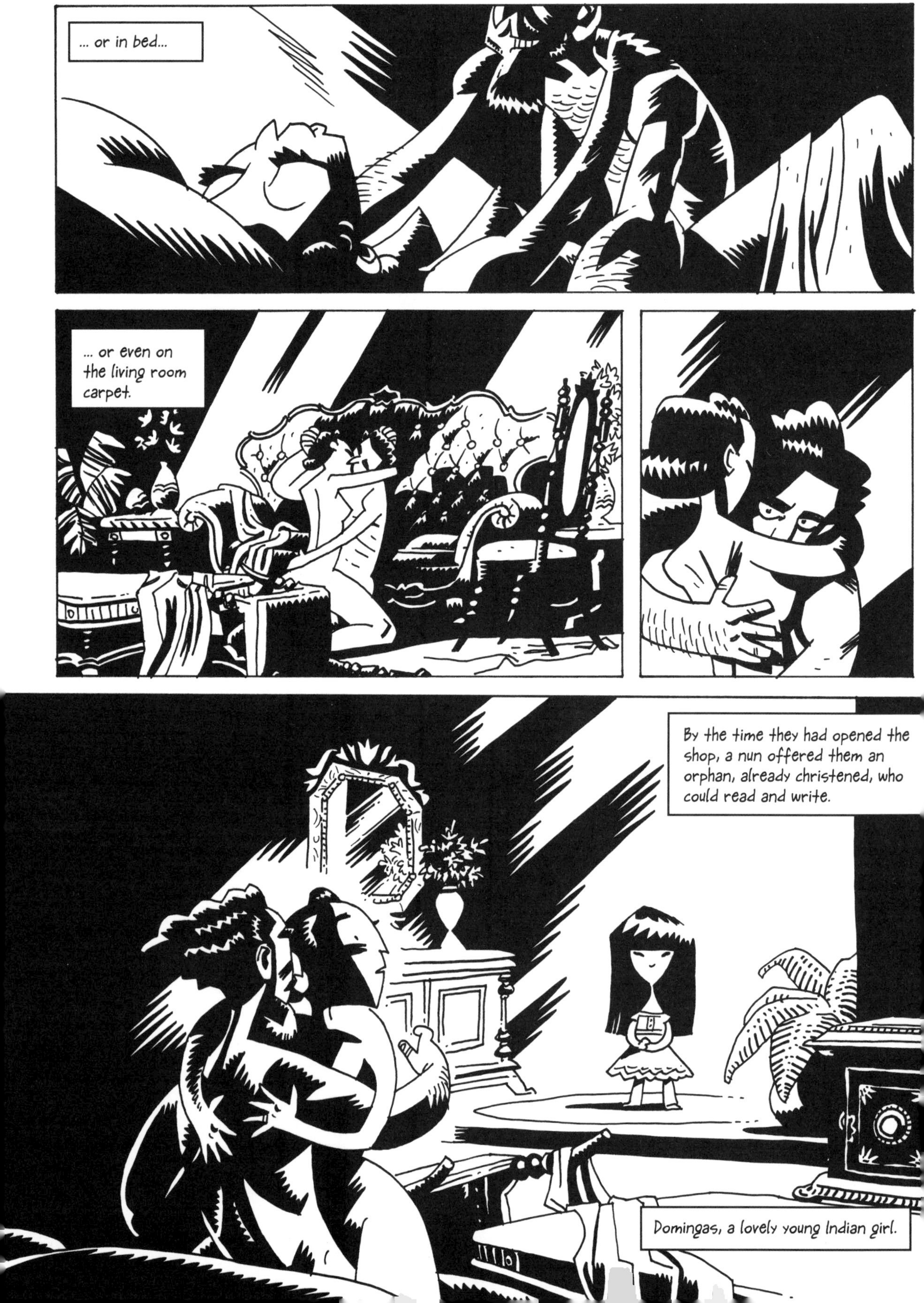
... or in bed...
... or even on the living room carpet.
By the time they had opened the shop, a nun offered them an orphan, already christened, who could read and write.
Domingas, a lovely young Indian girl.

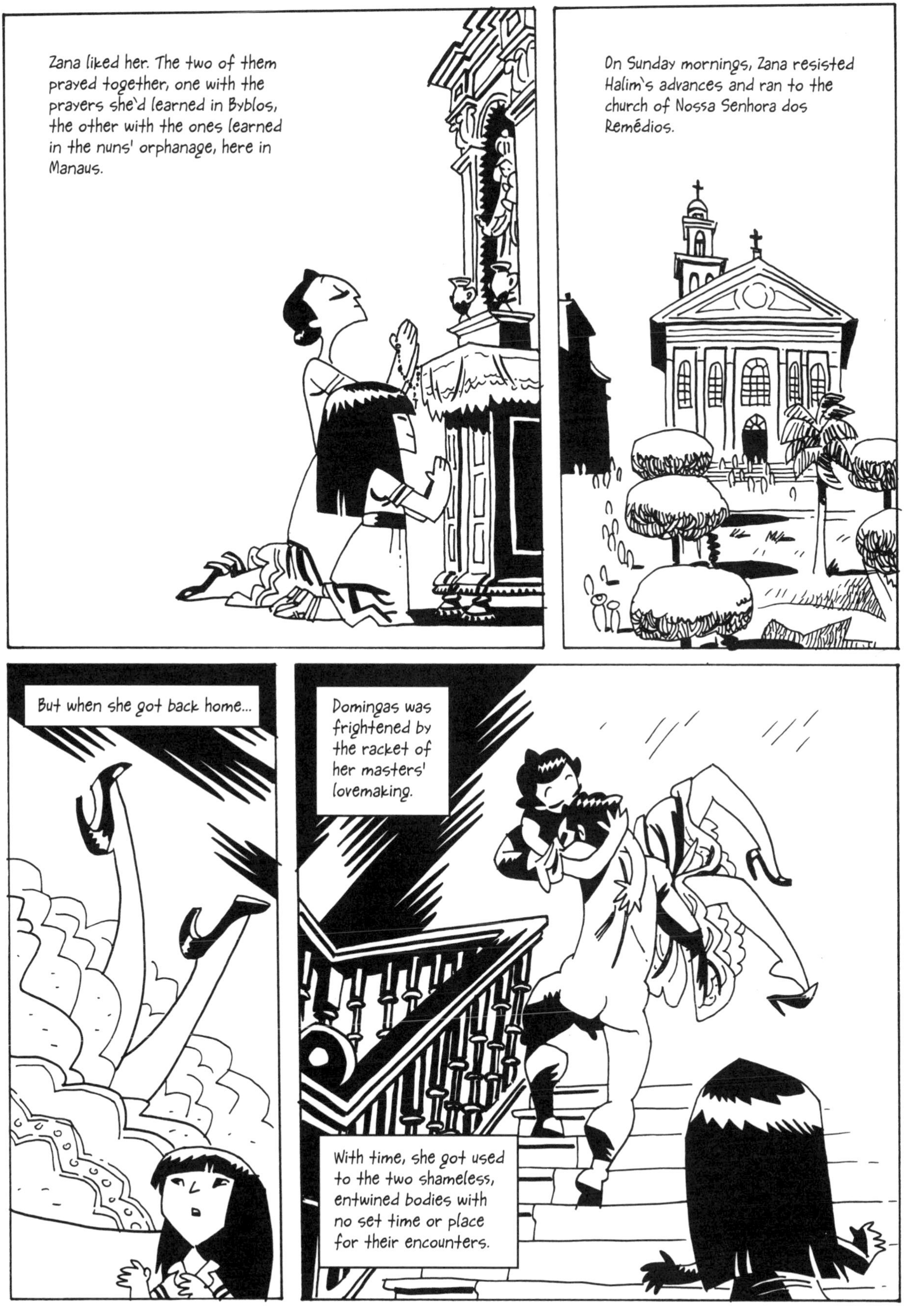
Zana liked her. The two of them prayed together, one with the prayers she'd learned in Byblos, the other with the ones learned in the nuns' orphanage, here in Manaus.
On Sunday mornings, Zana resisted Halim's advances and ran to the church of Nossa Senhora dos Remédios.
But when she got back home...
Domingas was frightened by the racket of her masters' lovemaking.
With time, she got used to the two shameless, entwined bodies with no set time or place for their encounters.

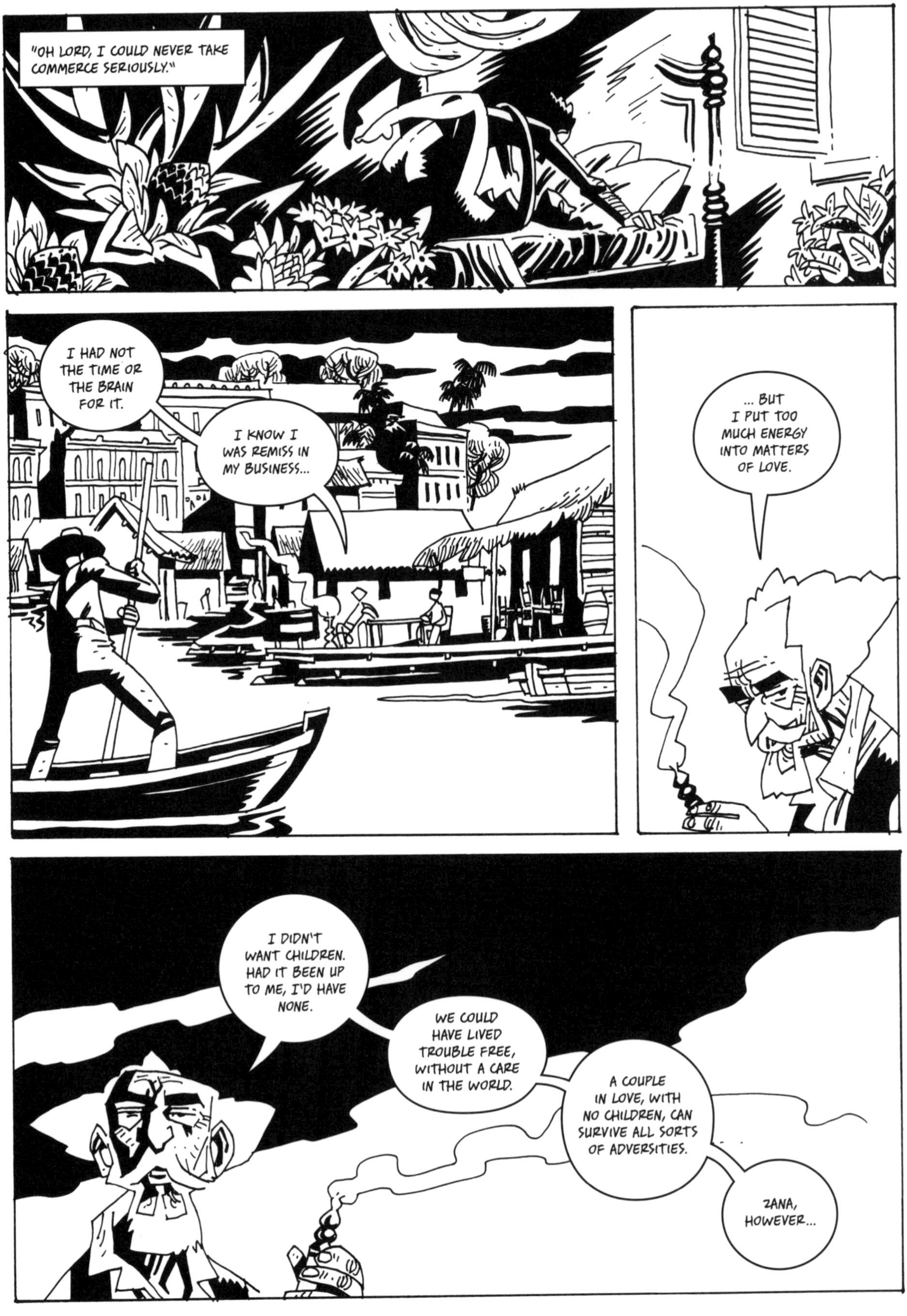
"OH LORD, I COULD NEVER TAKE COMMERCE SERIOUSLY."
I HAD NOT THE TIME OR THE BRAIN FOR IT.
I KNOW I WAS REMISS IN MY BUSINESS...
... BUT I PUT TOO MUCH ENERGY INTO MATTERS OF LOVE.
I DIDN'T WANT CHILDREN. HAD IT BEEN UP TO ME, I'D HAVE NONE.
WE COULD HAVE LIVED TROUBLE FREE, WITHOUT A CARE IN THE WORLD.
A COUPLE IN LOVE, WITH NO CHILDREN, CAN SURVIVE ALL SORTS OF ADVERSITIES.
ZANA, HOWEVER...

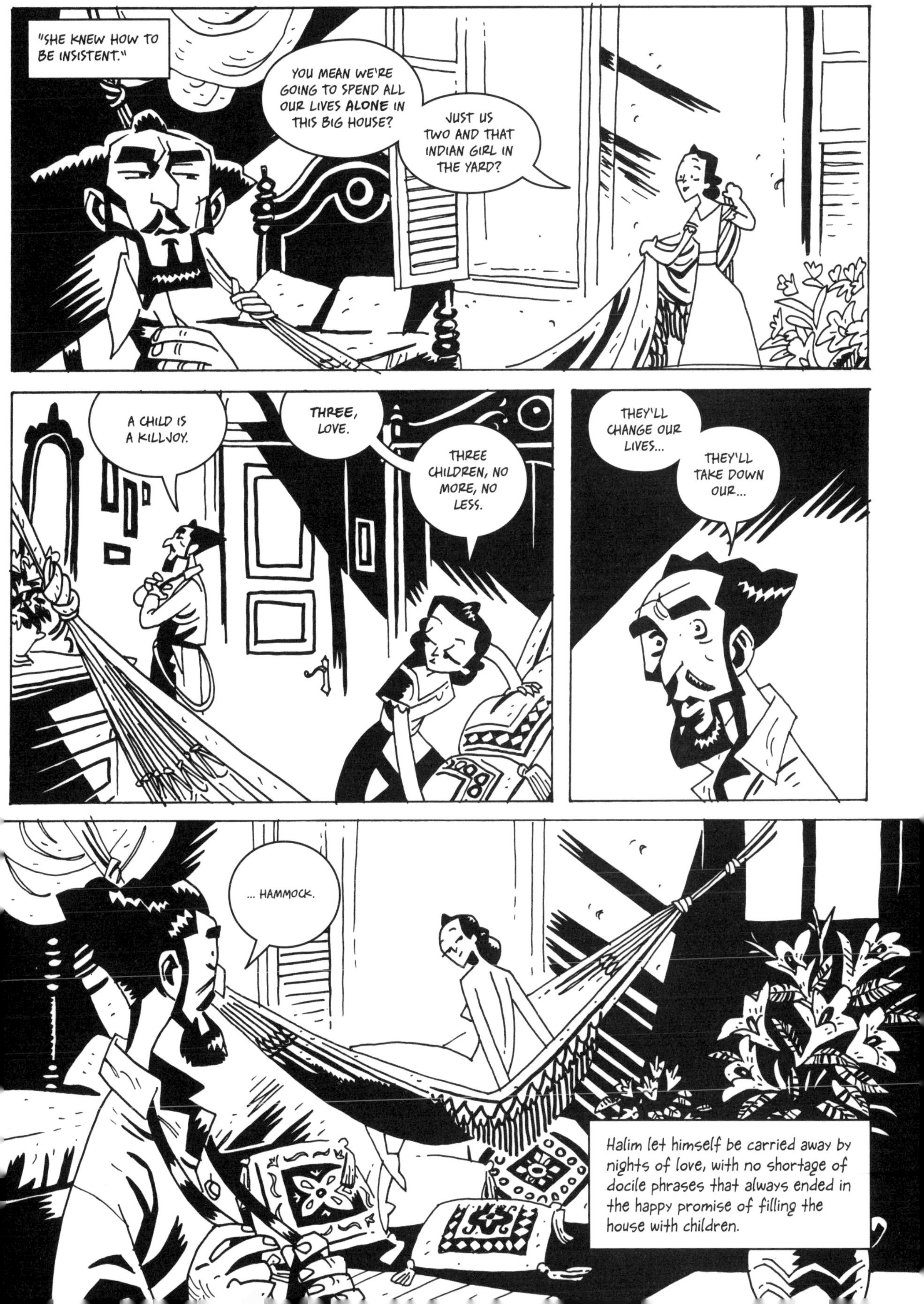
"SHE KNEW HOW TO BE INSISTENT."
YOU MEAN WE'RE GOING TO SPEND ALL OUR LIVES ALONE IN THIS BIG HOUSE?
JUST US TWO AND THAT INDIAN GIRL IN THE YARD?
A CHILD IS A KILLJOY.
THREE, LOVE.
THREE CHILDREN, NO MORE, NO LESS.
THEY'LL CHANGE OUR LIVES...
THEY'LL TAKE DOWN OUR...
... HAMMOCK.
Halim let himself be carried away by nights of love, with no shortage of docile phrases that always ended in the happy promise of filling the house with children.

Yaqub and Omar were born two years after Domingas came to the house. Halim got a shock when he saw the midwife hold up two fingers, announcing the arrival of twins.

They were born at home, Omar a few minutes later.

He was the youngest, the *Caçula*.

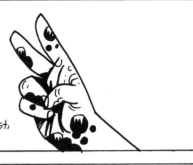

Omar was a little darker and had more hair.

"My little black monkey, my hairy little boy," Zana said.

He was often ill in the first few months of life and grew up in the jealous, excessive care of his mother.

Yaqub was left to the care of Domingas.

Halim spent two months forbidden from touching Zana's body.

He thought this time of prohibition and his wife's mad devotion to Omar absurd.

Slowly, he reconquered Zana, but said goodbye to the times when they shuddered with pleasure in every corner of the house.

Halim no longer had any peace when the boys began to walk.

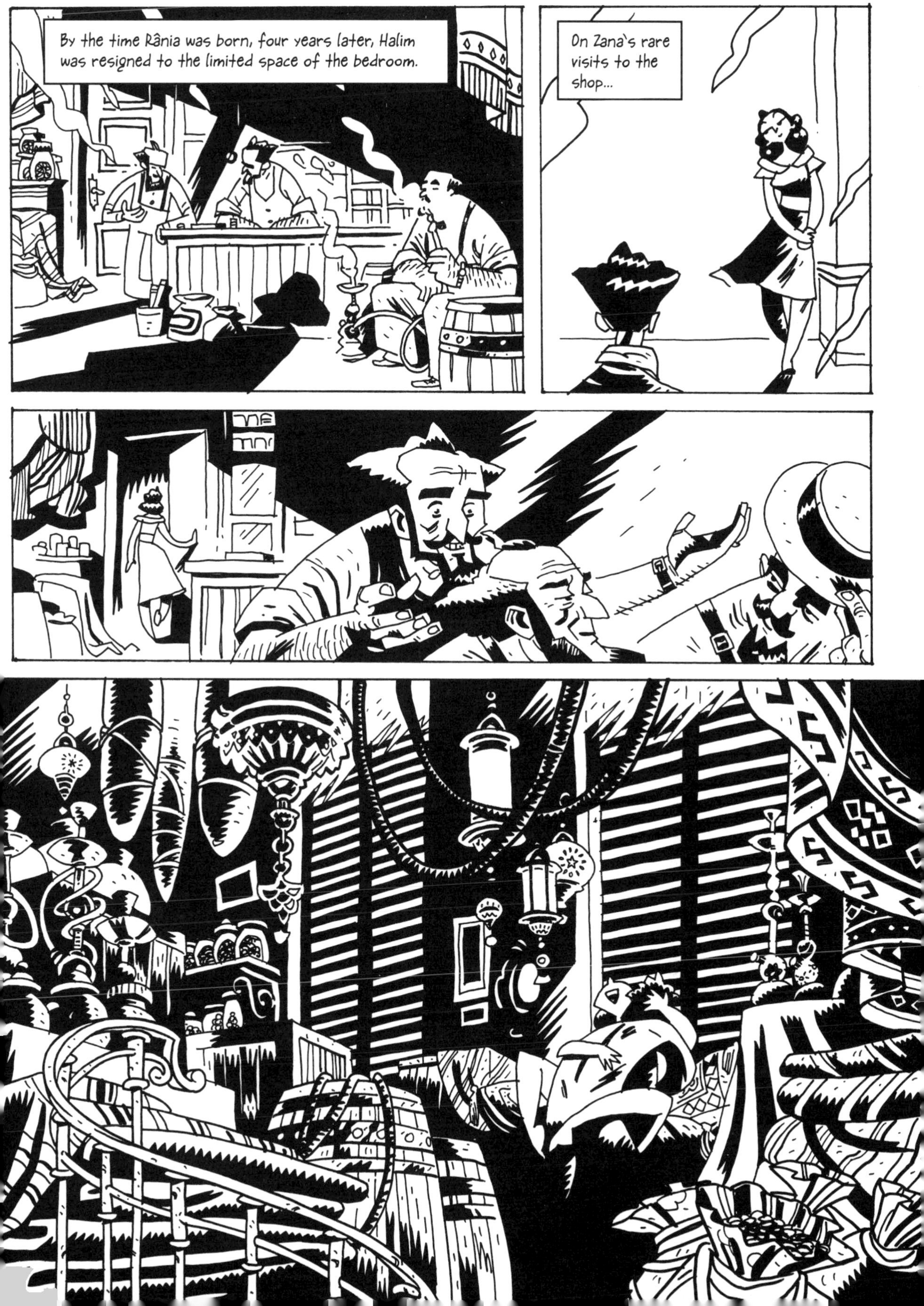
By the time Rânia was born, four years later, Halim was resigned to the limited space of the bedroom.
On Zana's rare visits to the shop...

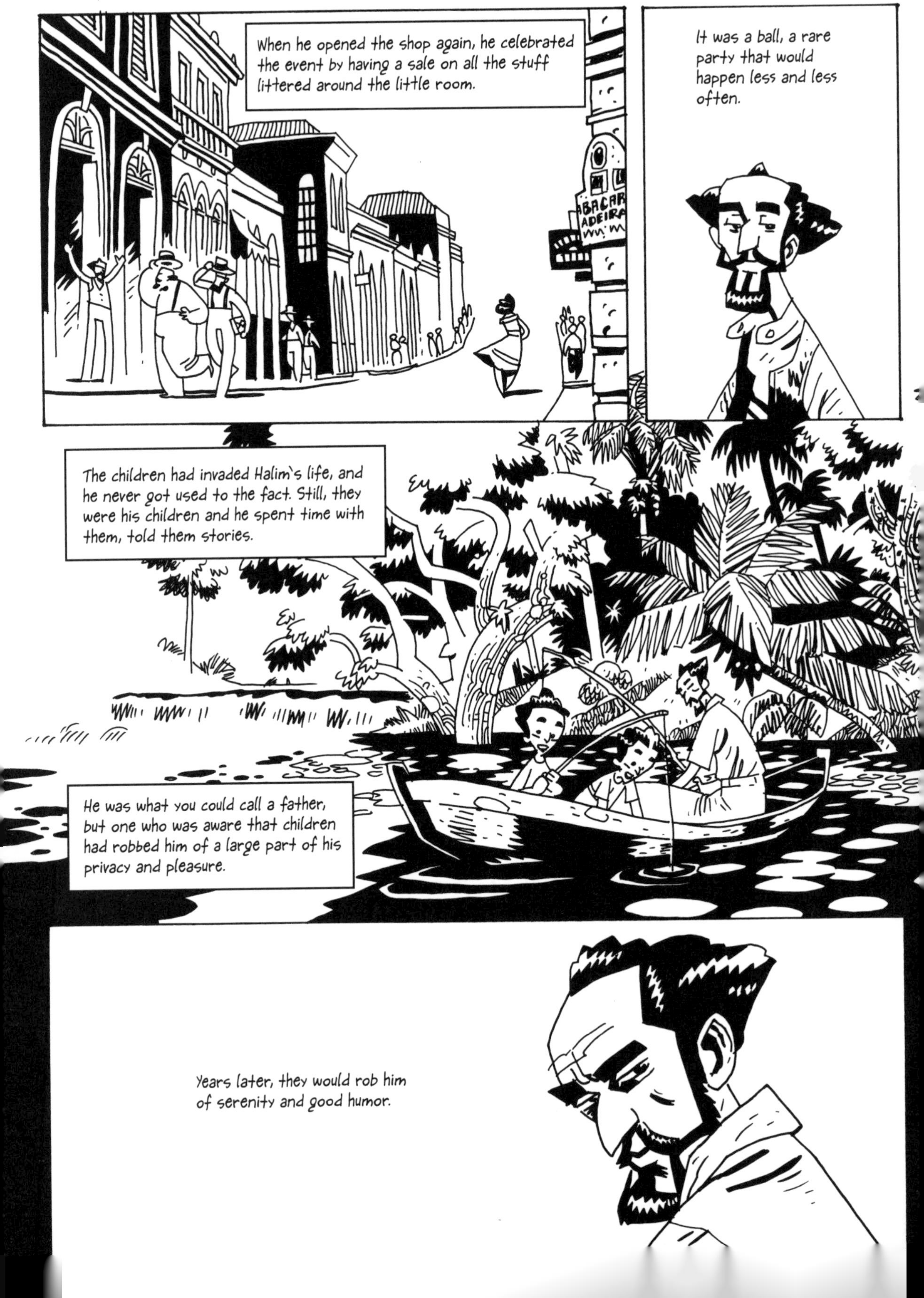
When he opened the shop again, he celebrated the event by having a sale on all the stuff littered around the little room.
It was a ball, a rare party that would happen less and less often.
The children had invaded Halim's life, and he never got used to the fact. Still, they were his children and he spent time with them, told them stories.
He was what you could call a father, but one who was aware that children had robbed him of a large part of his privacy and pleasure.
Years later, they would rob him of serenity and good humor.

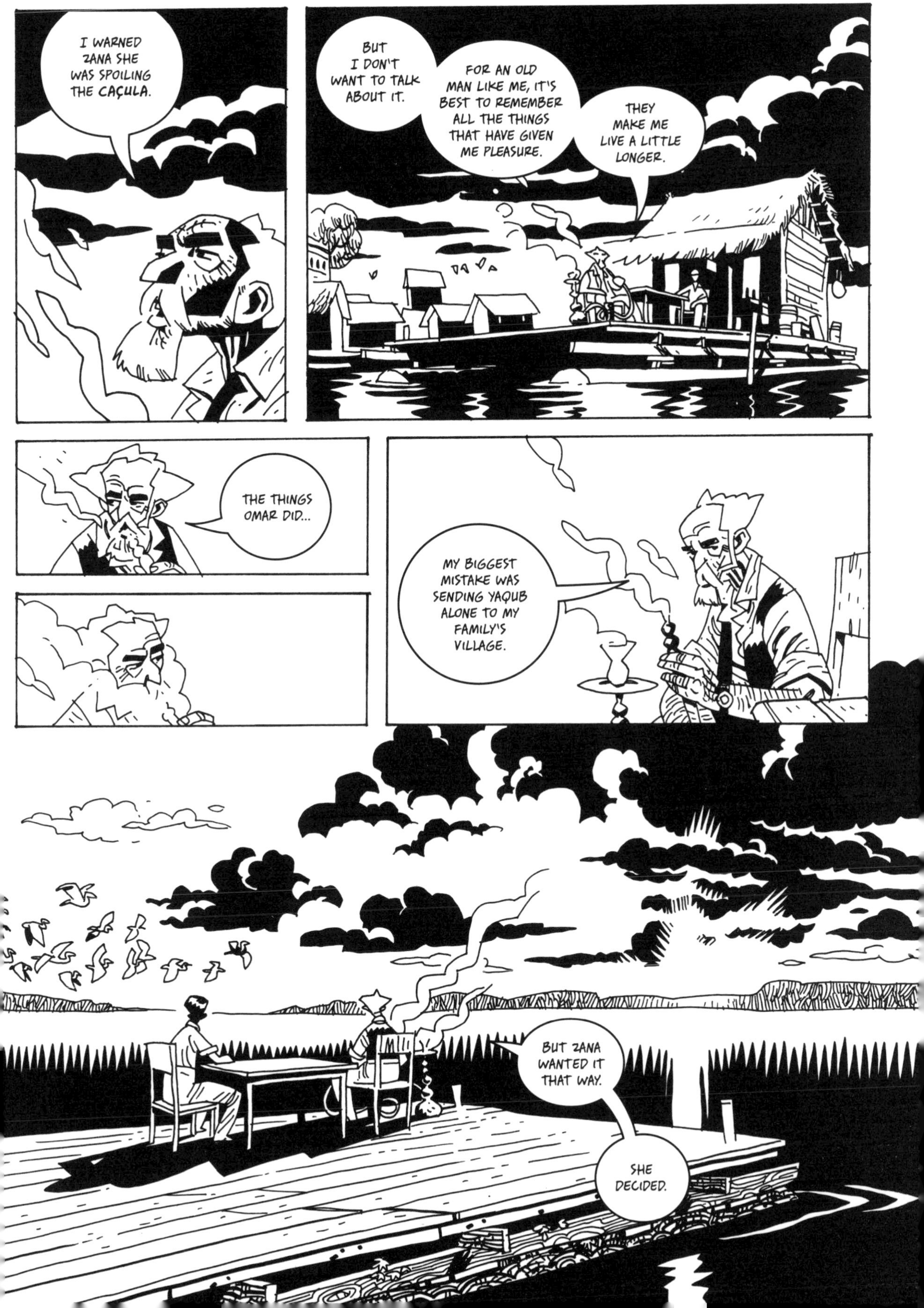
I WARNED ZANA SHE WAS SPOILING THE CAÇULA.
BUT I DON'T WANT TO TALK ABOUT IT.
FOR AN OLD MAN LIKE ME, IT'S BEST TO REMEMBER ALL THE THINGS THAT HAVE GIVEN ME PLEASURE.
THEY MAKE ME LIVE A LITTLE LONGER.
THE THINGS OMAR DID...
MY BIGGEST MISTAKE WAS SENDING YAQUB ALONE TO MY FAMILY'S VILLAGE.
BUT ZANA WANTED IT THAT WAY.
SHE DECIDED.

Chapter 3

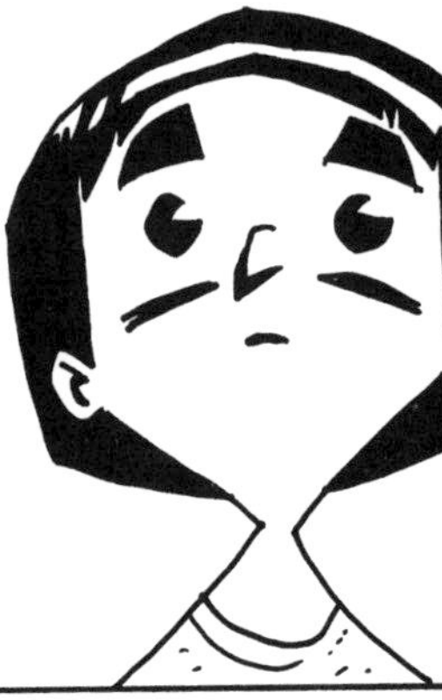

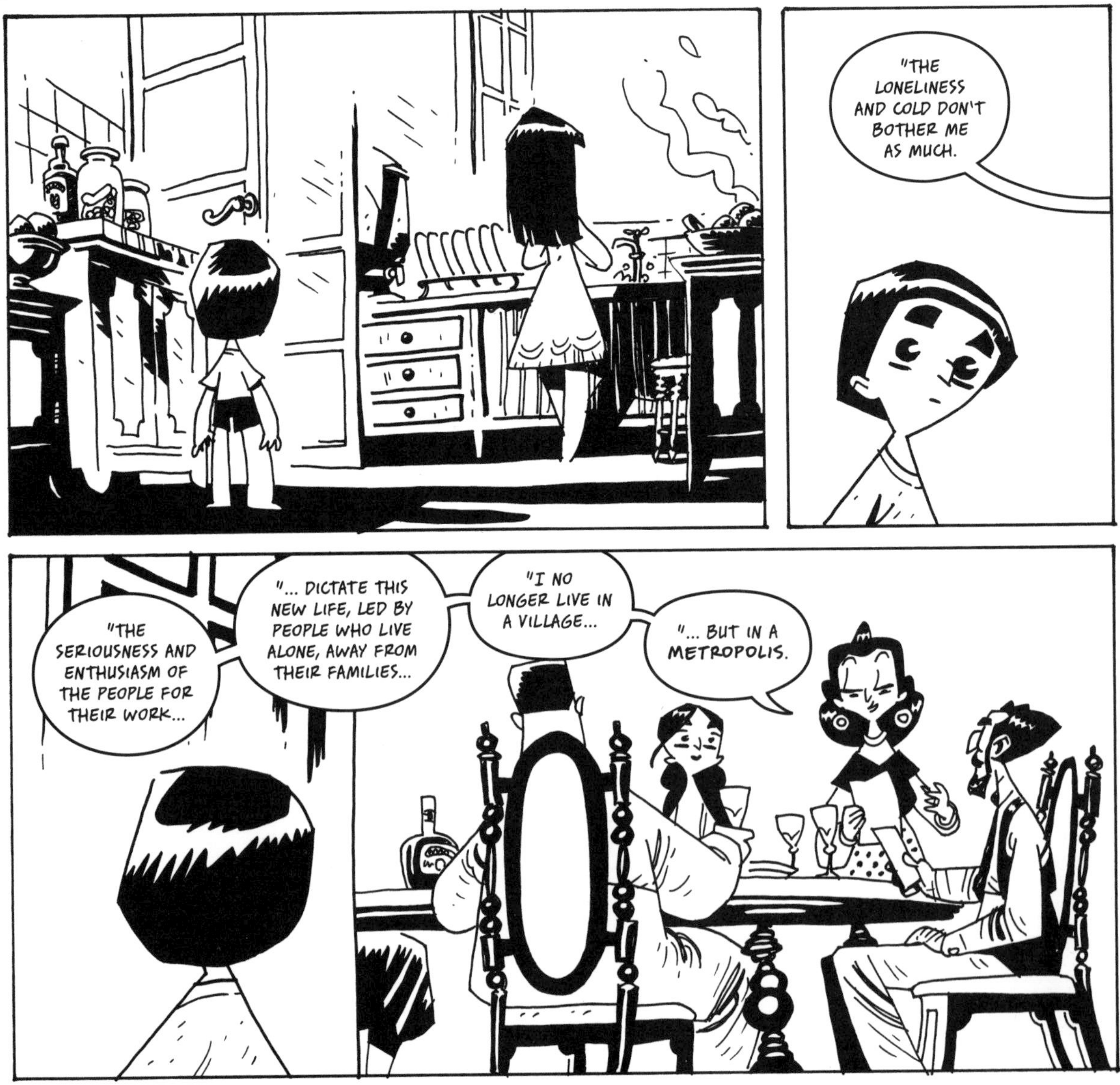
"THE LONELINESS AND COLD DON'T BOTHER ME AS MUCH.
"THE SERIOUSNESS AND ENTHUSIASM OF THE PEOPLE FOR THEIR WORK...
"... DICTATE THIS NEW LIFE, LED BY PEOPLE WHO LIVE ALONE, AWAY FROM THEIR FAMILIES...
"I NO LONGER LIVE IN A VILLAGE...
"... BUT IN A METROPOLIS.

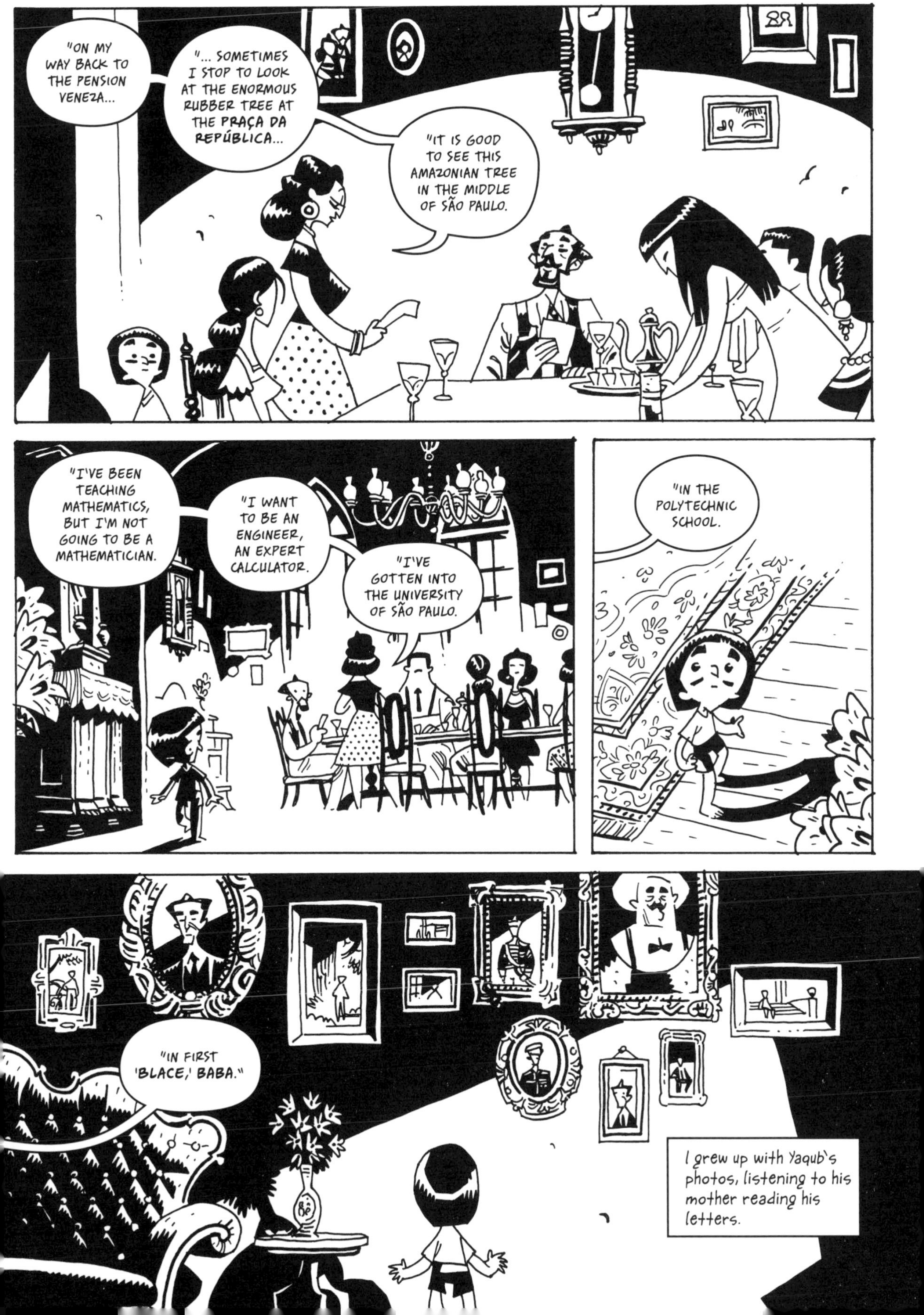
"ON MY WAY BACK TO THE PENSION VENEZA...
"... SOMETIMES I STOP TO LOOK AT THE ENORMOUS RUBBER TREE AT THE PRAÇA DA REPÚBLICA...
"IT IS GOOD TO SEE THIS AMAZONIAN TREE IN THE MIDDLE OF SÃO PAULO.
"I'VE BEEN TEACHING MATHEMATICS, BUT I'M NOT GOING TO BE A MATHEMATICIAN.
"I WANT TO BE AN ENGINEER, AN EXPERT CALCULATOR.
"I'VE GOTTEN INTO THE UNIVERSITY OF SÃO PAULO.
"IN THE POLYTECHNIC SCHOOL.
"IN FIRST 'BLACE,' BABA."
I grew up with Yaqub's photos, listening to his mother reading his letters.

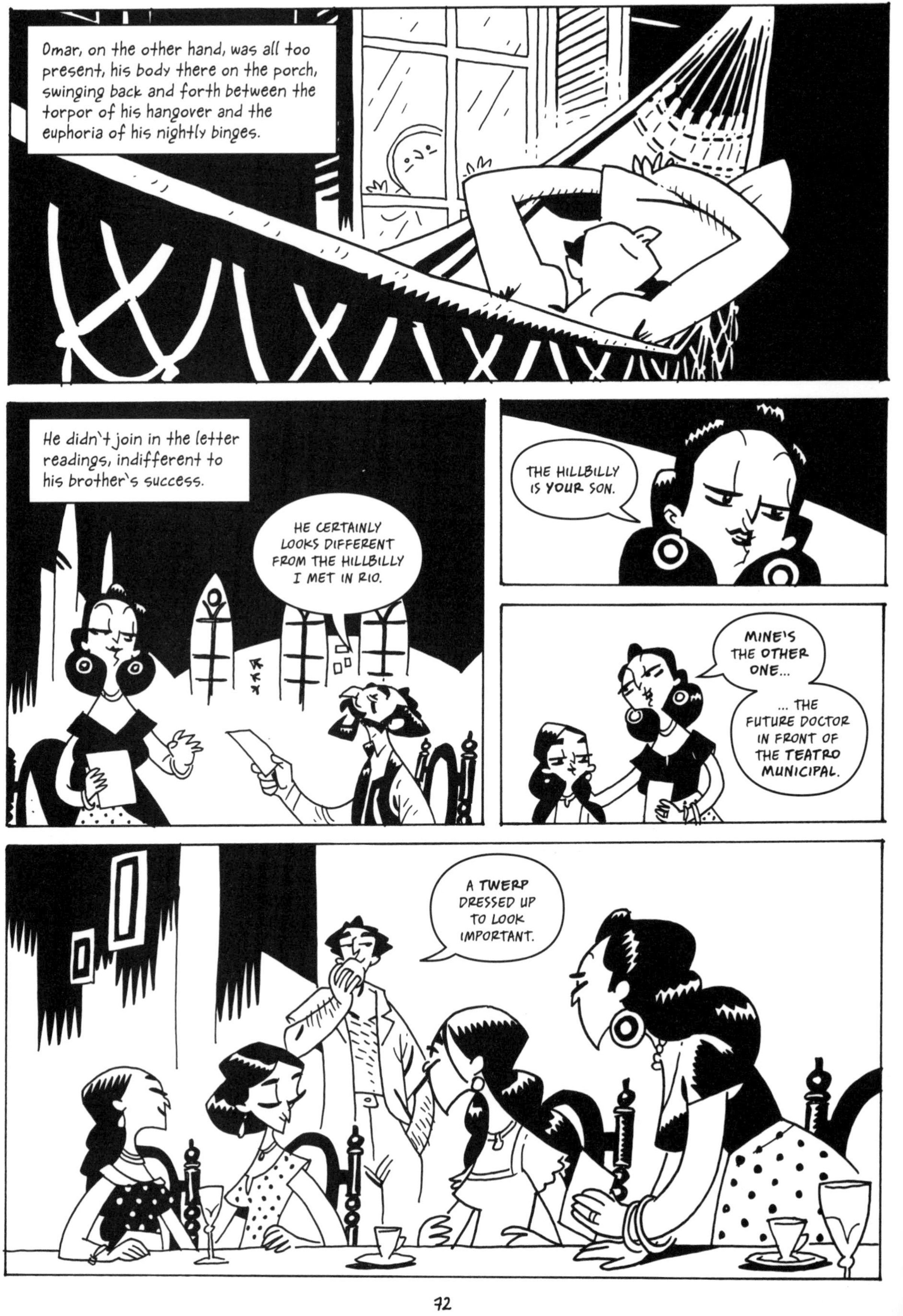
Omar, on the other hand, was all too present, his body there on the porch, swinging back and forth between the torpor of his hangover and the euphoria of his nightly binges.
He didn't join in the letter readings, indifferent to his brother's success.
HE CERTAINLY LOOKS DIFFERENT FROM THE HILLBILLY I MET IN RIO.
THE HILLBILLY IS YOUR SON.
MINE'S THE OTHER ONE...
... THE FUTURE DOCTOR IN FRONT OF THE TEATRO MUNICIPAL.
A TWERP DRESSED UP TO LOOK IMPORTANT.

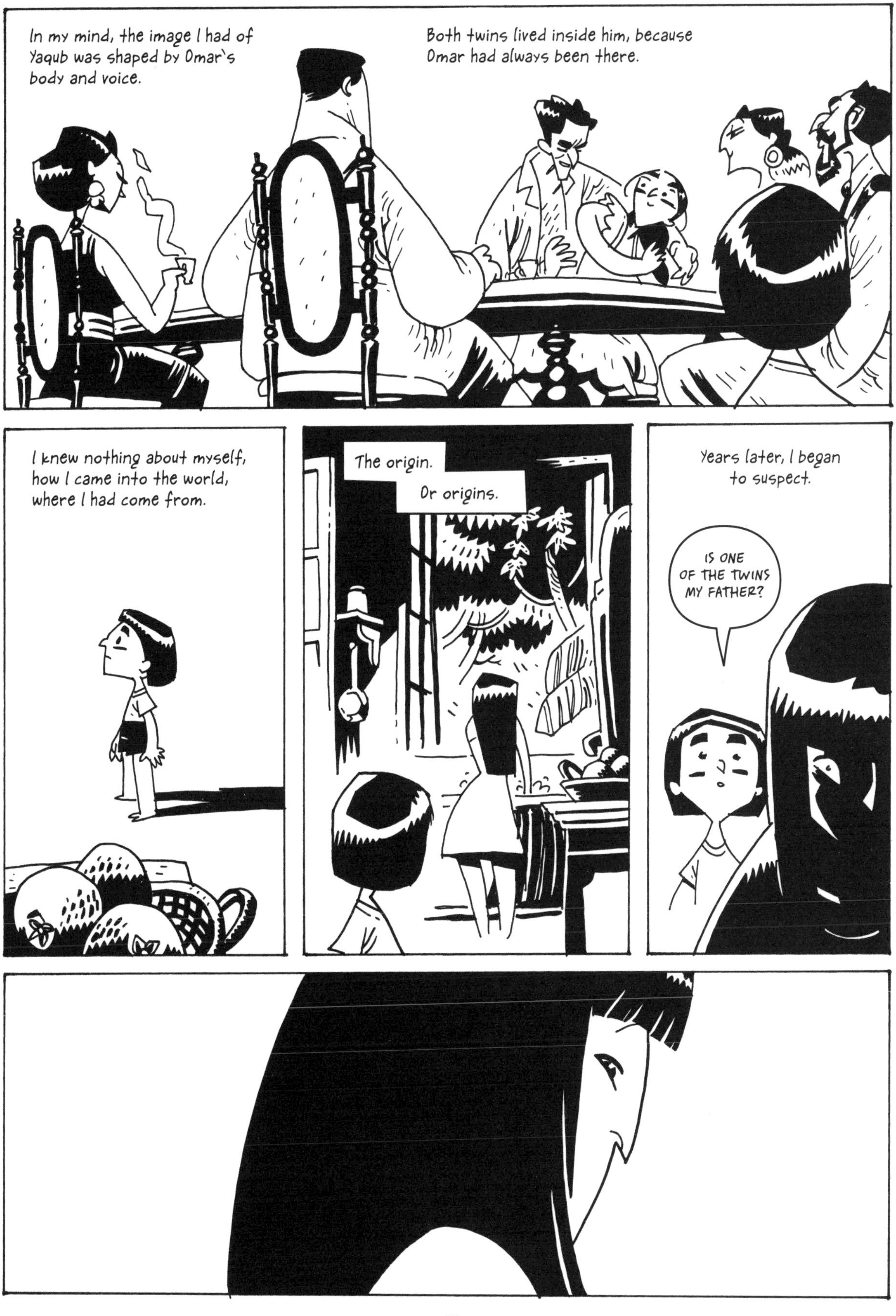
In my mind, the image I had of Yaqub was shaped by Omar's body and voice.
Both twins lived inside him, because Omar had always been there.
I knew nothing about myself, how I came into the world, where I had come from.
The origin.
Or origins.
Years later, I began to suspect.
IS ONE OF THE TWINS MY FATHER?

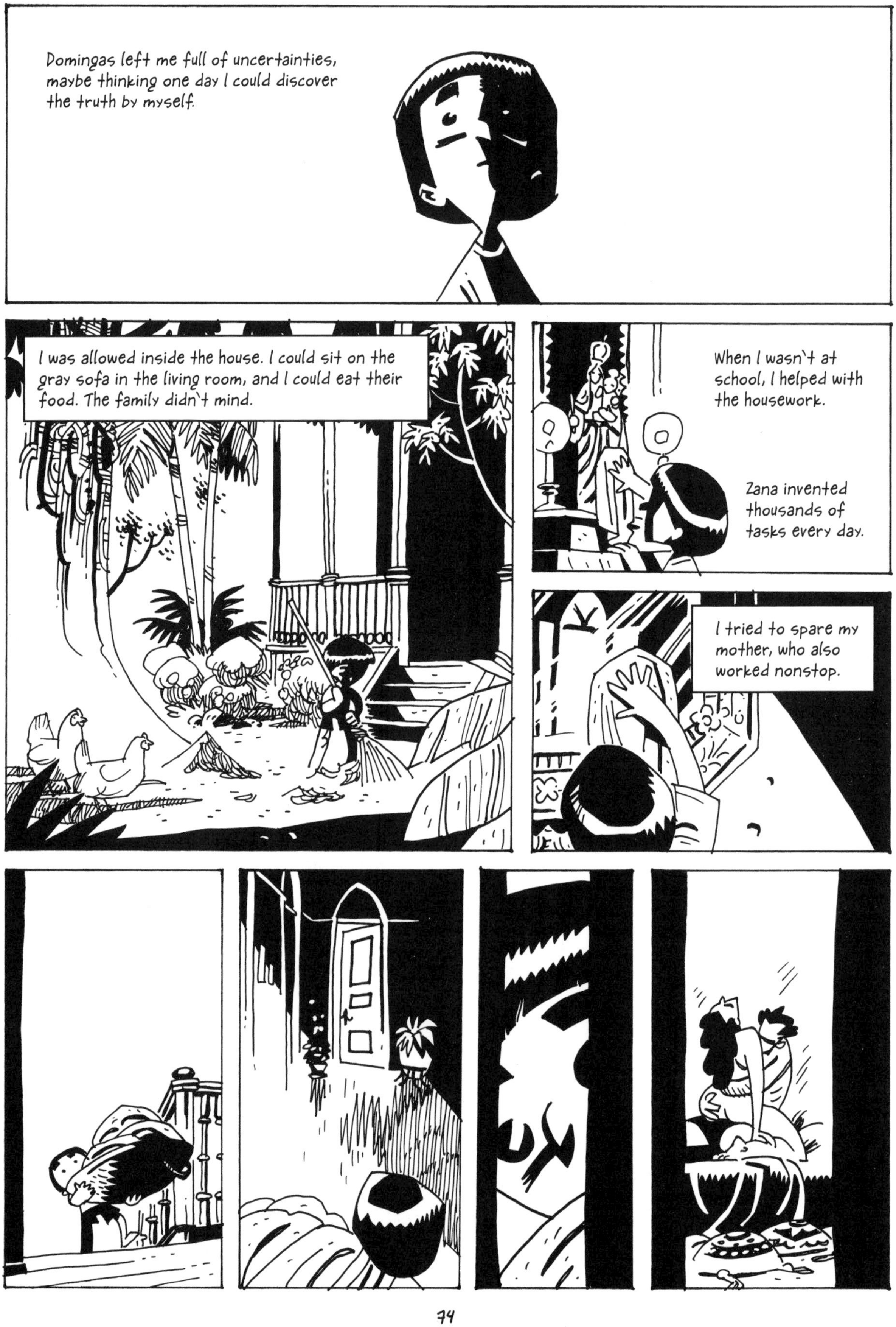
Domingas left me full of uncertainties, maybe thinking one day I could discover the truth by myself.
I was allowed inside the house. I could sit on the gray sofa in the living room, and I could eat their food. The family didn't mind.
When I wasn't at school, I helped with the housework.
Zana invented thousands of tasks every day.
I tried to spare my mother, who also worked nonstop.

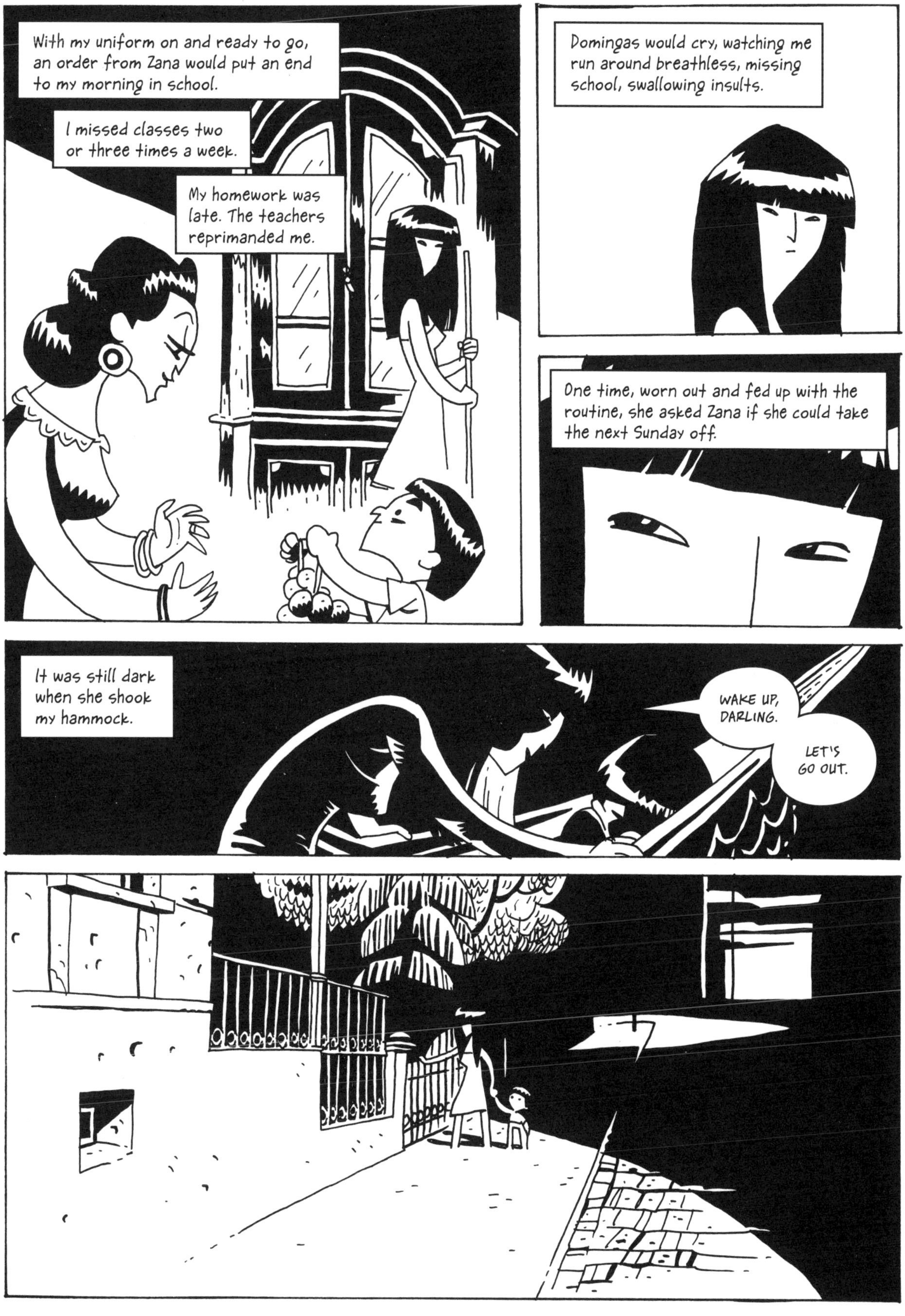
With my uniform on and ready to go, an order from Zana would put an end to my morning in school.
I missed classes two or three times a week.
My homework was late. The teachers reprimanded me.
Domingas would cry, watching me run around breathless, missing school, swallowing insults.
One time, worn out and fed up with the routine, she asked Zana if she could take the next Sunday off.
It was still dark when she shook my hammock.
WAKE UP, DARLING.
LET'S GO OUT.

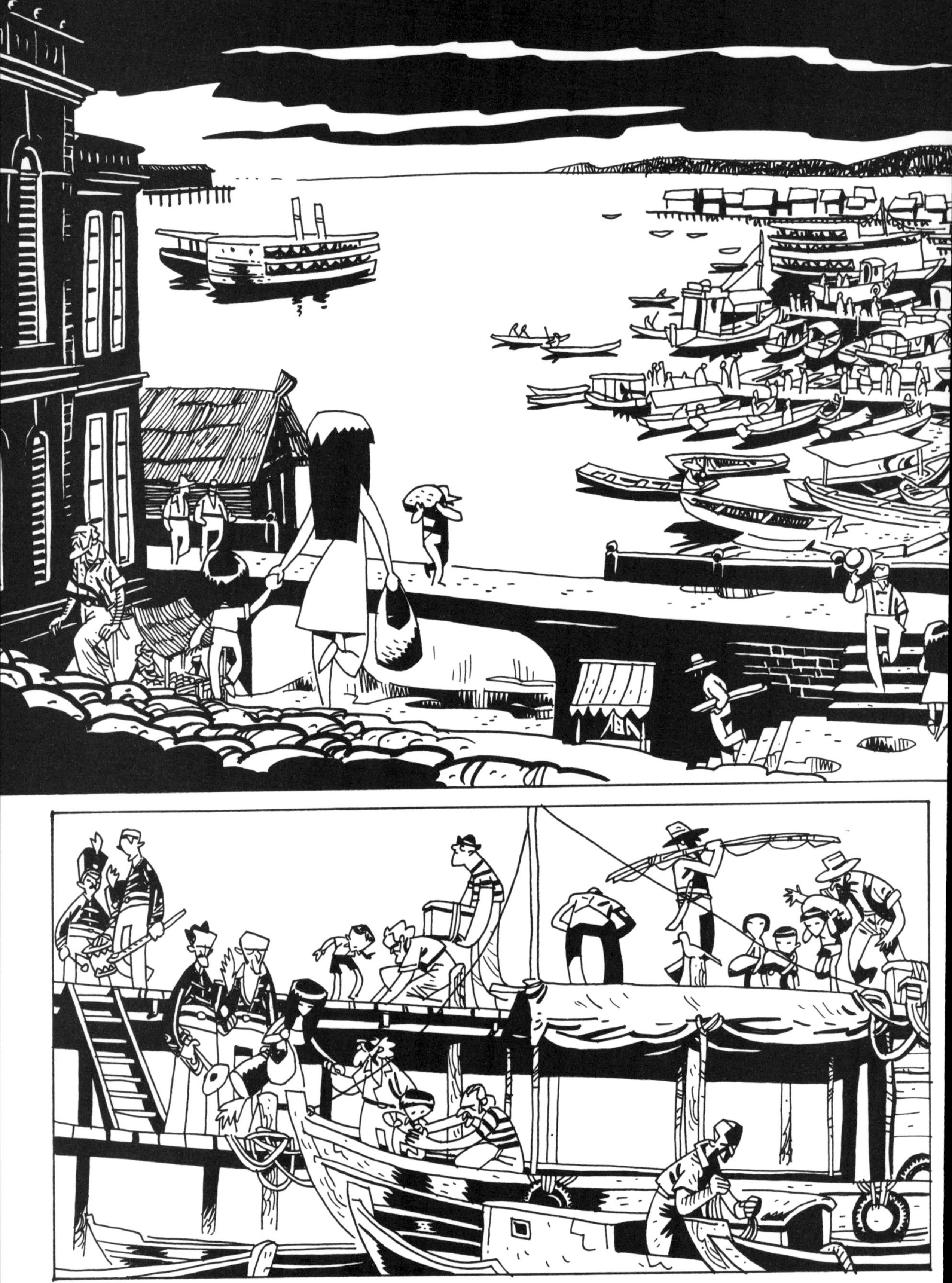

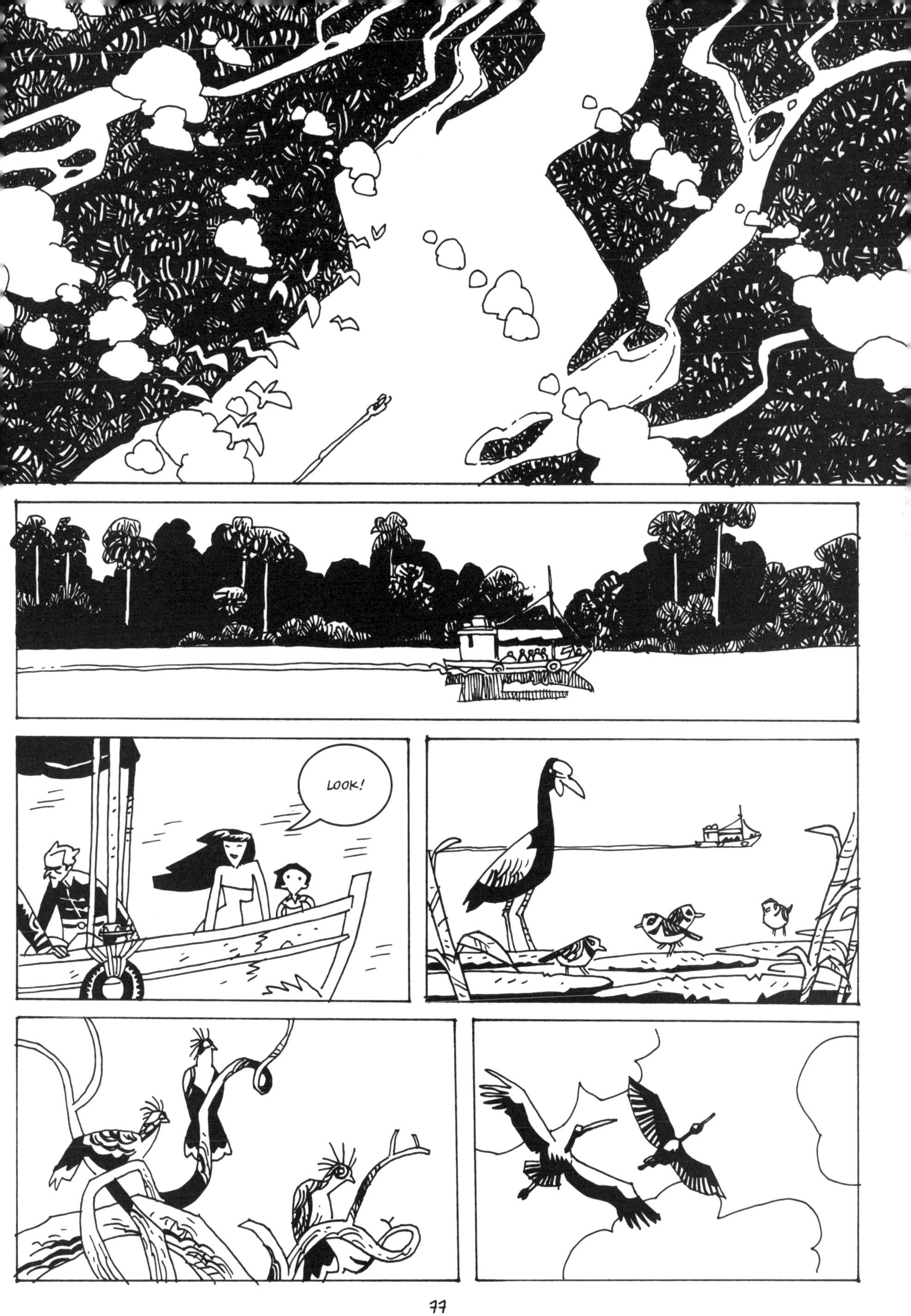
LOOK!

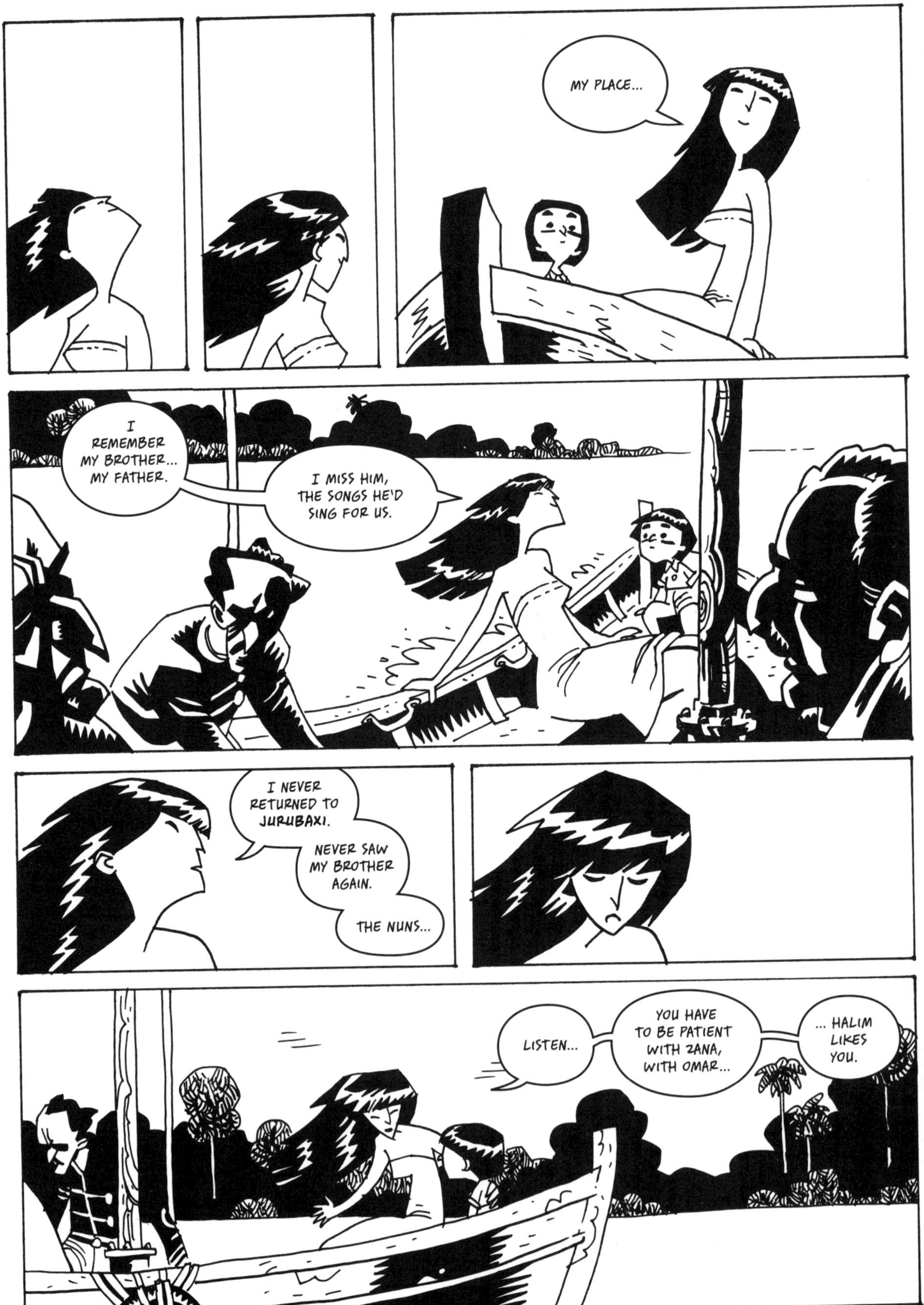
MY PLACE...
I REMEMBER MY BROTHER... MY FATHER.
I MISS HIM, THE SONGS HE'D SING FOR US.
I NEVER RETURNED TO JURUBAXI.
NEVER SAW MY BROTHER AGAIN.
THE NUNS...
LISTEN...
YOU HAVE TO BE PATIENT WITH ZANA, WITH OMAR...
... HALIM LIKES YOU.

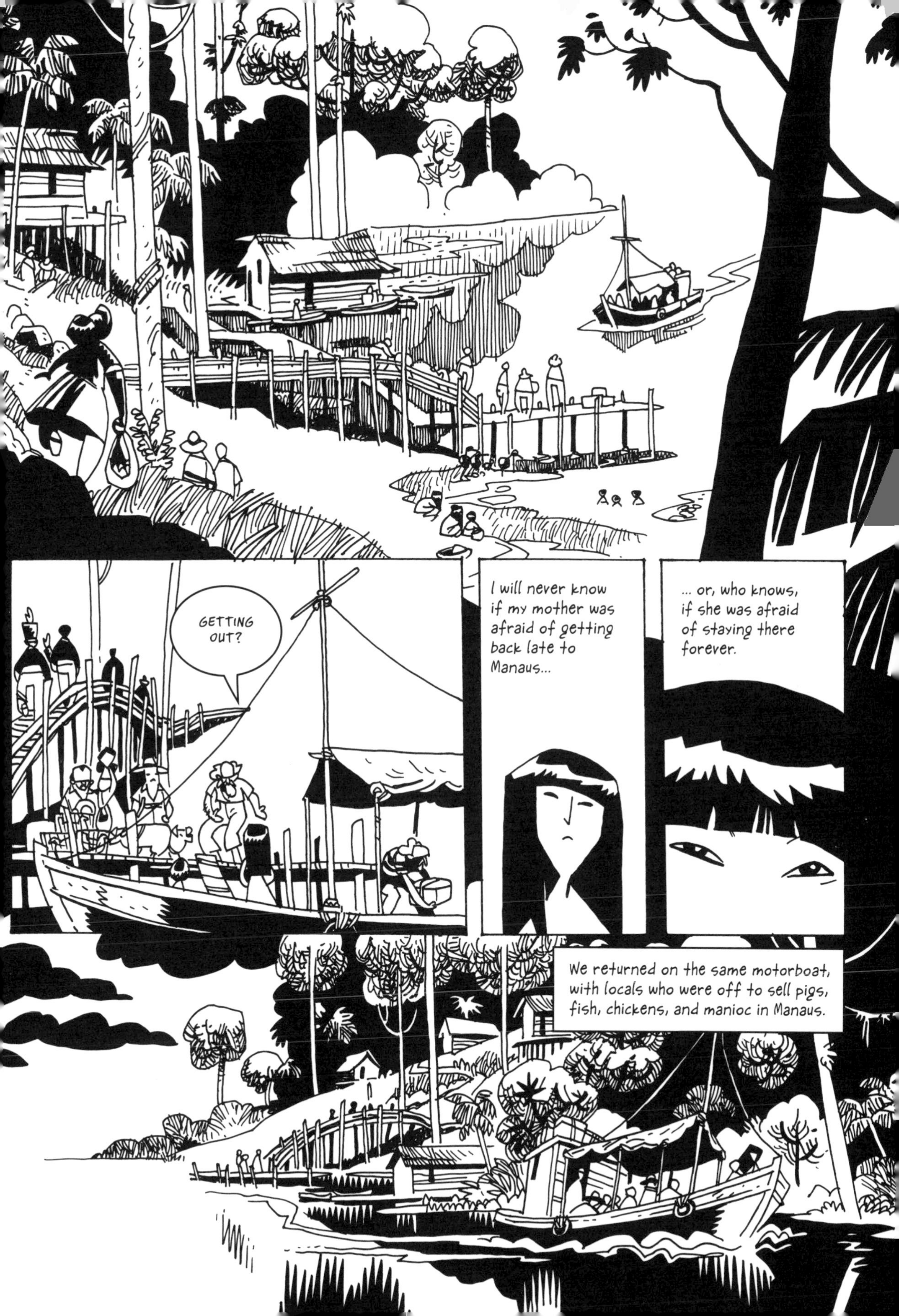
GETTING OUT?
I will never know if my mother was afraid of getting back late to Manaus...
... or, who knows, if she was afraid of staying there forever.
We returned on the same motorboat, with locals who were off to sell pigs, fish, chickens, and manioc in Manaus.

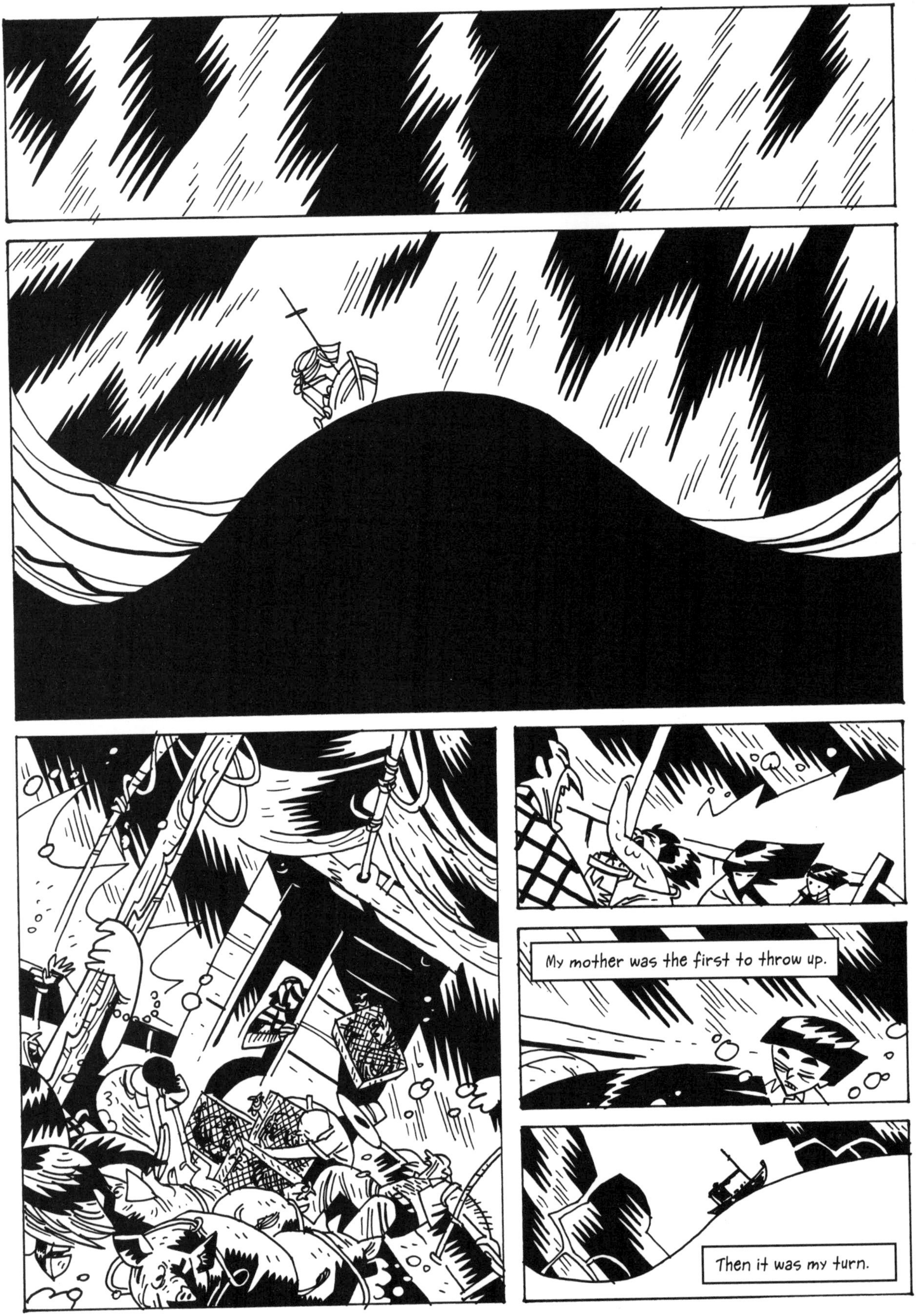
My mother was the first to throw up.
Then it was my turn.

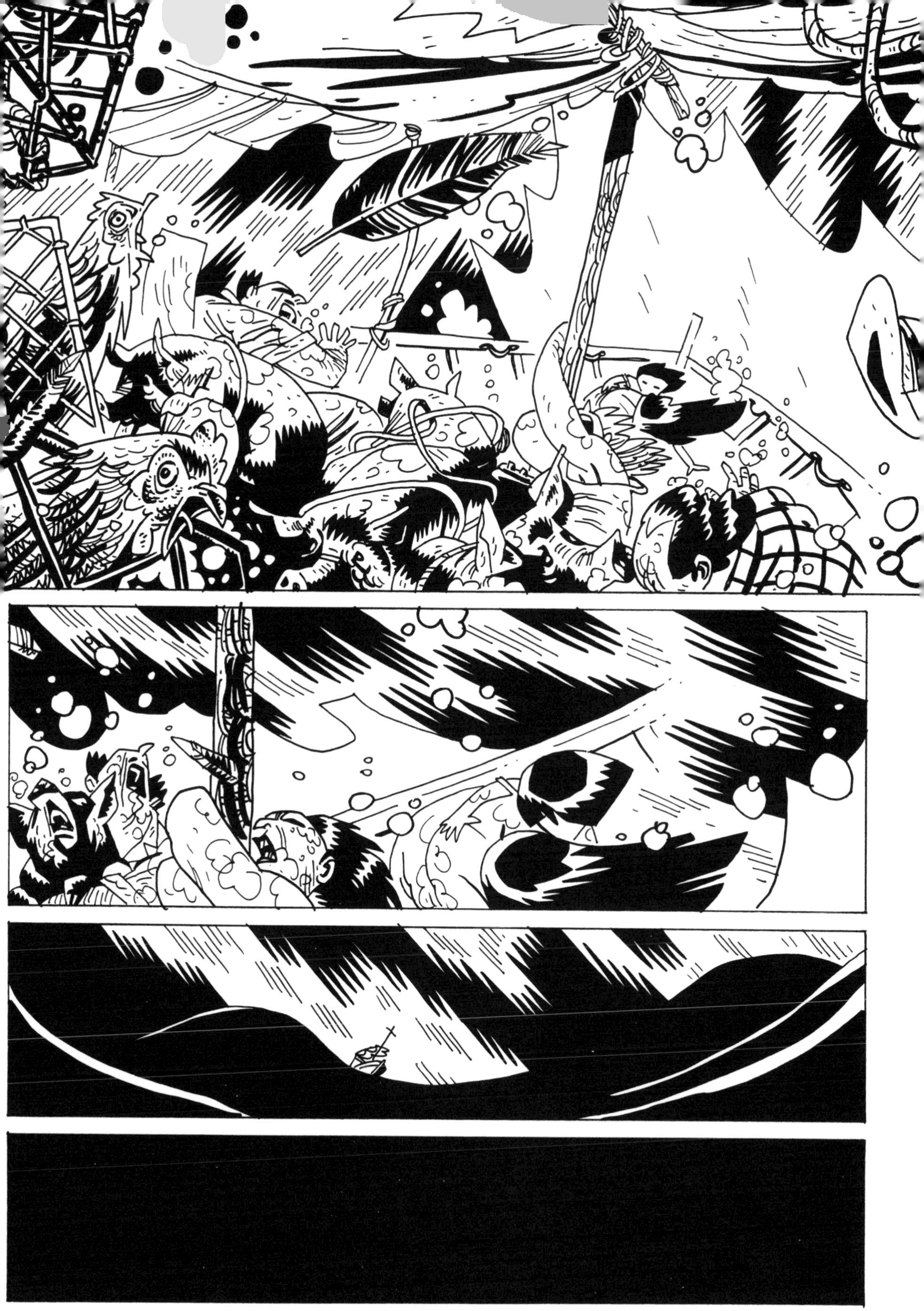

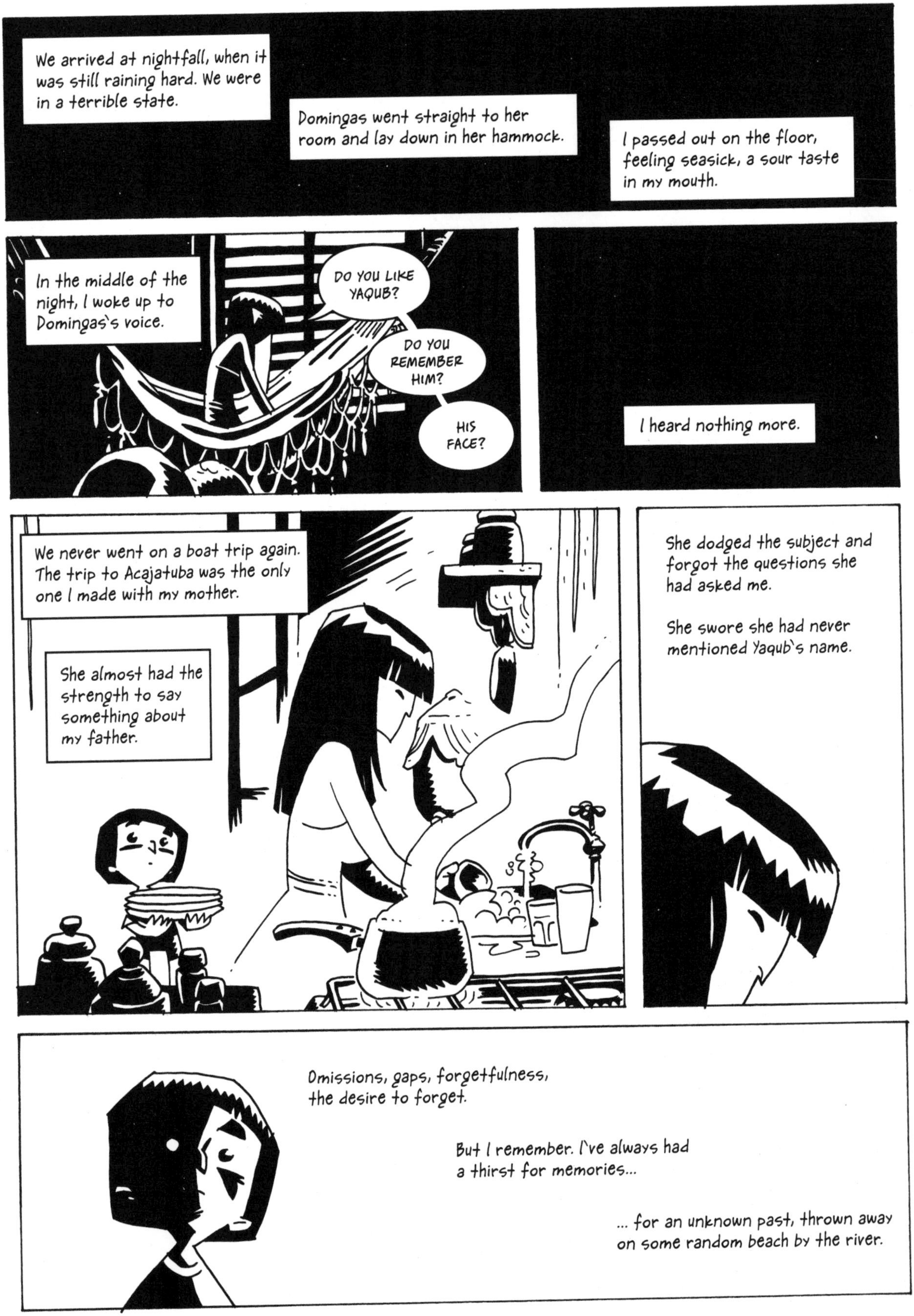
We arrived at nightfall, when it was still raining hard. We were in a terrible state.
Domingas went straight to her room and lay down in her hammock.
I passed out on the floor, feeling seasick, a sour taste in my mouth.
In the middle of the night, I woke up to Domingas's voice.
DO YOU LIKE YAQUB?
DO YOU REMEMBER HIM?
HIS FACE?
I heard nothing more.
We never went on a boat trip again. The trip to Acajatuba was the only one I made with my mother.
She almost had the strength to say something about my father.
She dodged the subject and forgot the questions she had asked me.
She swore she had never mentioned Yaqub's name.
Omissions, gaps, forgetfulness, the desire to forget.
But I remember. I've always had a thirst for memories...
... for an unknown past, thrown away on some random beach by the river.

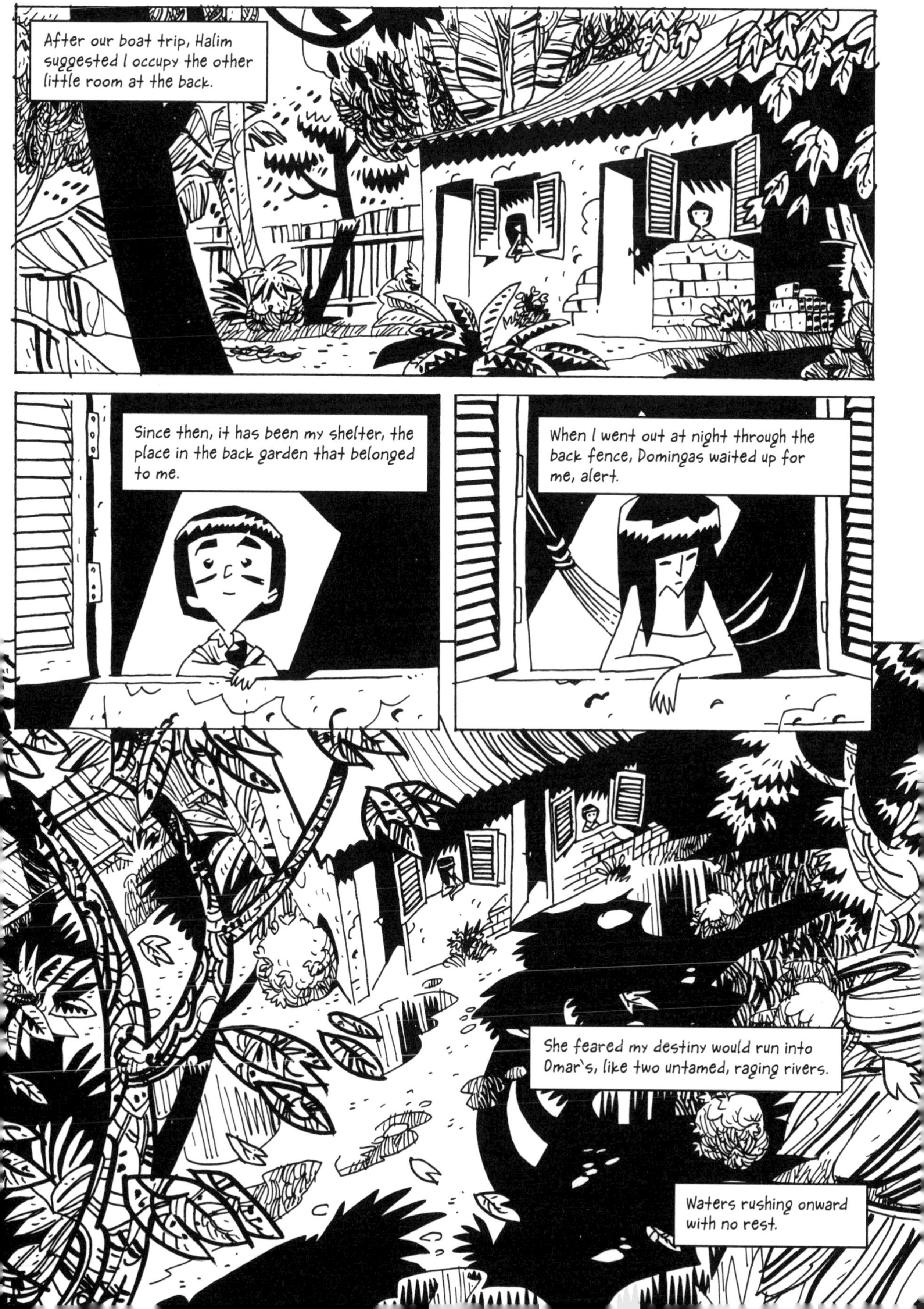
After our boat trip, Halim suggested I occupy the other little room at the back.
Since then, it has been my shelter, the place in the back garden that belonged to me.
When I went out at night through the back fence, Domingas waited up for me, alert.
She feared my destiny would run into Omar's, like two untamed, raging rivers.
Waters rushing onward with no rest.

Chapter 4

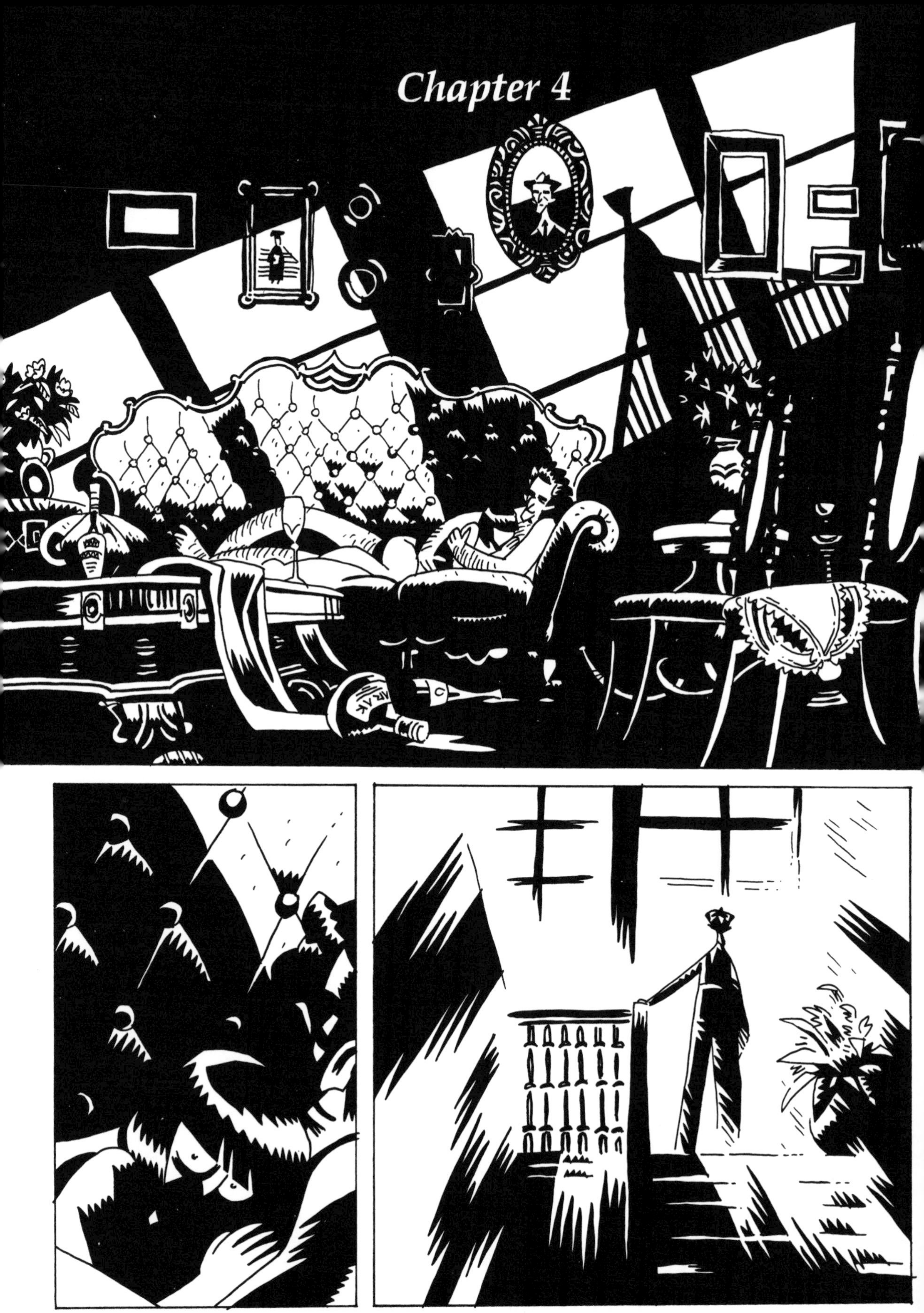

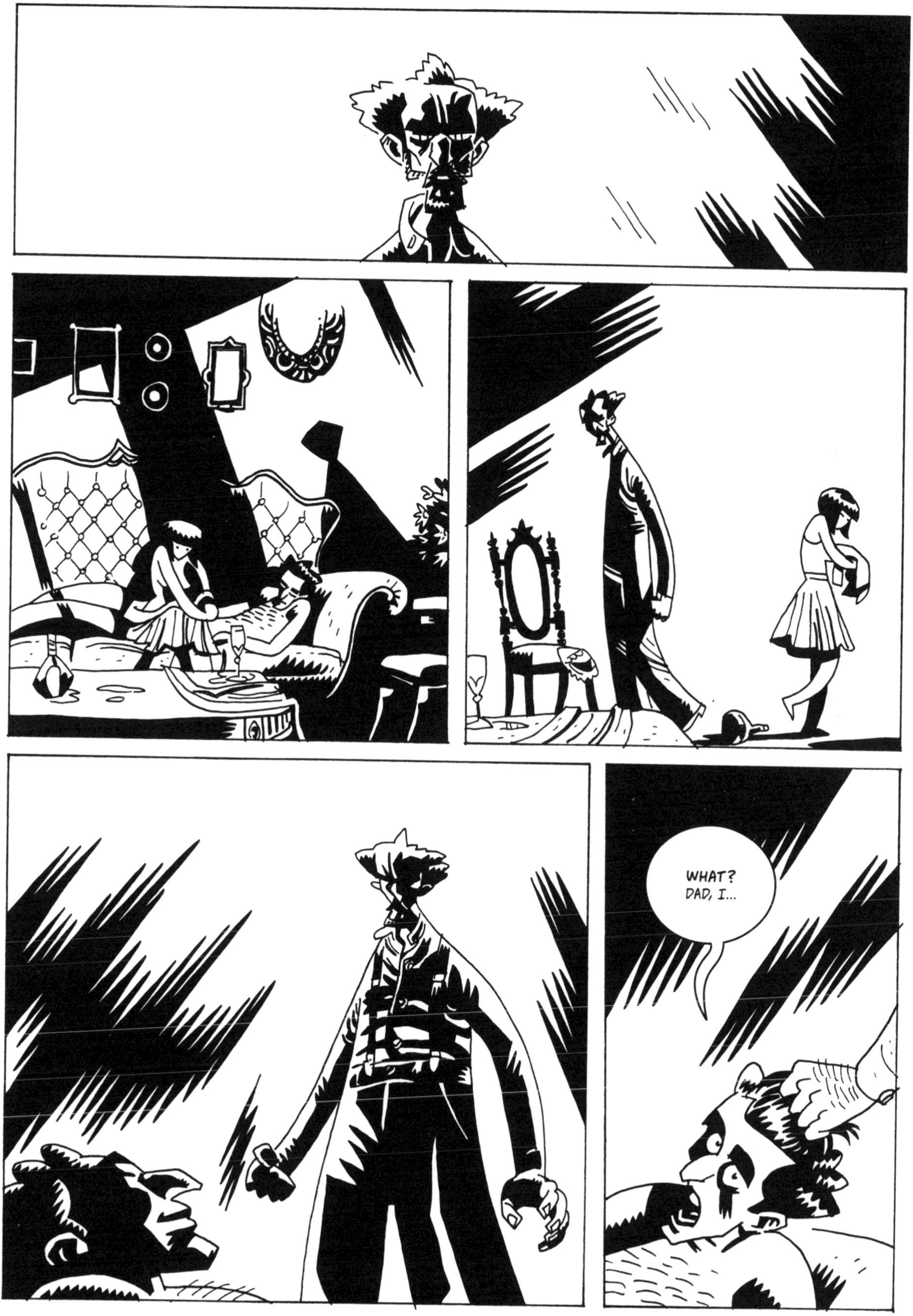
WHAT?
DAD, I...

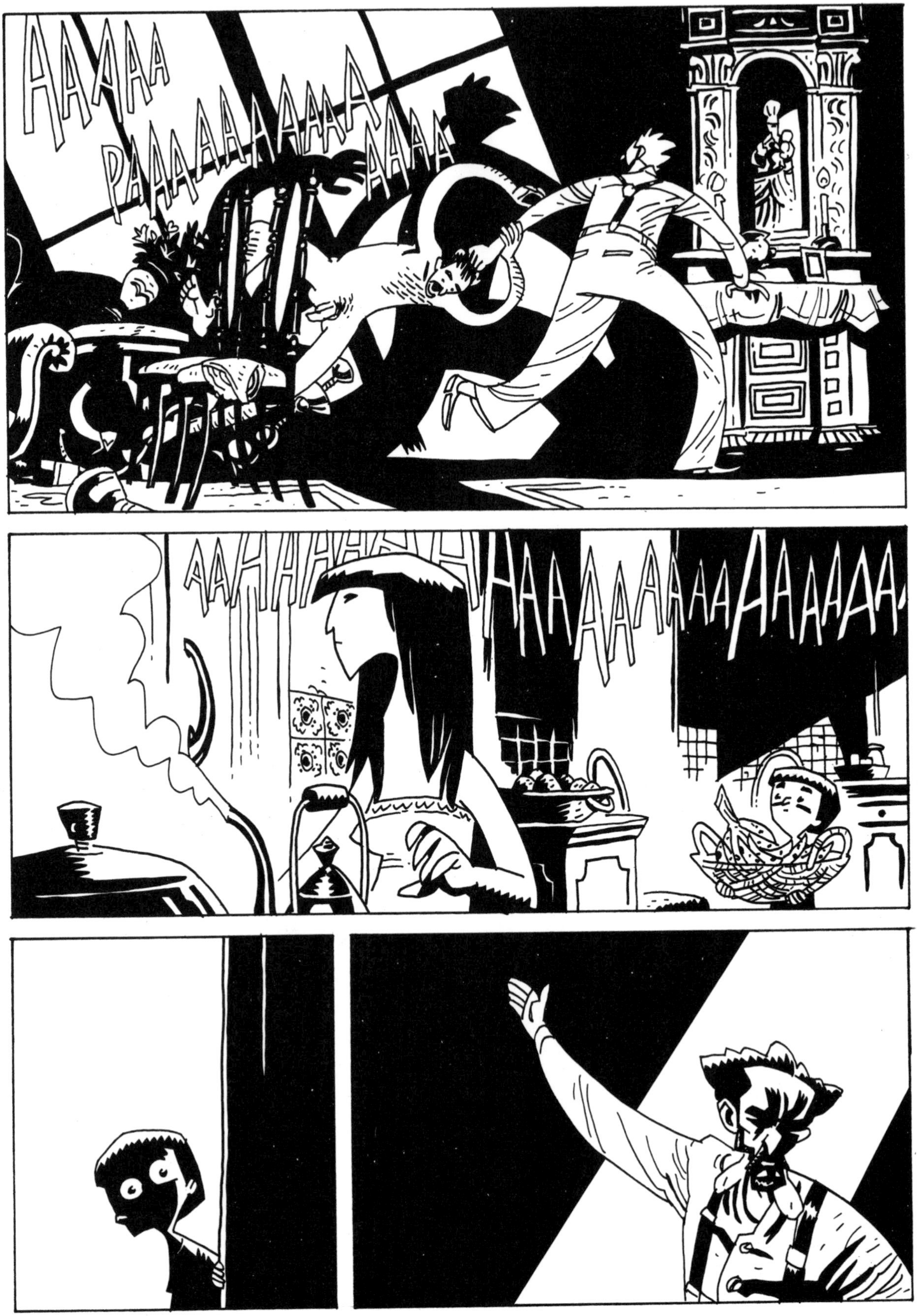
AAAAA
PAAAAAAAAAAA
AAAA
AAHHHHHHHHAAAAAAAAAAAAA,

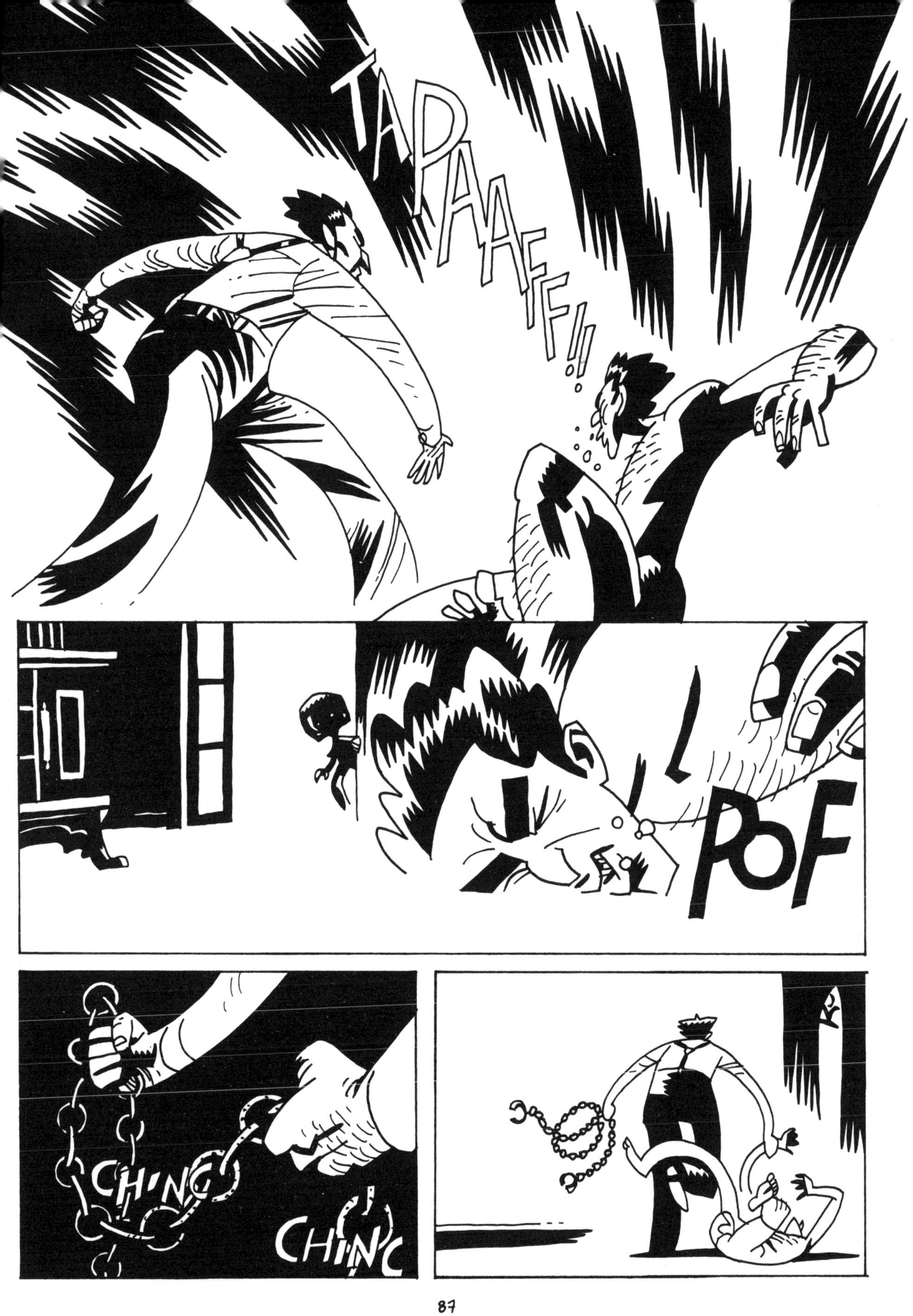
TAPAAAFFF!!
POF
CHING
CHING

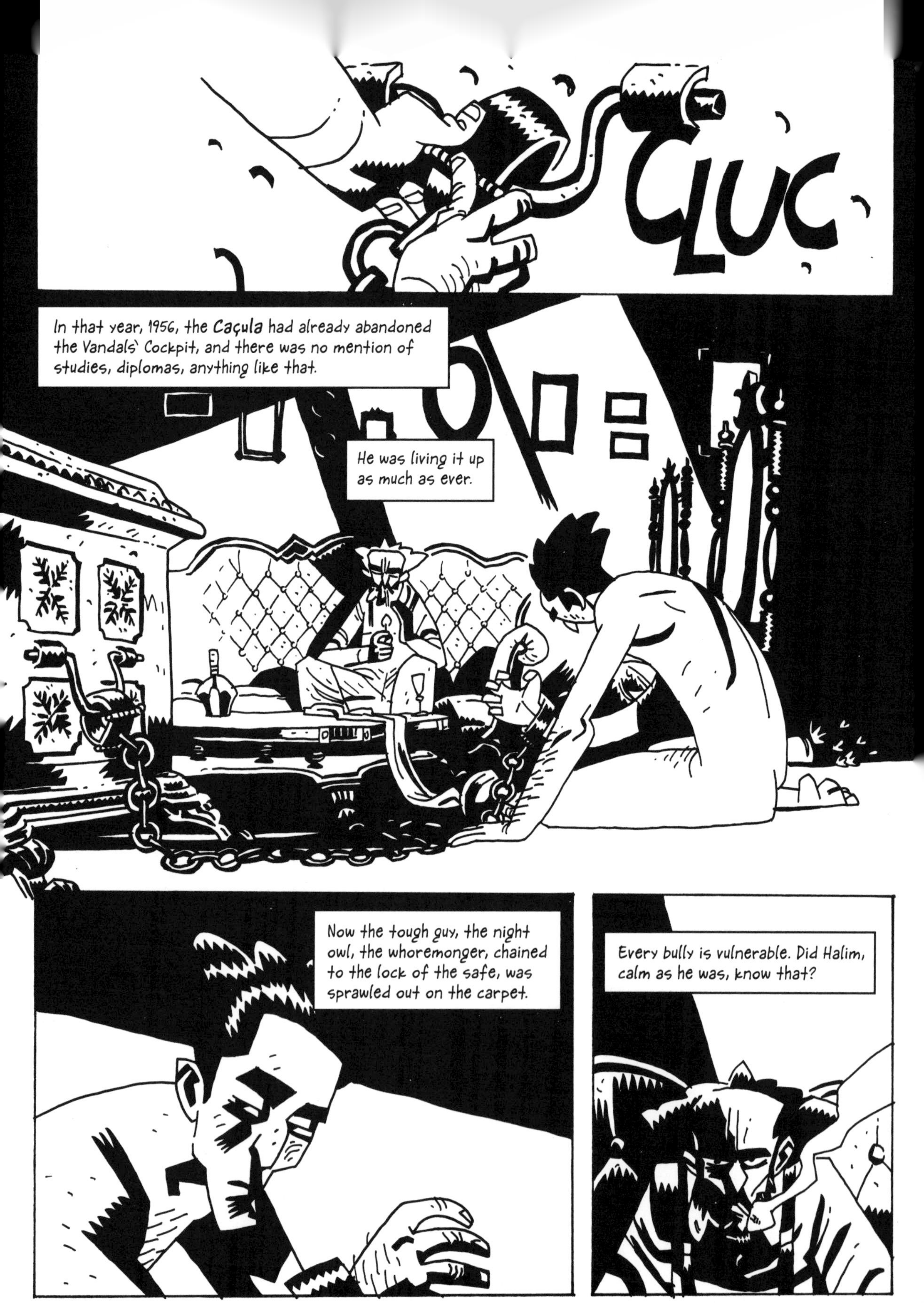
CLUC
In that year, 1956, the Caçula had already abandoned the Vandals' Cockpit, and there was no mention of studies, diplomas, anything like that.
He was living it up as much as ever.
Now the tough guy, the night owl, the whoremonger, chained to the lock of the safe, was sprawled out on the carpet.
Every bully is vulnerable. Did Halim, calm as he was, know that?

He hit his son hard and went out. He disappeared for two days. Zana couldn't interfere. She'd had no time to come to her son's aid.

I was in charge of going after Halim, combing the city center, searching in the stalls scattered around the harbor, in the little restaurants, in the cheap bars of the Floating City.

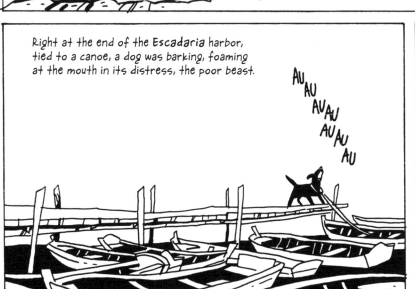

Right at the end of the **Escadaria** harbor, tied to a canoe, a dog was barking, foaming at the mouth in its distress, the poor beast.

AU
AU
AUAU
AUAU
AU

The sight of the tethered dog reminded me of the prisoner with the swollen face.

AU
AU
AUAUAUAUAU

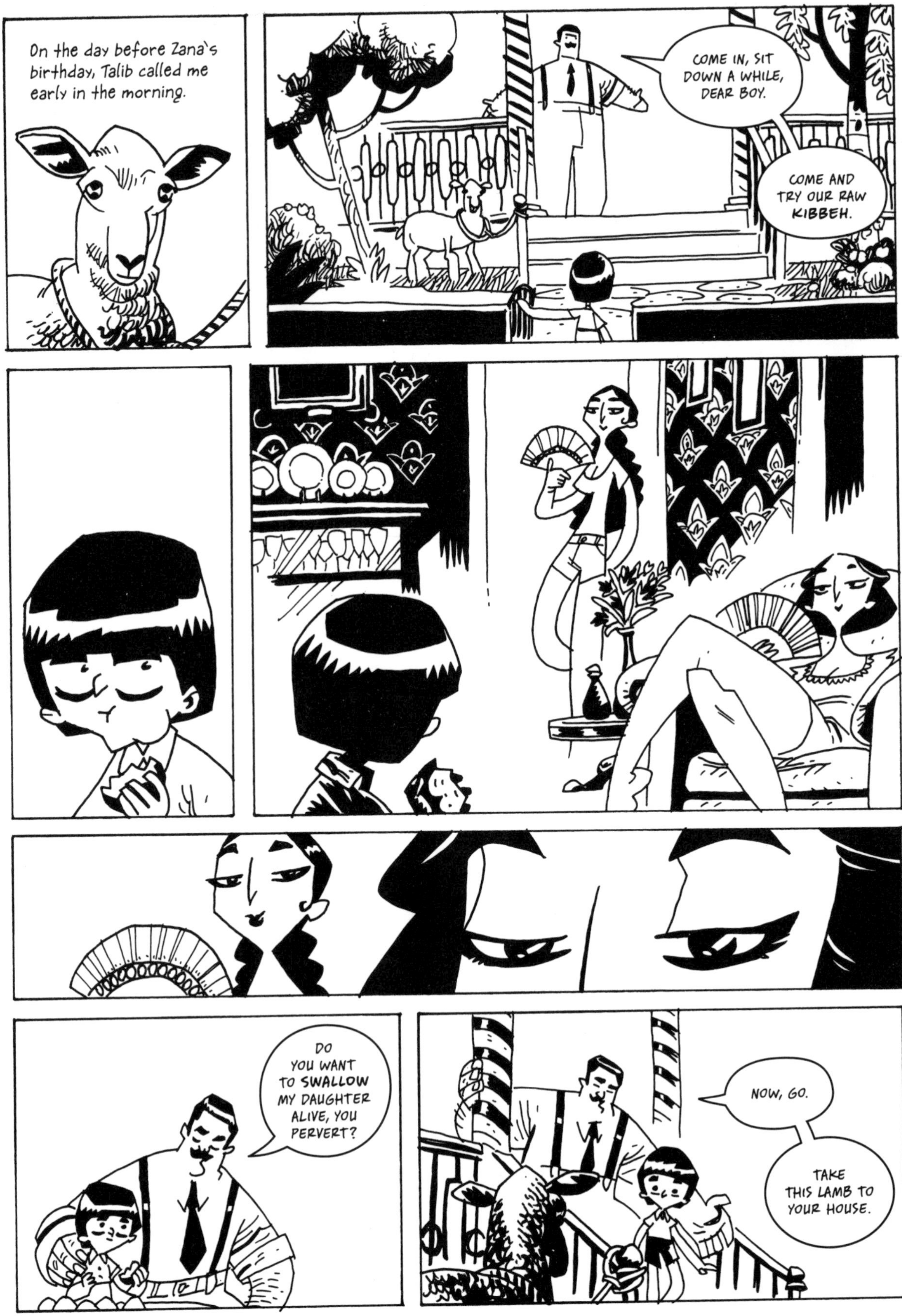

On the day before Zana's birthday, Talib called me early in the morning.
COME IN, SIT DOWN A WHILE, DEAR BOY.
COME AND TRY OUR RAW KIBBEH.
DO YOU WANT TO SWALLOW MY DAUGHTER ALIVE, YOU PERVERT?
NOW, GO.
TAKE THIS LAMB TO YOUR HOUSE.

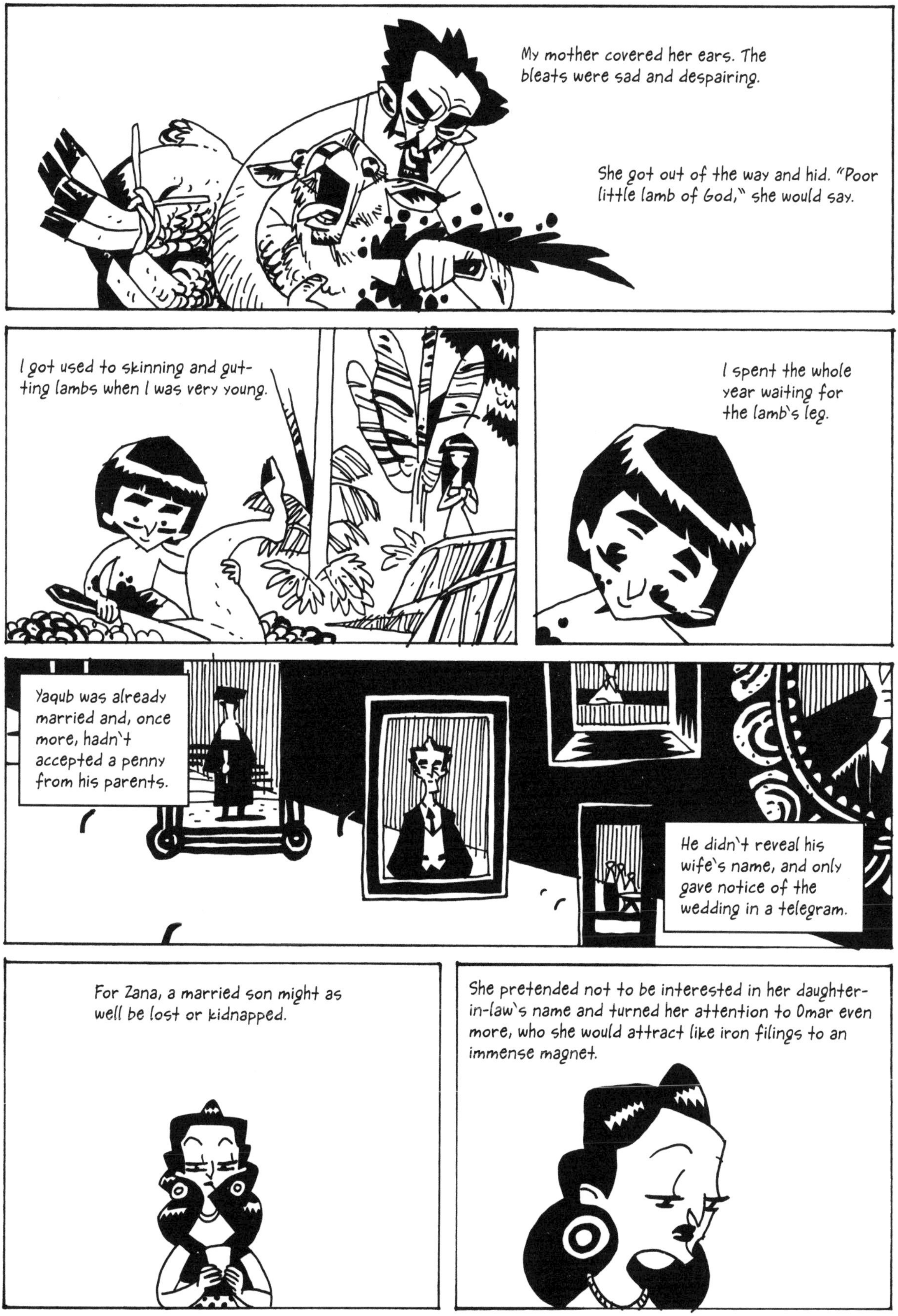
My mother covered her ears. The bleats were sad and despairing.
She got out of the way and hid. "Poor little lamb of God," she would say.
I got used to skinning and gutting lambs when I was very young.
I spent the whole year waiting for the lamb's leg.
Yaqub was already married and, once more, hadn't accepted a penny from his parents.
He didn't reveal his wife's name, and only gave notice of the wedding in a telegram.
For Zana, a married son might as well be lost or kidnapped.
She pretended not to be interested in her daughter-in-law's name and turned her attention to Omar even more, who she would attract like iron filings to an immense magnet.

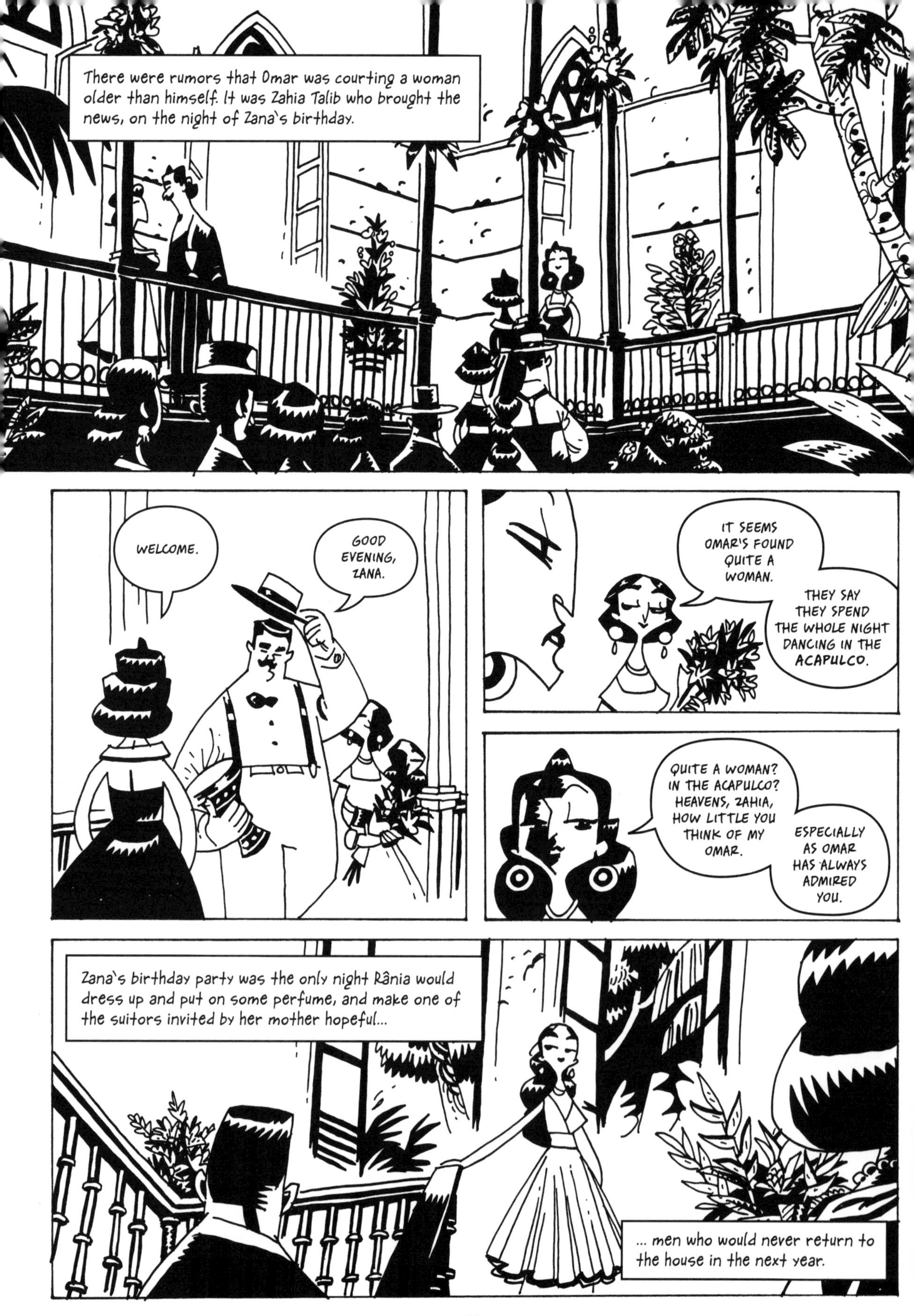
There were rumors that Omar was courting a woman older than himself. It was Zahia Talib who brought the news, on the night of Zana's birthday.
WELCOME.
GOOD EVENING, ZANA.
IT SEEMS OMAR'S FOUND QUITE A WOMAN.
THEY SAY THEY SPEND THE WHOLE NIGHT DANCING IN THE ACAPULCO.
QUITE A WOMAN? IN THE ACAPULCO? HEAVENS, ZAHIA, HOW LITTLE YOU THINK OF MY OMAR.
ESPECIALLY AS OMAR HAS ALWAYS ADMIRED YOU.
Zana's birthday party was the only night Rânia would dress up and put on some perfume, and make one of the suitors invited by her mother hopeful...
... men who would never return to the house in the next year.

Talib had the hots for her.

BY GOD, HALIM.

I'D GIVE MY TWO DAUGHTERS FOR YOURS.

Rânia brought shivers to my almost-adolescent body.

I awaited dearly her close embrace, the only one of the year.

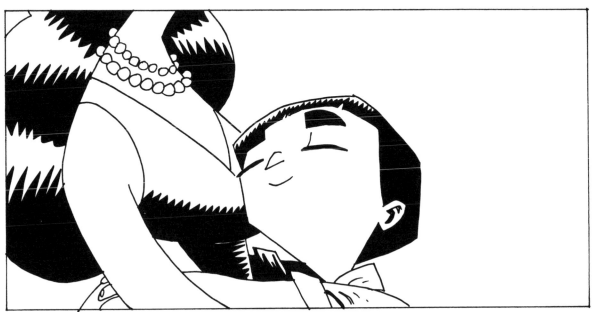

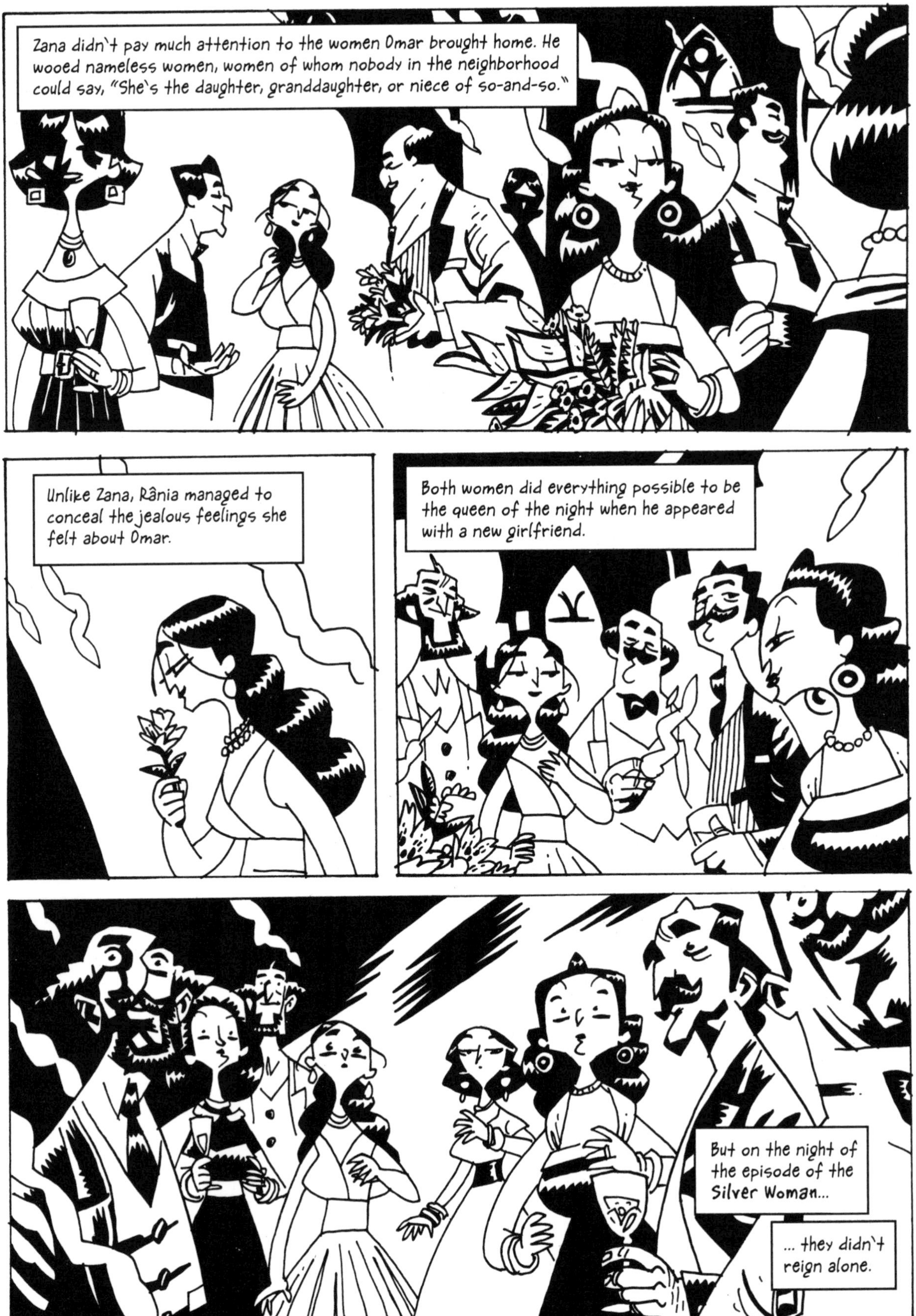
Zana didn't pay much attention to the women Omar brought home. He wooed nameless women, women of whom nobody in the neighborhood could say, "She's the daughter, granddaughter, or niece of so-and-so."
Unlike Zana, Rânia managed to conceal the jealous feelings she felt about Omar.
Both women did everything possible to be the queen of the night when he appeared with a new girlfriend.
But on the night of the episode of the Silver Woman...
... they didn't reign alone.

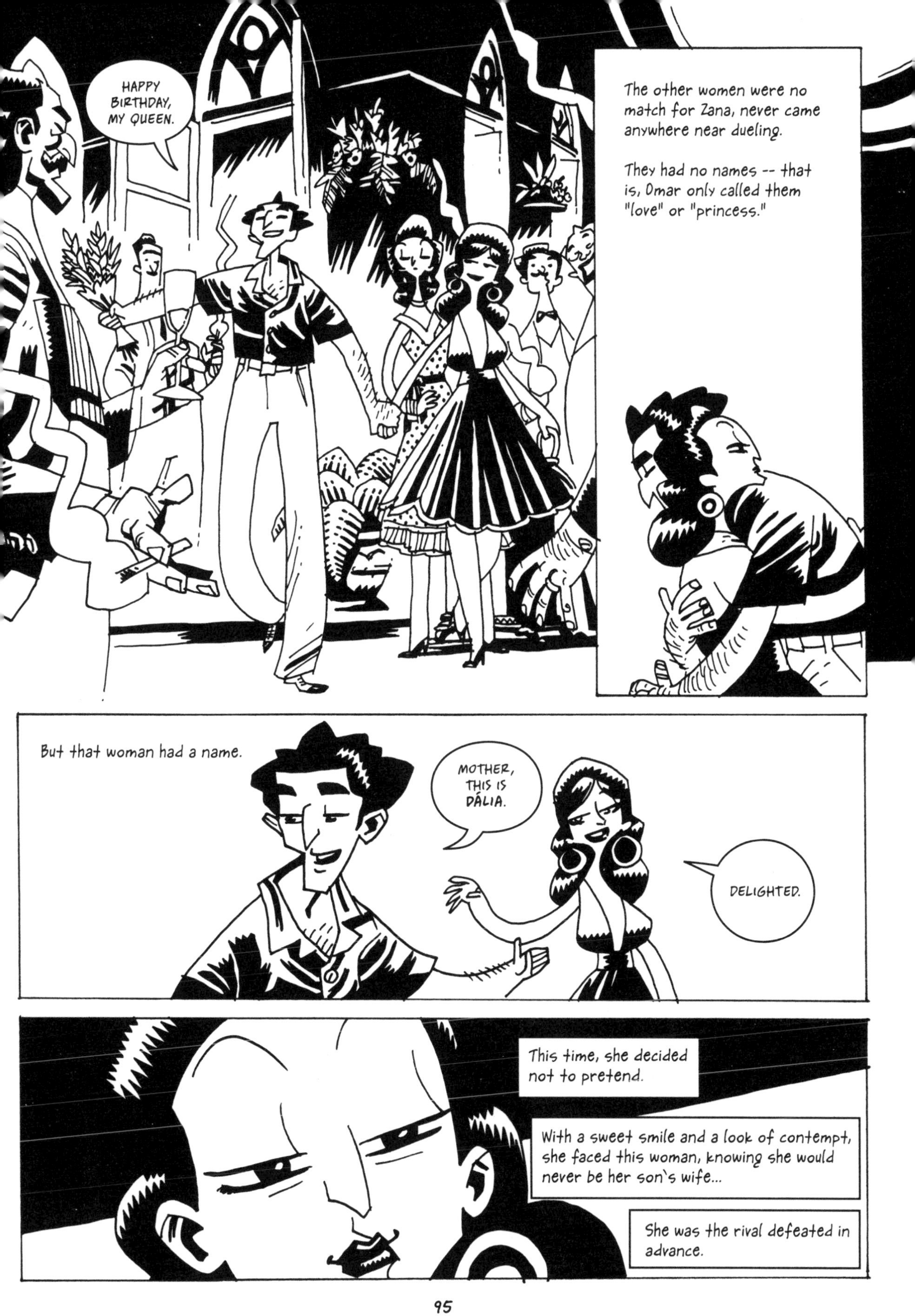
HAPPY BIRTHDAY, MY QUEEN.
The other women were no match for Zana, never came anywhere near dueling.
They had no names -- that is, Omar only called them "love" or "princess."
But that woman had a name.
MOTHER, THIS IS DÁLIA.
DELIGHTED.
This time, she decided not to pretend.
With a sweet smile and a look of contempt, she faced this woman, knowing she would never be her son's wife...
She was the rival defeated in advance.

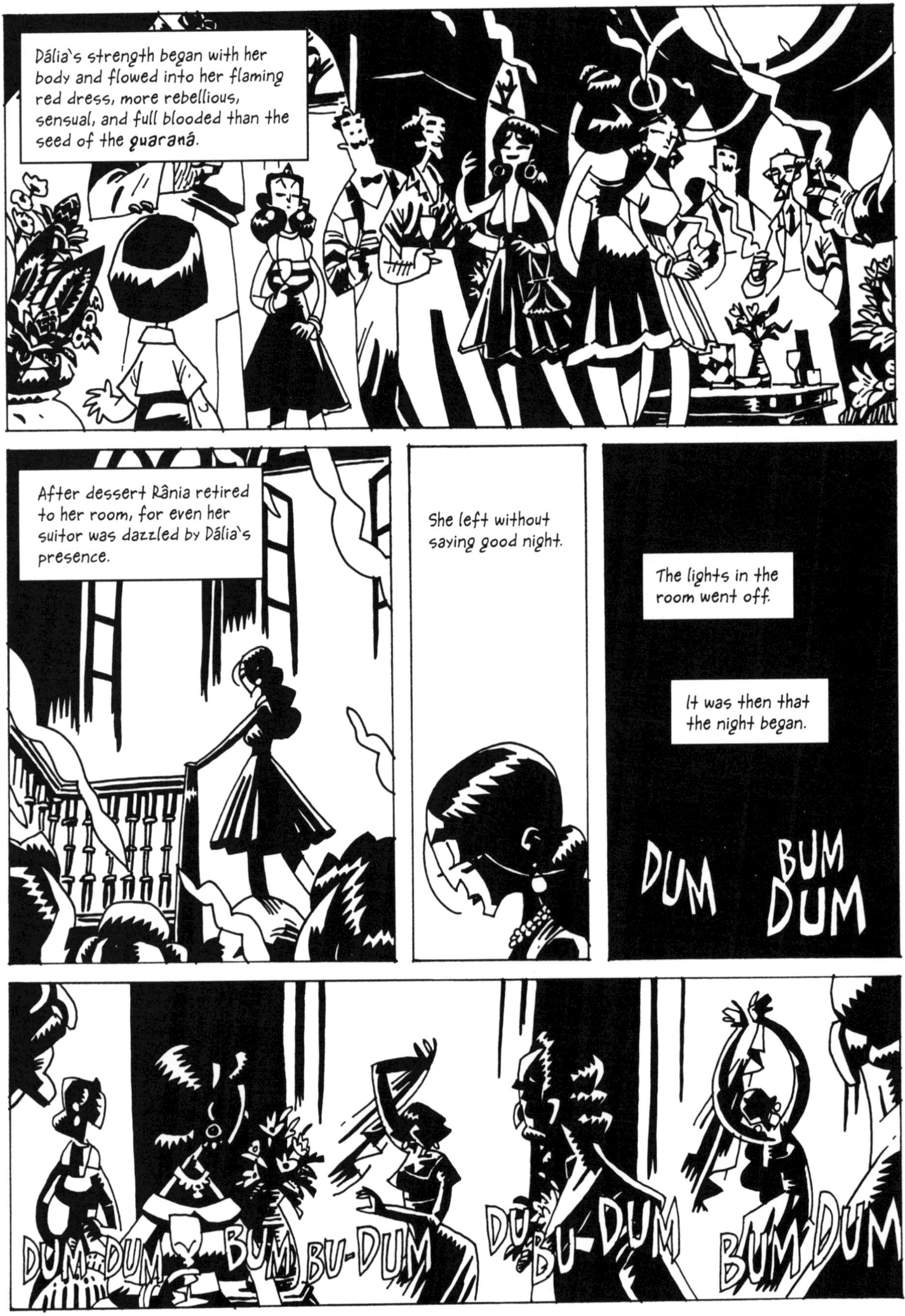
Dália's strength began with her body and flowed into her flaming red dress, more rebellious, sensual, and full blooded than the seed of the guaraná.
After dessert Rânia retired to her room, for even her suitor was dazzled by Dália's presence.
She left without saying good night.
The lights in the room went off.
It was then that the night began.
DUM
BUM DUM
DUM-DUM
BUM BU-DUM
DU BU-DUM
BUM DUM

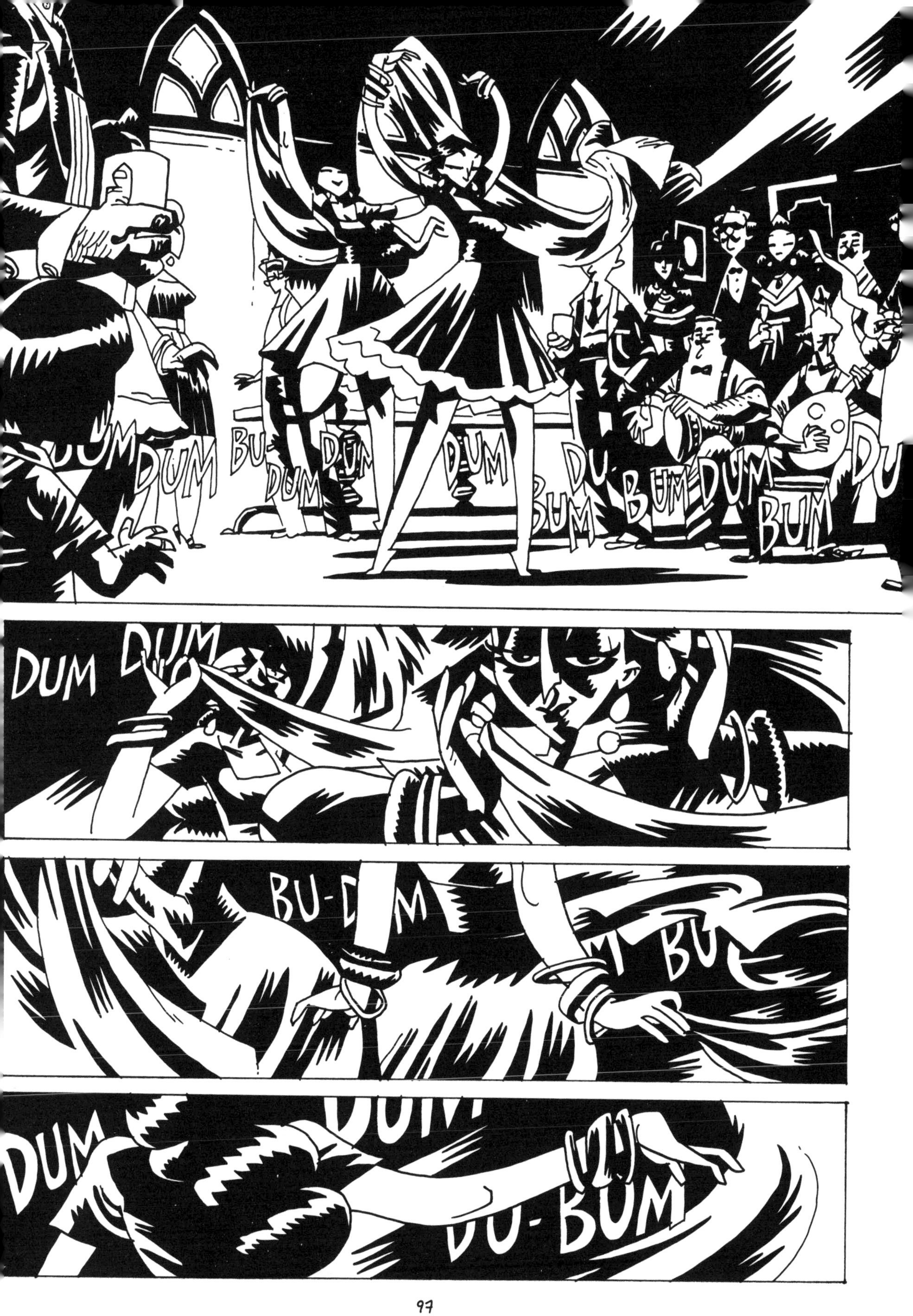
DUM
BU-
DUM
DUM
DUM
DU
BUM
BUM
DUM
BUM
DUM
DUM
BU
DUM
DU-BUM

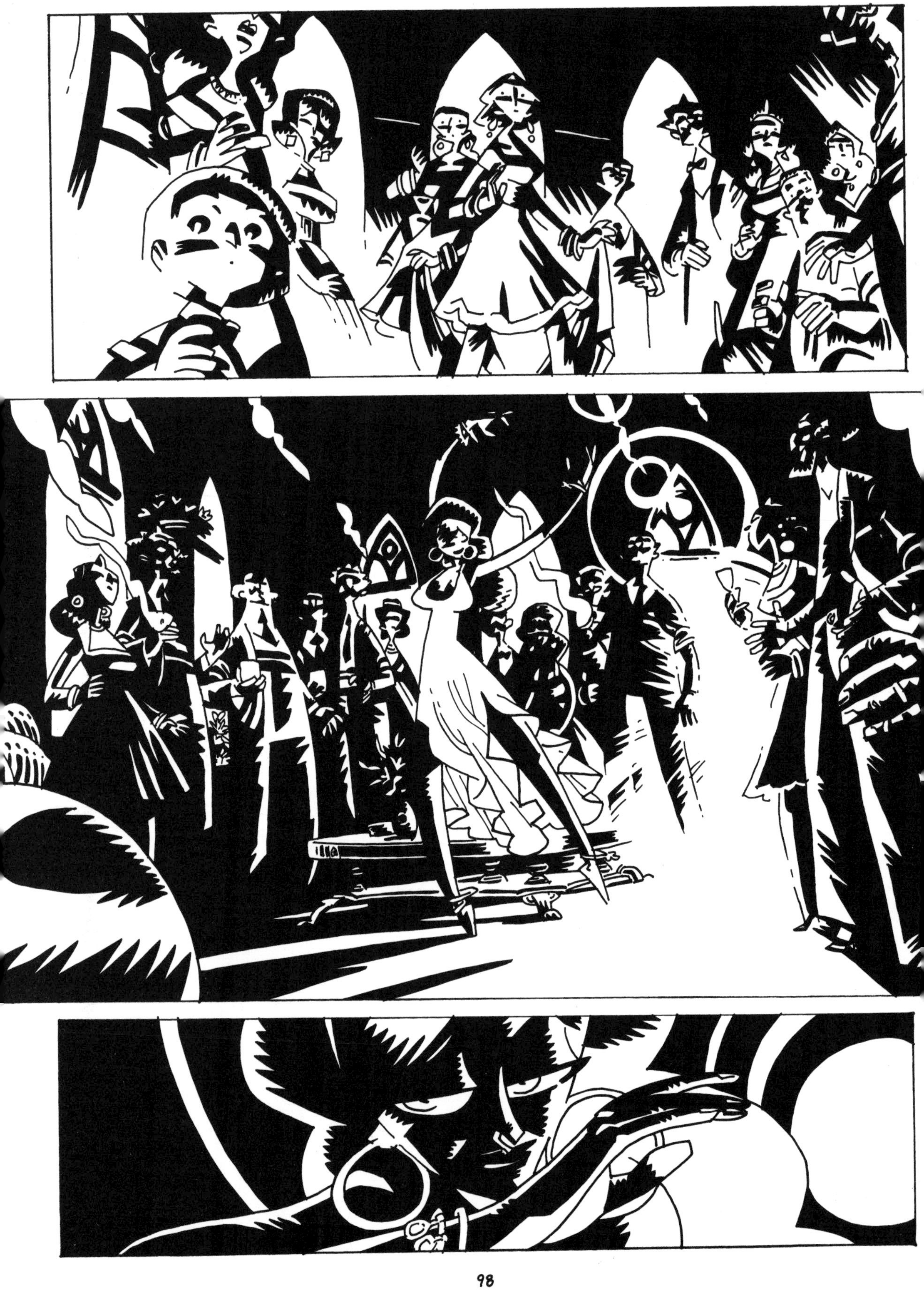

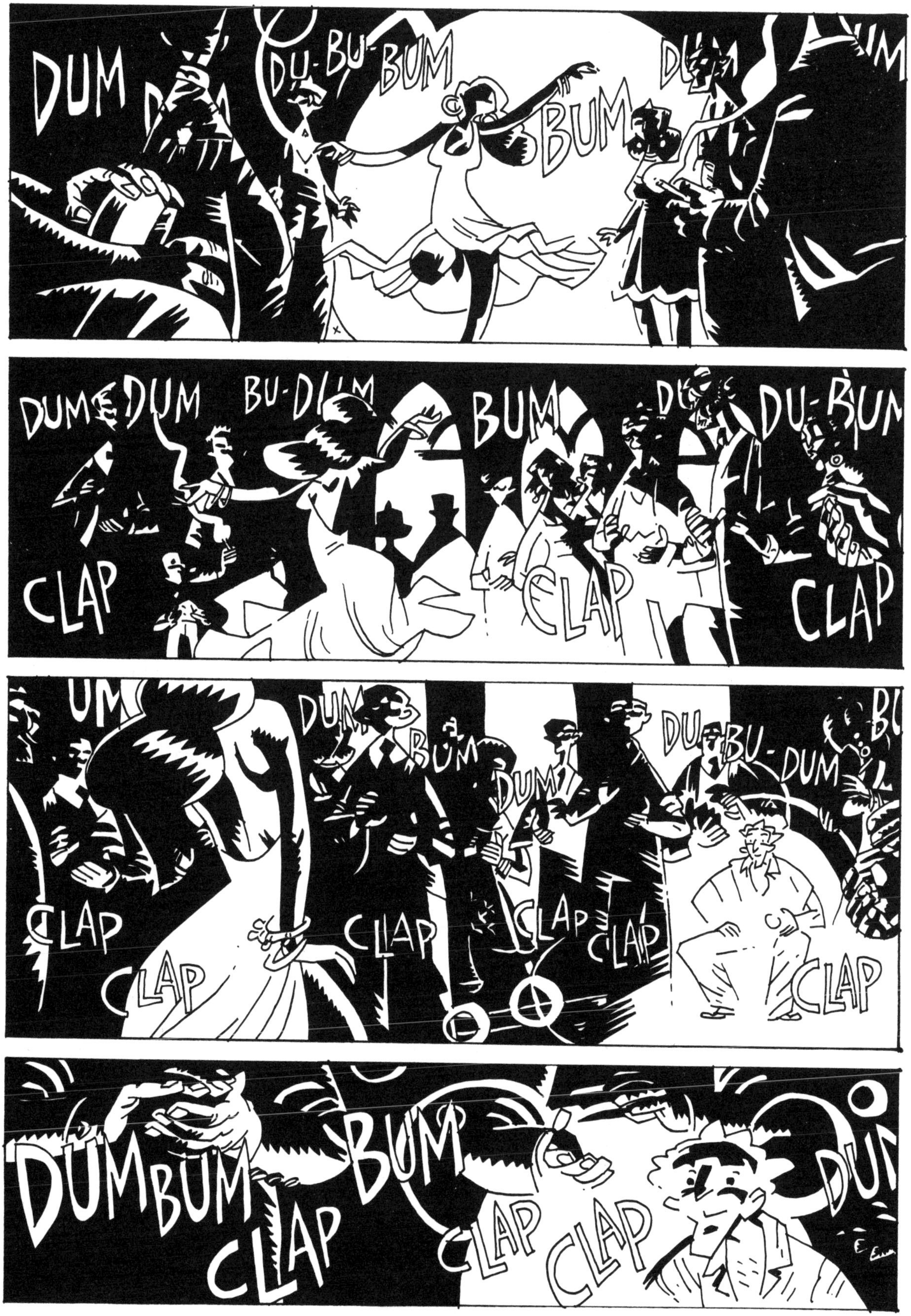
DUM
DU-BU
BUM
BUM
DUM
DUM
BU-DUM
BUM
DU-BUM
CLAP
CLAP
CLAP
DUM
BUM
DUM
DU-BU-BU-DUM
CLAP
CLAP
CLAP
CLAP
CLAP
CLAP
DUM
BUM
BUM
CLAP
CLAP
CLAP

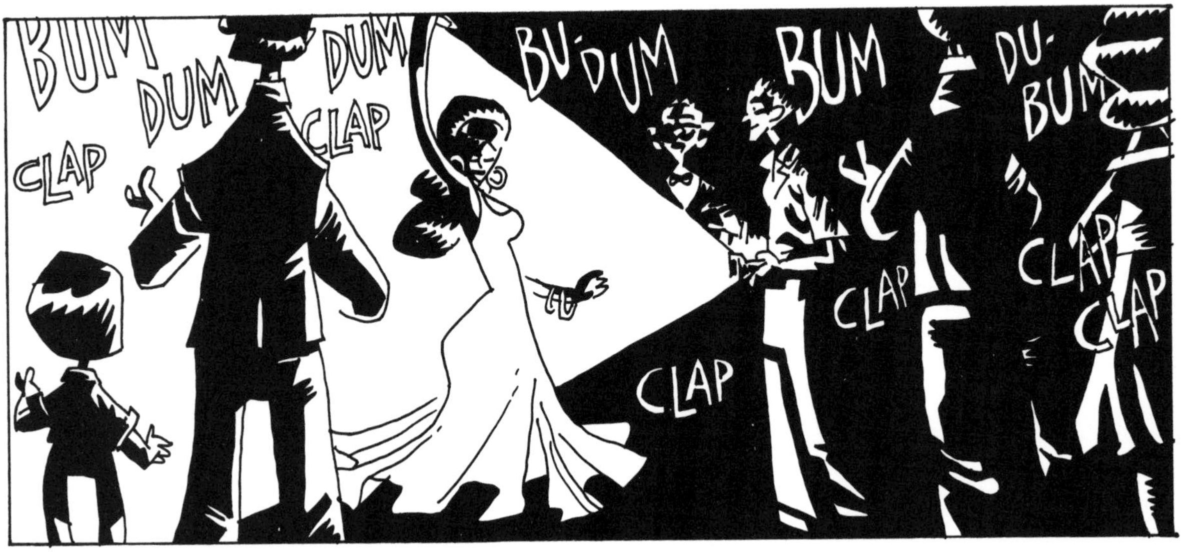
BUM
DUM
DUM
CLAP
CLAP
BU-DUM
BUM
DU-BUM
CLAP
CLAP
CLAP
CLAP

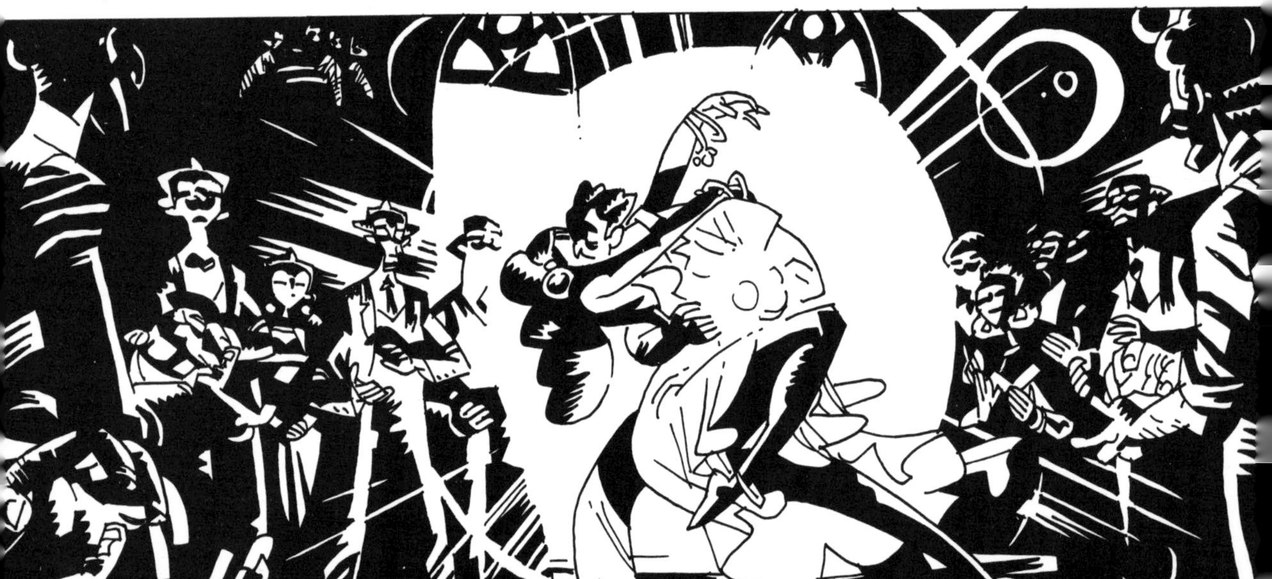
LAP CLAP CLAP CLAP CLAP CLAP

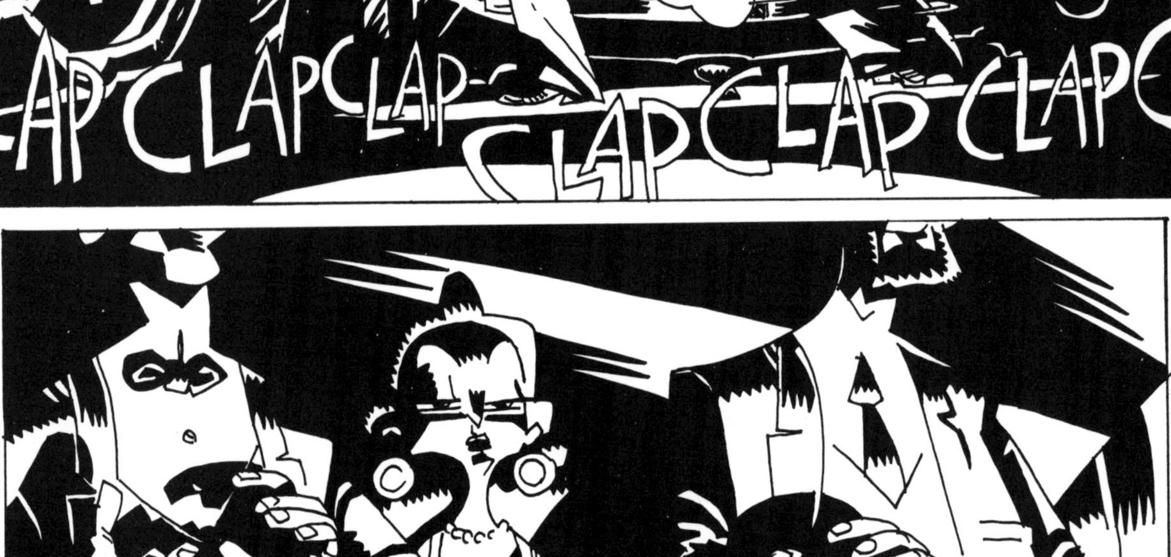

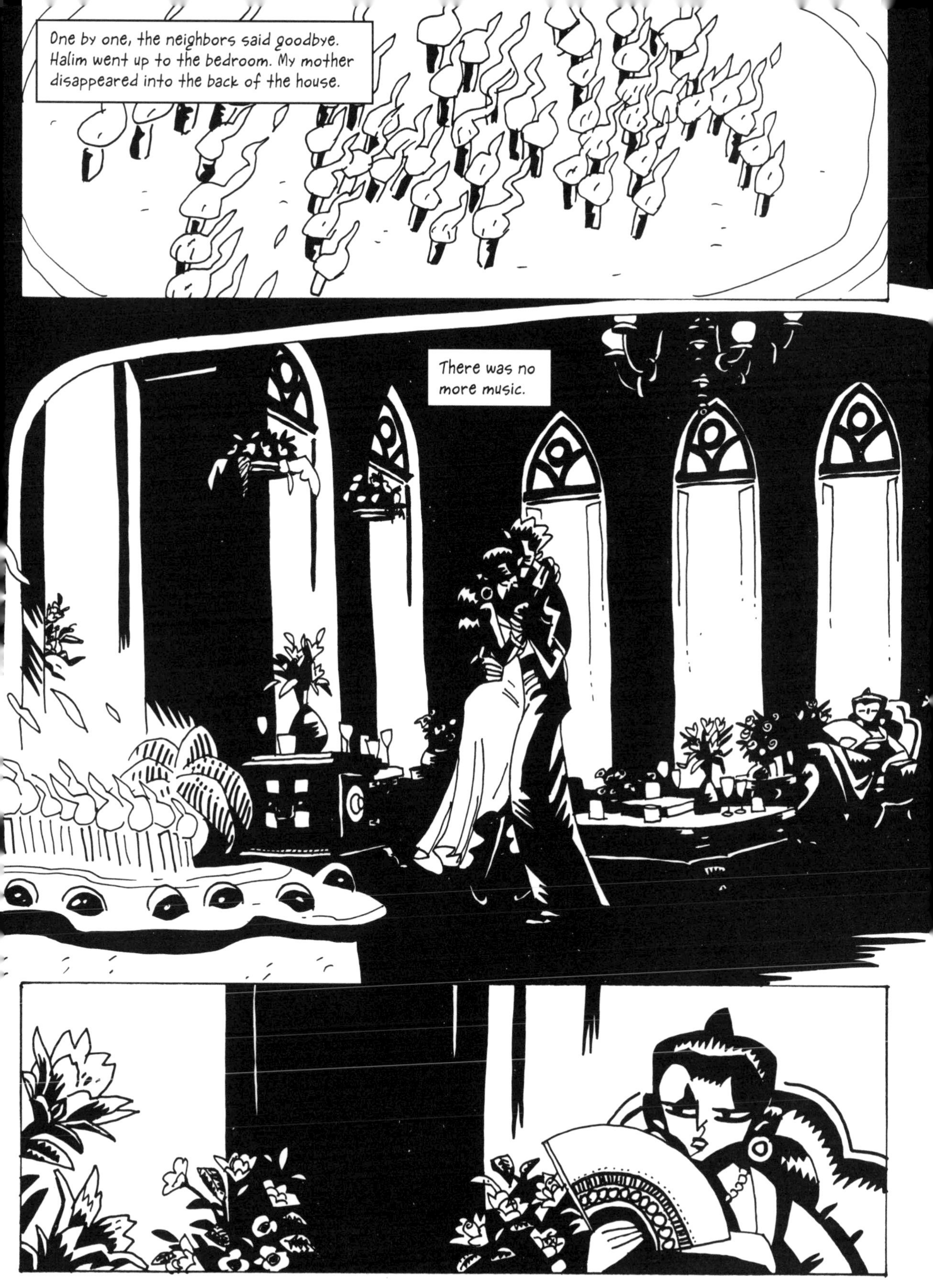
One by one, the neighbors said goodbye. Halim went up to the bedroom. My mother disappeared into the back of the house.
There was no more music.

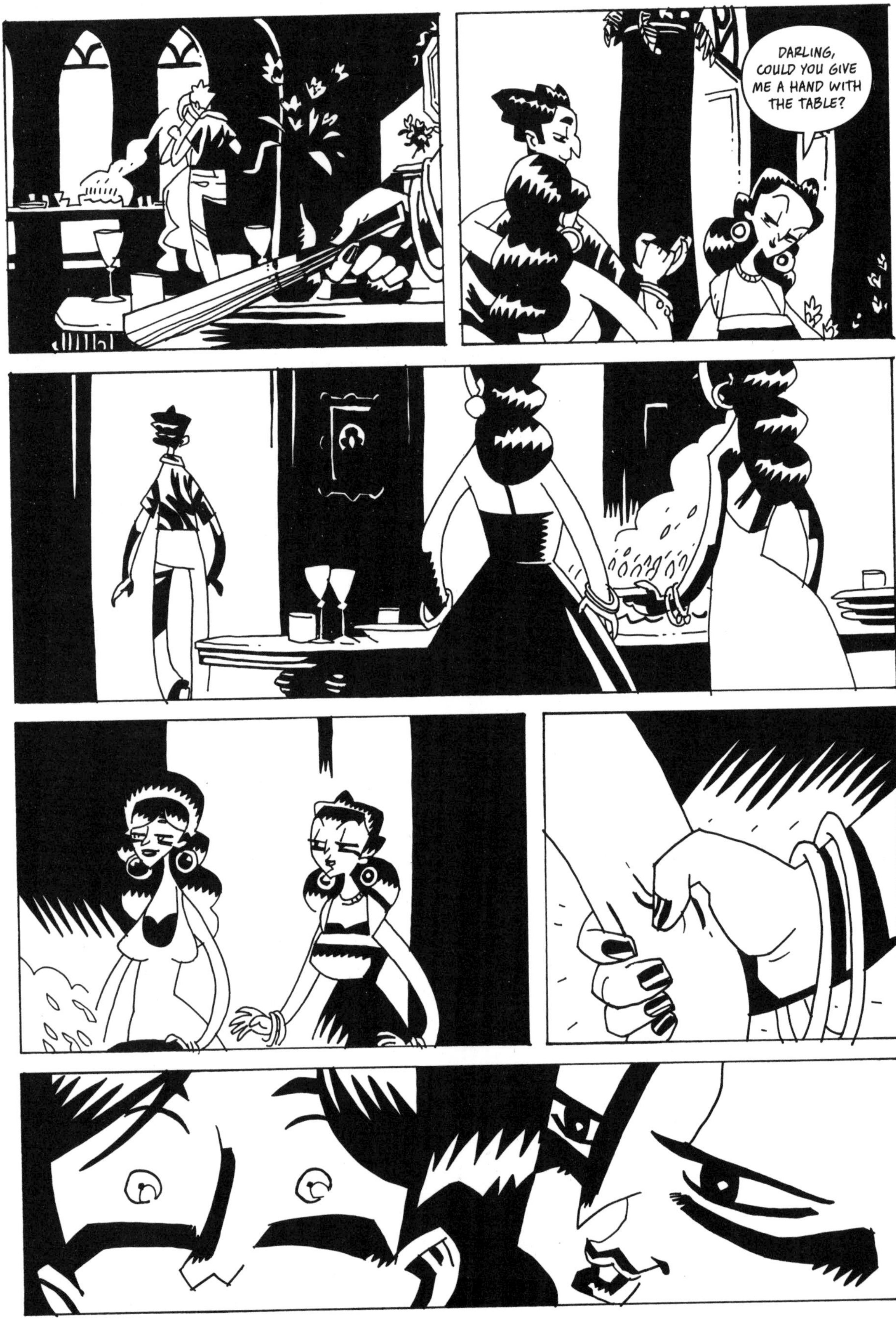
DARLING, COULD YOU GIVE ME A HAND WITH THE TABLE?

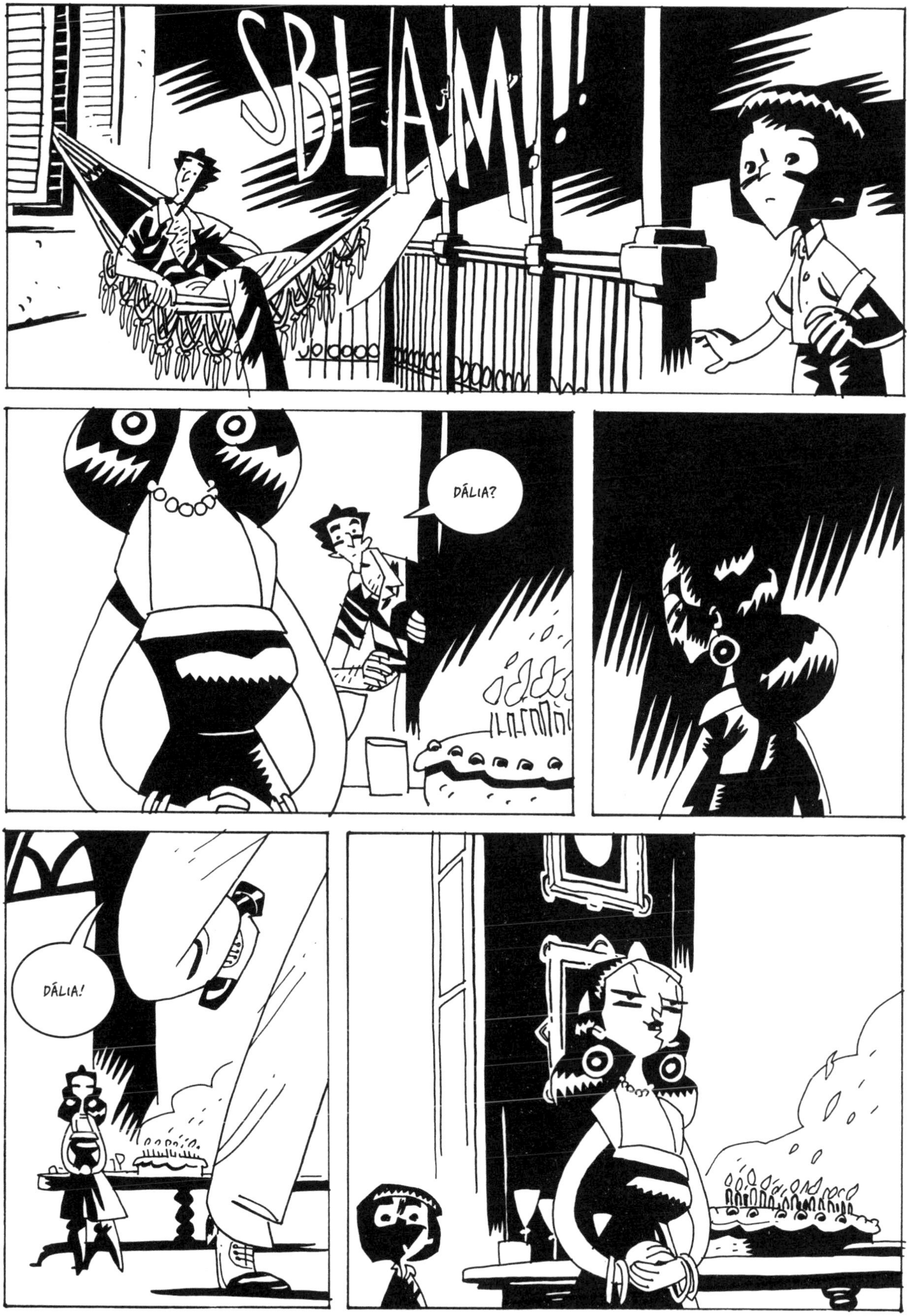
SBLAM!!
DÁLIA?
DÁLIA!

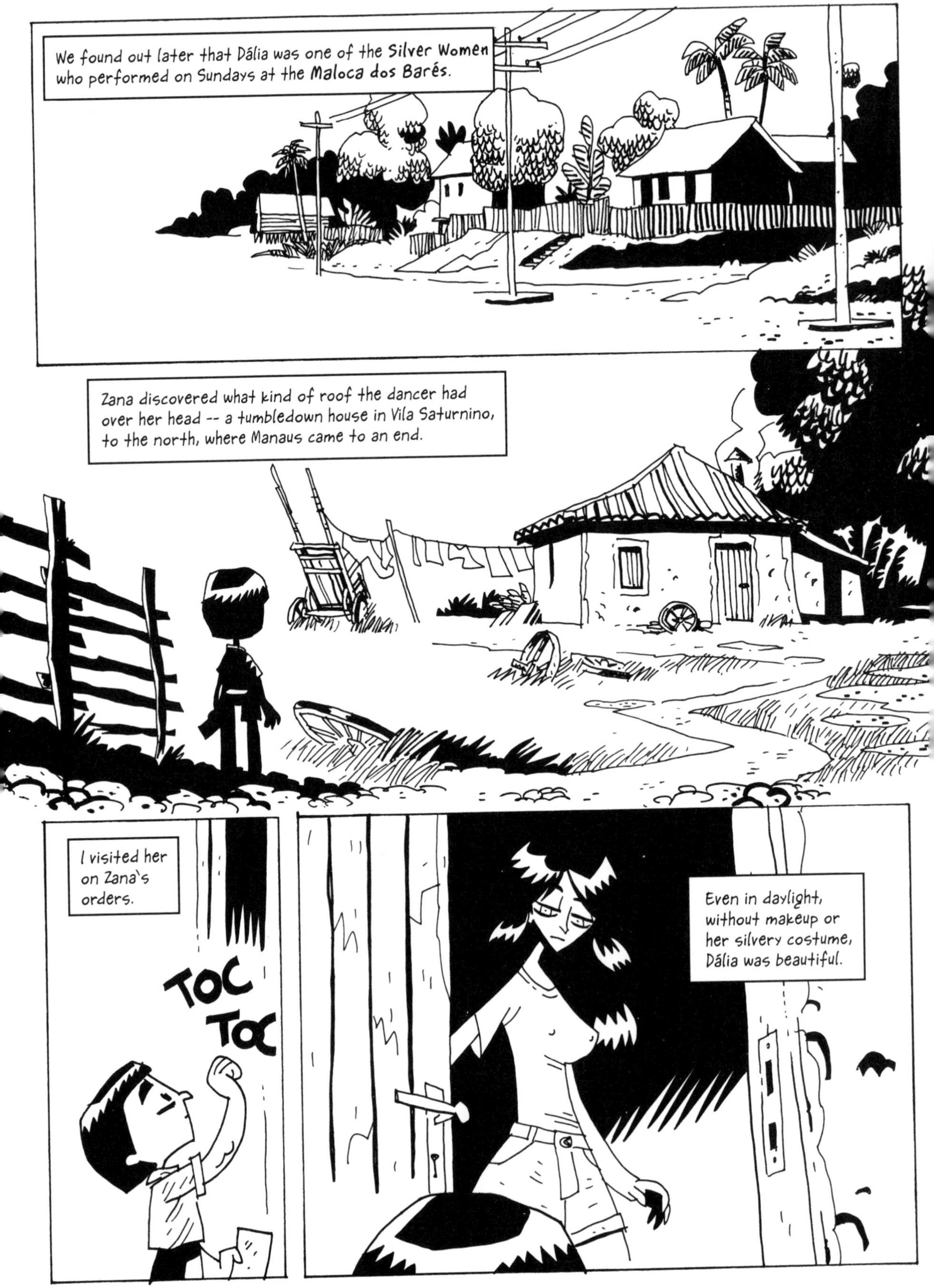
We found out later that Dália was one of the Silver Women who performed on Sundays at the Maloca dos Barés.
Zana discovered what kind of roof the dancer had over her head -- a tumbledown house in Vila Saturnino, to the north, where Manaus came to an end.
I visited her on Zana's orders.
TOC TOC
Even in daylight, without makeup or her silvery costume, Dália was beautiful.

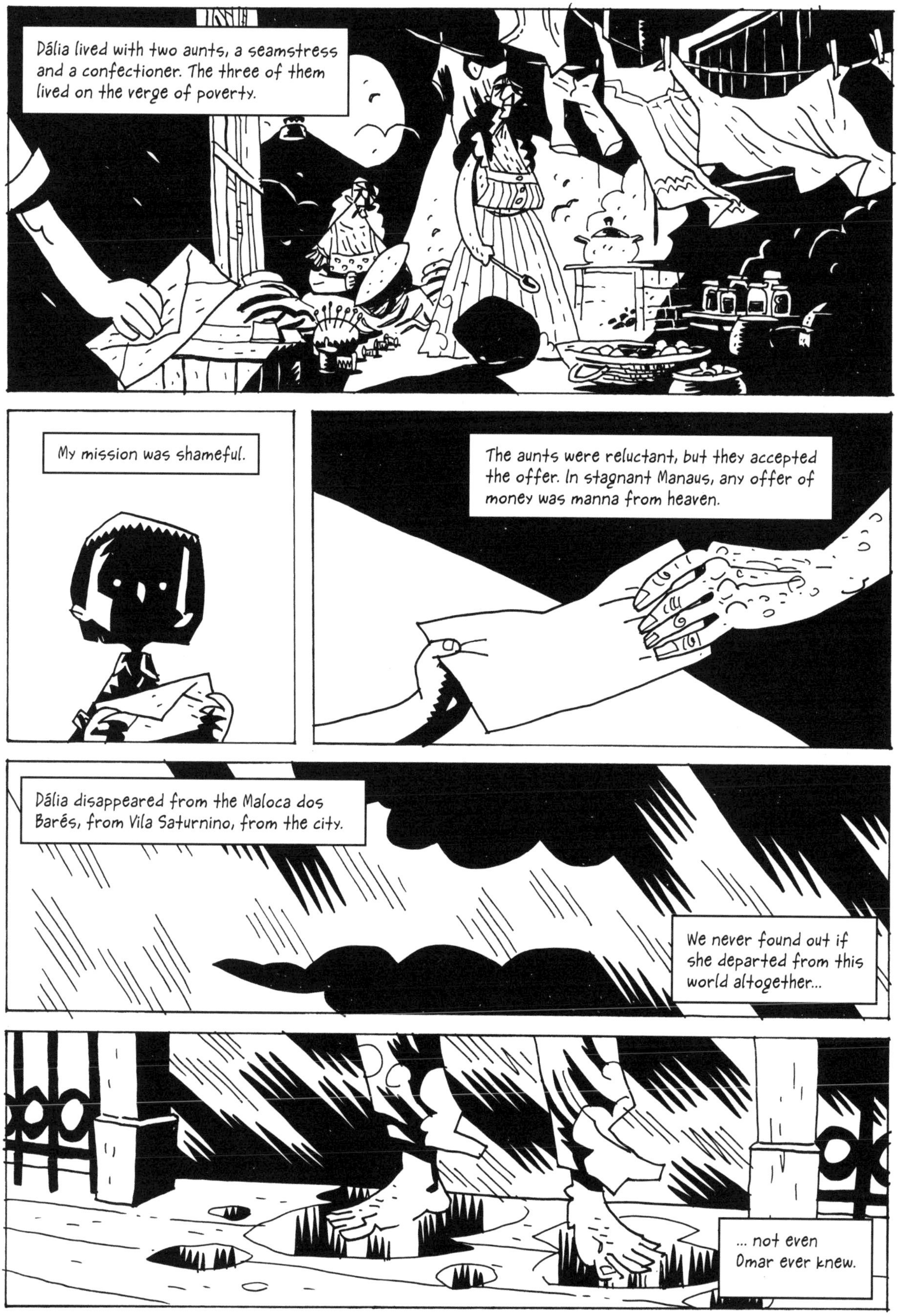
Dália lived with two aunts, a seamstress and a confectioner. The three of them lived on the verge of poverty.
My mission was shameful.
The aunts were reluctant, but they accepted the offer. In stagnant Manaus, any offer of money was manna from heaven.
Dália disappeared from the Maloca dos Barés, from Vila Saturnino, from the city.
We never found out if she departed from this world altogether...
... not even Omar ever knew.

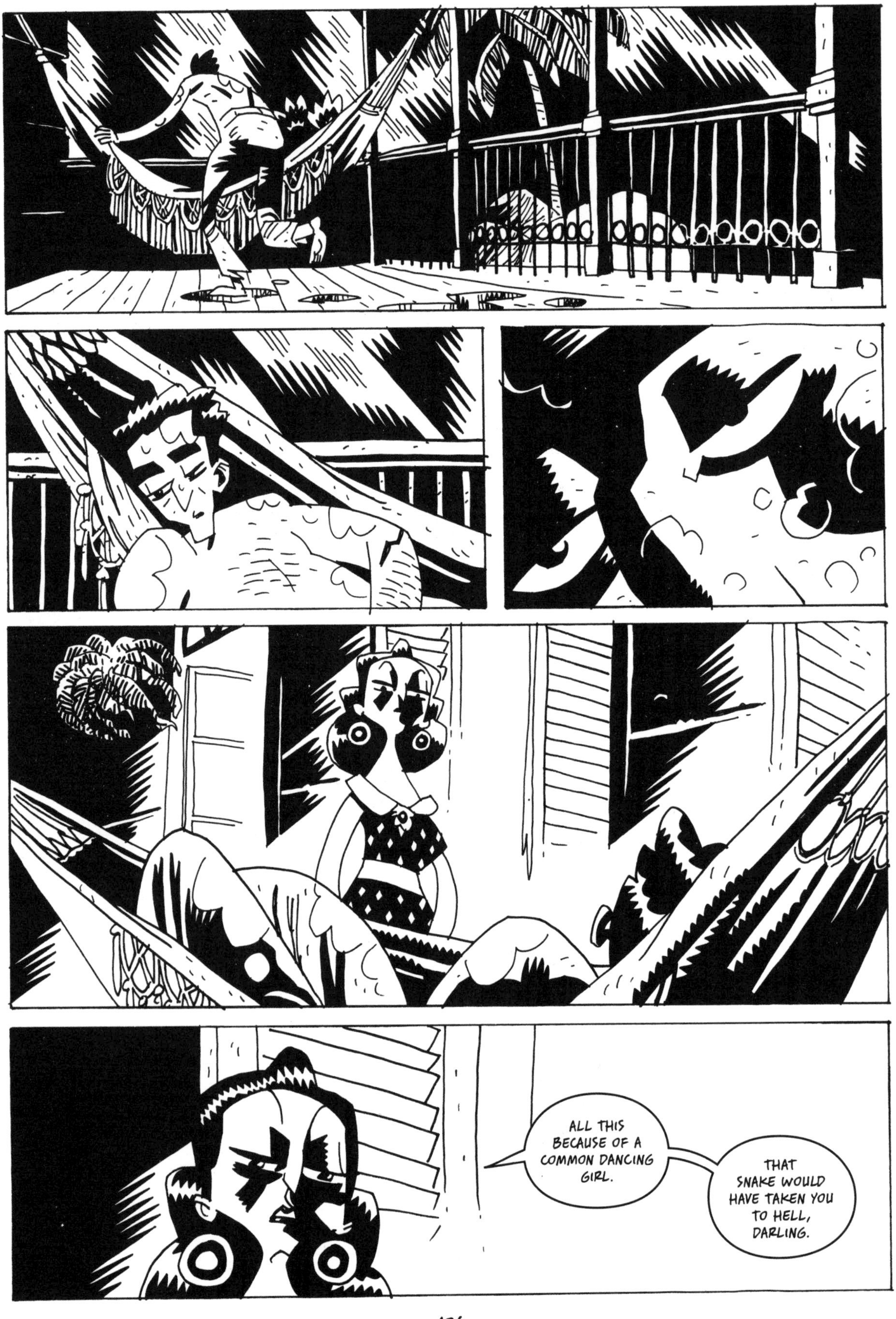
ALL THIS BECAUSE OF A COMMON DANCING GIRL.
THAT SNAKE WOULD HAVE TAKEN YOU TO HELL, DARLING.

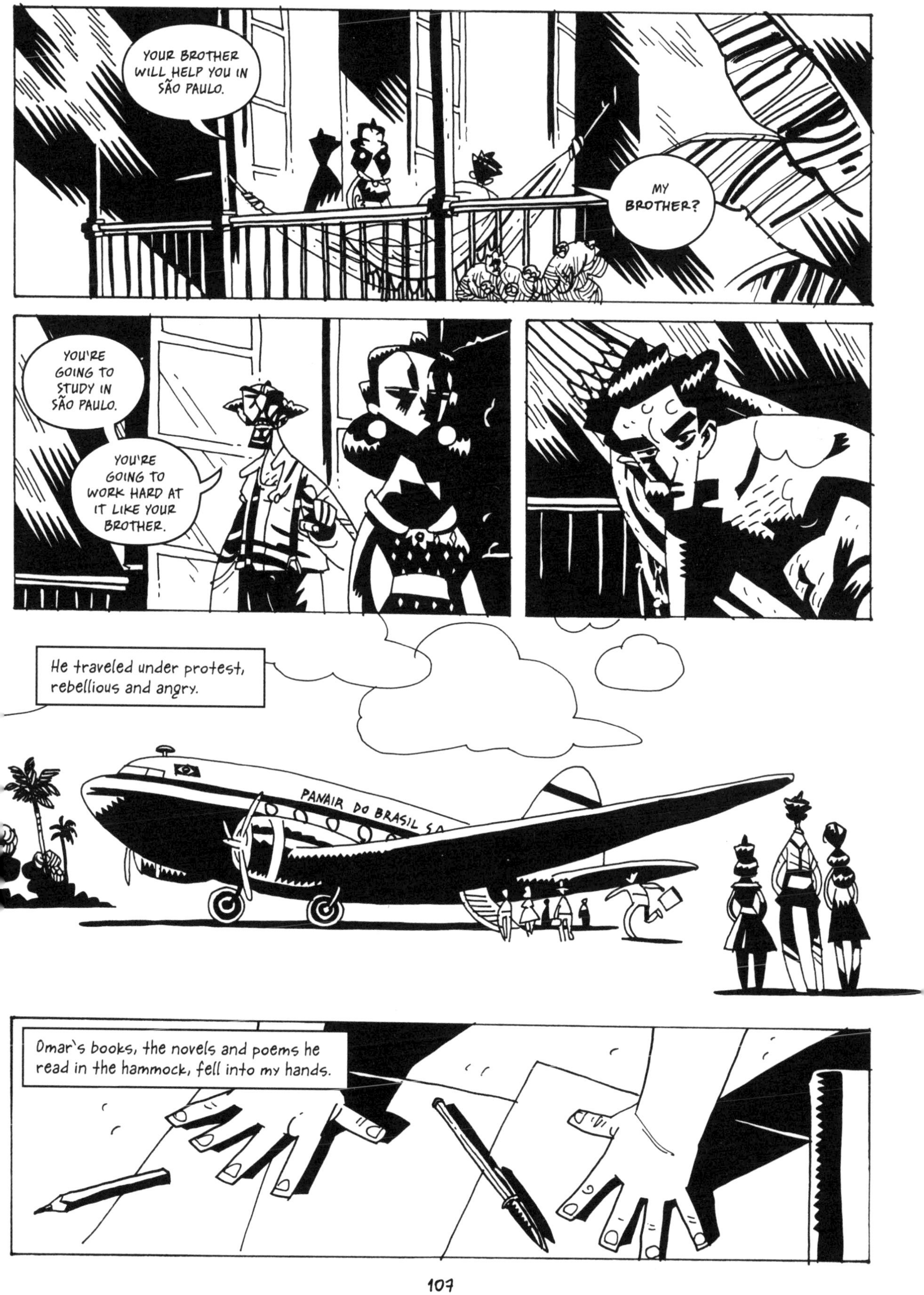
YOUR BROTHER WILL HELP YOU IN SÃO PAULO.
MY BROTHER?
YOU'RE GOING TO STUDY IN SÃO PAULO.
YOU'RE GOING TO WORK HARD AT IT LIKE YOUR BROTHER.
He traveled under protest, rebellious and angry.
PANAIR DO BRASIL S.A.
Omar's books, the novels and poems he read in the hammock, fell into my hands.

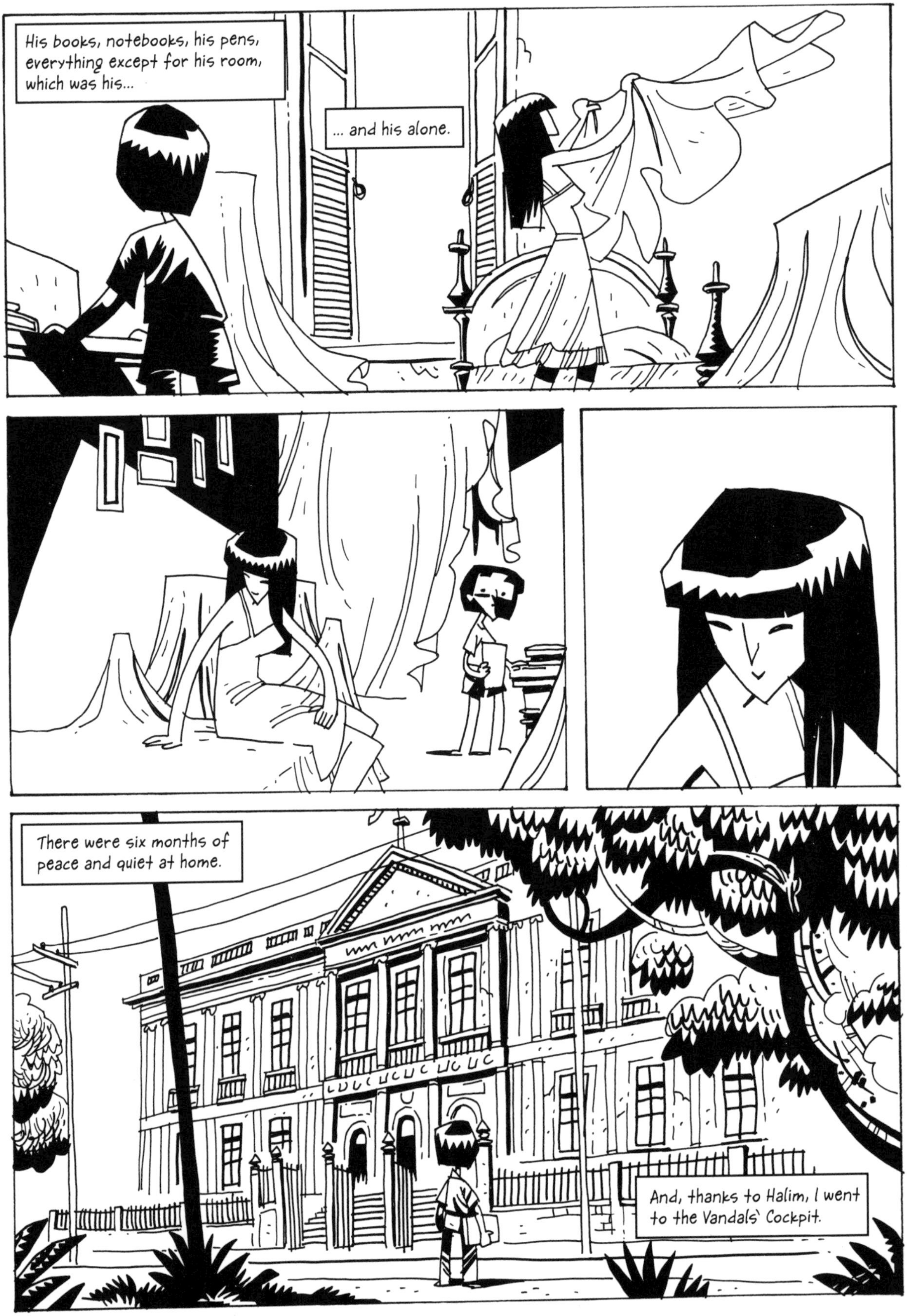
His books, notebooks, his pens, everything except for his room, which was his...
... and his alone.
There were six months of peace and quiet at home.
And, thanks to Halim, I went to the Vandals' Cockpit.

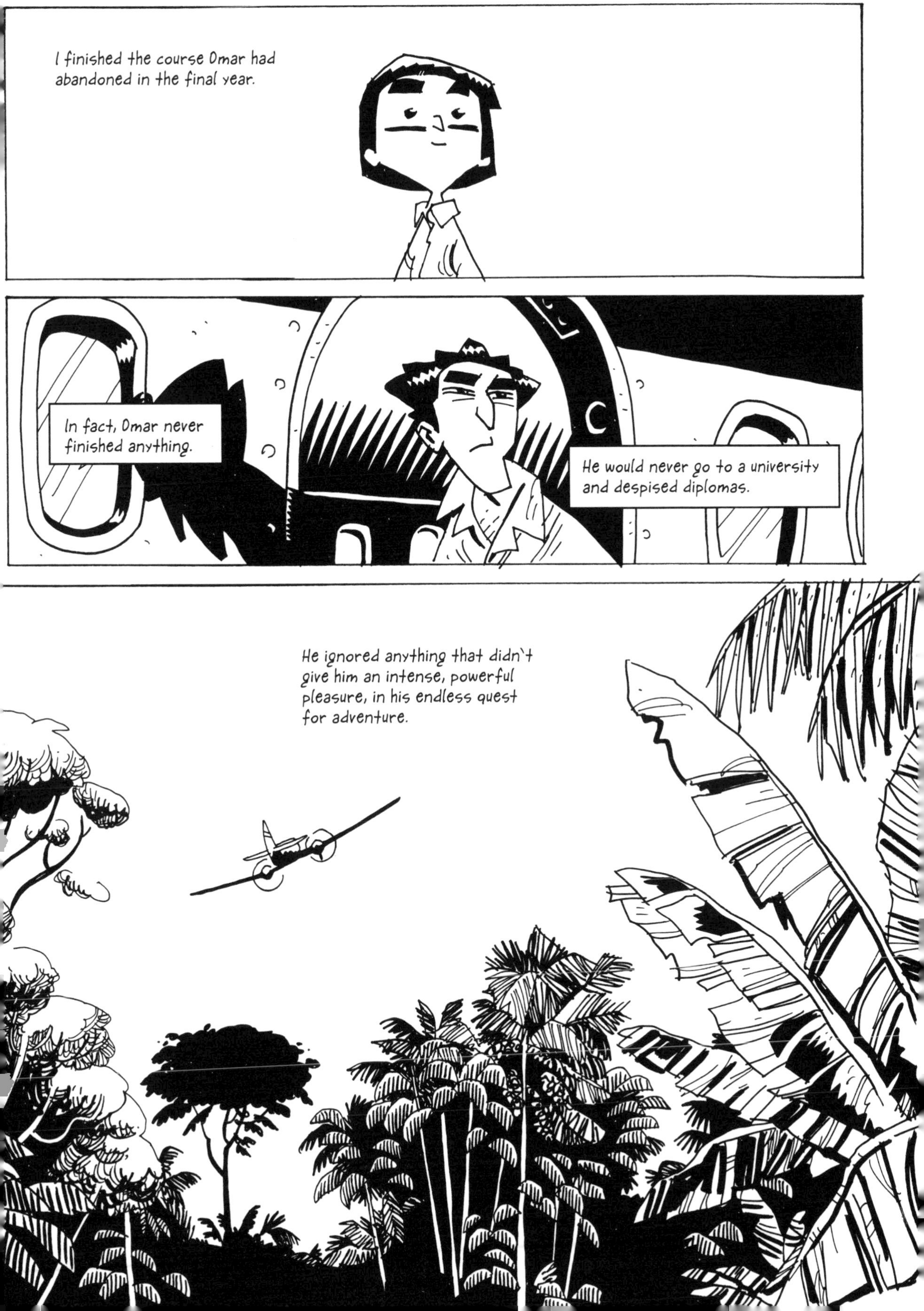
I finished the course Omar had abandoned in the final year.
In fact, Omar never finished anything.
He would never go to a university and despised diplomas.
He ignored anything that didn't give him an intense, powerful pleasure, in his endless quest for adventure.

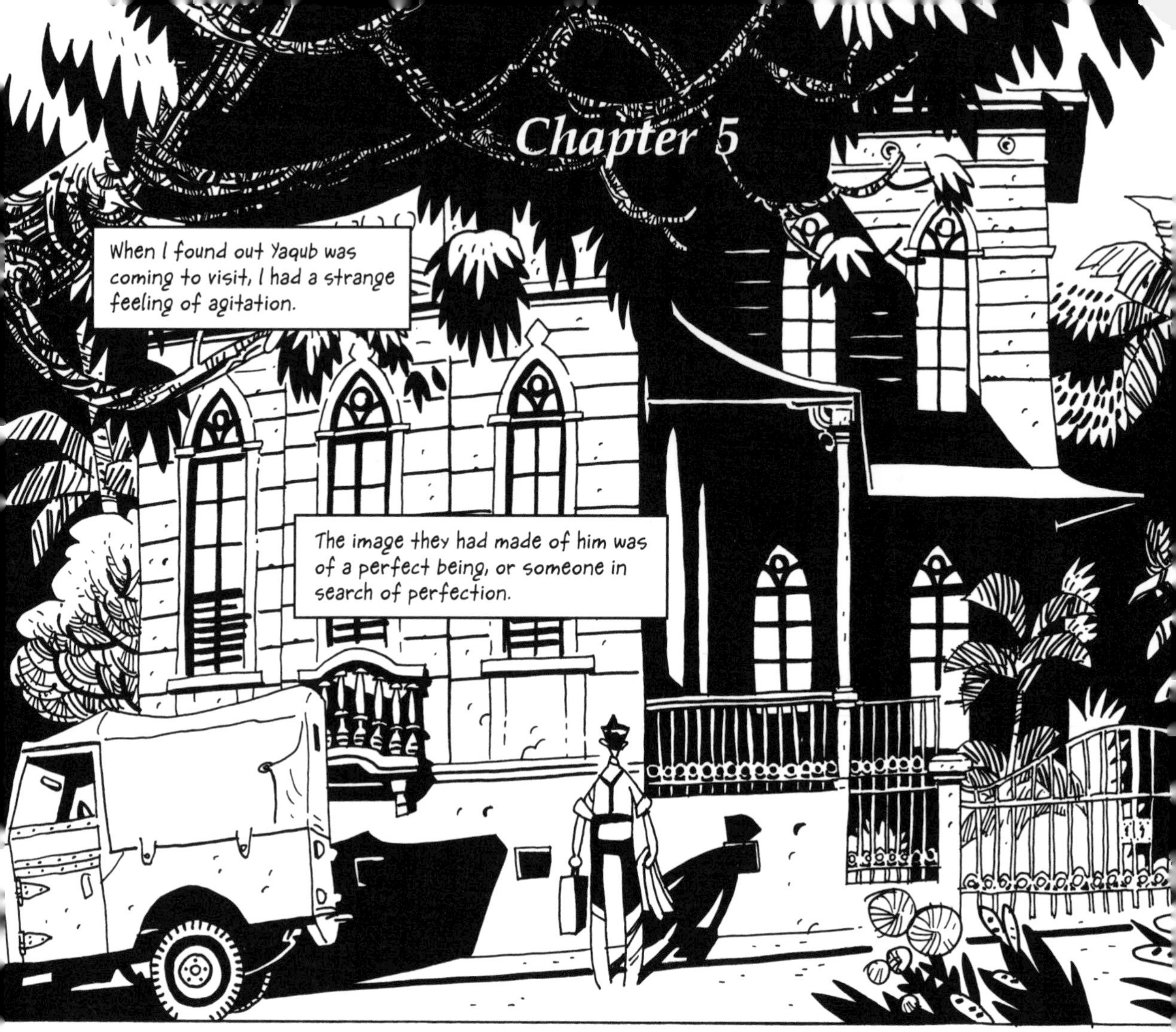
Chapter 5
When I found out Yaqub was coming to visit, I had a strange feeling of agitation.
The image they had made of him was of a perfect being, or someone in search of perfection.

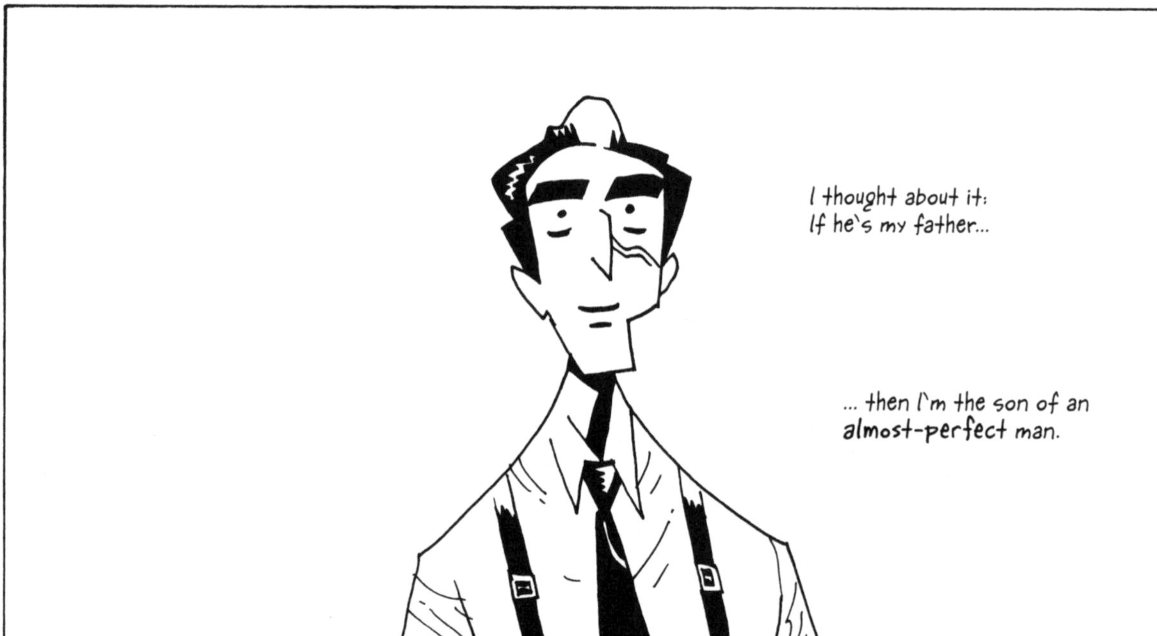
I thought about it: If he's my father...
... then I'm the son of an almost-perfect man.

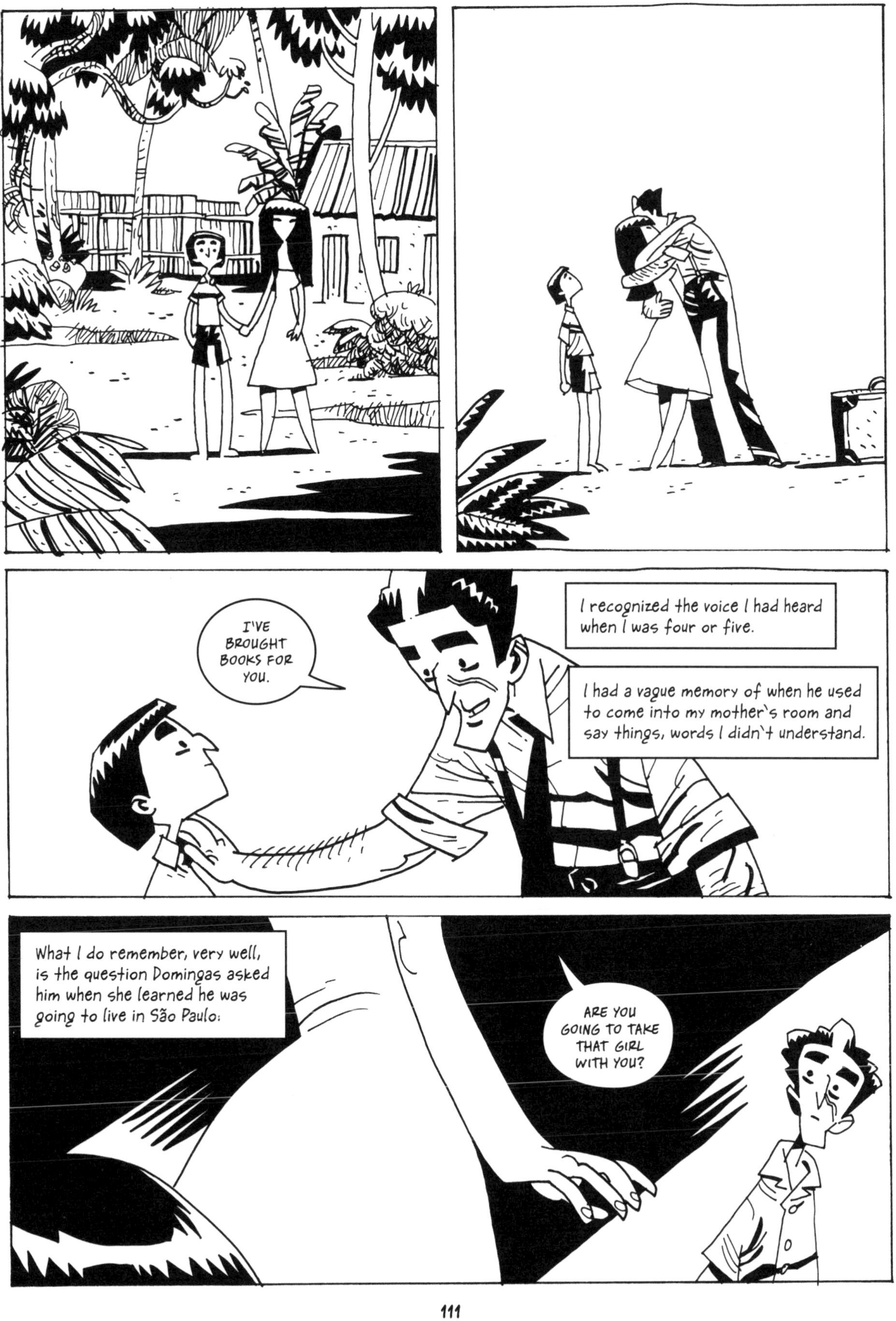
I recognized the voice I had heard when I was four or five.
I'VE BROUGHT BOOKS FOR YOU.
I had a vague memory of when he used to come into my mother's room and say things, words I didn't understand.
What I do remember, very well, is the question Domingas asked him when she learned he was going to live in São Paulo:
ARE YOU GOING TO TAKE THAT GIRL WITH YOU?

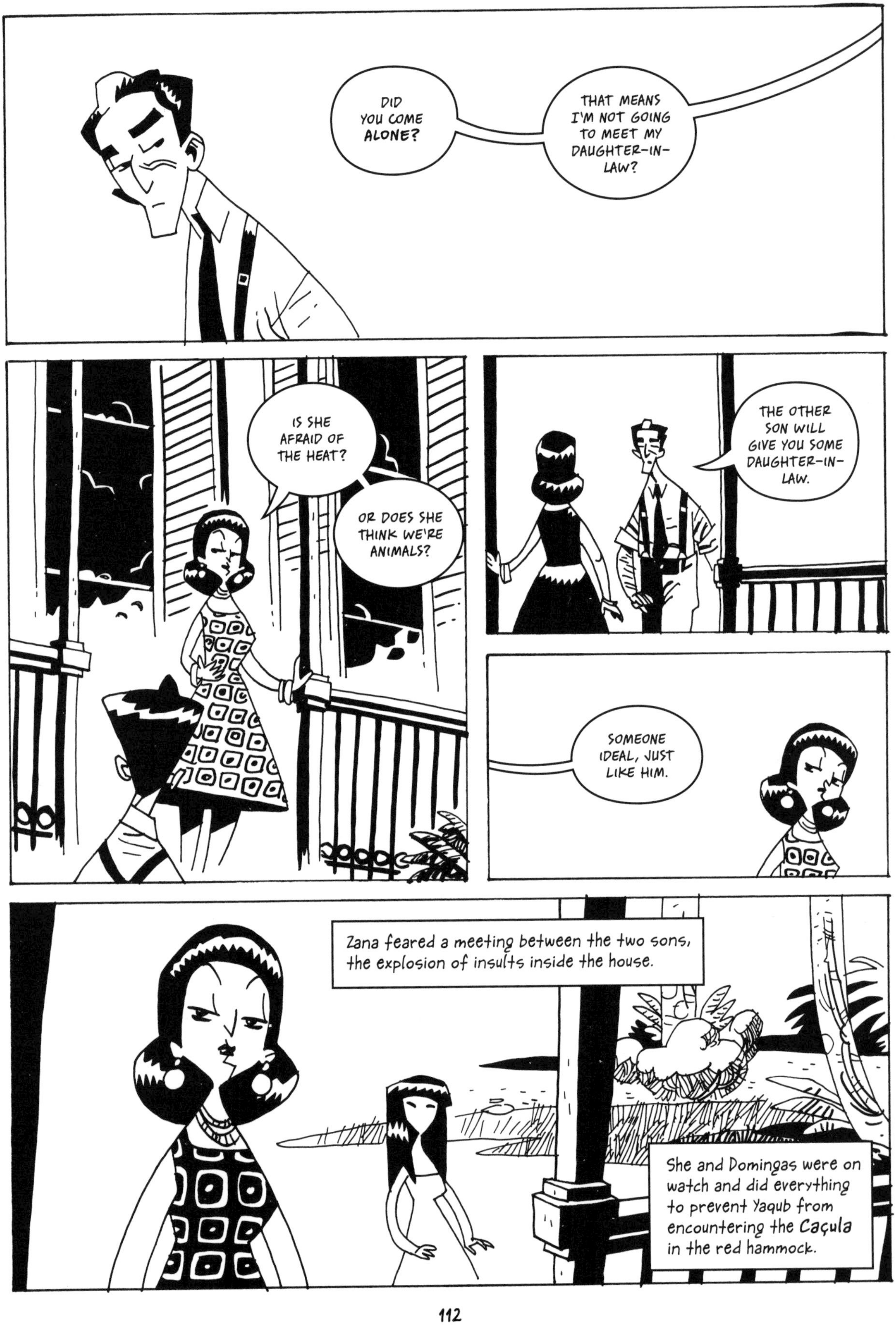
DID YOU COME ALONE?
THAT MEANS I'M NOT GOING TO MEET MY DAUGHTER-IN-LAW?
IS SHE AFRAID OF THE HEAT?
OR DOES SHE THINK WE'RE ANIMALS?
THE OTHER SON WILL GIVE YOU SOME DAUGHTER-IN-LAW.
SOMEONE IDEAL, JUST LIKE HIM.
Zana feared a meeting between the two sons, the explosion of insults inside the house.
She and Domingas were on watch and did everything to prevent Yaqub from encountering the Caçula in the red hammock.

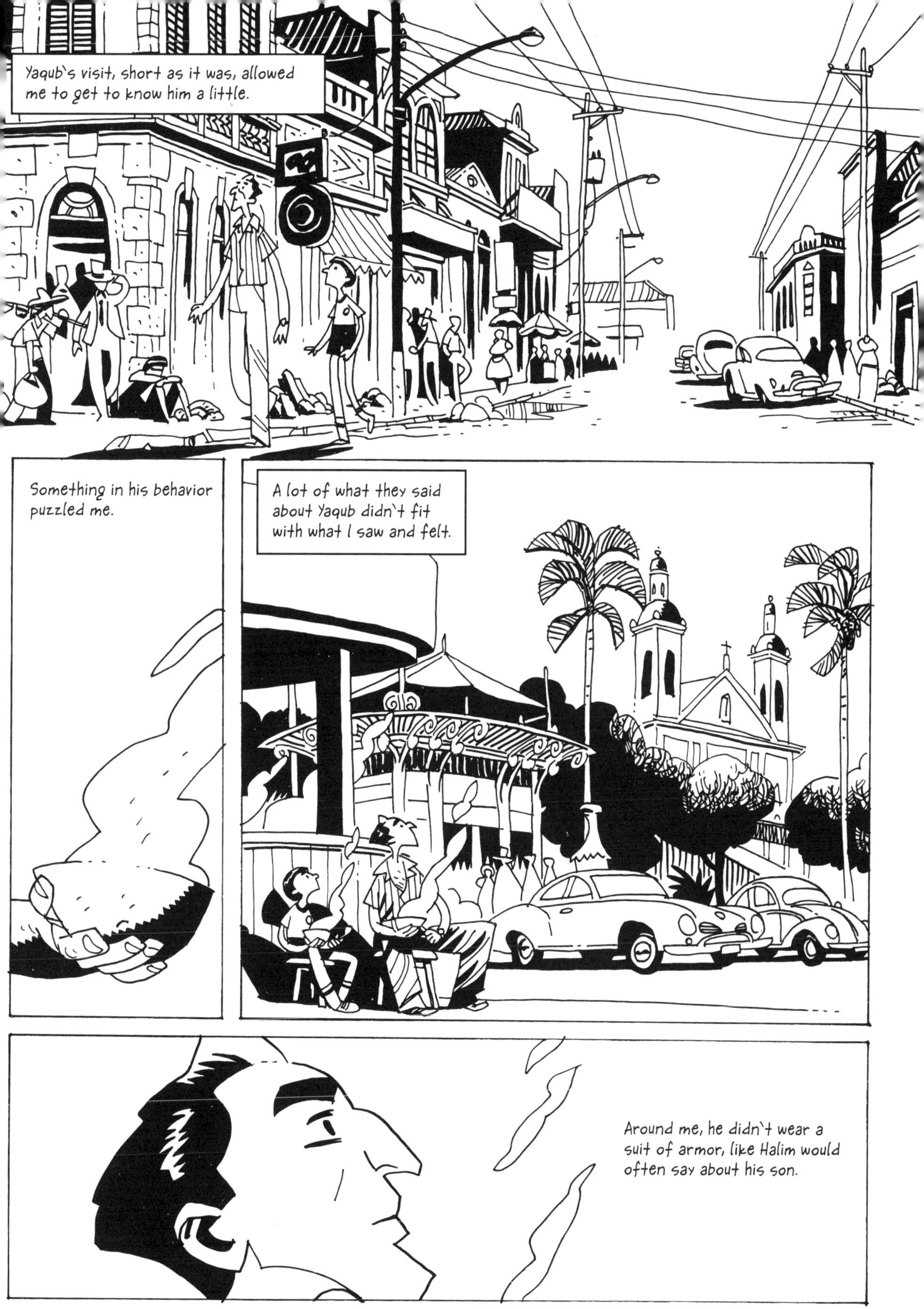
Yaqub's visit, short as it was, allowed me to get to know him a little.
Something in his behavior puzzled me.
A lot of what they said about Yaqub didn't fit with what I saw and felt.
Around me, he didn't wear a suit of armor, like Halim would often say about his son.

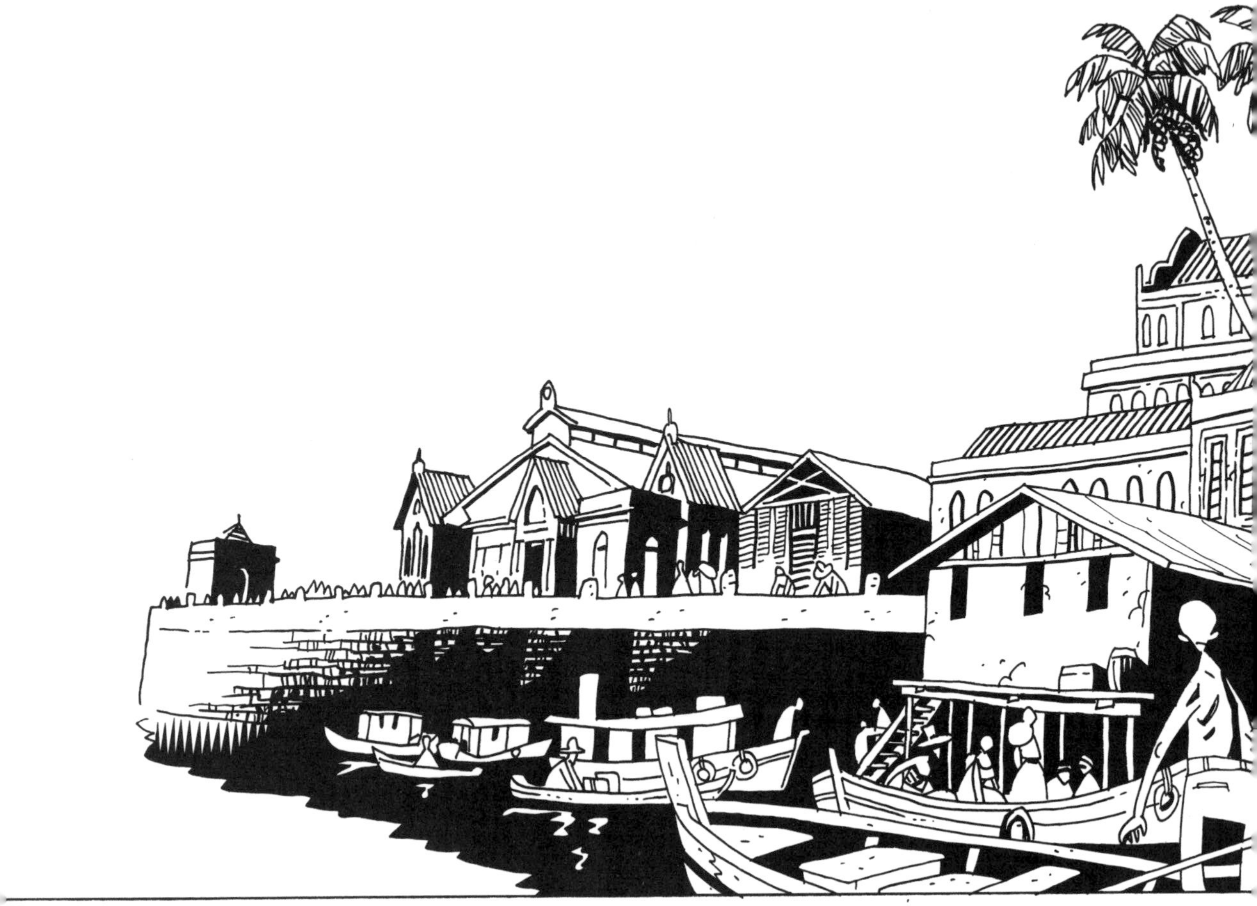

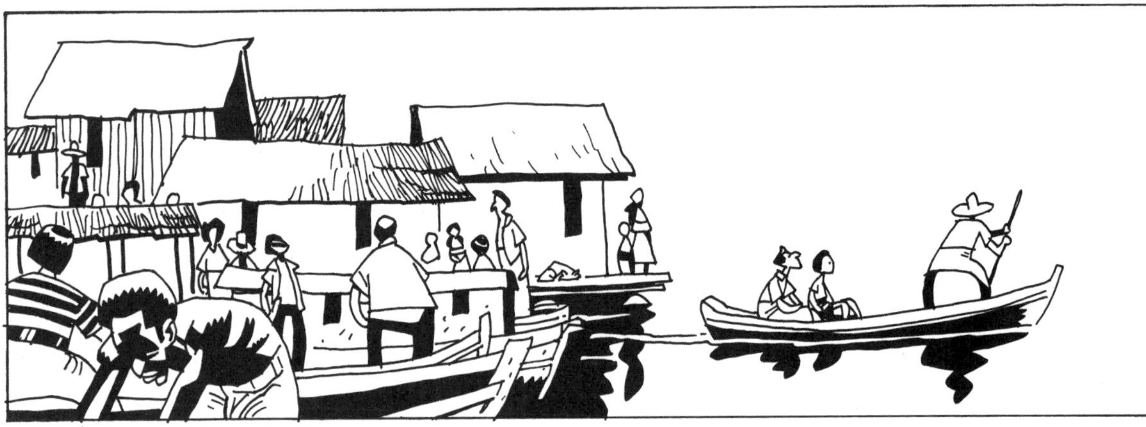

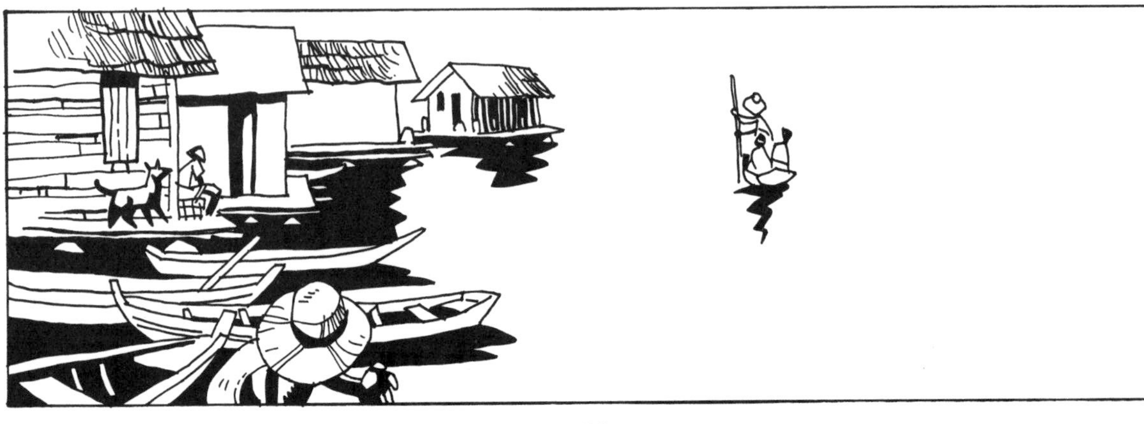

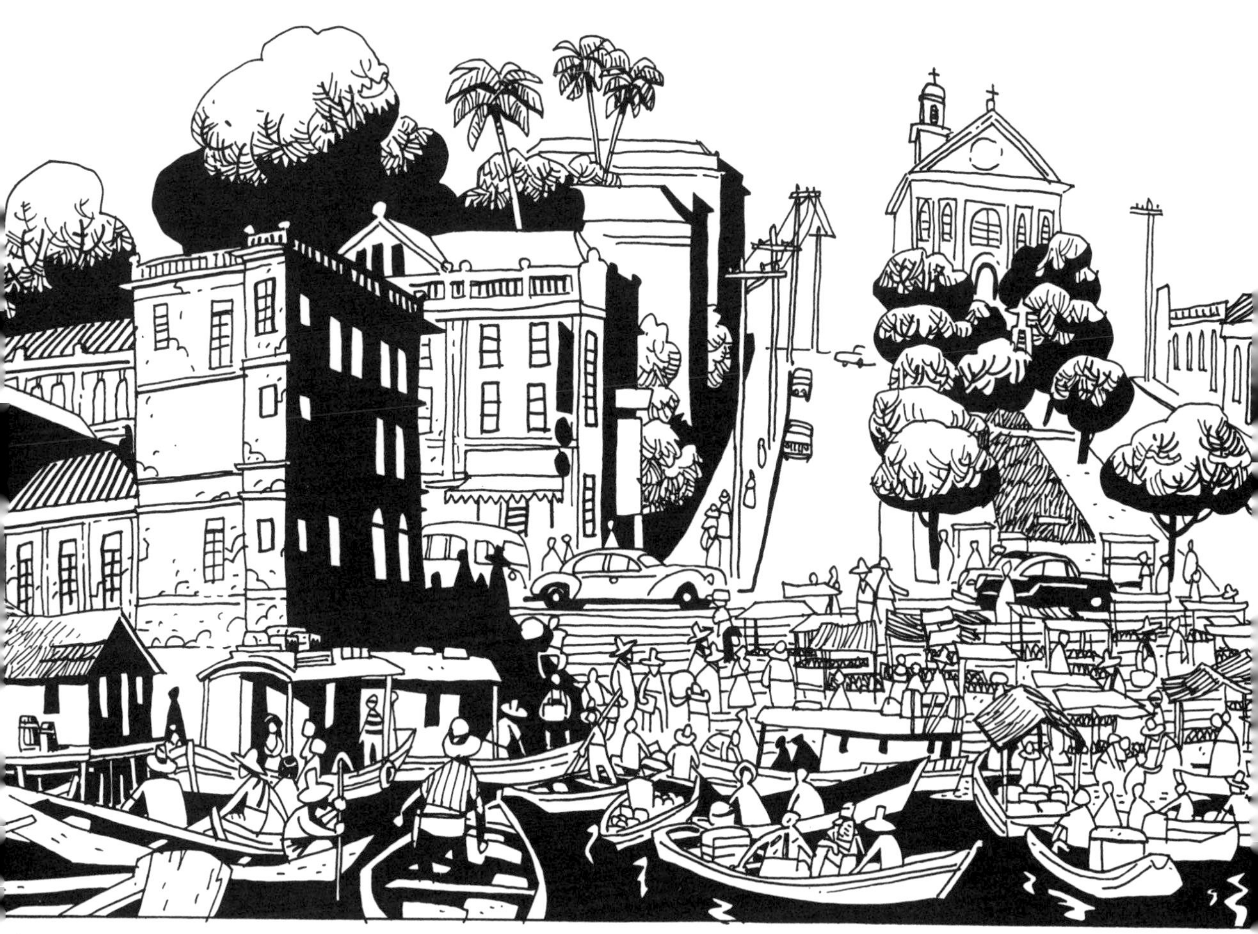

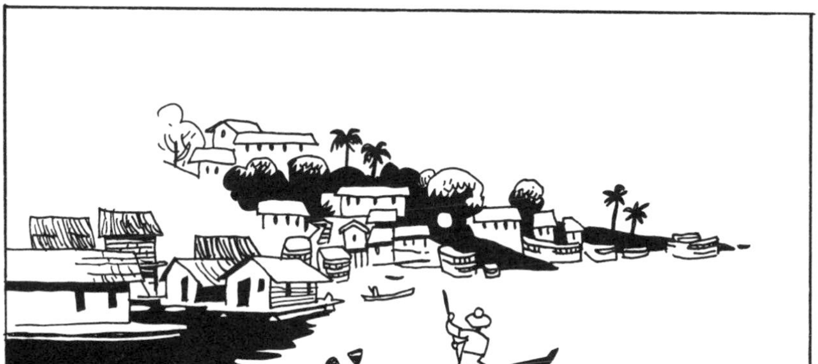

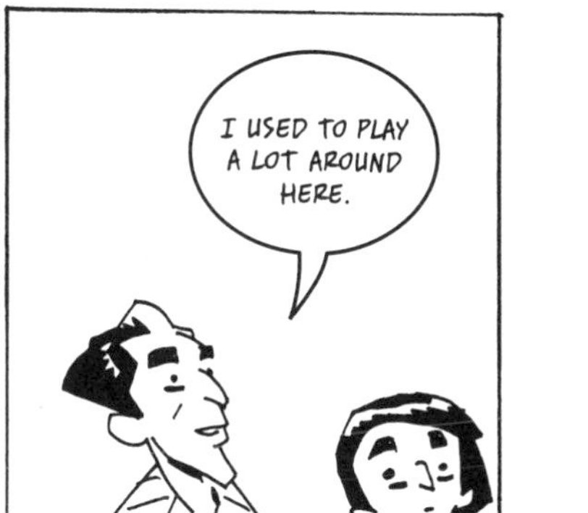
I USED TO PLAY A LOT AROUND HERE.

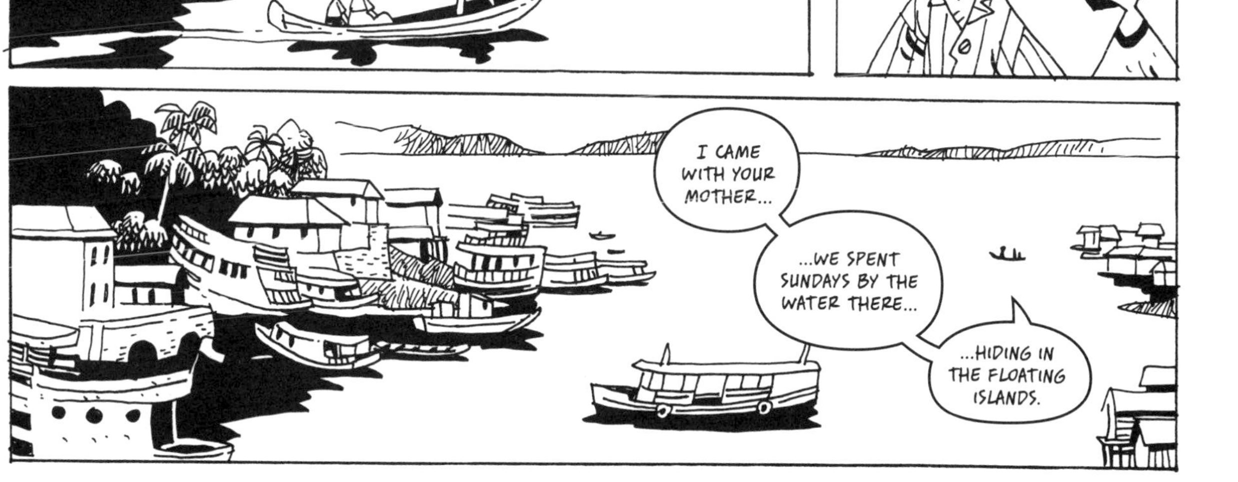
I CAME WITH YOUR MOTHER...
...WE SPENT SUNDAYS BY THE WATER THERE...
...HIDING IN THE FLOATING ISLANDS.

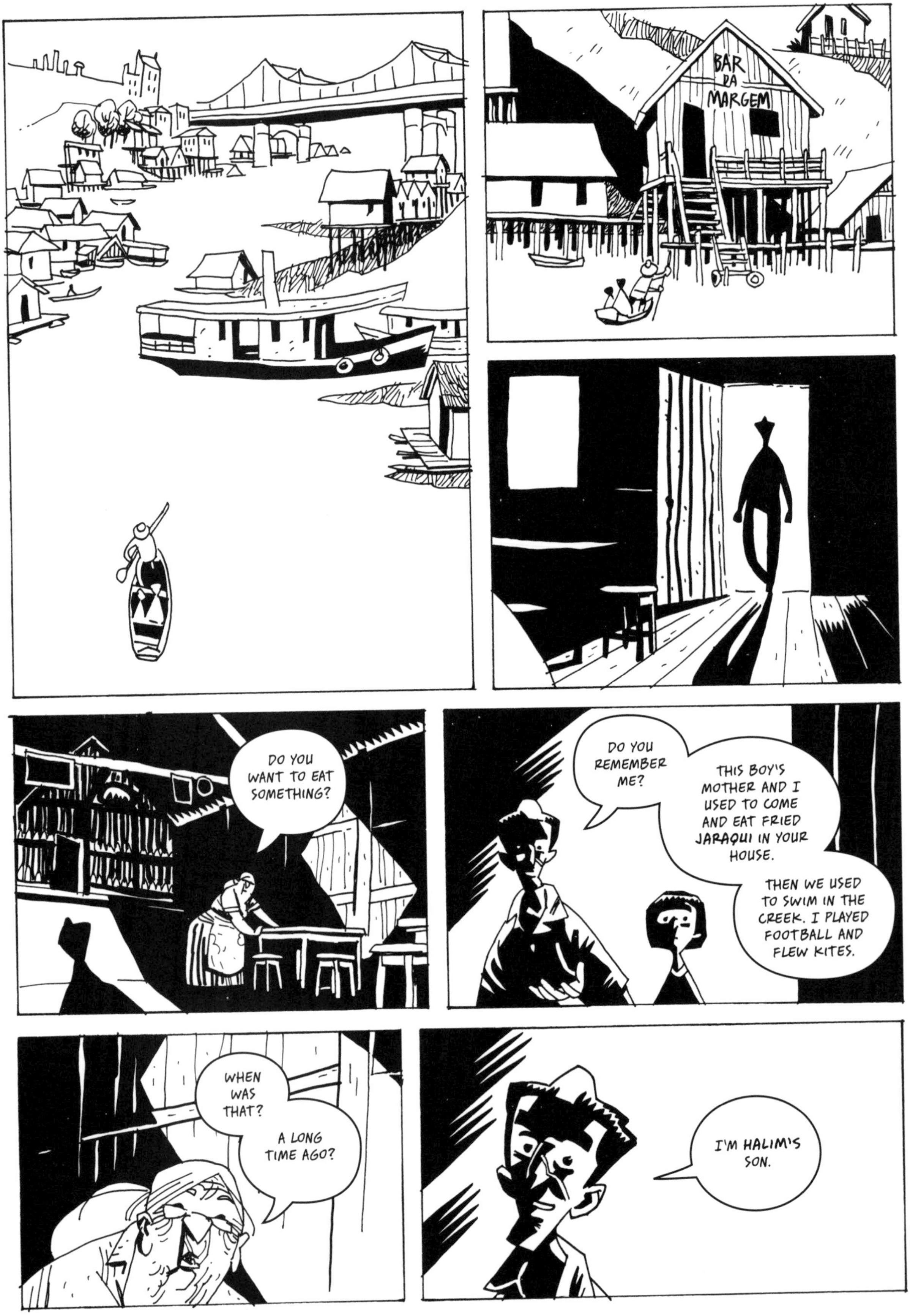
BAR DA MARGEM
DO YOU WANT TO EAT SOMETHING?
DO YOU REMEMBER ME?
THIS BOY'S MOTHER AND I USED TO COME AND EAT FRIED JARAQUI IN YOUR HOUSE.
THEN WE USED TO SWIM IN THE CREEK. I PLAYED FOOTBALL AND FLEW KITES.
WHEN WAS THAT?
A LONG TIME AGO?
I'M HALIM'S SON.

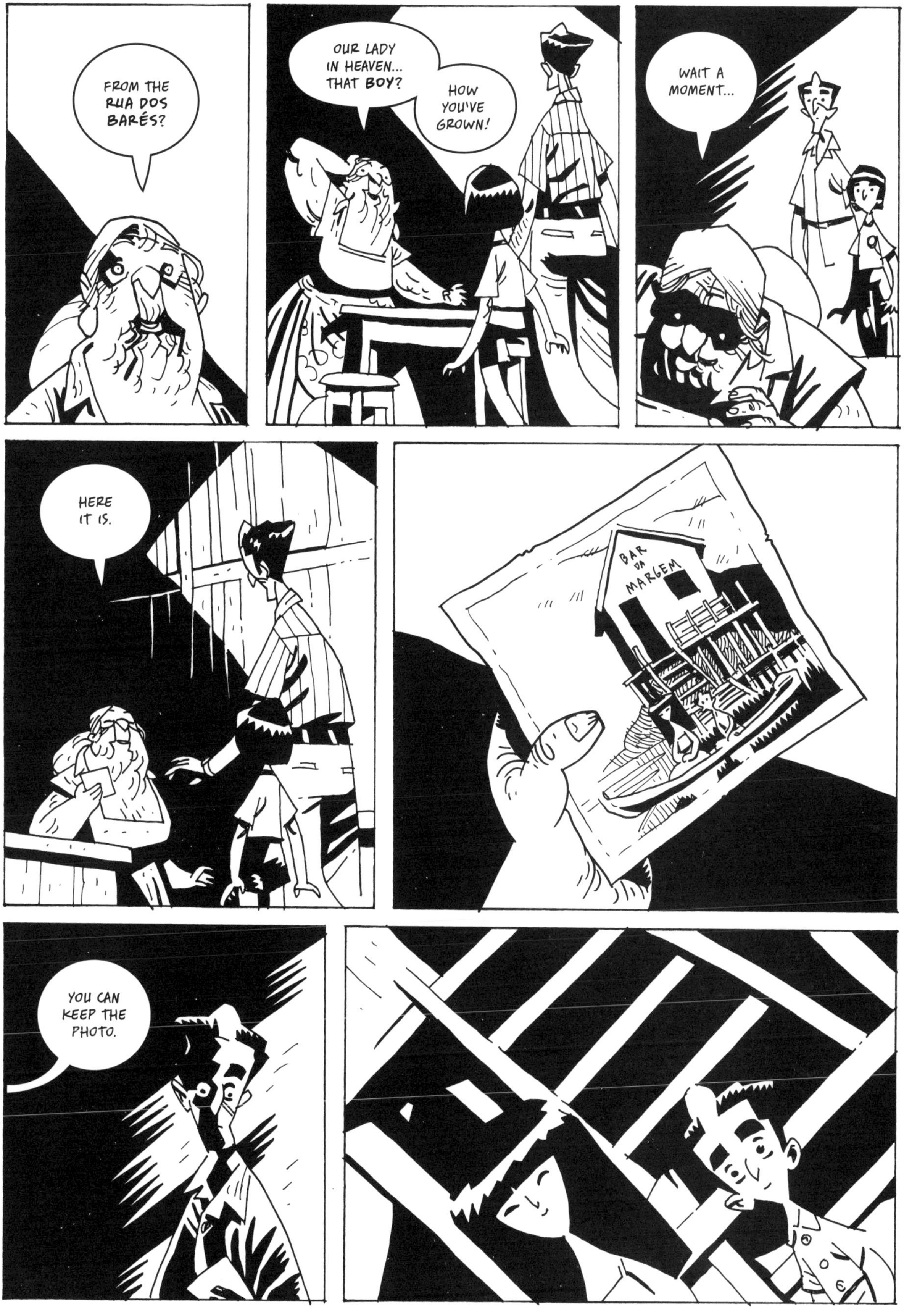
FROM THE RUA DOS BARÉS?
OUR LADY IN HEAVEN... THAT BOY?
HOW YOU'VE GROWN!
WAIT A MOMENT...
HERE IT IS.
BAR DA MARGEM
YOU CAN KEEP THE PHOTO.

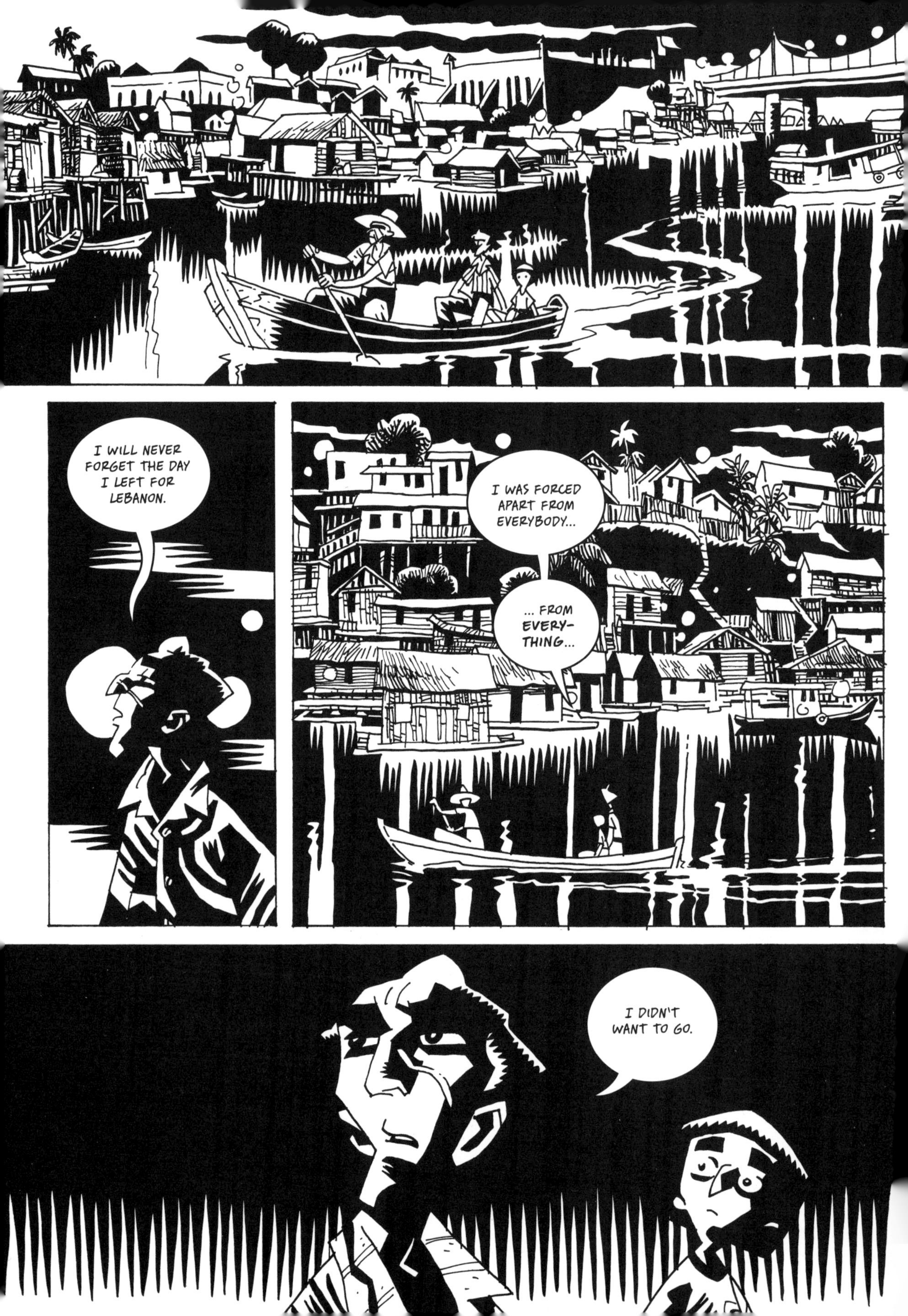
I WILL NEVER FORGET THE DAY I LEFT FOR LEBANON.
I WAS FORCED APART FROM EVERYBODY...
... FROM EVERY-THING...
I DIDN'T WANT TO GO.

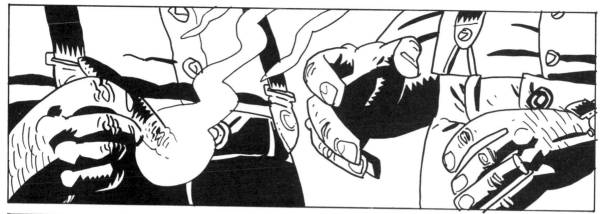

GOOD EVENING, SON.

I DON'T UNDERSTAND HOW YOU STILL SELL THESE PRODUCTS...

...THIS ANACHRONISTIC STUFF.

AND YOUR FRIENDS GET IN THE WAY OF THE CUSTOMERS.

THEY'RE LIKE VULTURES ON CARRION, WAITING FOR THE AFTERNOON SNACK.

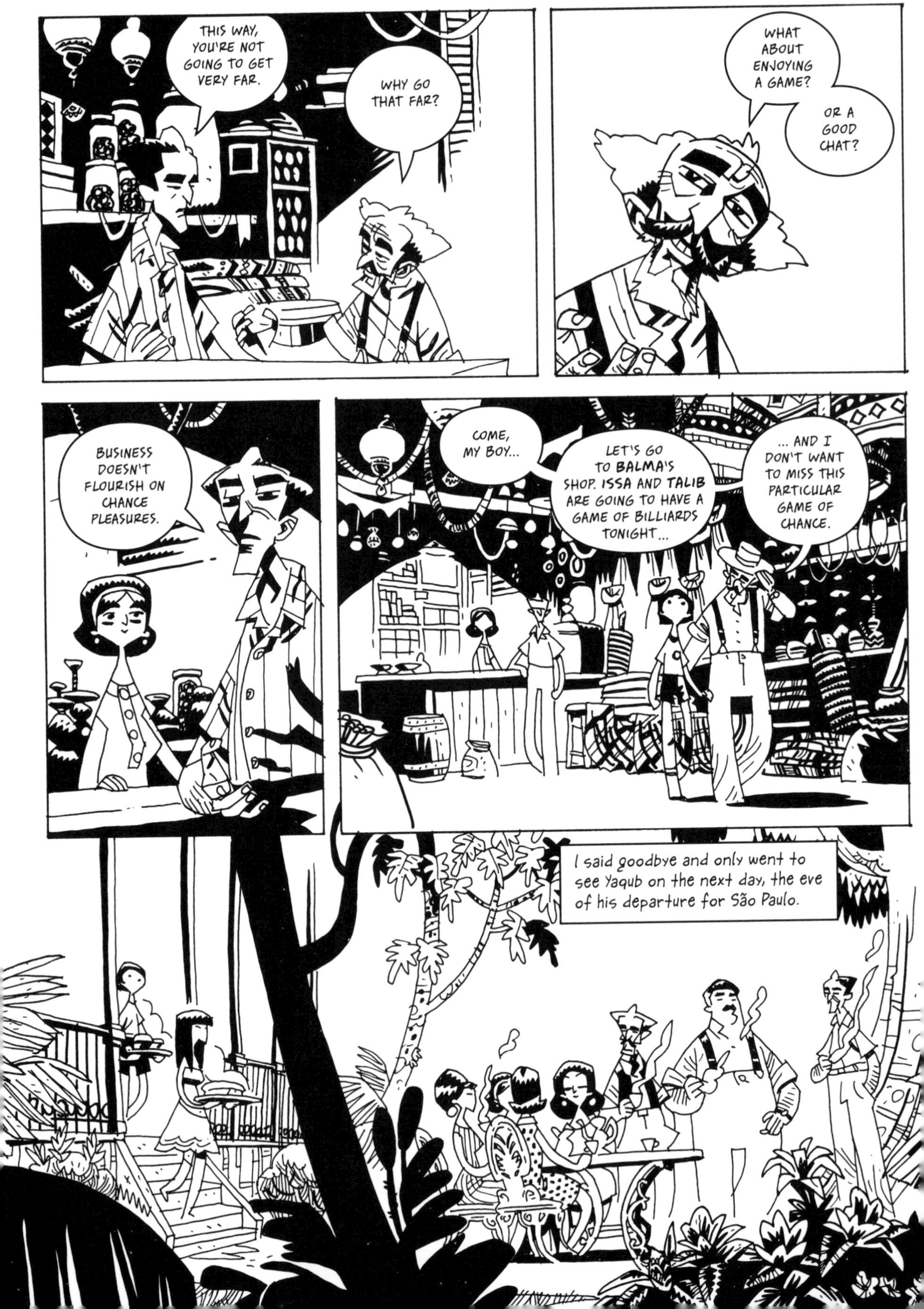
THIS WAY, YOU'RE NOT GOING TO GET VERY FAR.
WHY GO THAT FAR?
WHAT ABOUT ENJOYING A GAME?
OR A GOOD CHAT?
BUSINESS DOESN'T FLOURISH ON CHANCE PLEASURES.
COME, MY BOY...
LET'S GO TO BALMA'S SHOP. ISSA AND TALIB ARE GOING TO HAVE A GAME OF BILLIARDS TONIGHT...
... AND I DON'T WANT TO MISS THIS PARTICULAR GAME OF CHANCE.
I said goodbye and only went to see Yaqub on the next day, the eve of his departure for São Paulo.

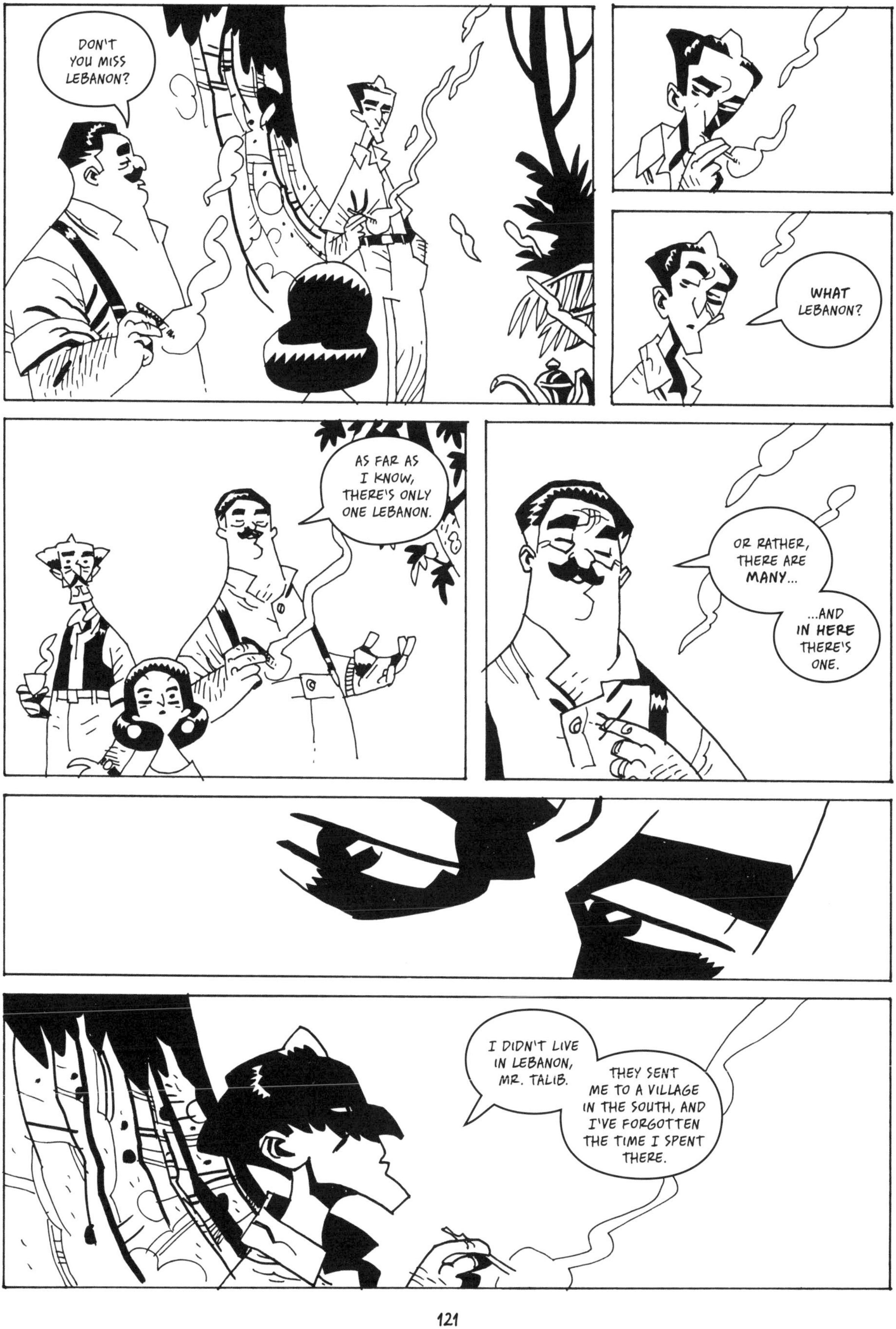
DON'T YOU MISS LEBANON?
WHAT LEBANON?
AS FAR AS I KNOW, THERE'S ONLY ONE LEBANON.
OR RATHER, THERE ARE **MANY**...
...AND **IN HERE** THERE'S ONE.
I DIDN'T LIVE IN LEBANON, MR. TALIB.
THEY SENT ME TO A VILLAGE IN THE SOUTH, AND I'VE FORGOTTEN THE TIME I SPENT THERE.

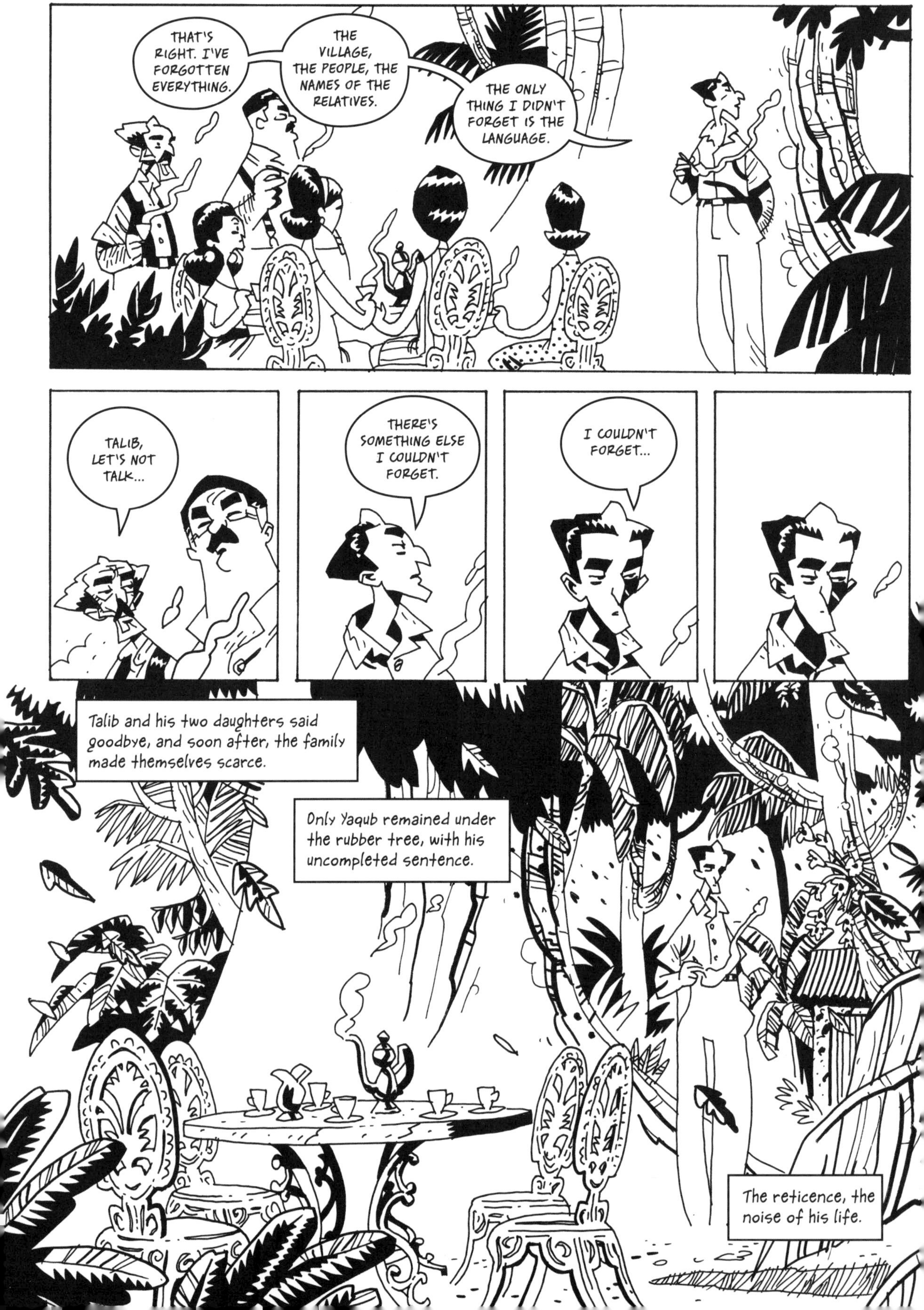
THAT'S RIGHT. I'VE FORGOTTEN EVERYTHING.
THE VILLAGE, THE PEOPLE, THE NAMES OF THE RELATIVES.
THE ONLY THING I DIDN'T FORGET IS THE LANGUAGE.
TALIB, LET'S NOT TALK...
THERE'S SOMETHING ELSE I COULDN'T FORGET.
I COULDN'T FORGET...
Talib and his two daughters said goodbye, and soon after, the family made themselves scarce.
Only Yaqub remained under the rubber tree, with his uncompleted sentence.
The reticence, the noise of his life.

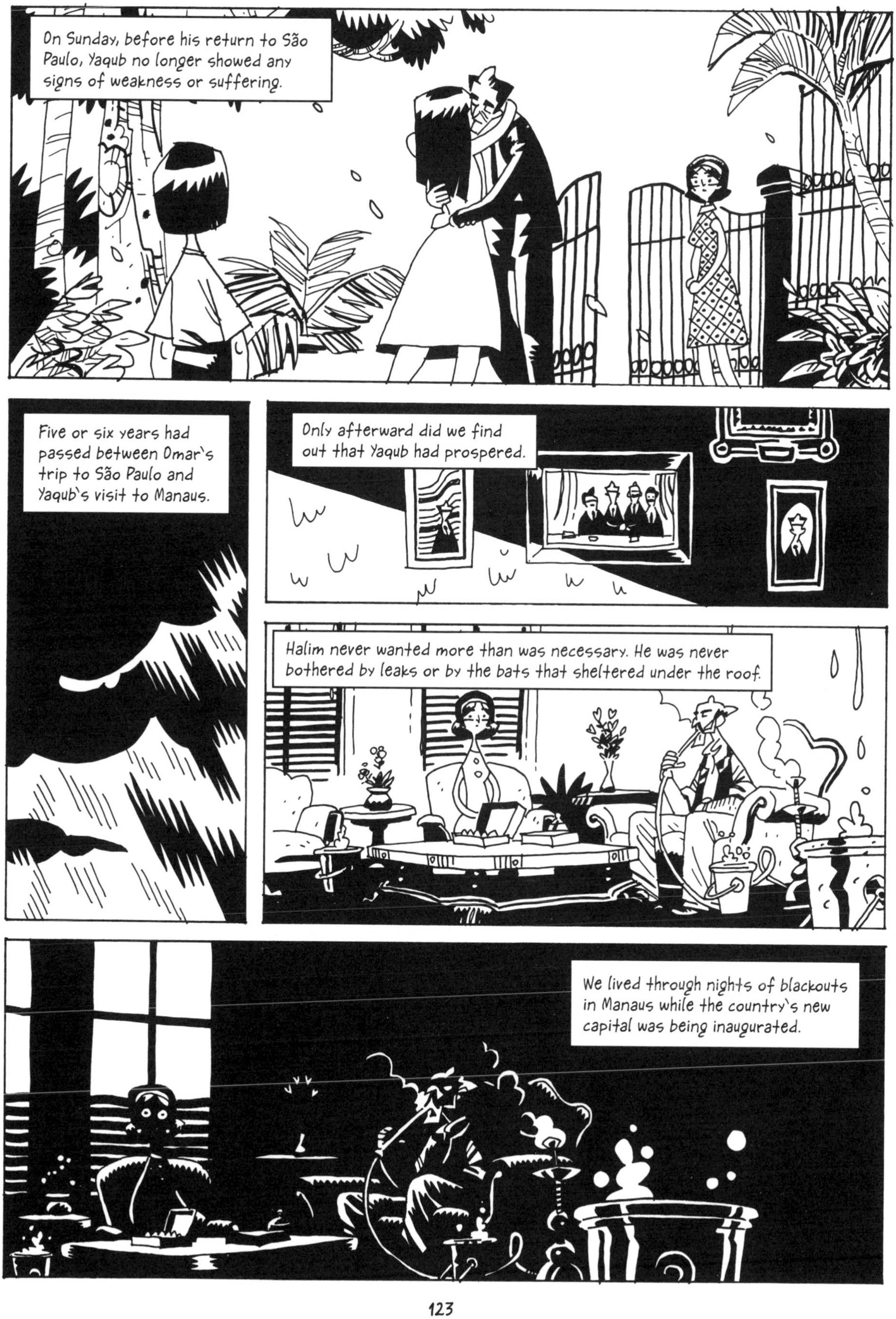
On Sunday, before his return to São Paulo, Yaqub no longer showed any signs of weakness or suffering.
Five or six years had passed between Omar's trip to São Paulo and Yaqub's visit to Manaus.
Only afterward did we find out that Yaqub had prospered.
Halim never wanted more than was necessary. He was never bothered by leaks or by the bats that sheltered under the roof.
We lived through nights of blackouts in Manaus while the country's new capital was being inaugurated.

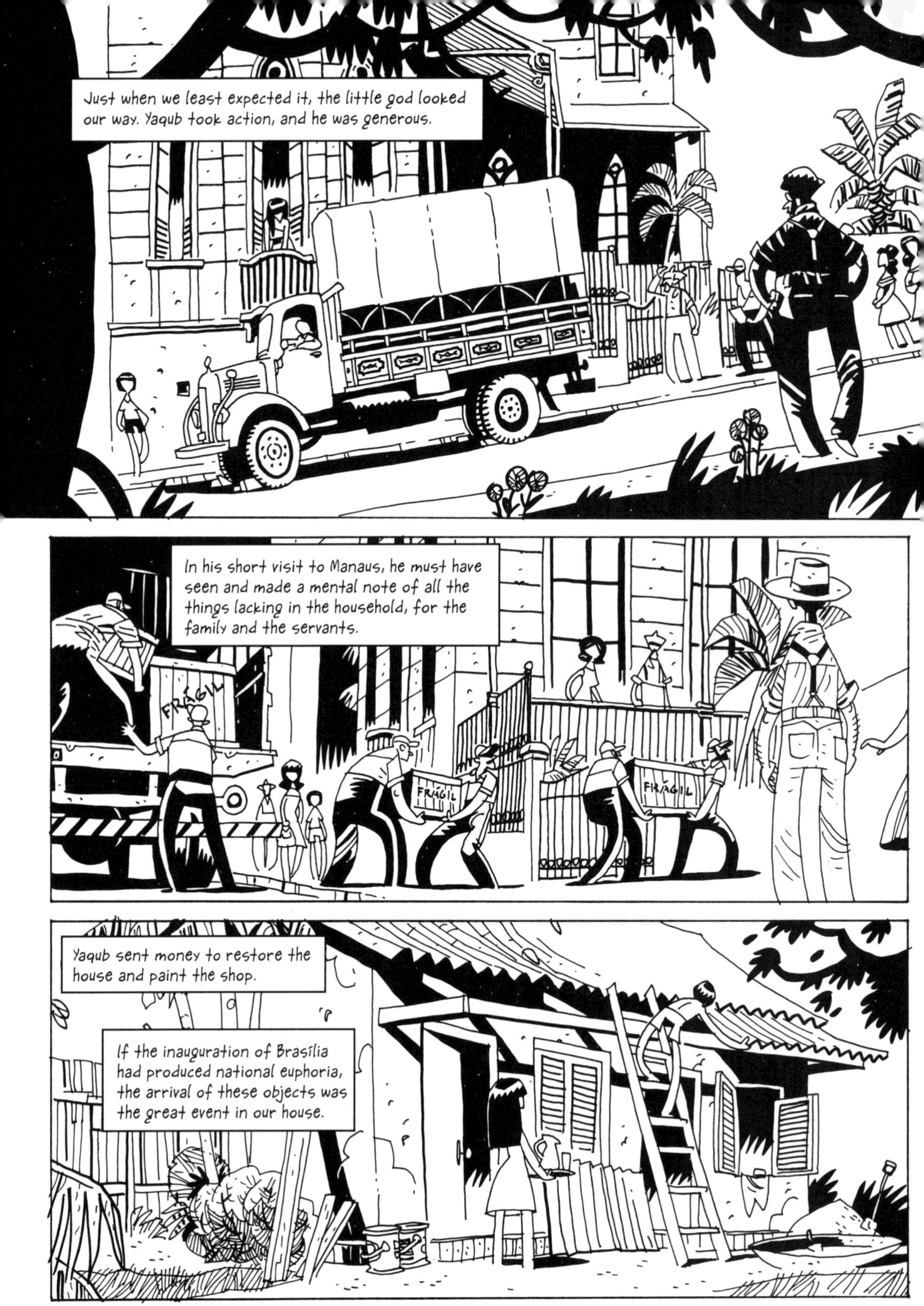

Just when we least expected it, the little god looked our way. Yaqub took action, and he was generous.
In his short visit to Manaus, he must have seen and made a mental note of all the things lacking in the household, for the family and the servants.
FRÁGIL
FRÁGIL
FRÁGIL
Yaqub sent money to restore the house and paint the shop.
If the inauguration of Brasília had produced national euphoria, the arrival of these objects was the great event in our house.

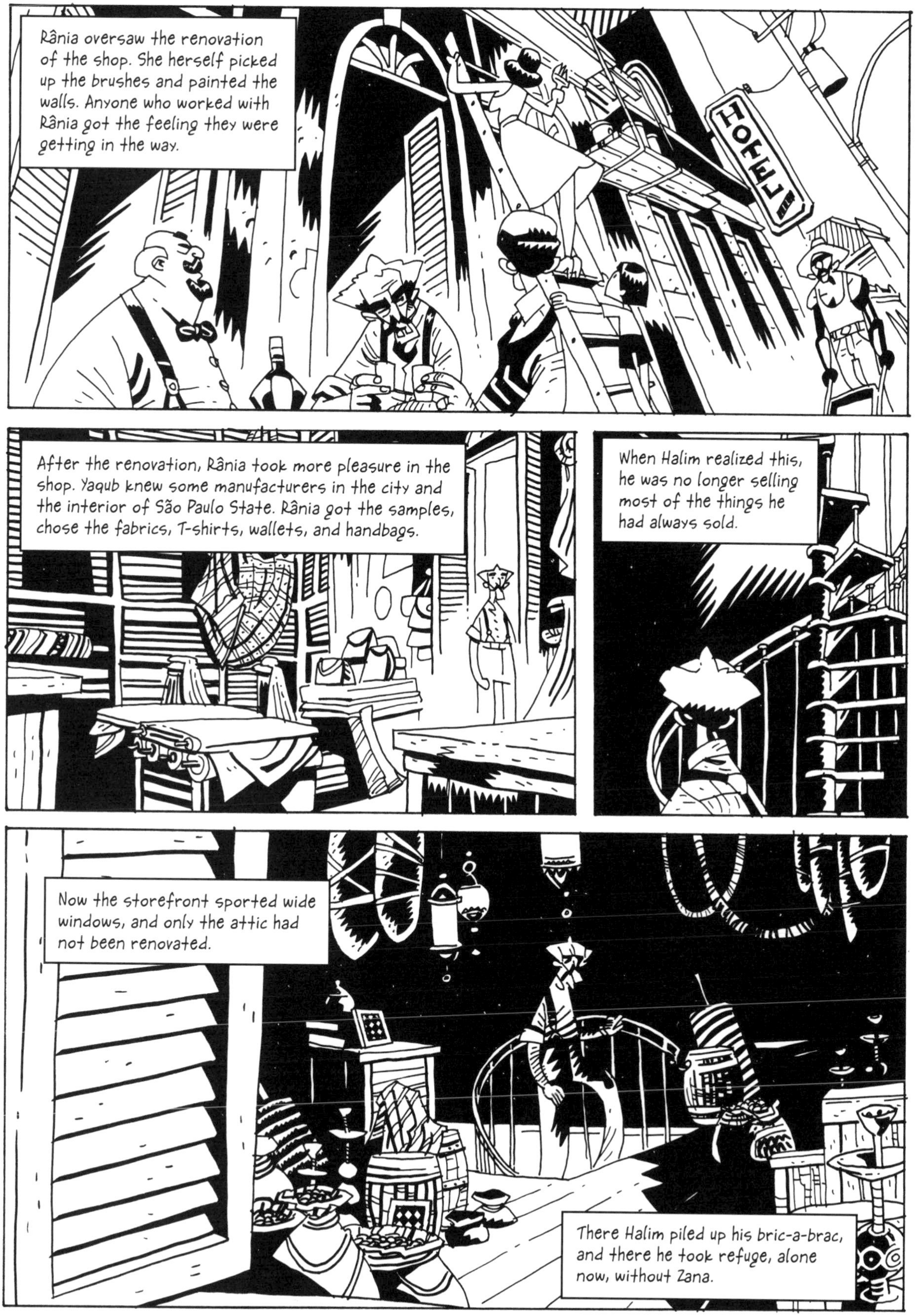
Rânia oversaw the renovation of the shop. She herself picked up the brushes and painted the walls. Anyone who worked with Rânia got the feeling they were getting in the way.
HOTEL
After the renovation, Rânia took more pleasure in the shop. Yaqub knew some manufacturers in the city and the interior of São Paulo State. Rânia got the samples, chose the fabrics, T-shirts, wallets, and handbags.
When Halim realized this, he was no longer selling most of the things he had always sold.
Now the storefront sported wide windows, and only the attic had not been renovated.
There Halim piled up his bric-a-brac, and there he took refuge, alone now, without Zana.

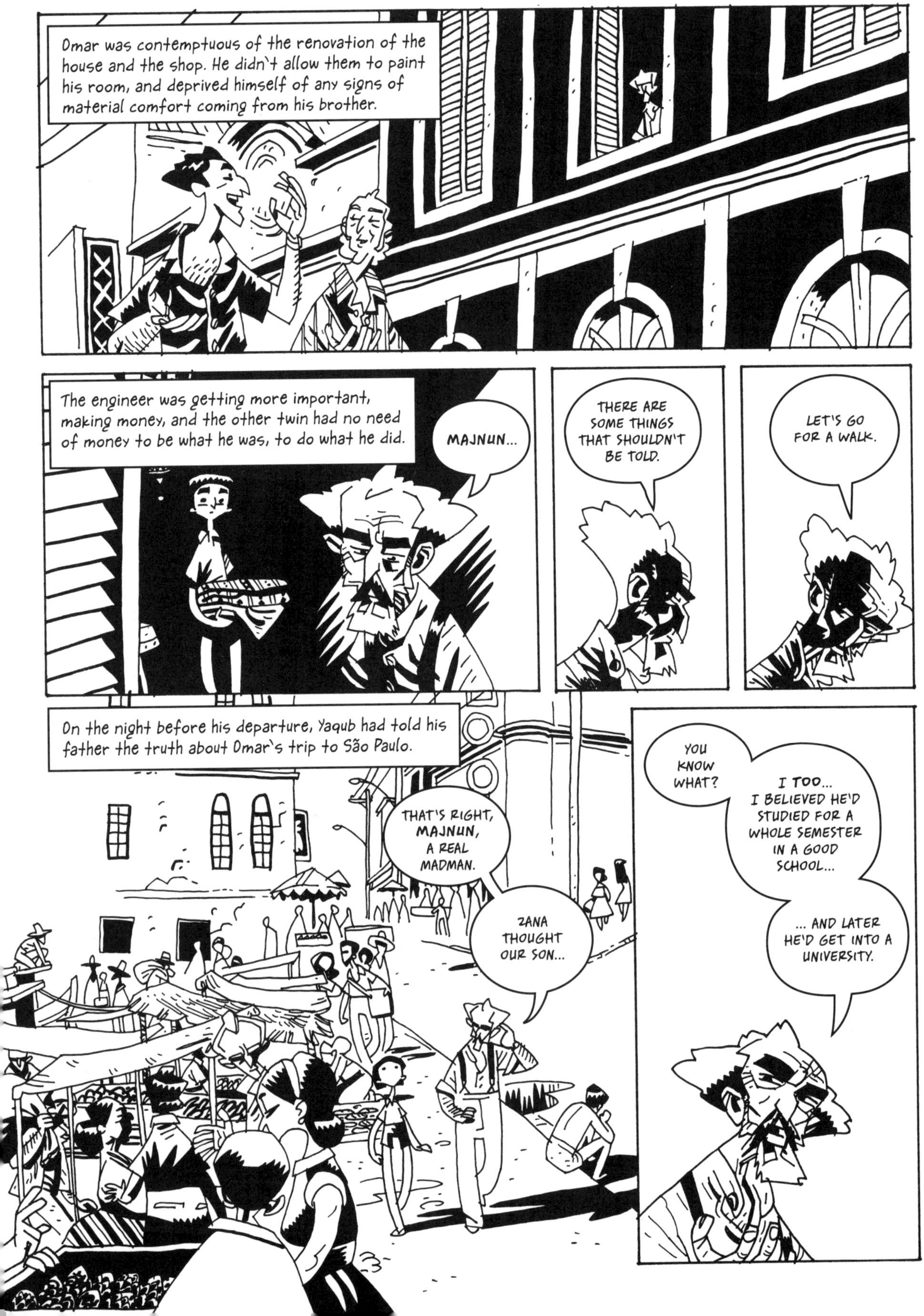

Omar was contemptuous of the renovation of the house and the shop. He didn't allow them to paint his room, and deprived himself of any signs of material comfort coming from his brother.
The engineer was getting more important, making money, and the other twin had no need of money to be what he was, to do what he did.
MAJNUN...
THERE ARE SOME THINGS THAT SHOULDN'T BE TOLD.
LET'S GO FOR A WALK.
On the night before his departure, Yaqub had told his father the truth about Omar's trip to São Paulo.
THAT'S RIGHT, MAJNUN, A REAL MADMAN.
ZANA THOUGHT OUR SON...
YOU KNOW WHAT?
I TOO... I BELIEVED HE'D STUDIED FOR A WHOLE SEMESTER IN A GOOD SCHOOL...
... AND LATER HE'D GET INTO A UNIVERSITY.

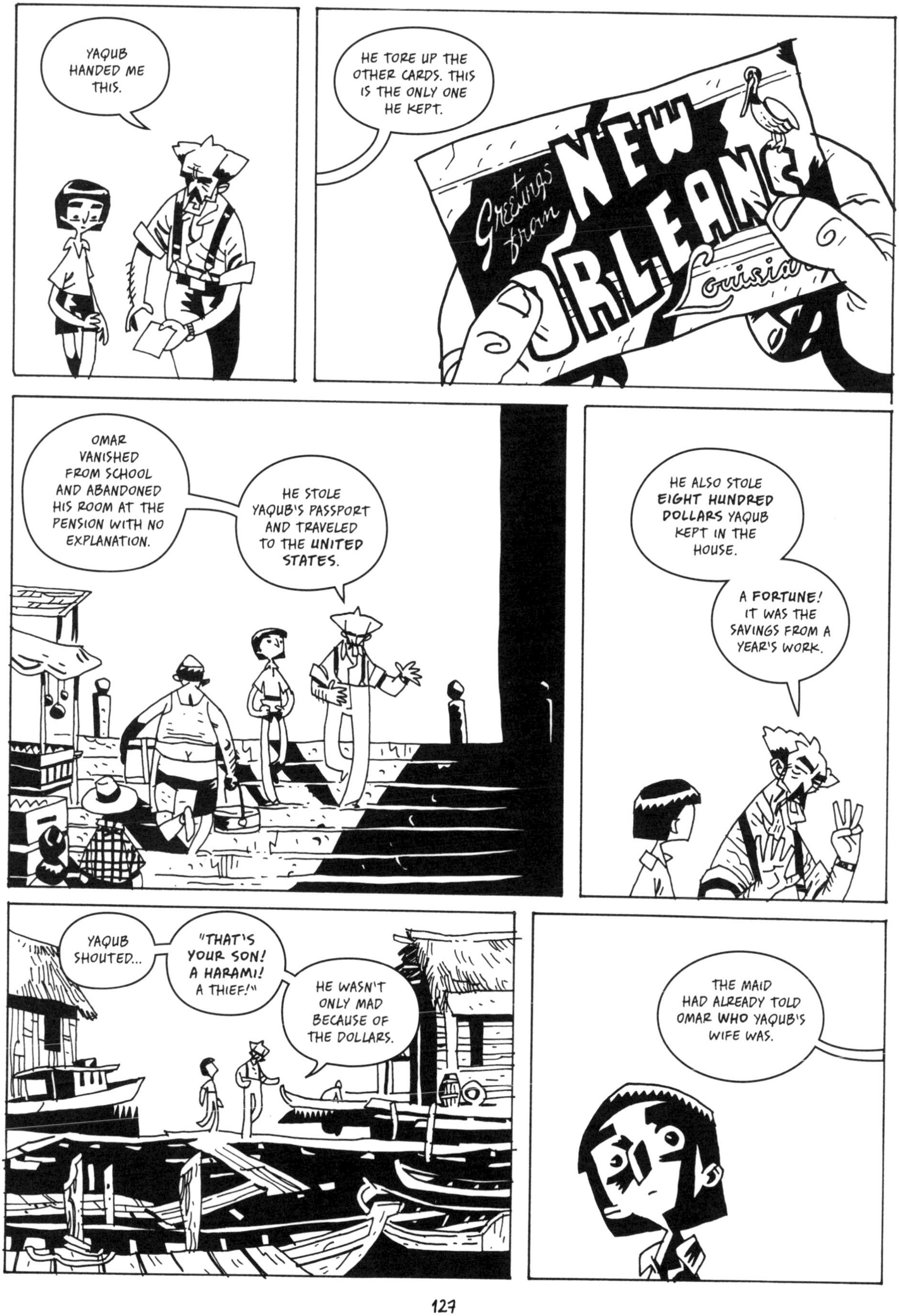
YAQUB HANDED ME THIS.
HE TORE UP THE OTHER CARDS. THIS IS THE ONLY ONE HE KEPT.
Greetings from NEW ORLEANS
OMAR VANISHED FROM SCHOOL AND ABANDONED HIS ROOM AT THE PENSION WITH NO EXPLANATION.
HE STOLE YAQUB'S PASSPORT AND TRAVELED TO THE **UNITED STATES**.
HE ALSO STOLE **EIGHT HUNDRED DOLLARS** YAQUB KEPT IN THE HOUSE.
A **FORTUNE!** IT WAS THE SAVINGS FROM A YEAR'S WORK.
YAQUB SHOUTED...
"THAT'S YOUR SON! A HARAMI! A THIEF!"
HE WASN'T ONLY MAD BECAUSE OF THE DOLLARS.
THE MAID HAD ALREADY TOLD OMAR **WHO** YAQUB'S WIFE WAS.

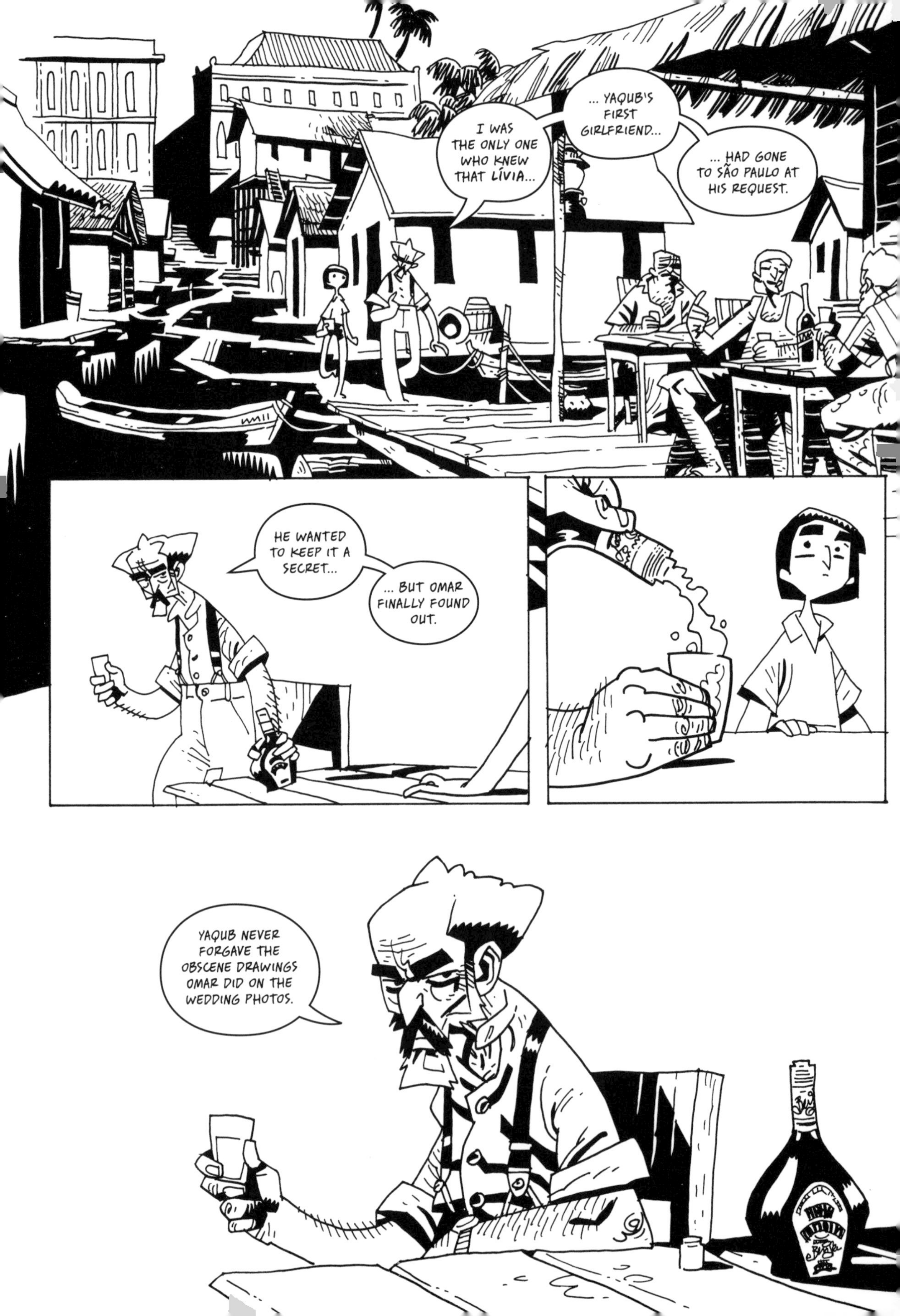
I WAS THE ONLY ONE WHO KNEW THAT LÍVIA...
... YAQUB'S FIRST GIRLFRIEND...
... HAD GONE TO SÃO PAULO AT HIS REQUEST.
HE WANTED TO KEEP IT A SECRET...
... BUT OMAR FINALLY FOUND OUT.
YAQUB NEVER FORGAVE THE OBSCENE DRAWINGS OMAR DID ON THE WEDDING PHOTOS.

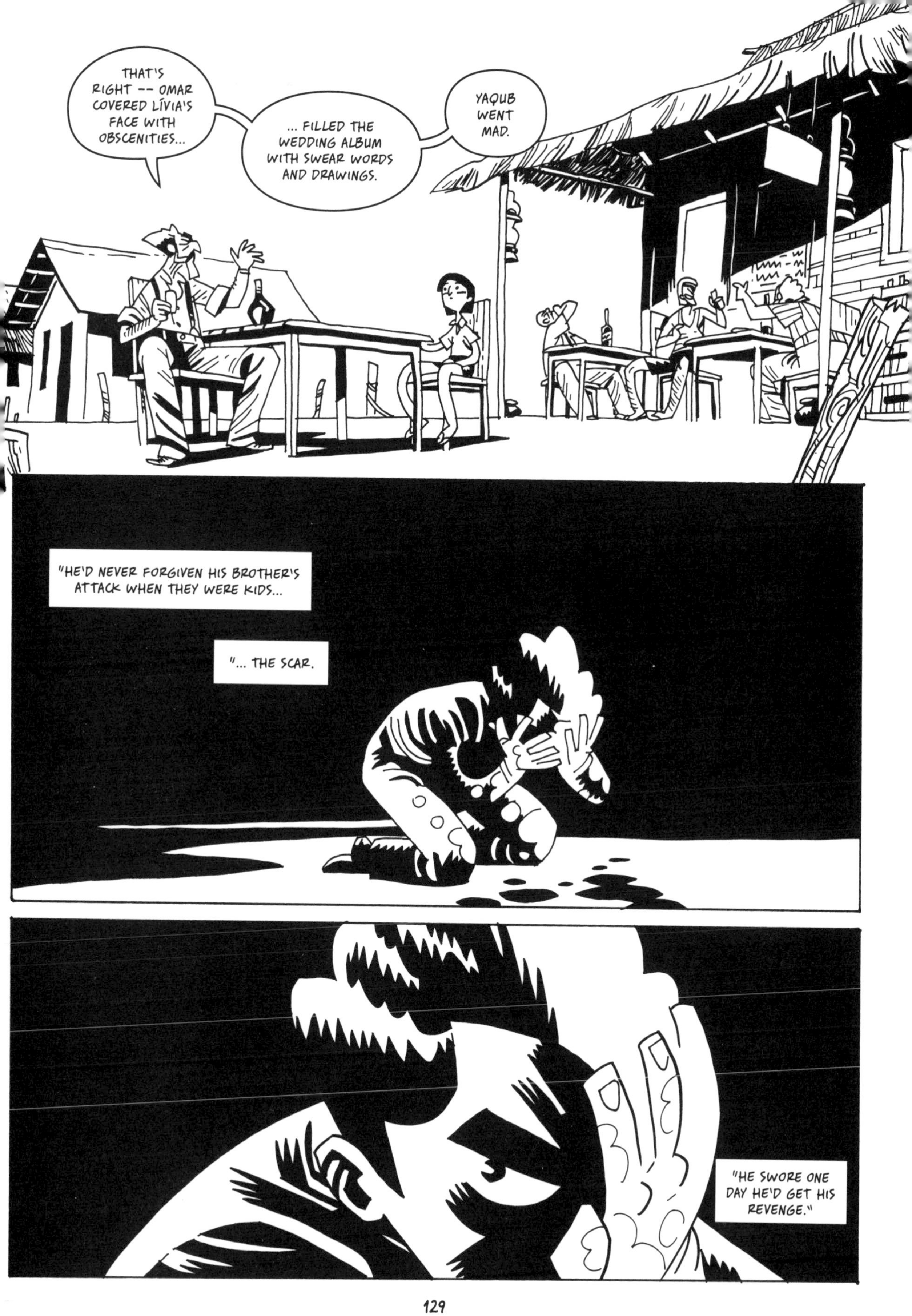

THAT'S RIGHT -- OMAR COVERED LÍVIA'S FACE WITH OBSCENITIES...
... FILLED THE WEDDING ALBUM WITH SWEAR WORDS AND DRAWINGS.
YAQUB WENT MAD.
"HE'D NEVER FORGIVEN HIS BROTHER'S ATTACK WHEN THEY WERE KIDS...
"... THE SCAR.
"HE SWORE ONE DAY HE'D GET HIS REVENGE."

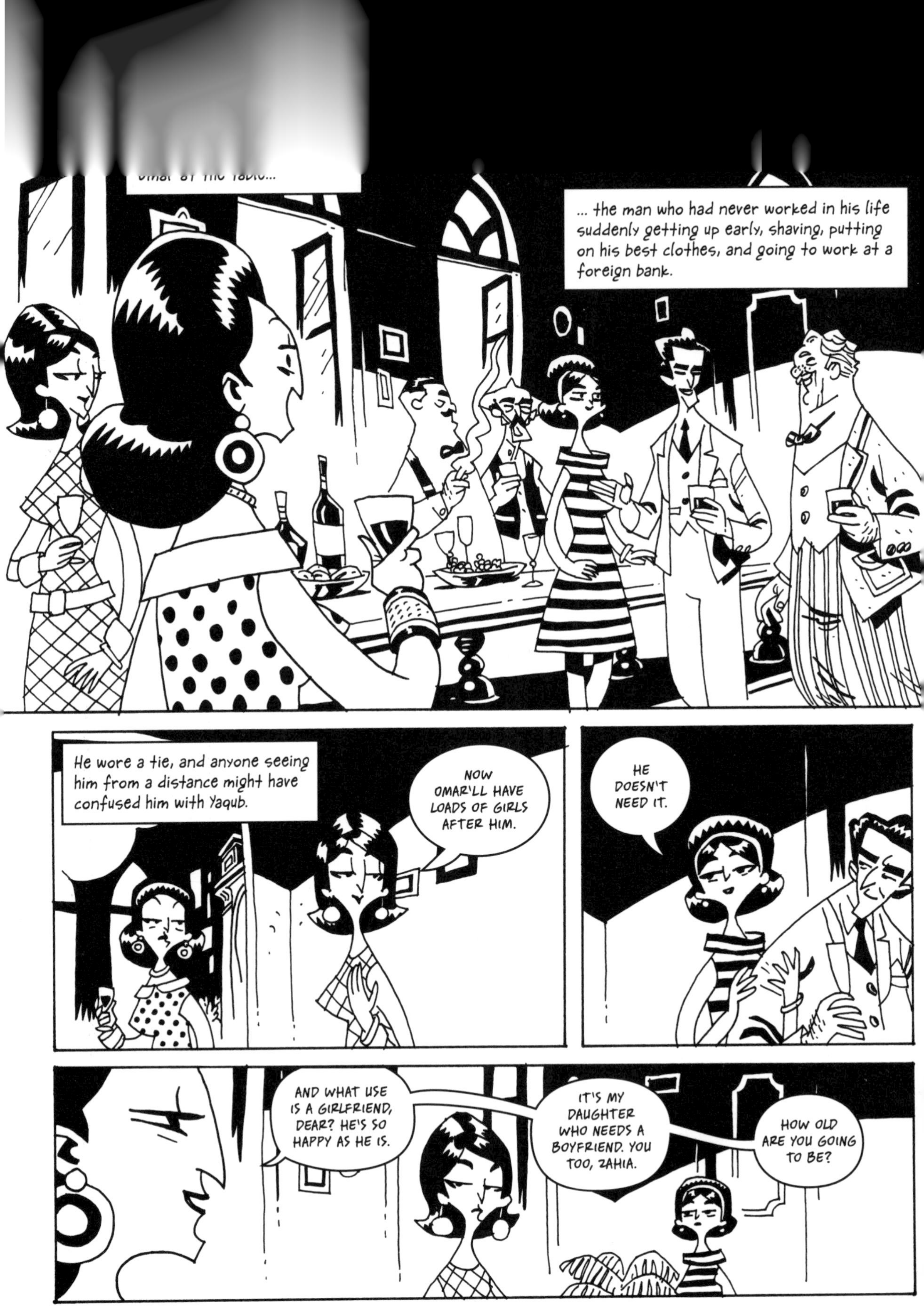
... the man who had never worked in his life suddenly getting up early, shaving, putting on his best clothes, and going to work at a foreign bank.
He wore a tie, and anyone seeing him from a distance might have confused him with Yaqub.
NOW OMAR'LL HAVE LOADS OF GIRLS AFTER HIM.
HE DOESN'T NEED IT.
AND WHAT USE IS A GIRLFRIEND, DEAR? HE'S SO HAPPY AS HE IS.
IT'S MY DAUGHTER WHO NEEDS A BOYFRIEND. YOU TOO, ZAHIA.
HOW OLD ARE YOU GOING TO BE?

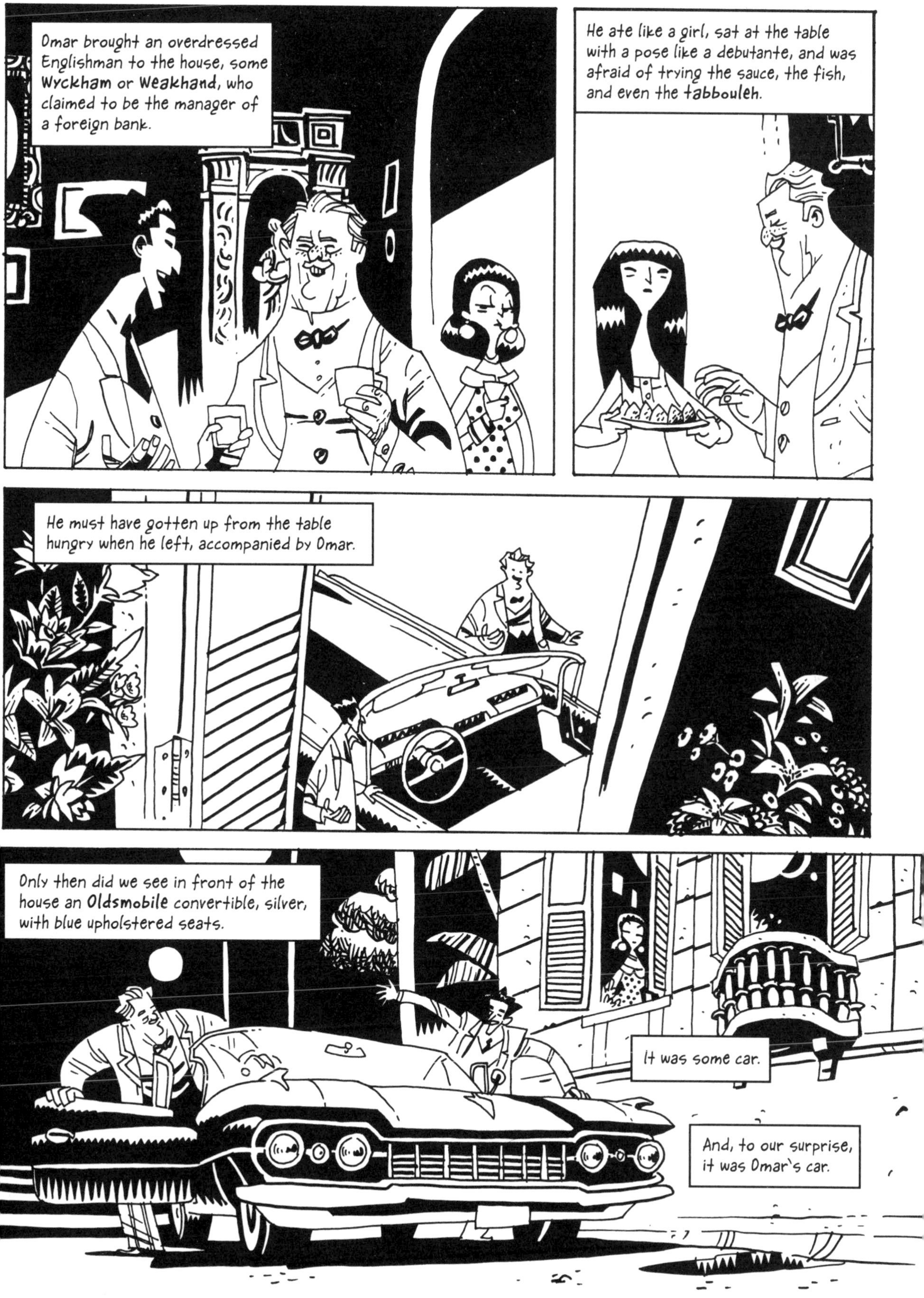
Omar brought an overdressed Englishman to the house, some **Wyckham** or **Weakhand**, who claimed to be the manager of a foreign bank.
He ate like a girl, sat at the table with a pose like a debutante, and was afraid of trying the sauce, the fish, and even the **tabbouleh**.
He must have gotten up from the table hungry when he left, accompanied by Omar.
Only then did we see in front of the house an **Oldsmobile** convertible, silver, with blue upholstered seats.
It was some car.
And, to our surprise, it was Omar's car.

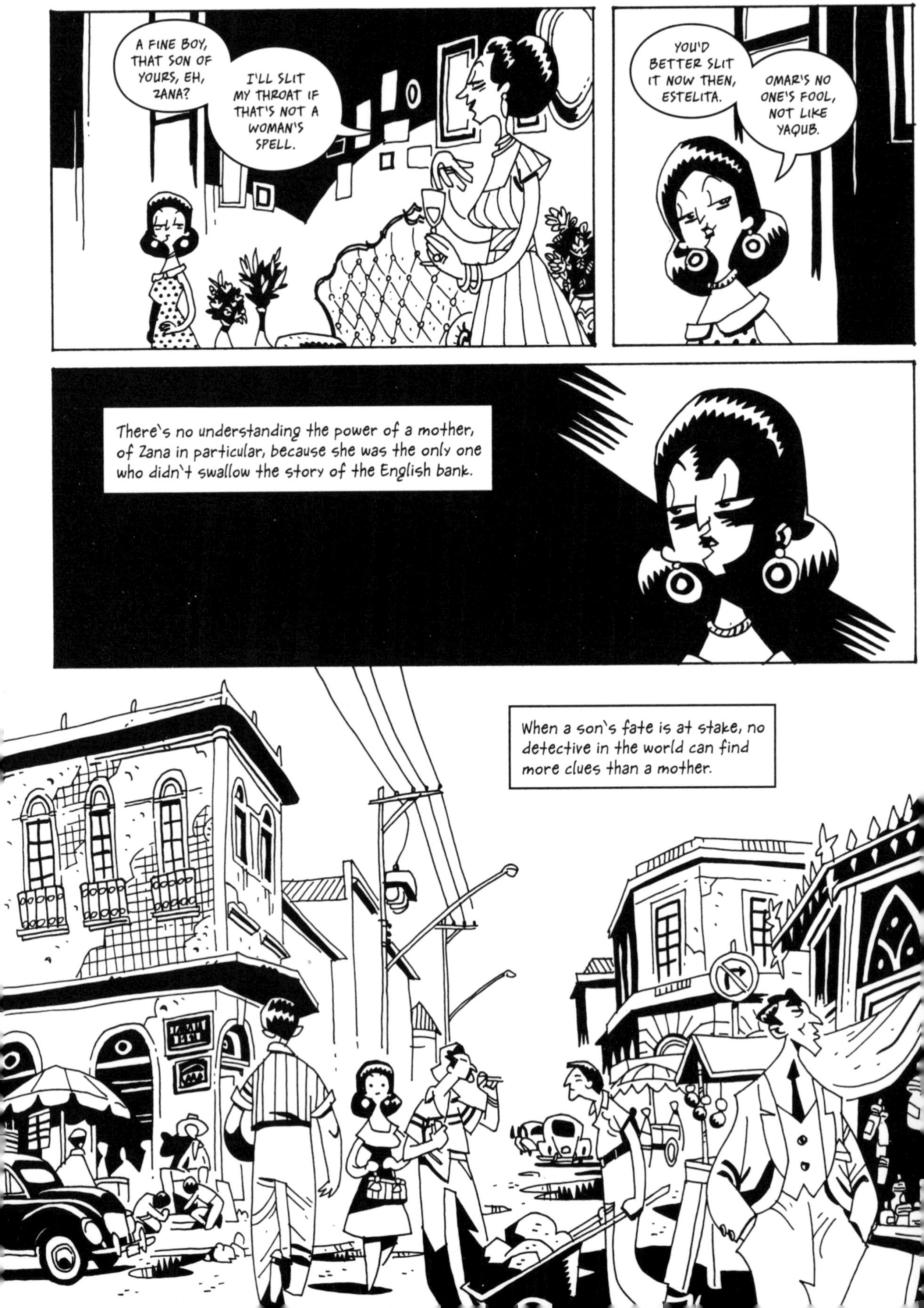
A FINE BOY, THAT SON OF YOURS, EH, ZANA?
I'LL SLIT MY THROAT IF THAT'S NOT A WOMAN'S SPELL.
YOU'D BETTER SLIT IT NOW THEN, ESTELITA.
OMAR'S NO ONE'S FOOL, NOT LIKE YAQUB.
There's no understanding the power of a mother, of Zana in particular, because she was the only one who didn't swallow the story of the English bank.
When a son's fate is at stake, no detective in the world can find more clues than a mother.

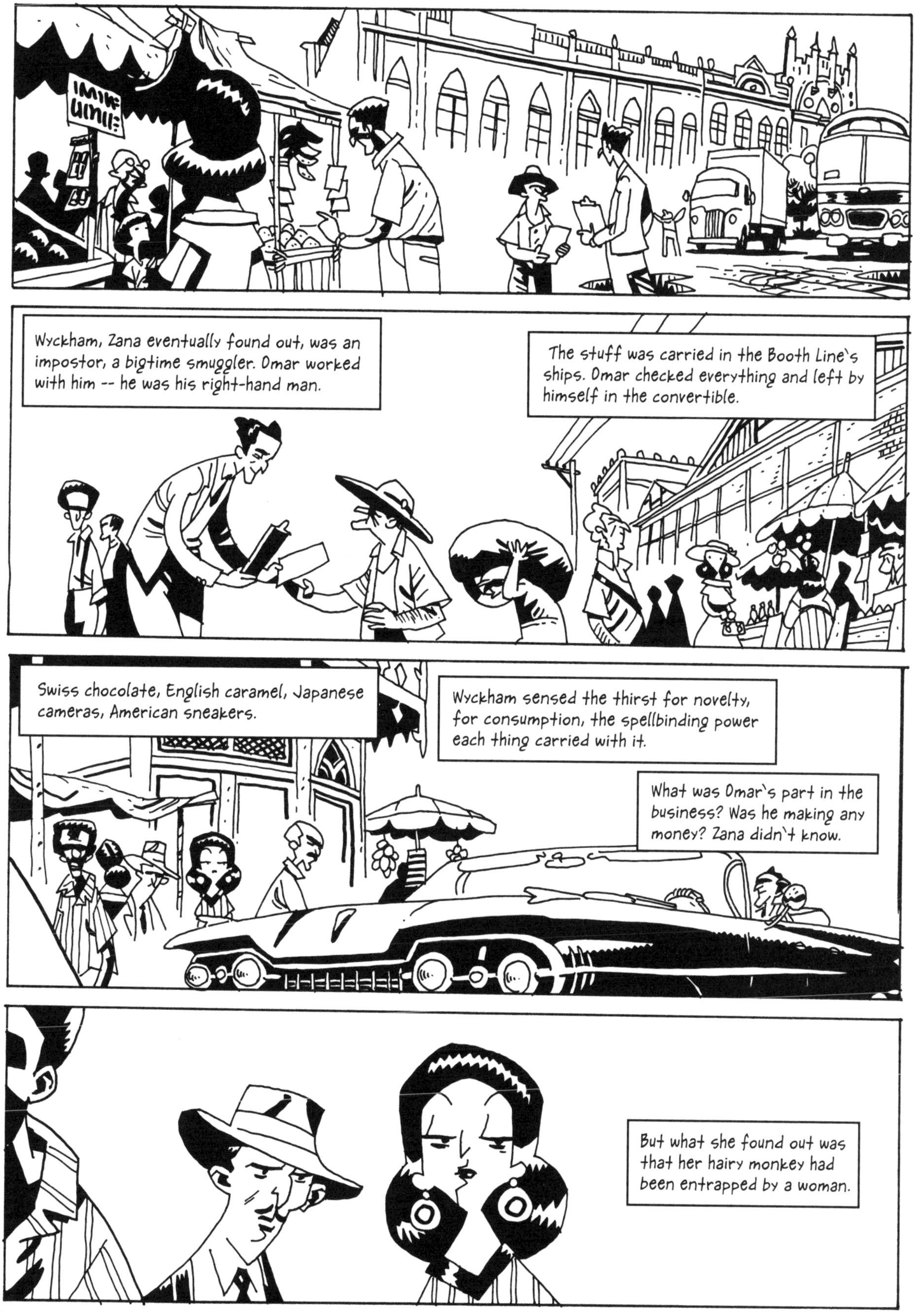
Wyckham, Zana eventually found out, was an impostor, a bigtime smuggler. Omar worked with him -- he was his right-hand man.
The stuff was carried in the Booth Line's ships. Omar checked everything and left by himself in the convertible.
Swiss chocolate, English caramel, Japanese cameras, American sneakers.
Wyckham sensed the thirst for novelty, for consumption, the spellbinding power each thing carried with it.
What was Omar's part in the business? Was he making any money? Zana didn't know.
But what she found out was that her hairy monkey had been entrapped by a woman.

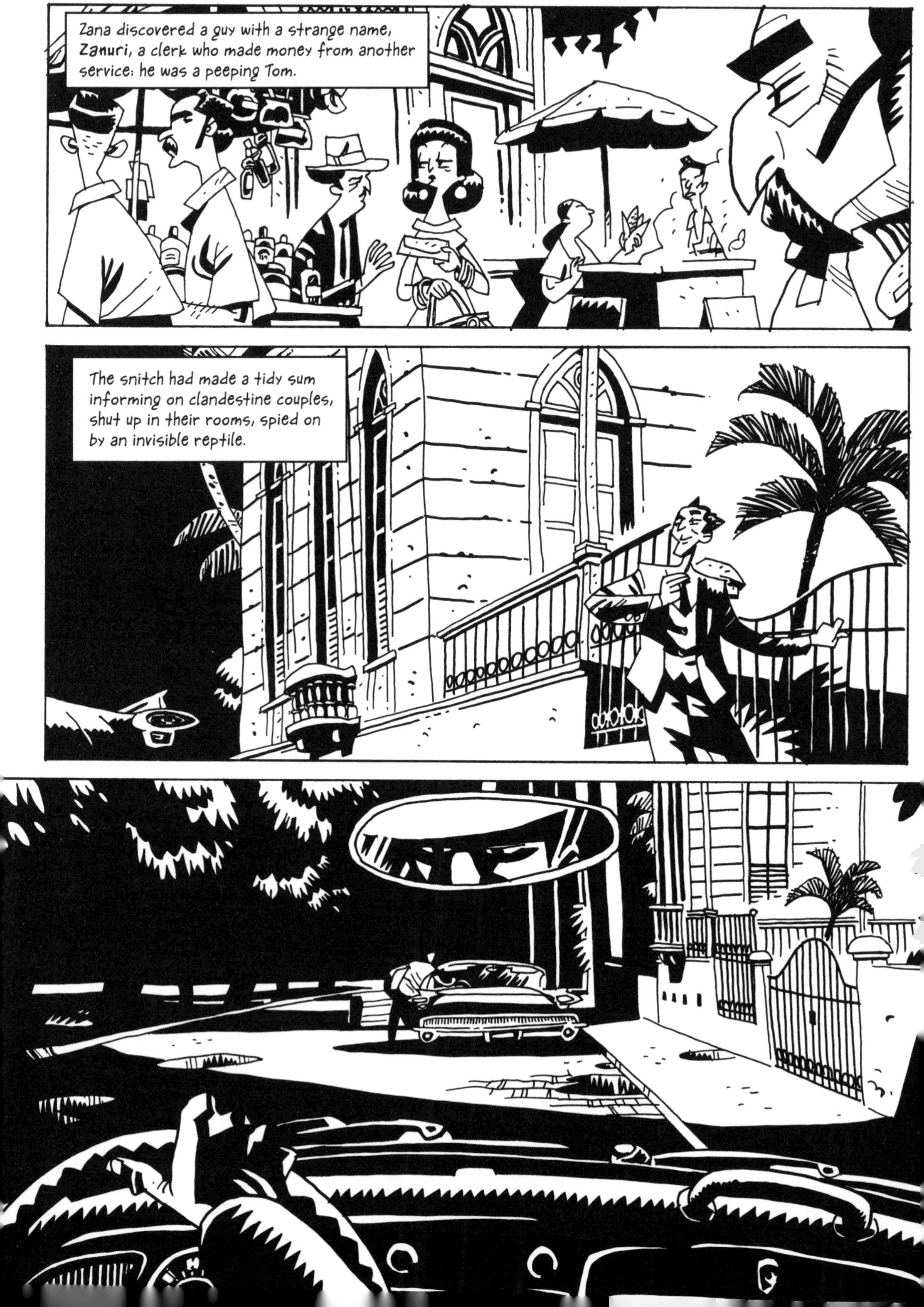
Zana discovered a guy with a strange name, **Zanuri**, a clerk who made money from another service: he was a peeping Tom.
The snitch had made a tidy sum informing on clandestine couples, shut up in their rooms, spied on by an invisible reptile.

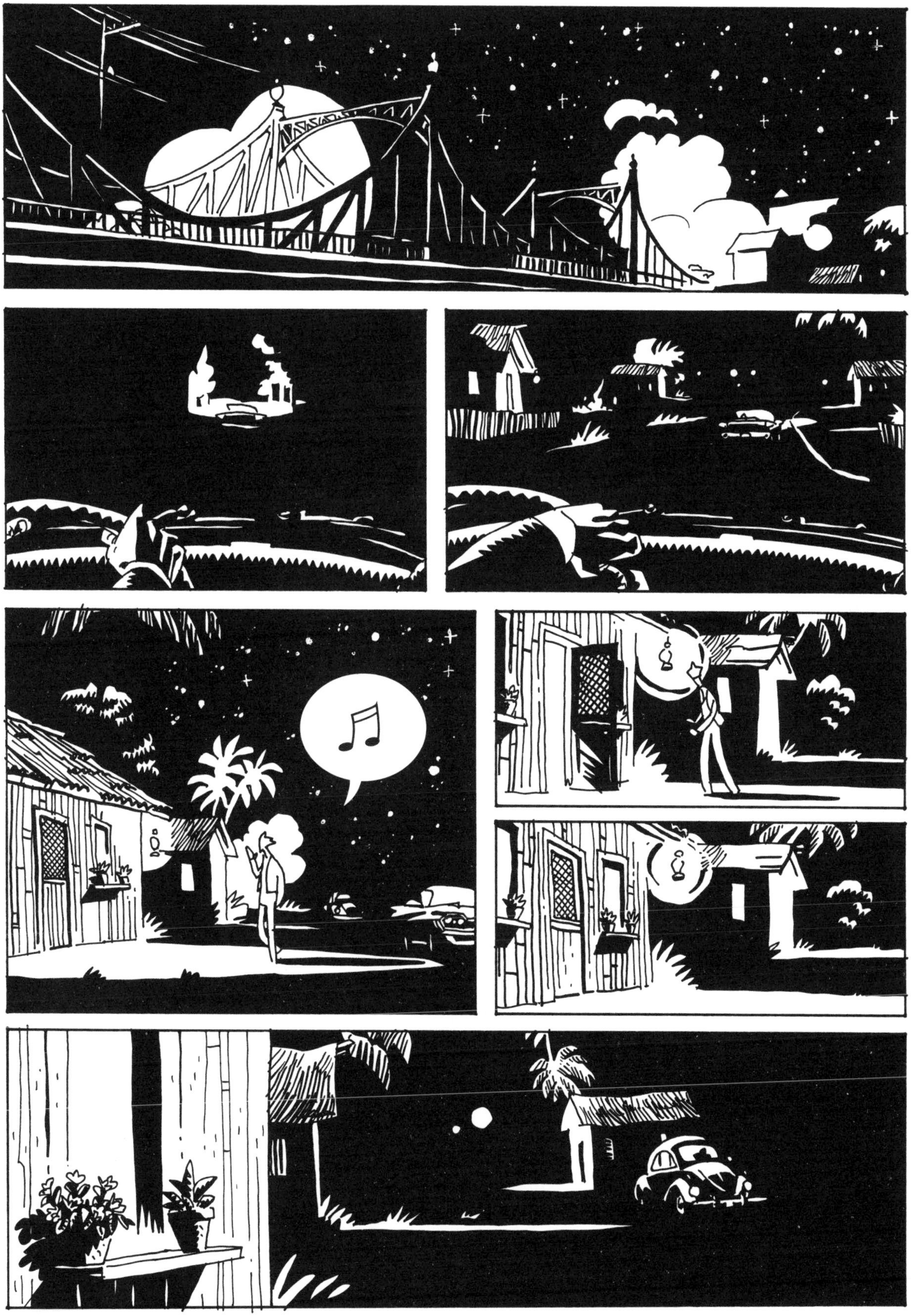

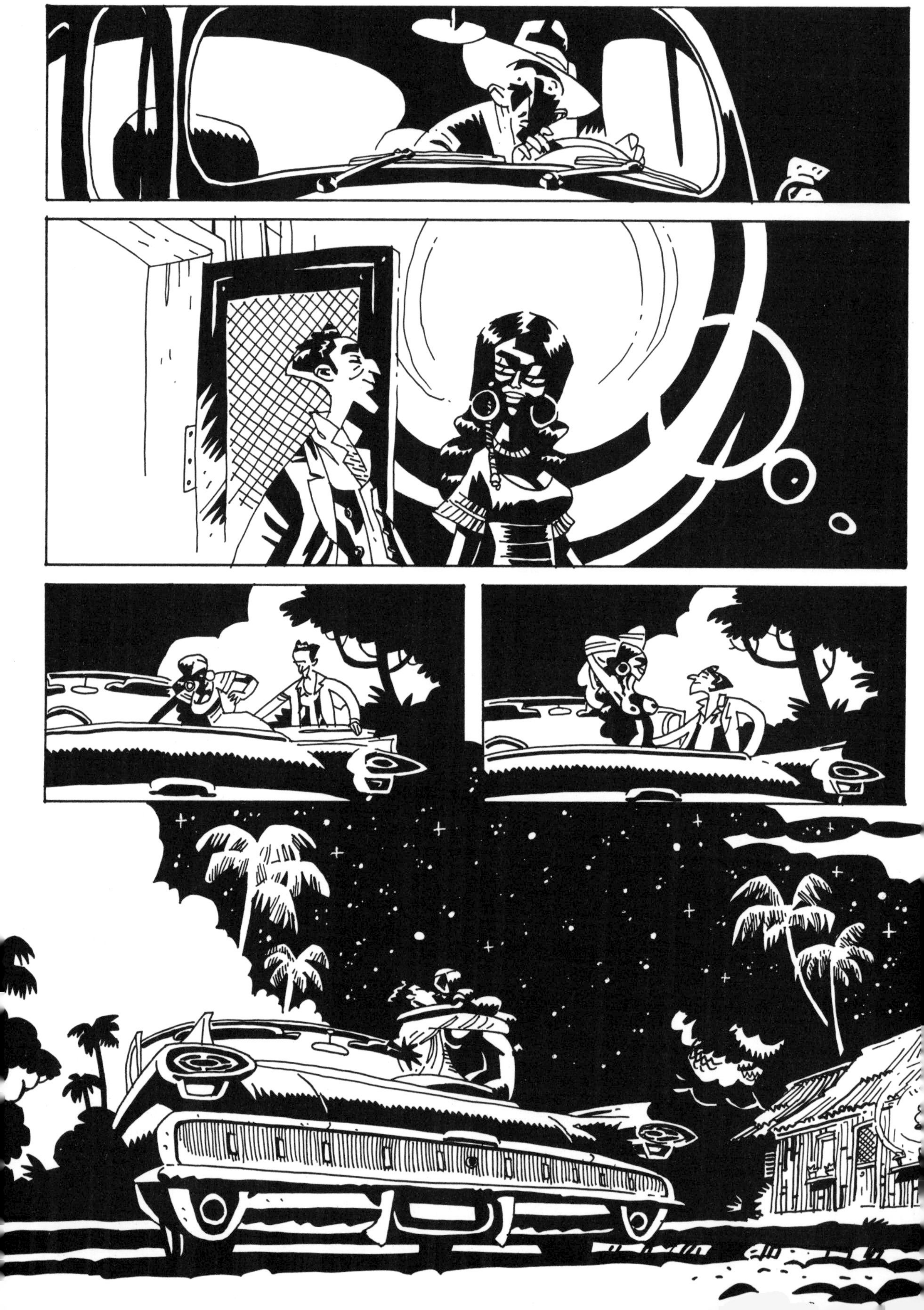

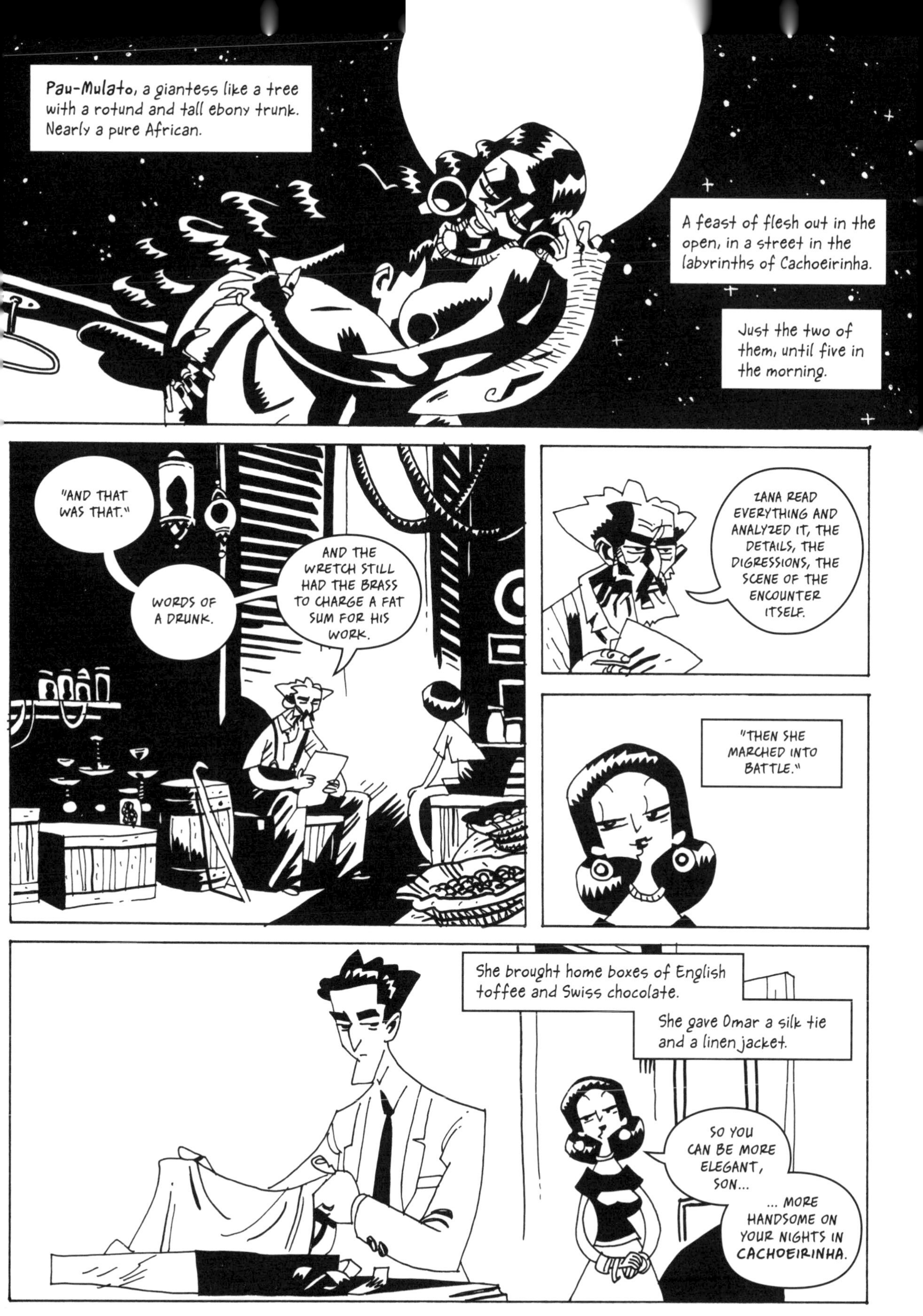
Pau-Mulato, a giantess like a tree with a rotund and tall ebony trunk. Nearly a pure African.
A feast of flesh out in the open, in a street in the labyrinths of Cachoeirinha.
Just the two of them, until five in the morning.
"AND THAT WAS THAT."
WORDS OF A DRUNK.
AND THE WRETCH STILL HAD THE BRASS TO CHARGE A FAT SUM FOR HIS WORK.
ZANA READ EVERYTHING AND ANALYZED IT, THE DETAILS, THE DIGRESSIONS, THE SCENE OF THE ENCOUNTER ITSELF.
"THEN SHE MARCHED INTO BATTLE."
She brought home boxes of English toffee and Swiss chocolate.
She gave Omar a silk tie and a linen jacket.
SO YOU CAN BE MORE ELEGANT, SON...
... MORE HANDSOME ON YOUR NIGHTS IN CACHOEIRINHA.

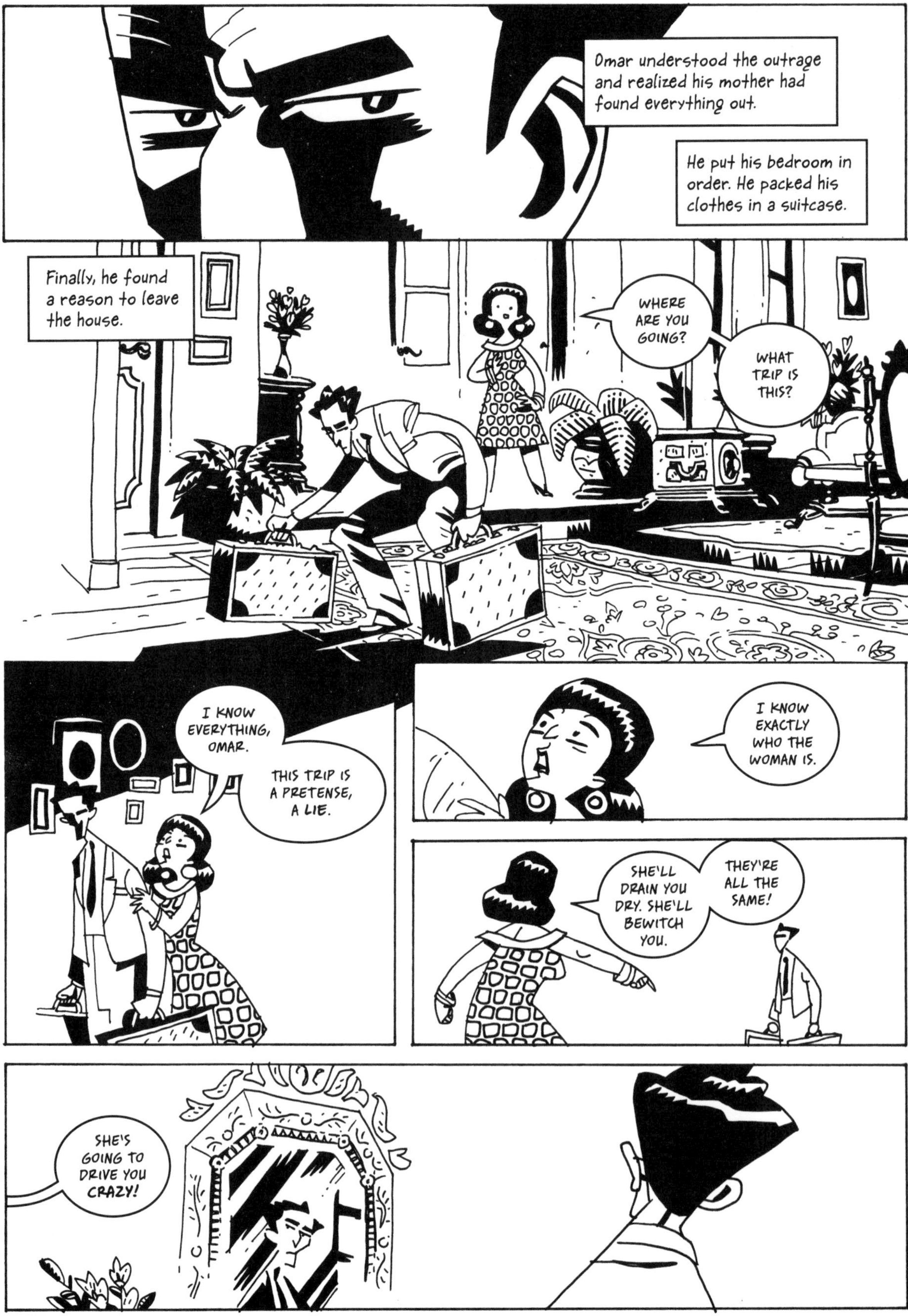

Omar understood the outrage and realized his mother had found everything out.
He put his bedroom in order. He packed his clothes in a suitcase.
Finally, he found a reason to leave the house.
WHERE ARE YOU GOING?
WHAT TRIP IS THIS?
I KNOW EVERYTHING, OMAR.
THIS TRIP IS A PRETENSE, A LIE.
I KNOW EXACTLY WHO THE WOMAN IS.
SHE'LL DRAIN YOU DRY. SHE'LL BEWITCH YOU.
THEY'RE ALL THE SAME!
SHE'S GOING TO DRIVE YOU CRAZY!

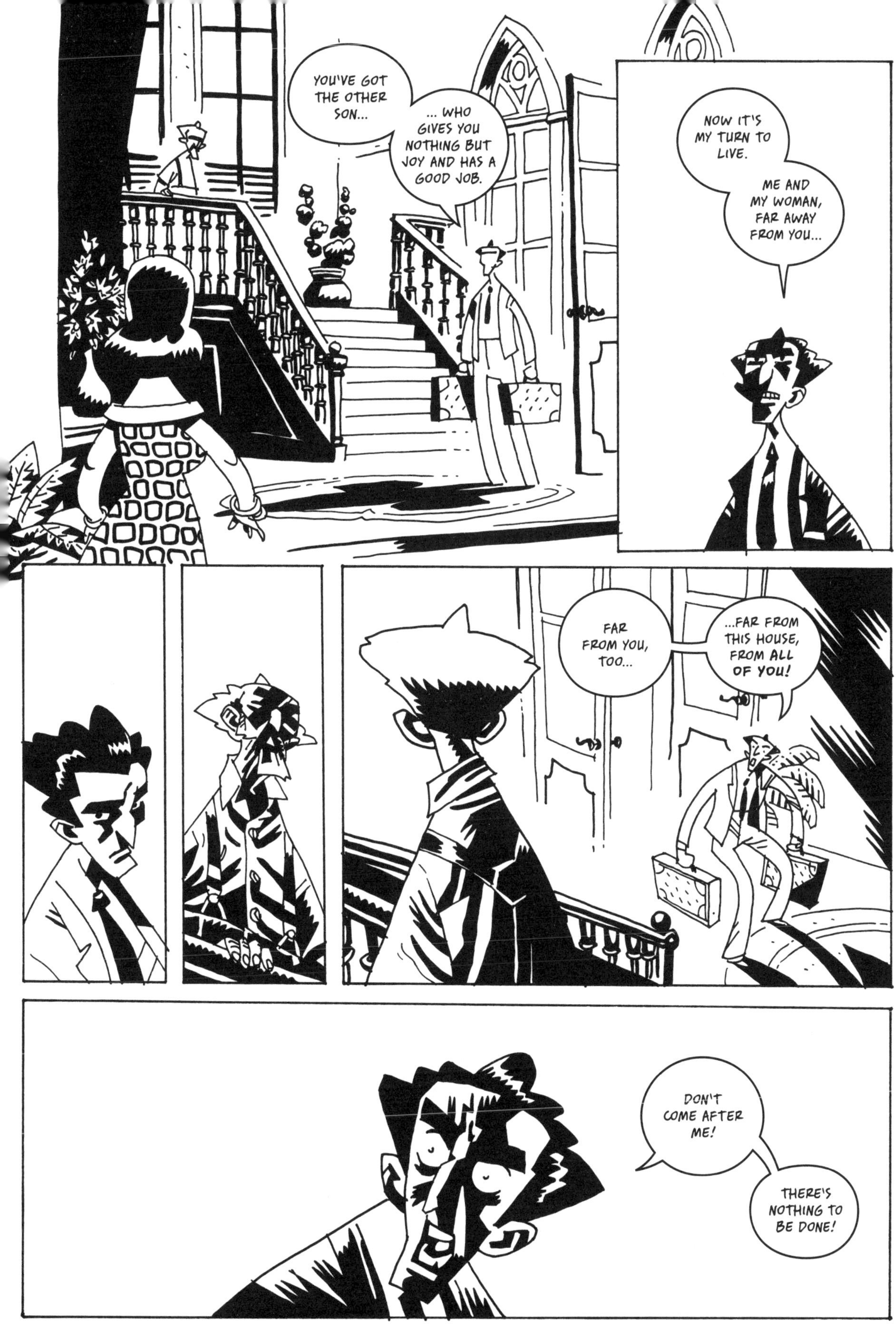
YOU'VE GOT THE OTHER SON...
... WHO GIVES YOU NOTHING BUT JOY AND HAS A GOOD JOB.
NOW IT'S MY TURN TO LIVE.
ME AND MY WOMAN, FAR AWAY FROM YOU...
FAR FROM YOU, TOO...
...FAR FROM THIS HOUSE, FROM ALL OF YOU!
DON'T COME AFTER ME!
THERE'S NOTHING TO BE DONE!

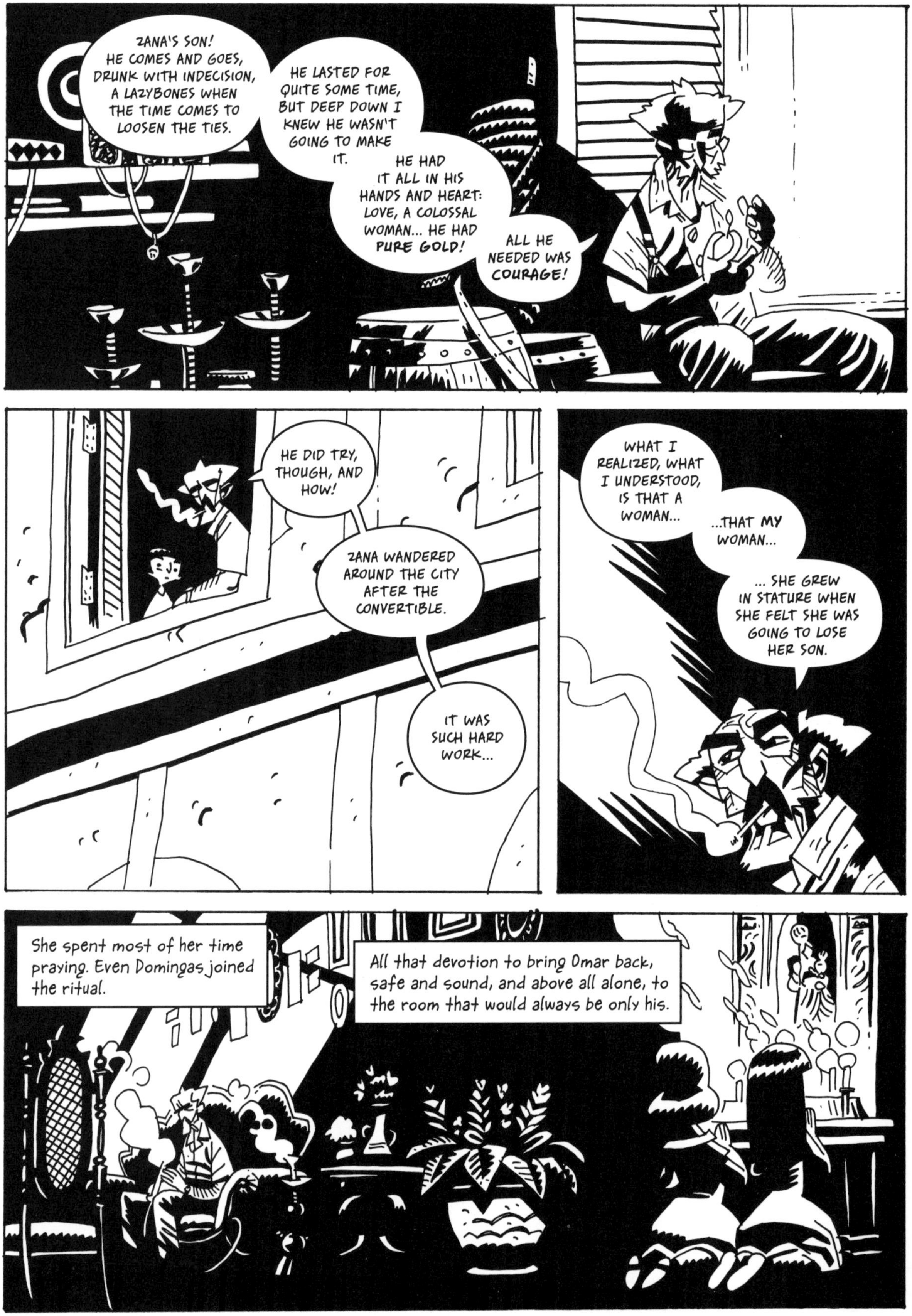
ZANA'S SON! HE COMES AND GOES, DRUNK WITH INDECISION, A LAZYBONES WHEN THE TIME COMES TO LOOSEN THE TIES.
HE LASTED FOR QUITE SOME TIME, BUT DEEP DOWN I KNEW HE WASN'T GOING TO MAKE IT.
HE HAD IT ALL IN HIS HANDS AND HEART: LOVE, A COLOSSAL WOMAN... HE HAD PURE GOLD!
ALL HE NEEDED WAS COURAGE!
HE DID TRY, THOUGH, AND HOW!
ZANA WANDERED AROUND THE CITY AFTER THE CONVERTIBLE.
IT WAS SUCH HARD WORK...
WHAT I REALIZED, WHAT I UNDERSTOOD, IS THAT A WOMAN...
...THAT MY WOMAN...
... SHE GREW IN STATURE WHEN SHE FELT SHE WAS GOING TO LOSE HER SON.
She spent most of her time praying. Even Domingas joined the ritual.
All that devotion to bring Omar back, safe and sound, and above all alone, to the room that would always be only his.

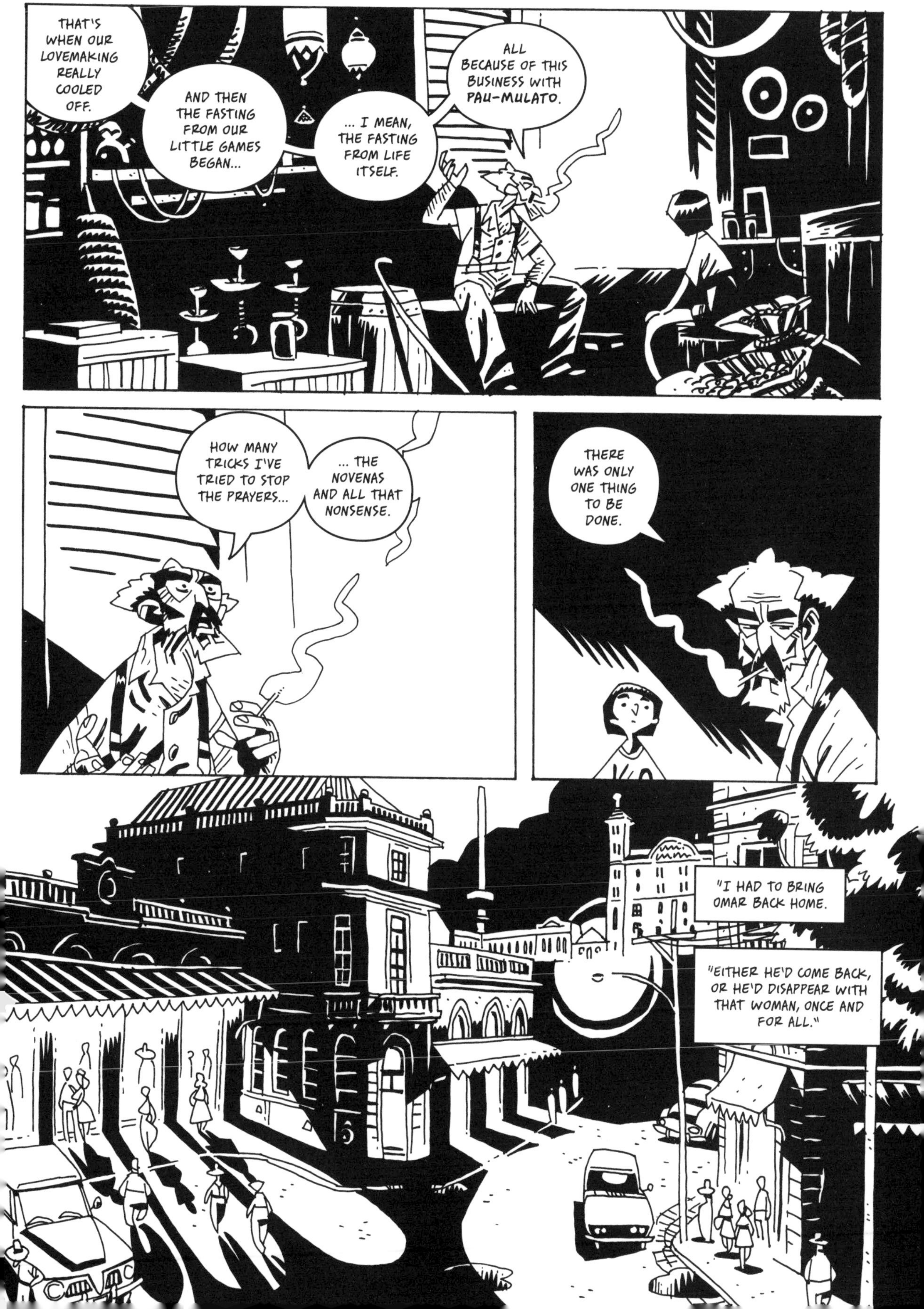
THAT'S WHEN OUR LOVEMAKING REALLY COOLED OFF.
AND THEN THE FASTING FROM OUR LITTLE GAMES BEGAN...
... I MEAN, THE FASTING FROM LIFE ITSELF.
ALL BECAUSE OF THIS BUSINESS WITH **PAU-MULATO**.
HOW MANY TRICKS I'VE TRIED TO STOP THE PRAYERS...
... THE NOVENAS AND ALL THAT NONSENSE.
THERE WAS ONLY ONE THING TO BE DONE.
"I HAD TO BRING OMAR BACK HOME.
"EITHER HE'D COME BACK, OR HE'D DISAPPEAR WITH THAT WOMAN, ONCE AND FOR ALL."

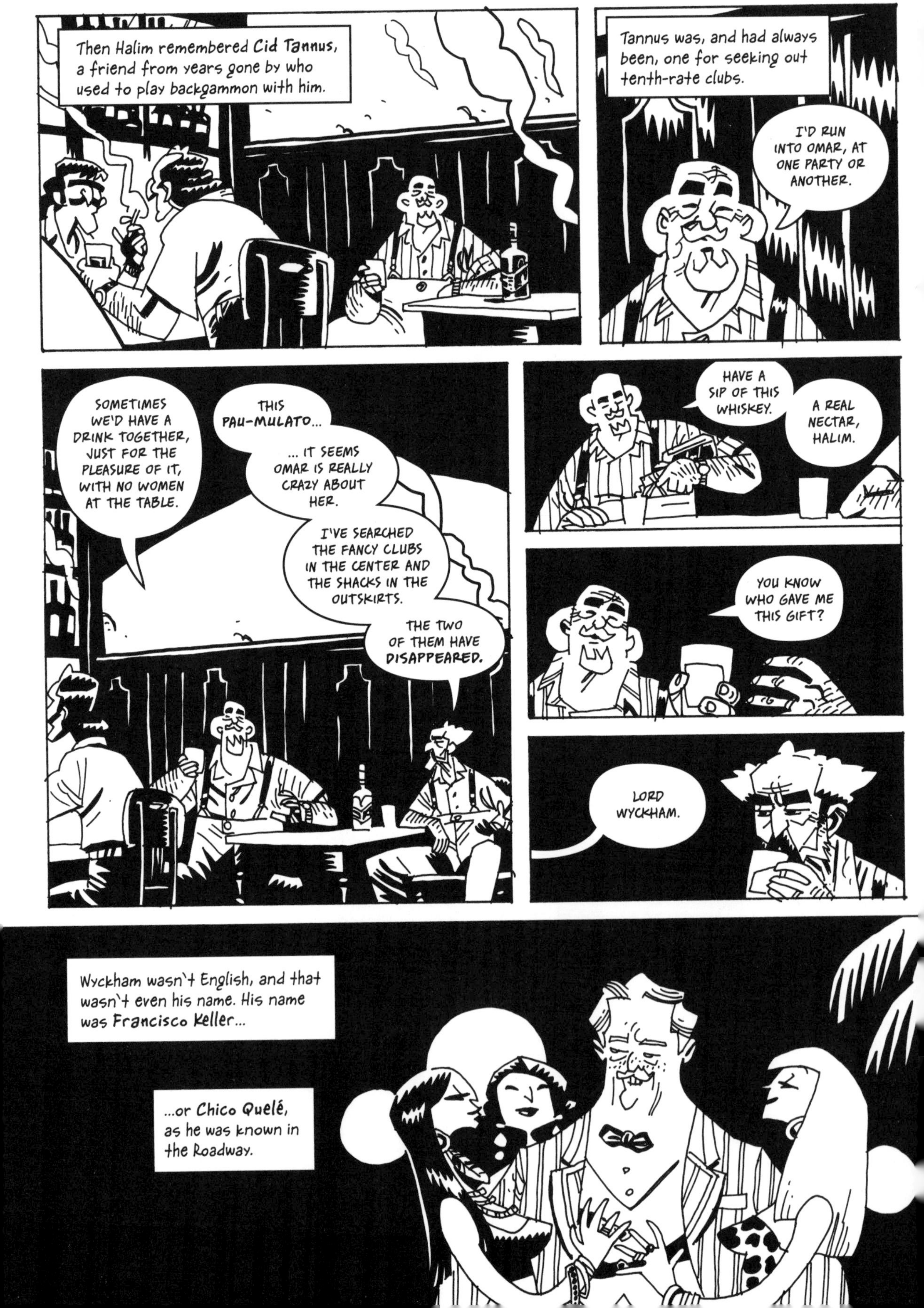

Then Halim remembered Cid Tannus, a friend from years gone by who used to play backgammon with him.
Tannus was, and had always been, one for seeking out tenth-rate clubs.
I'D RUN INTO OMAR, AT ONE PARTY OR ANOTHER.
SOMETIMES WE'D HAVE A DRINK TOGETHER, JUST FOR THE PLEASURE OF IT, WITH NO WOMEN AT THE TABLE.
THIS PAU-MULATO...
... IT SEEMS OMAR IS REALLY CRAZY ABOUT HER.
I'VE SEARCHED THE FANCY CLUBS IN THE CENTER AND THE SHACKS IN THE OUTSKIRTS.
THE TWO OF THEM HAVE DISAPPEARED.
HAVE A SIP OF THIS WHISKEY.
A REAL NECTAR, HALIM.
YOU KNOW WHO GAVE ME THIS GIFT?
LORD WYCKHAM.
Wyckham wasn't English, and that wasn't even his name. His name was Francisco Keller...
...or Chico Quelé, as he was known in the Roadway.

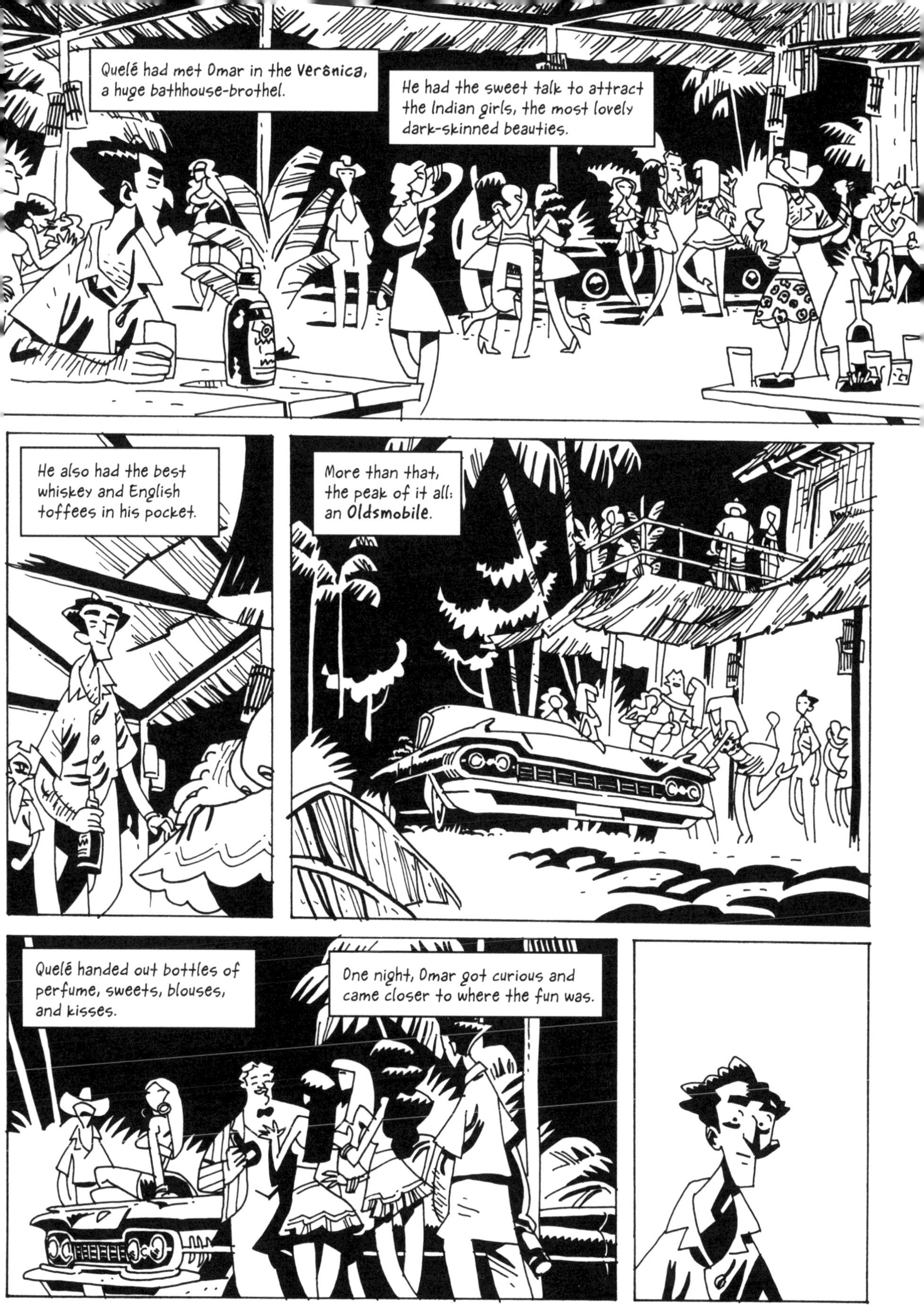
Quelé had met Omar in the **Verônica**, a huge bathhouse-brothel.
He had the sweet talk to attract the Indian girls, the most lovely dark-skinned beauties.
He also had the best whiskey and English toffees in his pocket.
More than that, the peak of it all: an **Oldsmobile**.
Quelé handed out bottles of perfume, sweets, blouses, and kisses.
One night, Omar got curious and came closer to where the fun was.

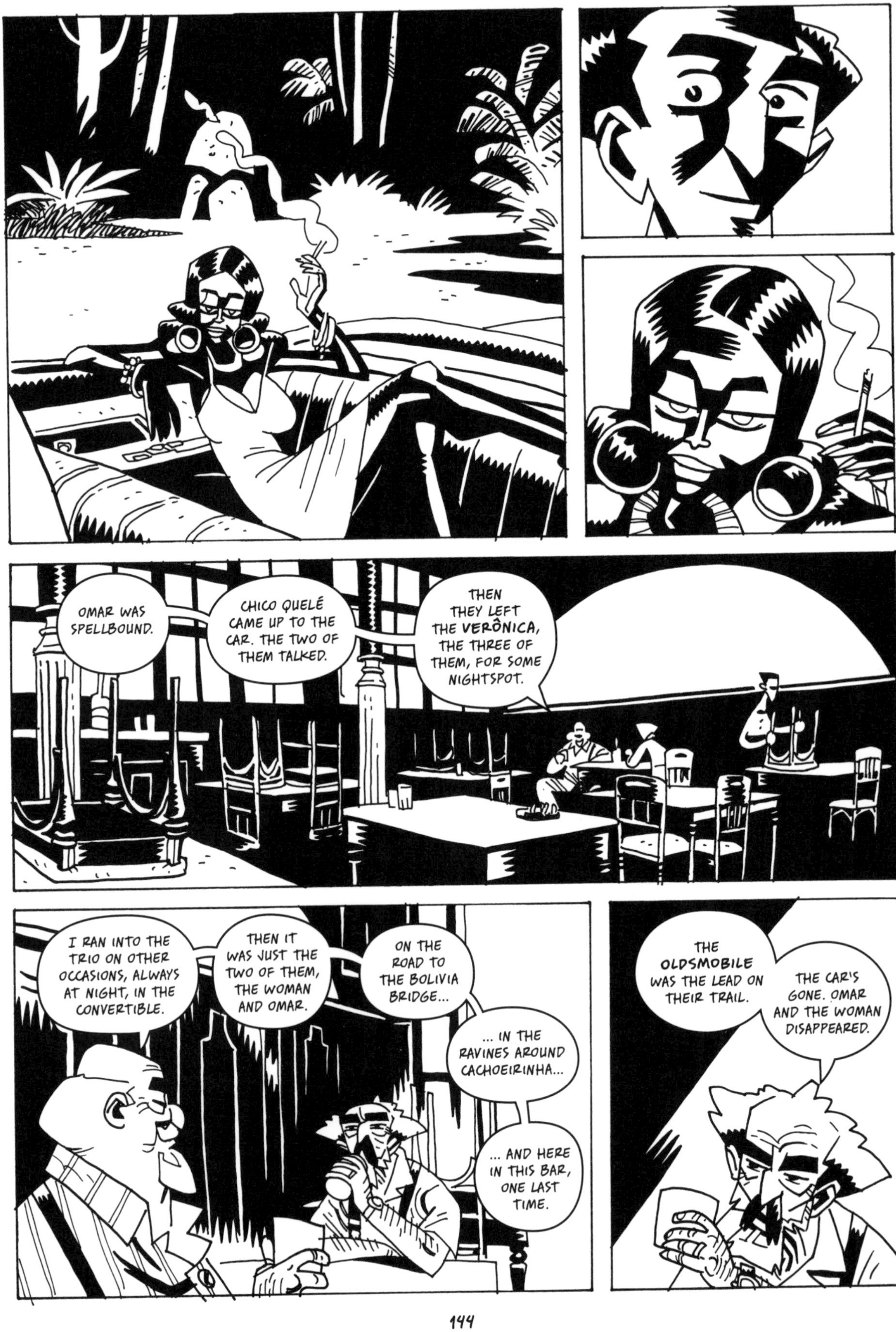
OMAR WAS SPELLBOUND.
CHICO QUELÉ CAME UP TO THE CAR. THE TWO OF THEM TALKED.
THEN THEY LEFT THE **VERÔNICA**, THE THREE OF THEM, FOR SOME NIGHTSPOT.
I RAN INTO THE TRIO ON OTHER OCCASIONS, ALWAYS AT NIGHT, IN THE CONVERTIBLE.
THEN IT WAS JUST THE TWO OF THEM, THE WOMAN AND OMAR.
ON THE ROAD TO THE BOLIVIA BRIDGE...
... IN THE RAVINES AROUND CACHOEIRINHA...
... AND HERE IN THIS BAR, ONE LAST TIME.
THE **OLDSMOBILE** WAS THE LEAD ON THEIR TRAIL.
THE CAR'S GONE. OMAR AND THE WOMAN DISAPPEARED.

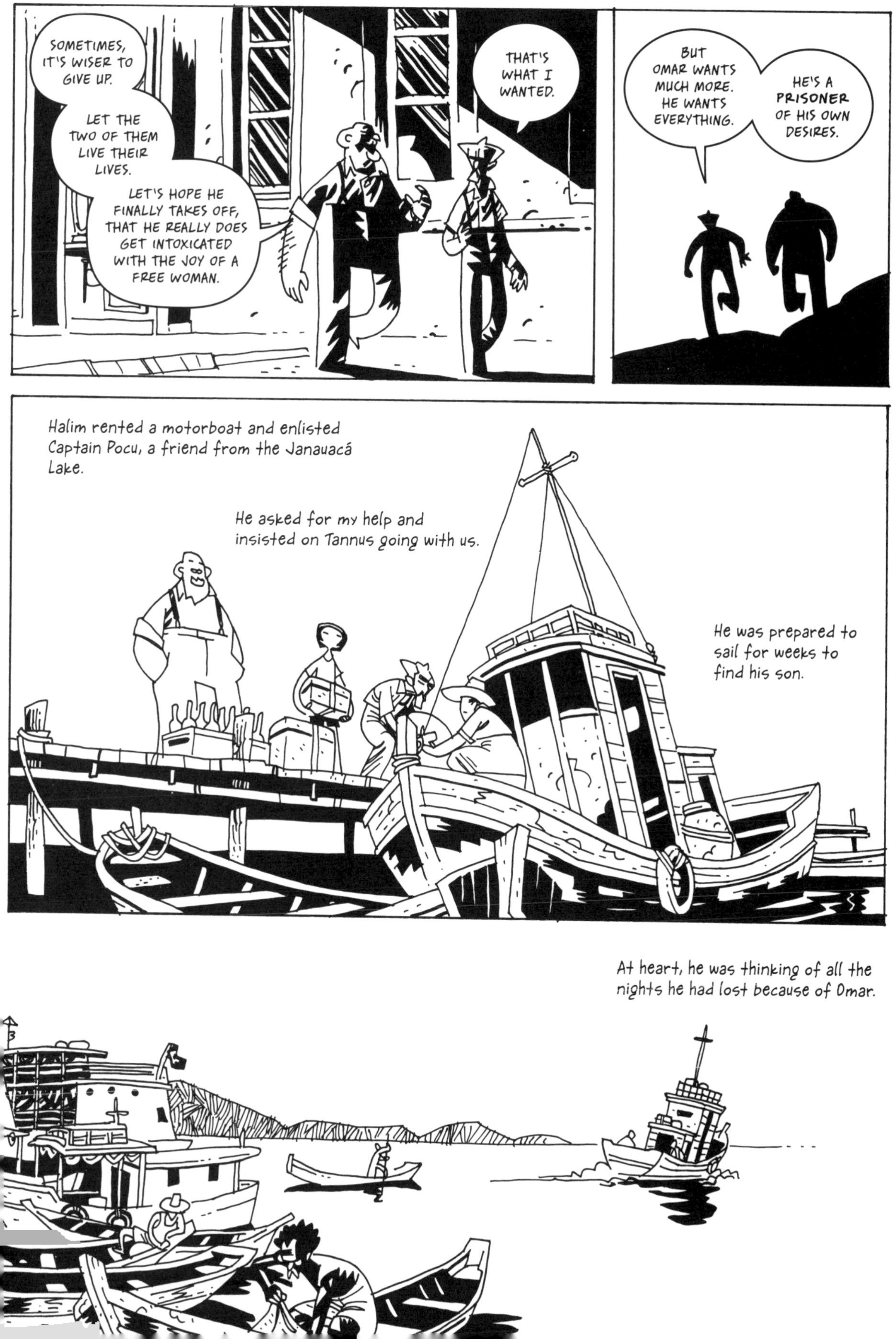
SOMETIMES, IT'S WISER TO GIVE UP.
LET THE TWO OF THEM LIVE THEIR LIVES.
LET'S HOPE HE FINALLY TAKES OFF, THAT HE REALLY DOES GET INTOXICATED WITH THE JOY OF A FREE WOMAN.
THAT'S WHAT I WANTED.
BUT OMAR WANTS MUCH MORE. HE WANTS EVERYTHING.
HE'S A **PRISONER** OF HIS OWN DESIRES.
Halim rented a motorboat and enlisted Captain Pocu, a friend from the Janauacá Lake.
He asked for my help and insisted on Tannus going with us.
He was prepared to sail for weeks to find his son.
At heart, he was thinking of all the nights he had lost because of Omar.

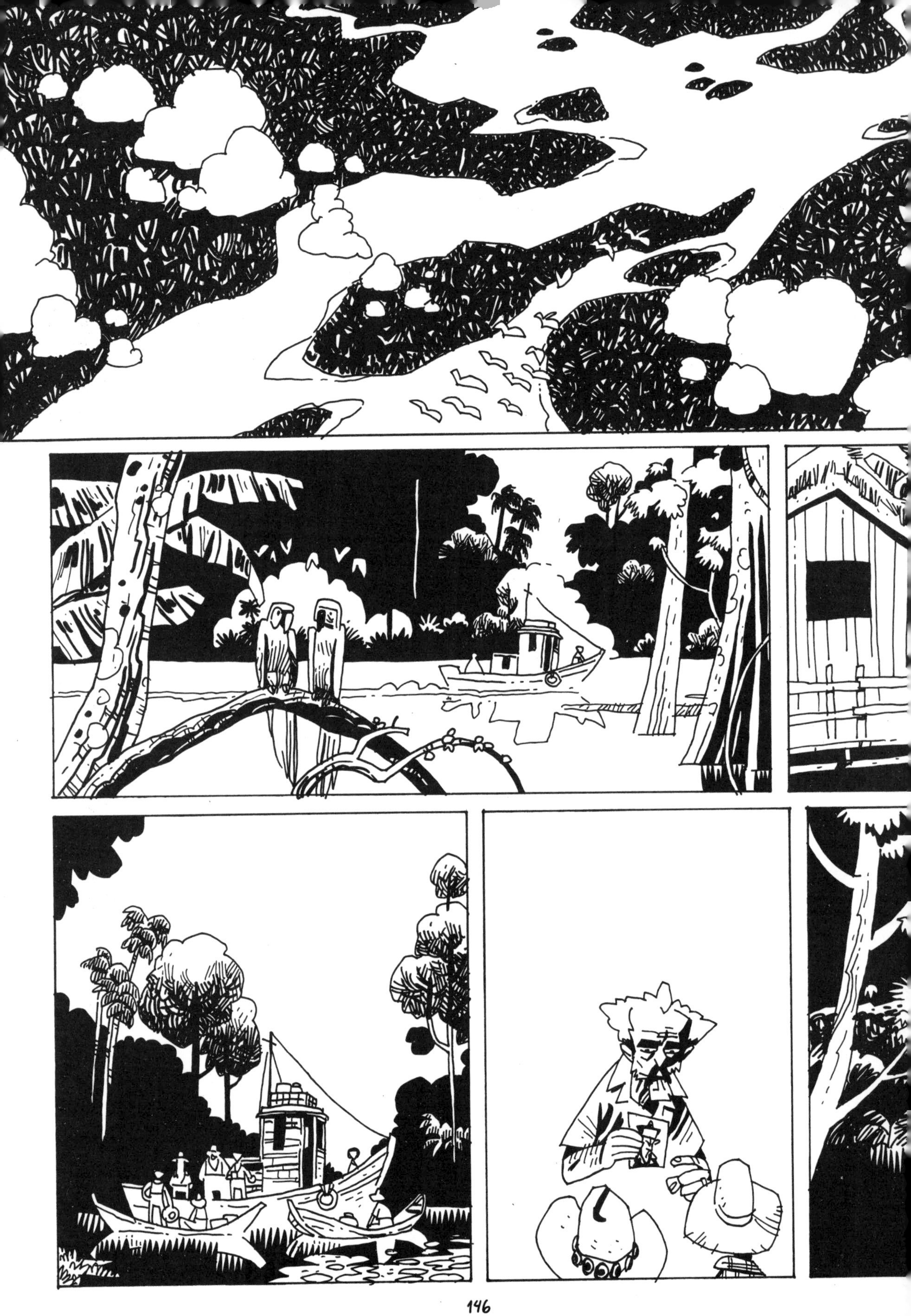

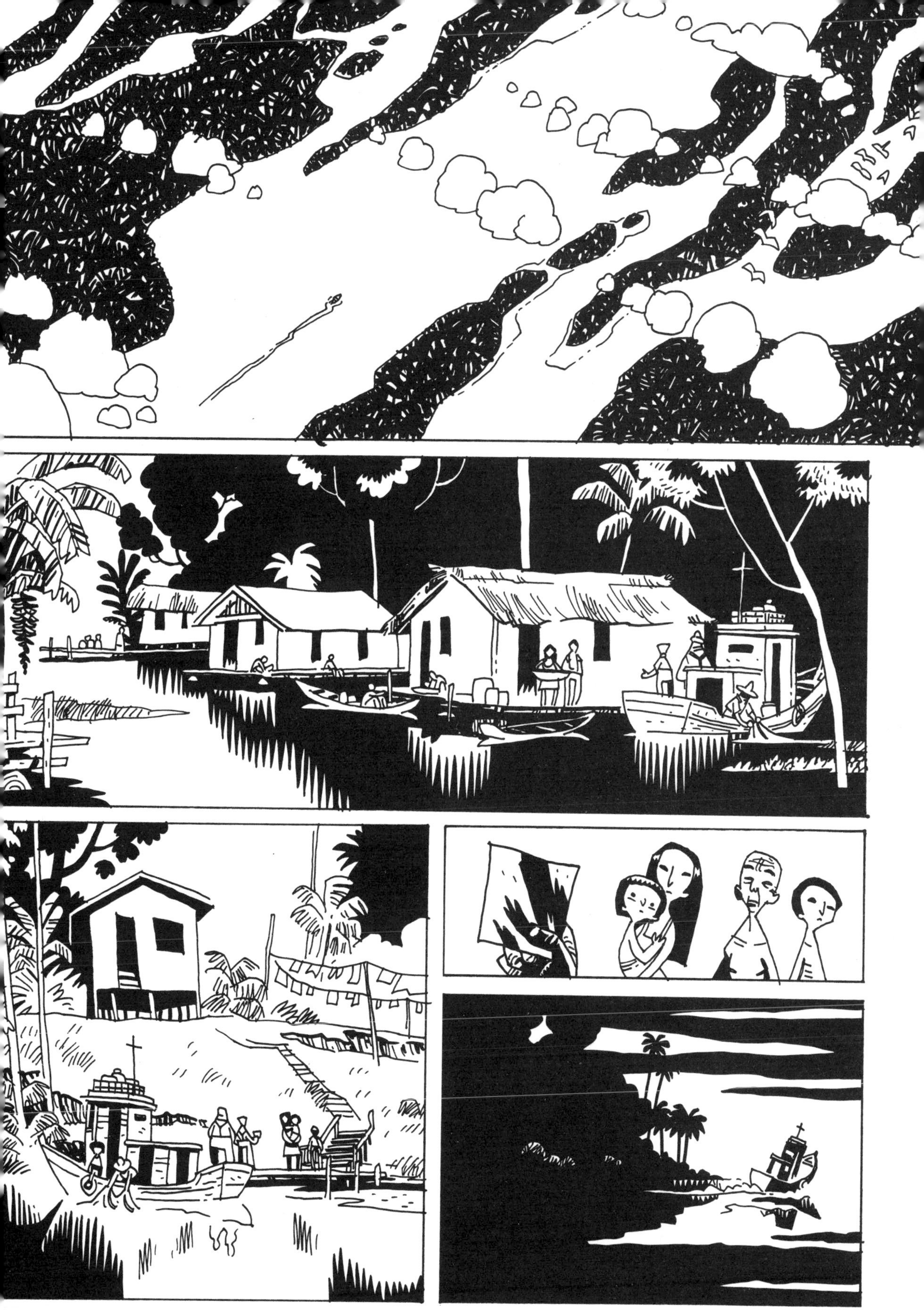

We spent weeks going around in circles. More than a month -- months. We lost track of what day of the week or what month it was.

MAYBE THE DOLPHIN HAS GOT THEM.

THEY MUST BE ENCHANTED, AT THE BOTTOM OF THE RIVER.

THEY'RE IN THE CLOUDS, HAVING A GOOD TIME UNDER A TREE...

... EATING FRIED FISH.

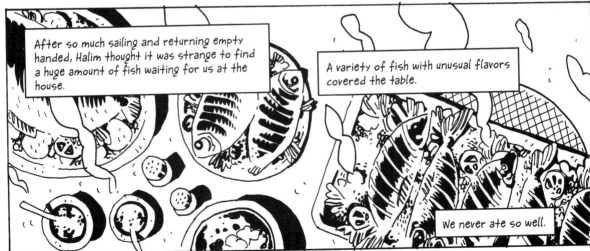

After so much sailing and returning empty handed, Halim thought it was strange to find a huge amount of fish waiting for us at the house.

A variety of fish with unusual flavors covered the table.

We never ate so well.

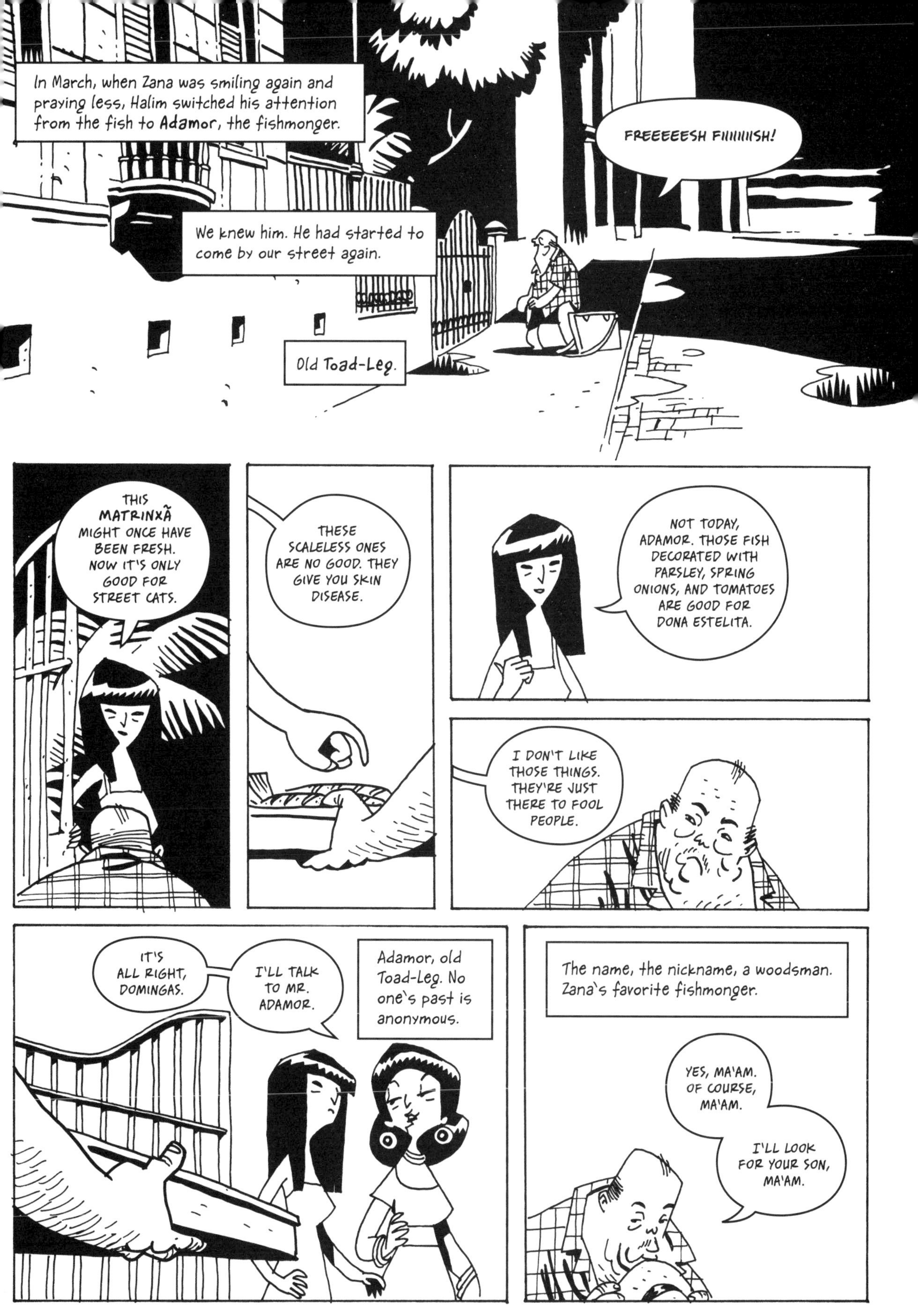

In March, when Zana was smiling again and praying less, Halim switched his attention from the fish to Adamor, the fishmonger.
FREEEEESH FIIIIIISH!
We knew him. He had started to come by our street again.
Old Toad-Leg.
THIS MATRINXÃ MIGHT ONCE HAVE BEEN FRESH. NOW IT'S ONLY GOOD FOR STREET CATS.
THESE SCALELESS ONES ARE NO GOOD. THEY GIVE YOU SKIN DISEASE.
NOT TODAY, ADAMOR. THOSE FISH DECORATED WITH PARSLEY, SPRING ONIONS, AND TOMATOES ARE GOOD FOR DONA ESTELITA.
I DON'T LIKE THOSE THINGS. THEY'RE JUST THERE TO FOOL PEOPLE.
IT'S ALL RIGHT, DOMINGAS.
I'LL TALK TO MR. ADAMOR.
Adamor, old Toad-Leg. No one's past is anonymous.
The name, the nickname, a woodsman. Zana's favorite fishmonger.
YES, MA'AM. OF COURSE, MA'AM.
I'LL LOOK FOR YOUR SON, MA'AM.

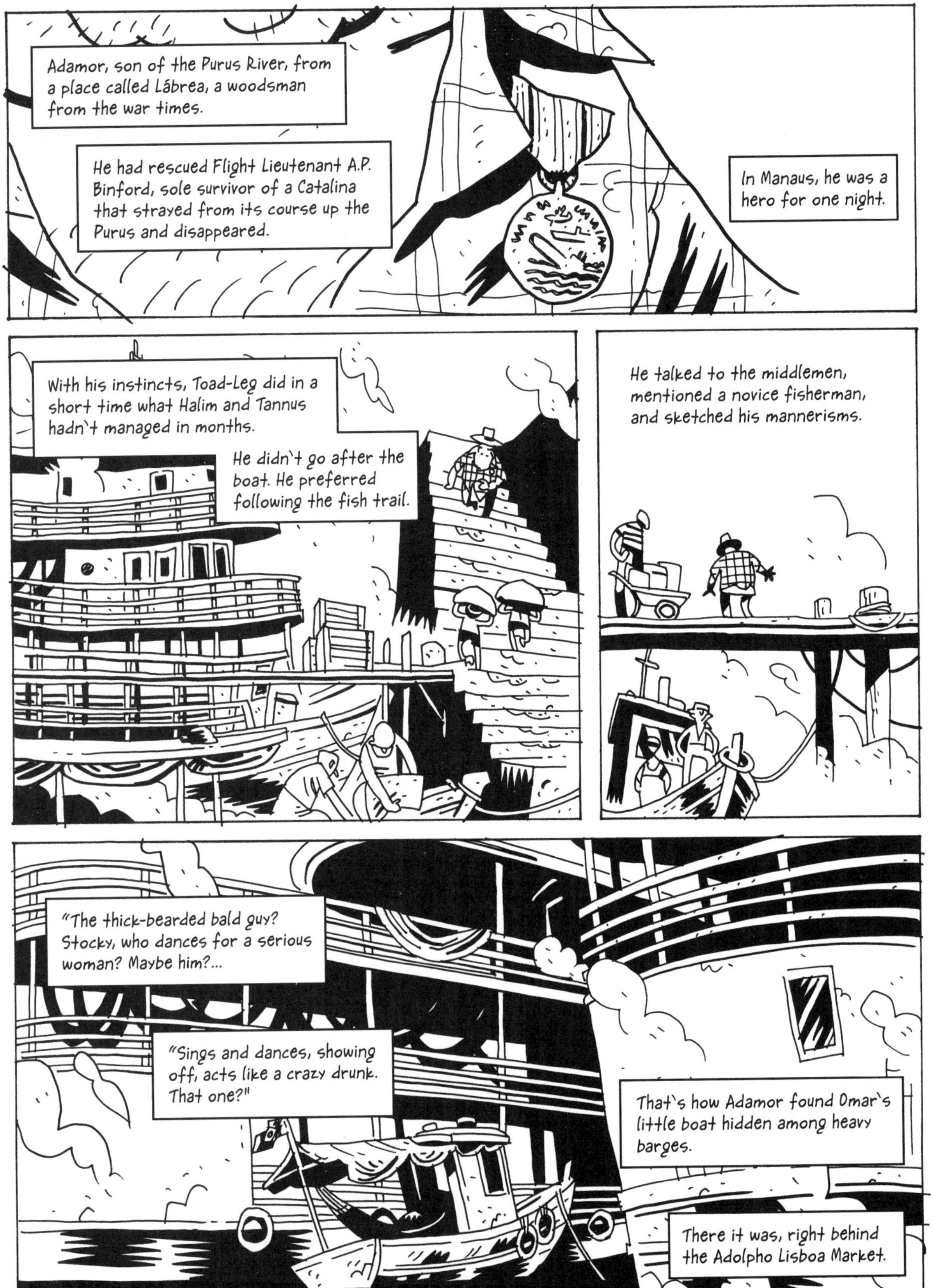
Adamor, son of the Purus River, from a place called Lábrea, a woodsman from the war times.
He had rescued Flight Lieutenant A.P. Binford, sole survivor of a Catalina that strayed from its course up the Purus and disappeared.
In Manaus, he was a hero for one night.
With his instincts, Toad-Leg did in a short time what Halim and Tannus hadn't managed in months.
He didn't go after the boat. He preferred following the fish trail.
He talked to the middlemen, mentioned a novice fisherman, and sketched his mannerisms.
"The thick-bearded bald guy? Stocky, who dances for a serious woman? Maybe him?...
"Sings and dances, showing off, acts like a crazy drunk. That one?"
That's how Adamor found Omar's little boat hidden among heavy barges.
There it was, right behind the Adolpho Lisboa Market.

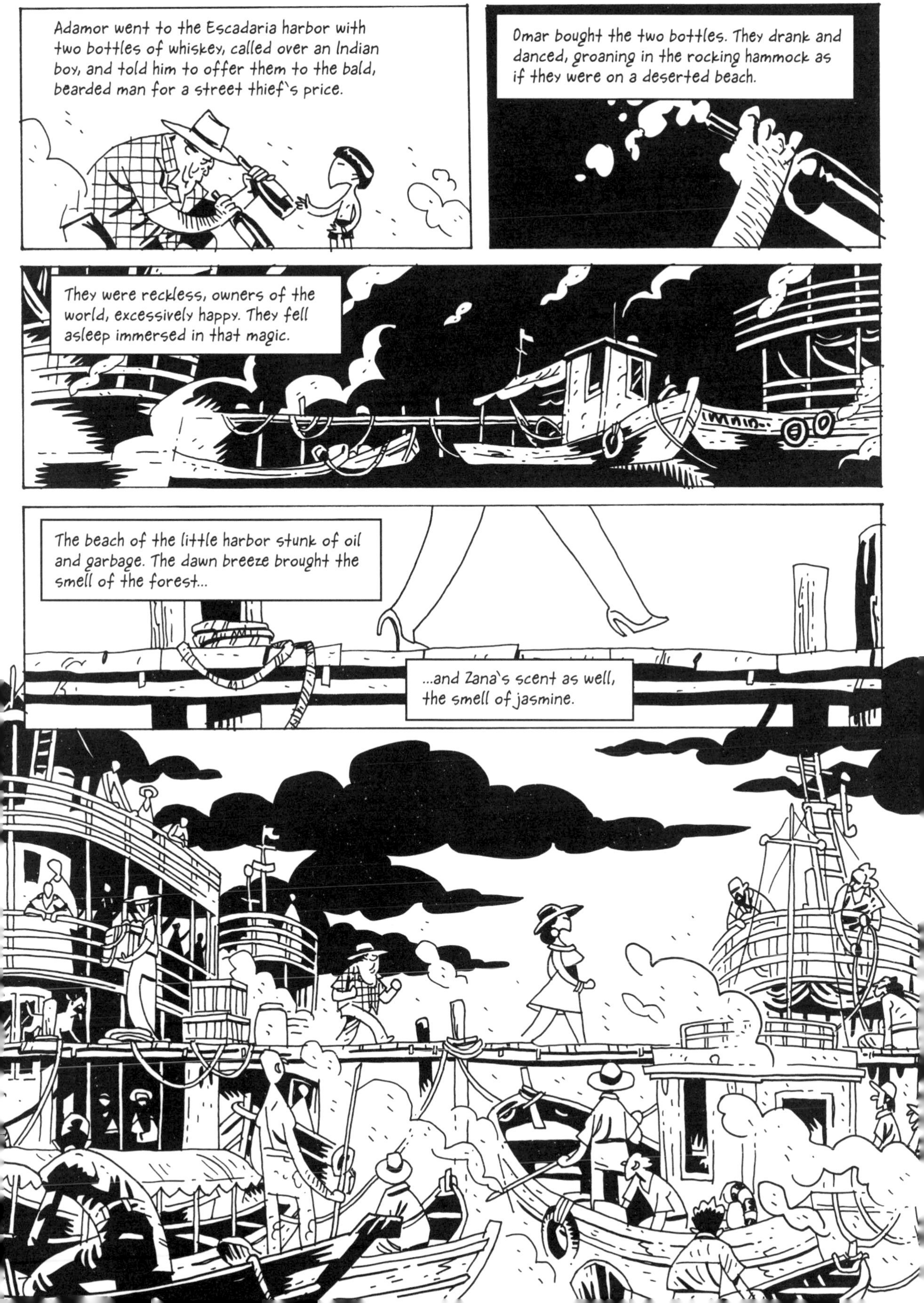
Adamor went to the Escadaria harbor with two bottles of whiskey, called over an Indian boy, and told him to offer them to the bald, bearded man for a street thief's price.
Omar bought the two bottles. They drank and danced, groaning in the rocking hammock as if they were on a deserted beach.
They were reckless, owners of the world, excessively happy. They fell asleep immersed in that magic.
The beach of the little harbor stunk of oil and garbage. The dawn breeze brought the smell of the forest...
...and Zana's scent as well, the smell of jasmine.

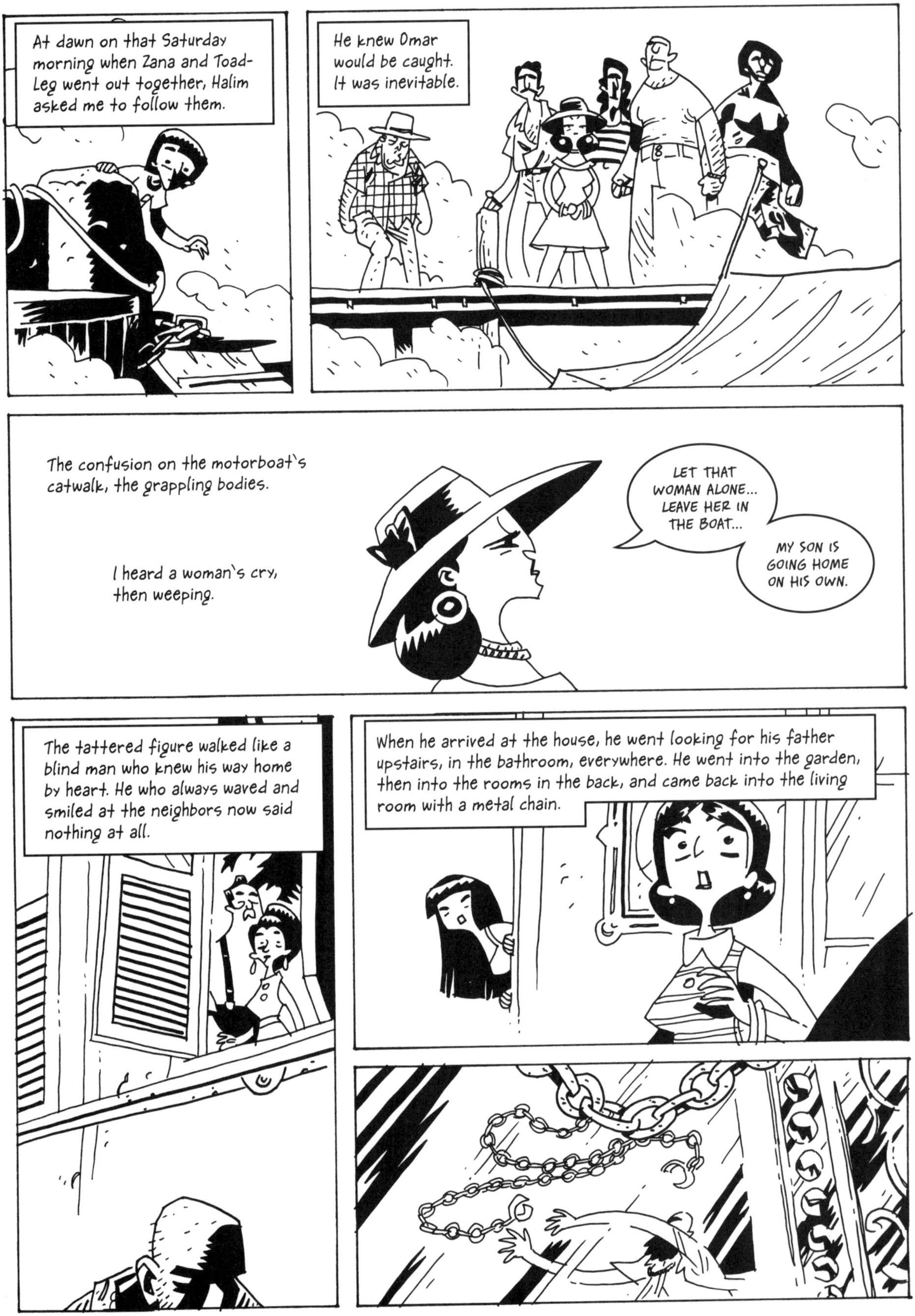
At dawn on that Saturday morning when Zana and Toad-Leg went out together, Halim asked me to follow them.
He knew Omar would be caught. It was inevitable.
The confusion on the motorboat's catwalk, the grappling bodies.
I heard a woman's cry, then weeping.
LET THAT WOMAN ALONE... LEAVE HER IN THE BOAT...
MY SON IS GOING HOME ON HIS OWN.
The tattered figure walked like a blind man who knew his way home by heart. He who always waved and smiled at the neighbors now said nothing at all.
When he arrived at the house, he went looking for his father upstairs, in the bathroom, everywhere. He went into the garden, then into the rooms in the back, and came back into the living room with a metal chain.

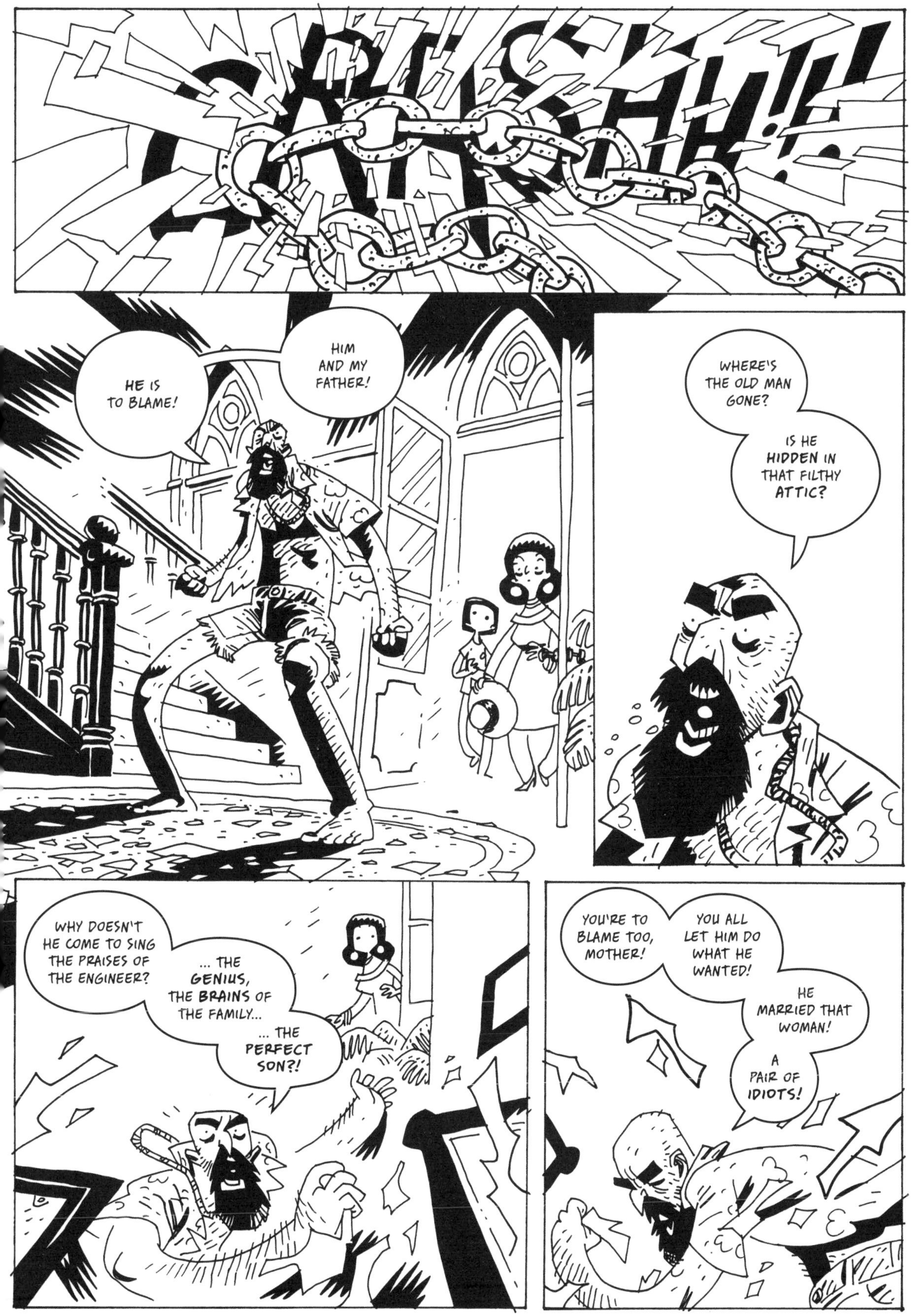
CRASHH!!
HE IS TO BLAME!
HIM AND MY FATHER!
WHERE'S THE OLD MAN GONE?
IS HE HIDDEN IN THAT FILTHY ATTIC?
WHY DOESN'T HE COME TO SING THE PRAISES OF THE ENGINEER?
... THE GENIUS, THE BRAINS OF THE FAMILY...
... THE PERFECT SON?!
YOU'RE TO BLAME TOO, MOTHER!
YOU ALL LET HIM DO WHAT HE WANTED!
HE MARRIED THAT WOMAN!
A PAIR OF IDIOTS!

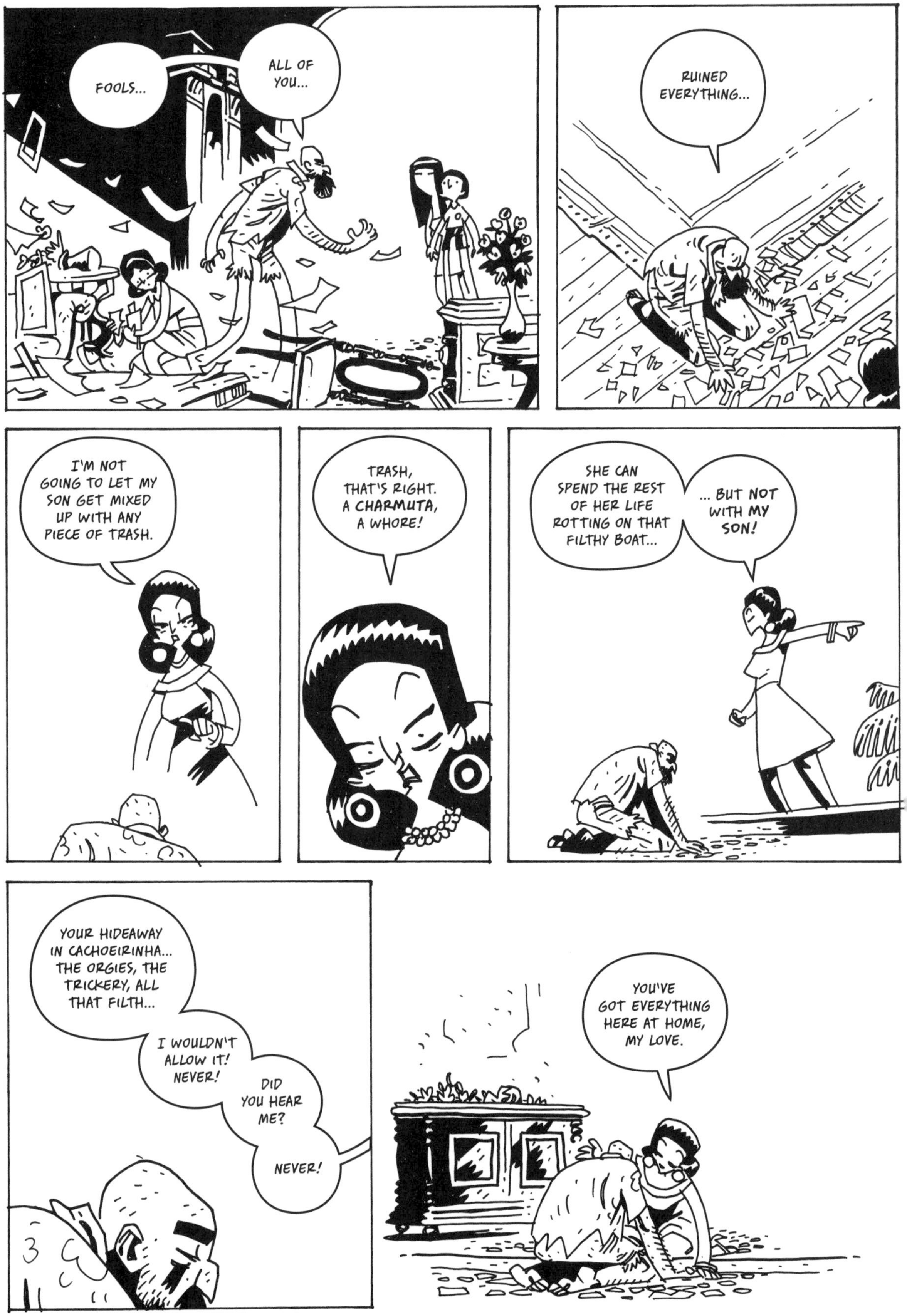
FOOLS...
ALL OF YOU...
RUINED EVERYTHING...
I'M NOT GOING TO LET MY SON GET MIXED UP WITH ANY PIECE OF TRASH.
TRASH, THAT'S RIGHT. A **CHARMUTA**, A WHORE!
SHE CAN SPEND THE REST OF HER LIFE ROTTING ON THAT FILTHY BOAT...
... BUT **NOT** WITH **MY SON**!
YOUR HIDEAWAY IN CACHOEIRINHA... THE ORGIES, THE TRICKERY, ALL THAT FILTH...
I WOULDN'T ALLOW IT! NEVER!
DID YOU HEAR ME?
NEVER!
YOU'VE GOT EVERYTHING HERE AT HOME, MY LOVE.

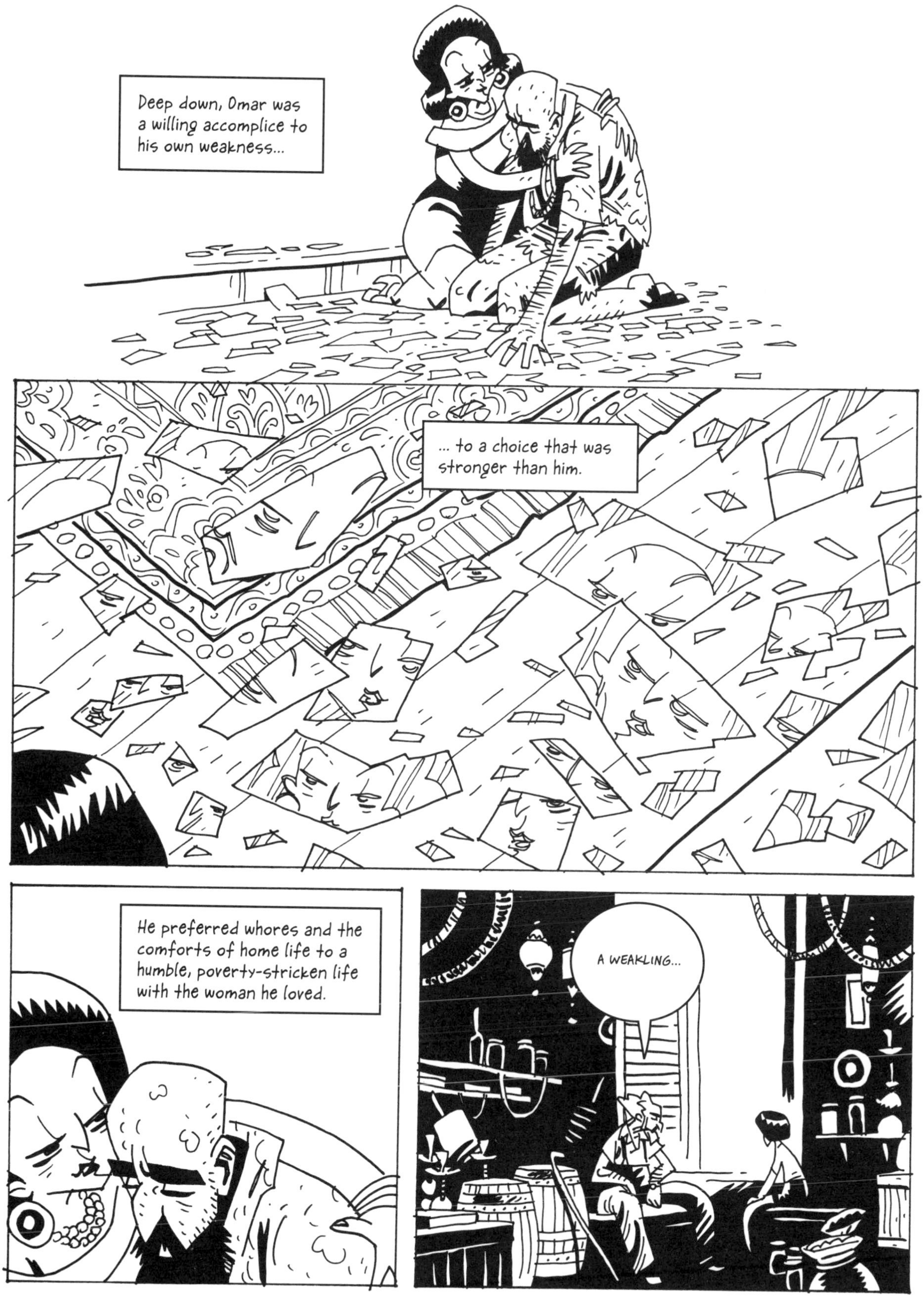
Deep down, Omar was a willing accomplice to his own weakness...
... to a choice that was stronger than him.
He preferred whores and the comforts of home life to a humble, poverty-stricken life with the woman he loved.
A WEAKLING...

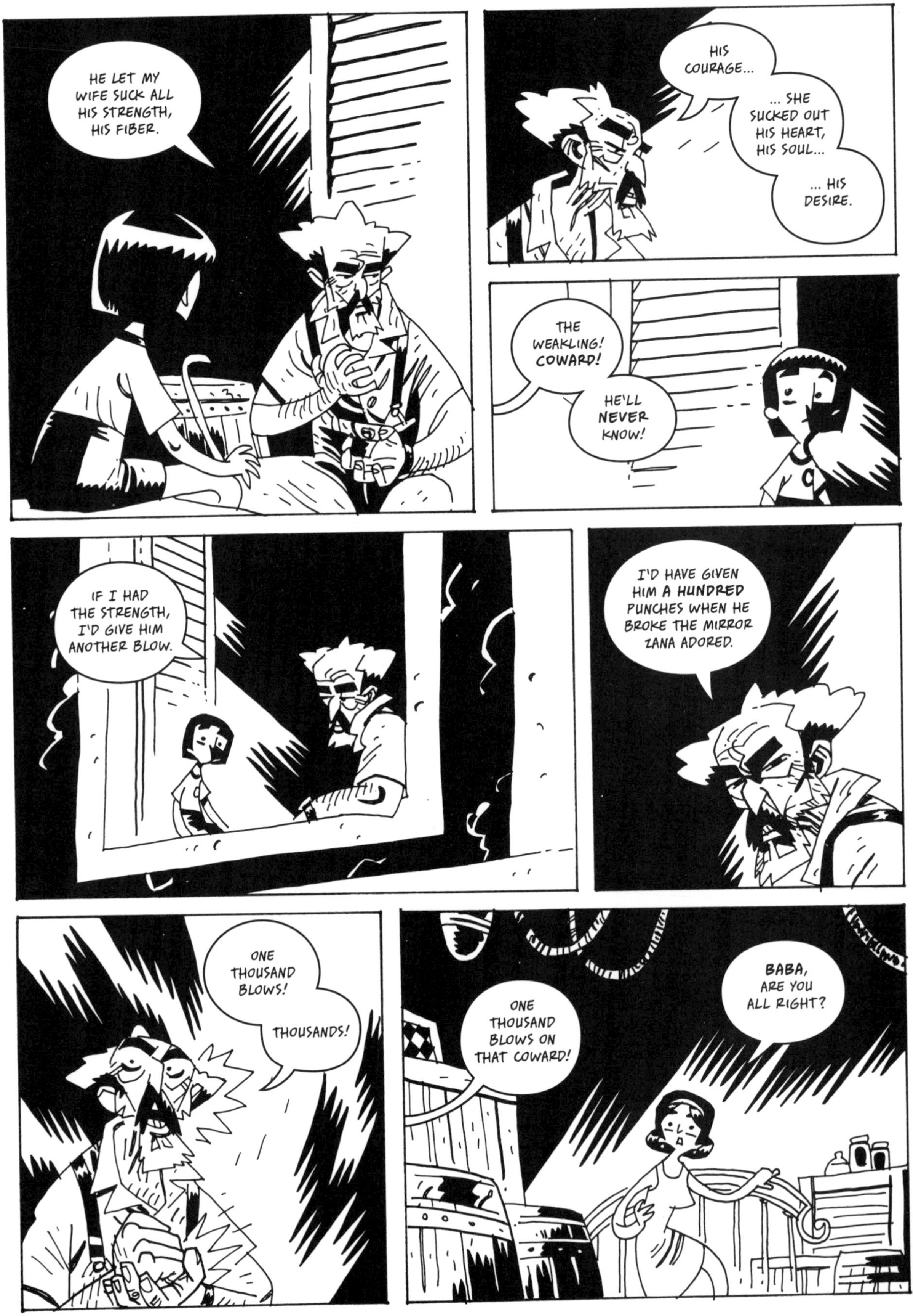
HE LET MY WIFE SUCK ALL HIS STRENGTH, HIS FIBER.
HIS COURAGE...
... SHE SUCKED OUT HIS HEART, HIS SOUL...
... HIS DESIRE.
THE WEAKLING! COWARD!
HE'LL NEVER KNOW!
IF I HAD THE STRENGTH, I'D GIVE HIM ANOTHER BLOW.
I'D HAVE GIVEN HIM A HUNDRED PUNCHES WHEN HE BROKE THE MIRROR ZANA ADORED.
ONE THOUSAND BLOWS!
THOUSANDS!
ONE THOUSAND BLOWS ON THAT COWARD!
BABA, ARE YOU ALL RIGHT?

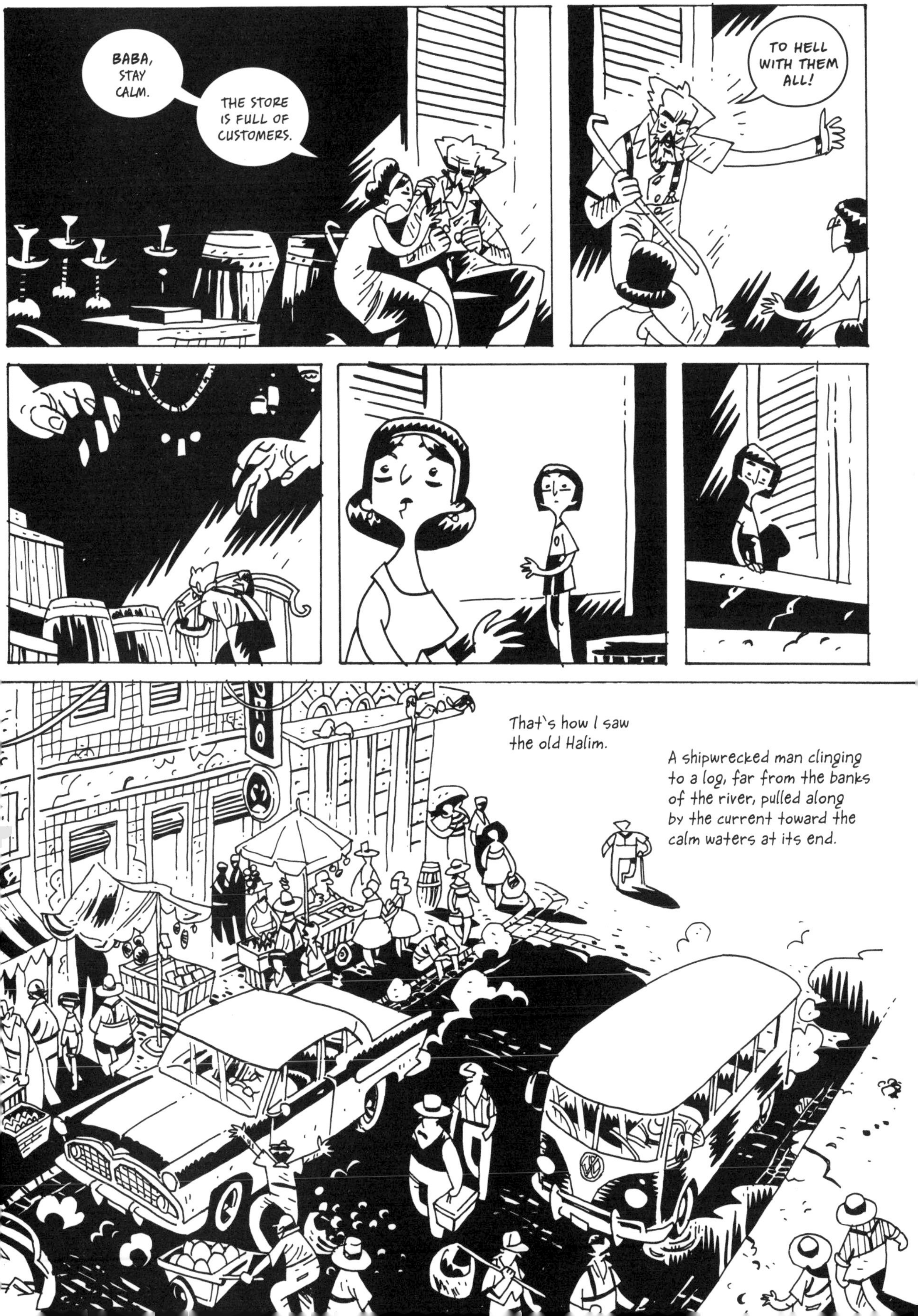
BABA, STAY CALM.
THE STORE IS FULL OF CUSTOMERS.
TO HELL WITH THEM ALL!
That's how I saw the old Halim.
A shipwrecked man clinging to a log, far from the banks of the river, pulled along by the current toward the calm waters at its end.

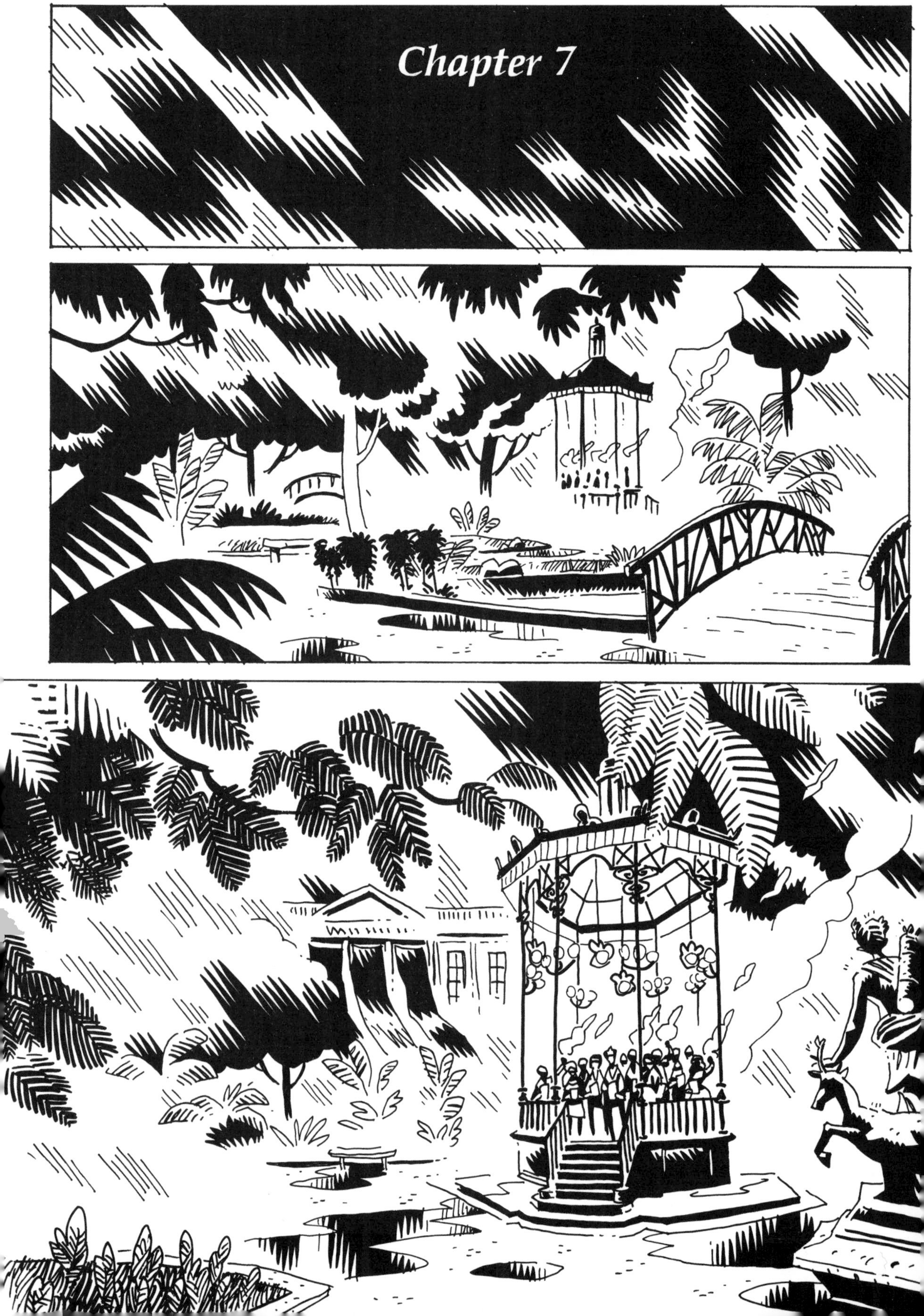
Chapter 7

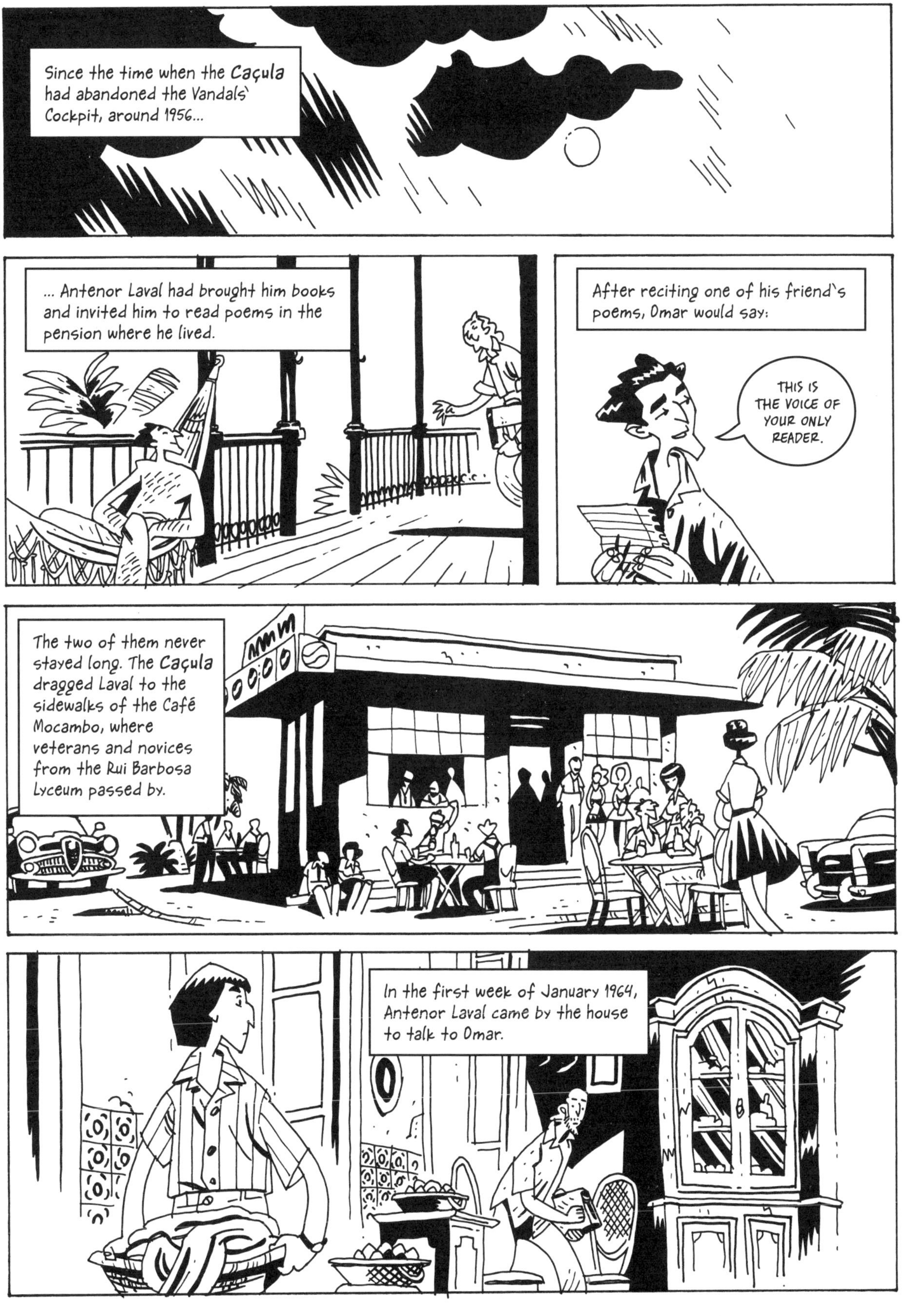
Since the time when the Caçula had abandoned the Vandals' Cockpit, around 1956...
... Antenor Laval had brought him books and invited him to read poems in the pension where he lived.
After reciting one of his friend's poems, Omar would say:
THIS IS THE VOICE OF YOUR ONLY READER.
The two of them never stayed long. The Caçula dragged Laval to the sidewalks of the Café Mocambo, where veterans and novices from the Rui Barbosa Lyceum passed by.
In the first week of January 1964, Antenor Laval came by the house to talk to Omar.

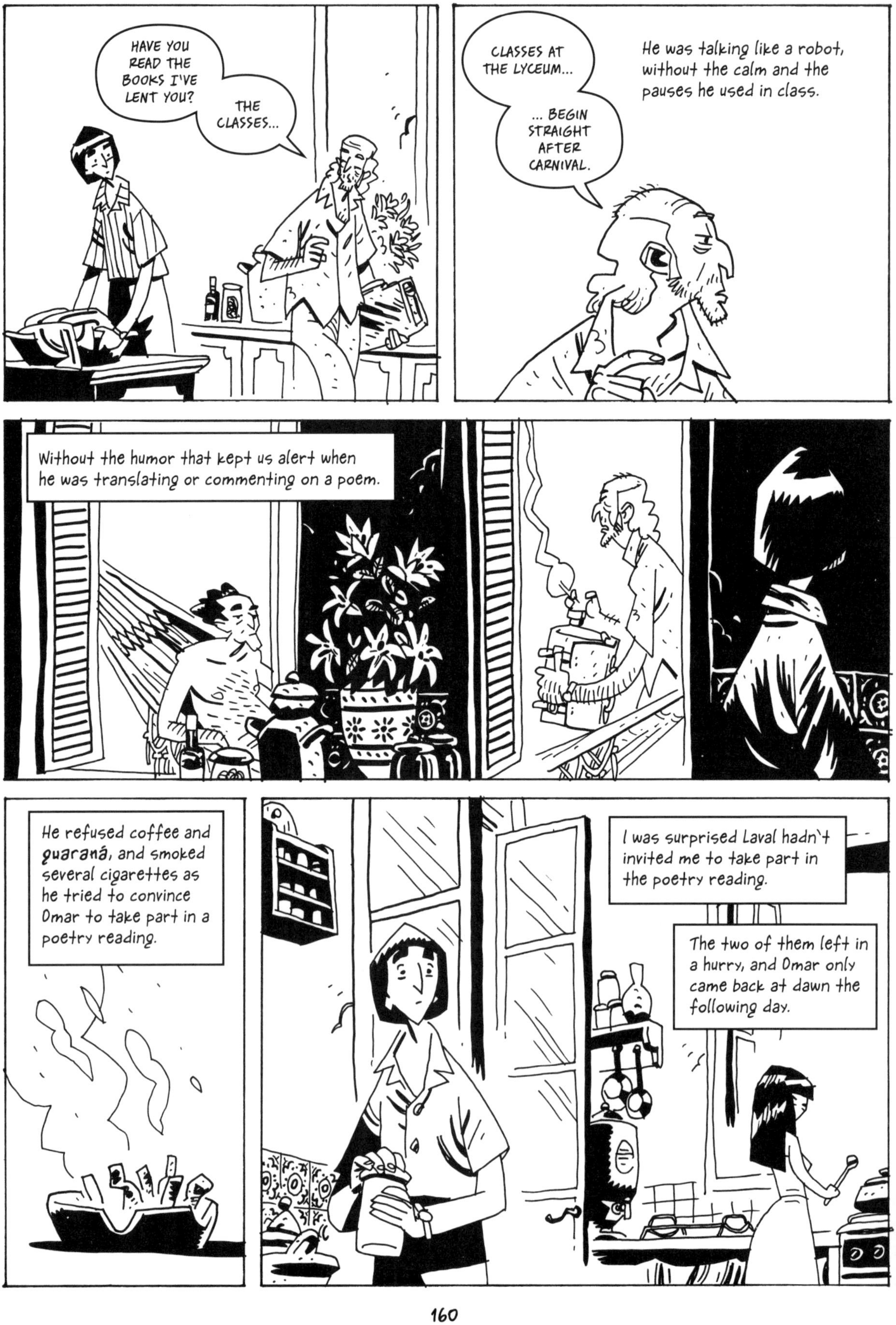
HAVE YOU READ THE BOOKS I'VE LENT YOU?
THE CLASSES...
CLASSES AT THE LYCEUM...
... BEGIN STRAIGHT AFTER CARNIVAL.
He was talking like a robot, without the calm and the pauses he used in class.
Without the humor that kept us alert when he was translating or commenting on a poem.
He refused coffee and guaraná, and smoked several cigarettes as he tried to convince Omar to take part in a poetry reading.
I was surprised Laval hadn't invited me to take part in the poetry reading.
The two of them left in a hurry, and Omar only came back at dawn the following day.

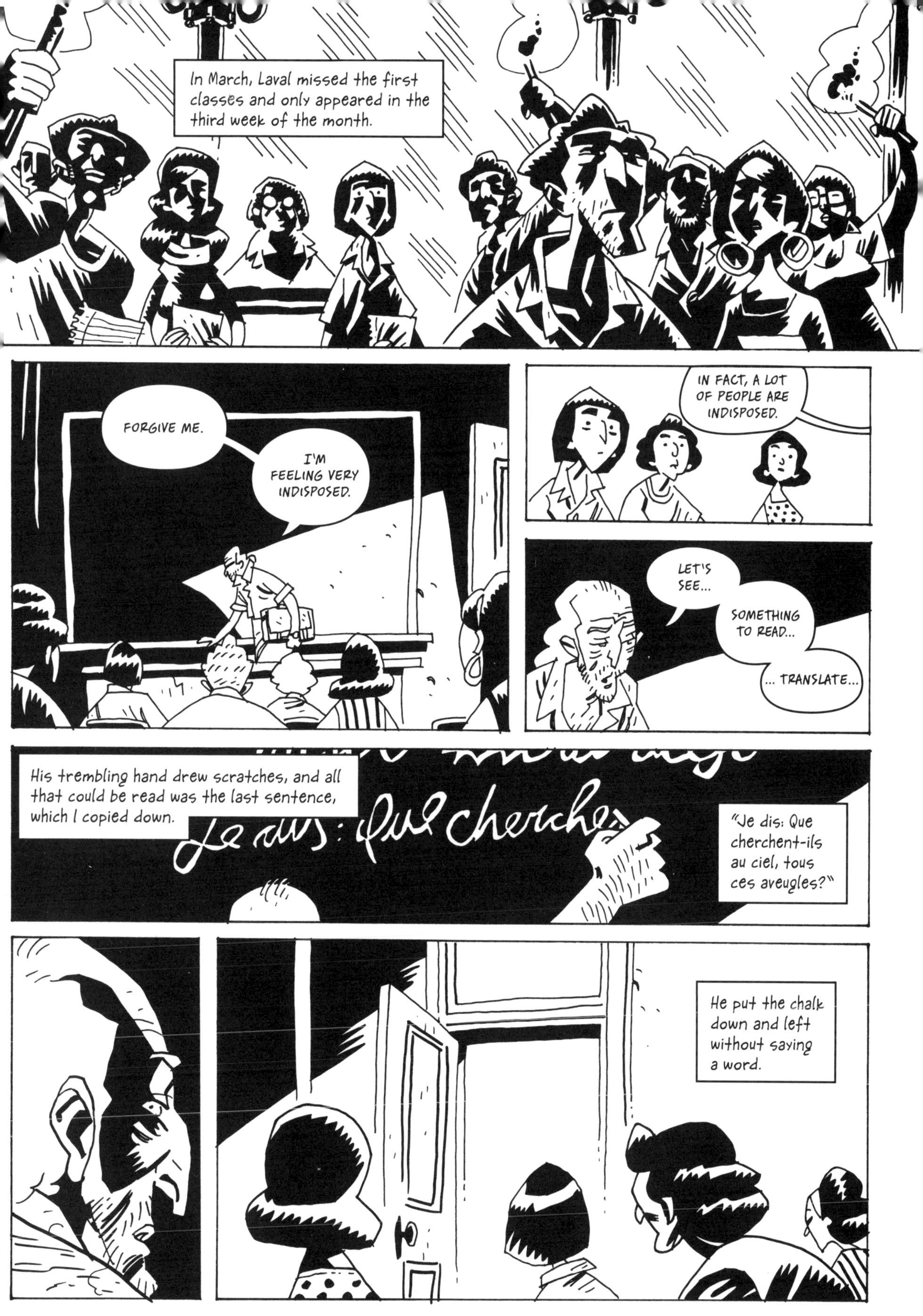
In March, Laval missed the first classes and only appeared in the third week of the month.
FORGIVE ME.
I'M FEELING VERY INDISPOSED.
IN FACT, A LOT OF PEOPLE ARE INDISPOSED.
LET'S SEE...
SOMETHING TO READ...
... TRANSLATE...
His trembling hand drew scratches, and all that could be read was the last sentence, which I copied down.
"Je dis: Que cherchent-ils au ciel, tous ces aveugles?"
He put the chalk down and left without saying a word.

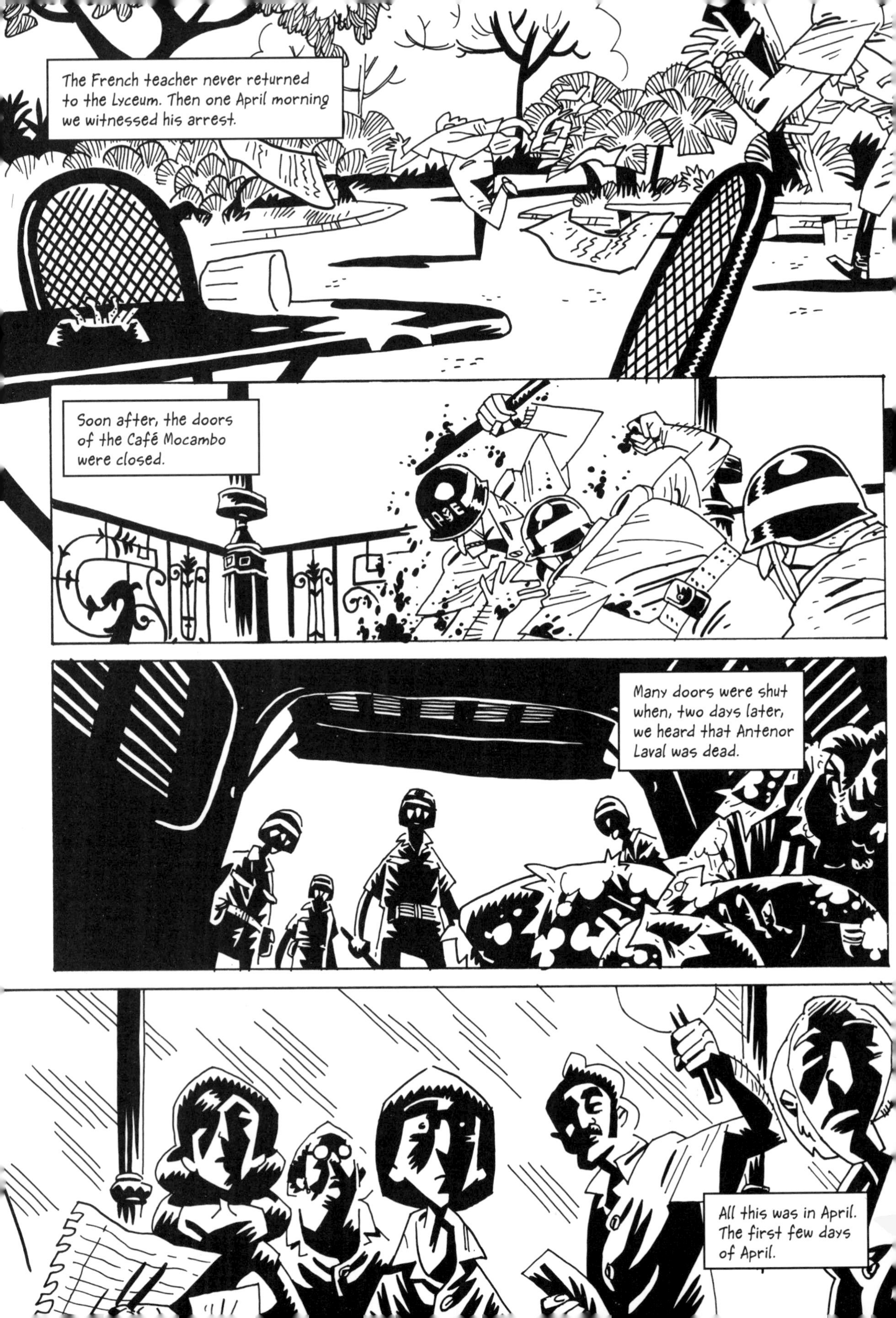
The French teacher never returned to the Lyceum. Then one April morning we witnessed his arrest.
Soon after, the doors of the Café Mocambo were closed.
Many doors were shut when, two days later, we heard that Antenor Laval was dead.
All this was in April. The first few days of April.

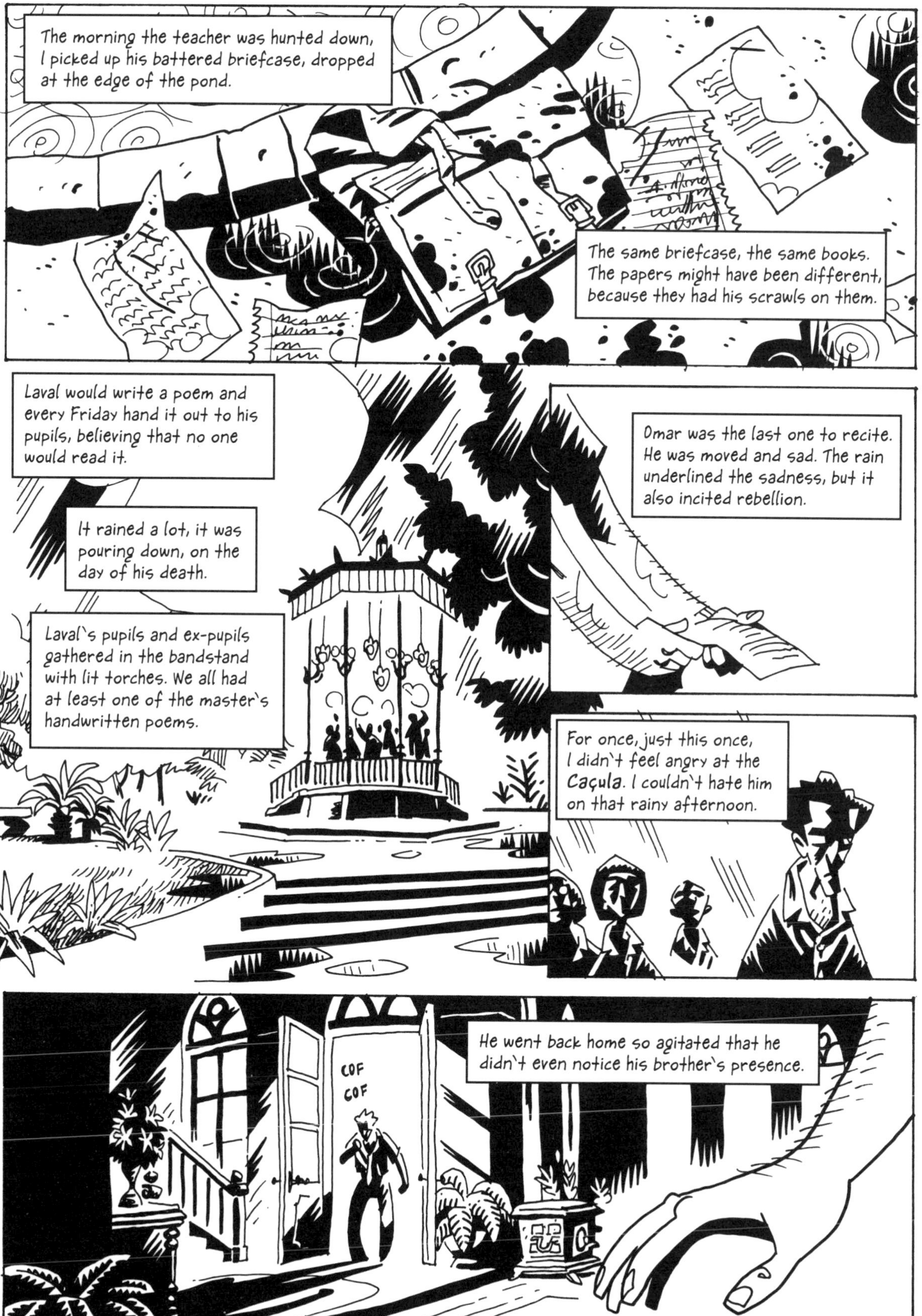

The morning the teacher was hunted down, I picked up his battered briefcase, dropped at the edge of the pond.
The same briefcase, the same books. The papers might have been different, because they had his scrawls on them.
Laval would write a poem and every Friday hand it out to his pupils, believing that no one would read it.
It rained a lot, it was pouring down, on the day of his death.
Laval's pupils and ex-pupils gathered in the bandstand with lit torches. We all had at least one of the master's handwritten poems.
Omar was the last one to recite. He was moved and sad. The rain underlined the sadness, but it also incited rebellion.
For once, just this once, I didn't feel angry at the **Caçula**. I couldn't hate him on that rainy afternoon.
He went back home so agitated that he didn't even notice his brother's presence.
COF
COF

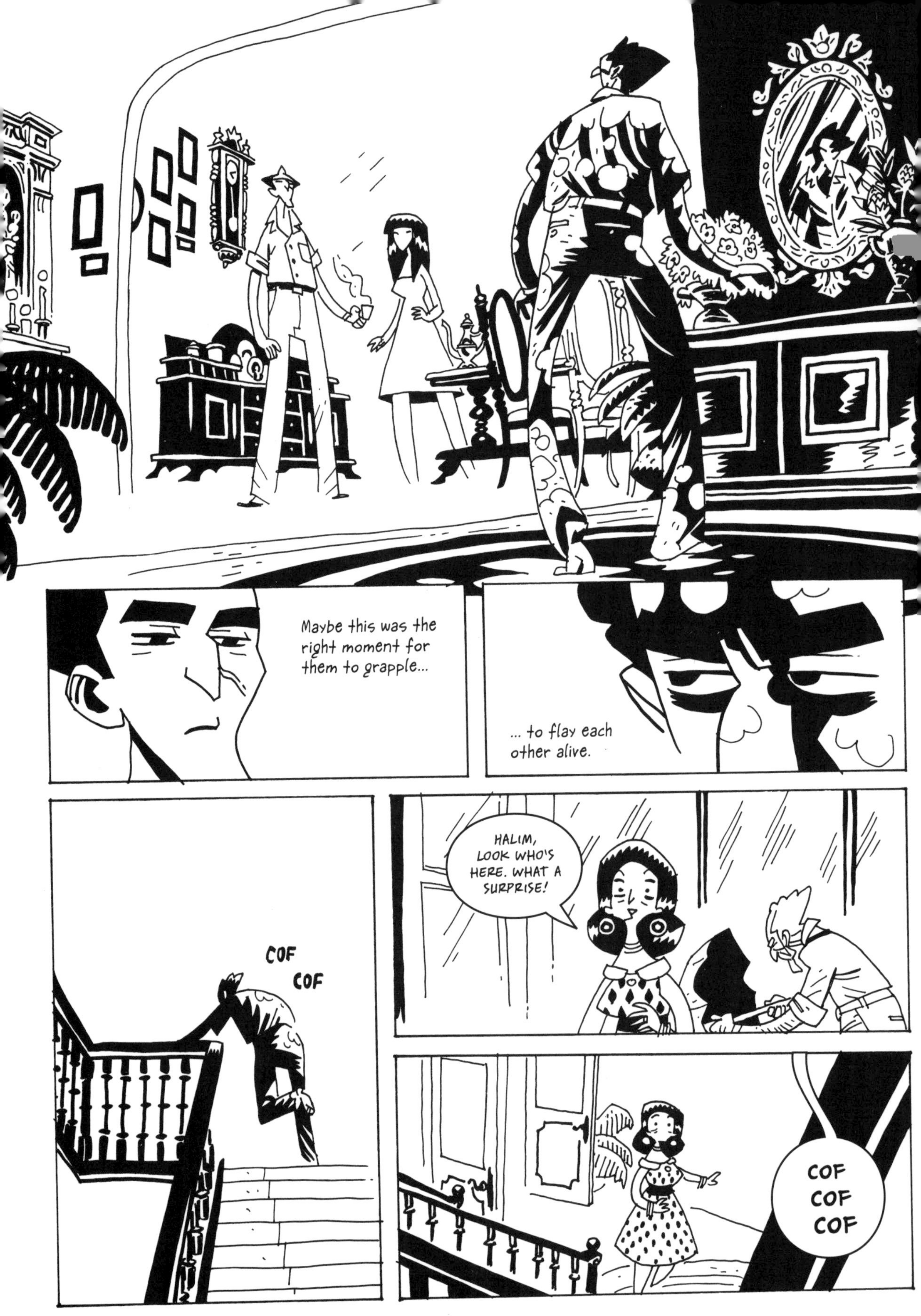

Maybe this was the right moment for them to grapple...
... to flay each other alive.
COF
COF
HALIM, LOOK WHO'S HERE. WHAT A SURPRISE!
COF COF COF

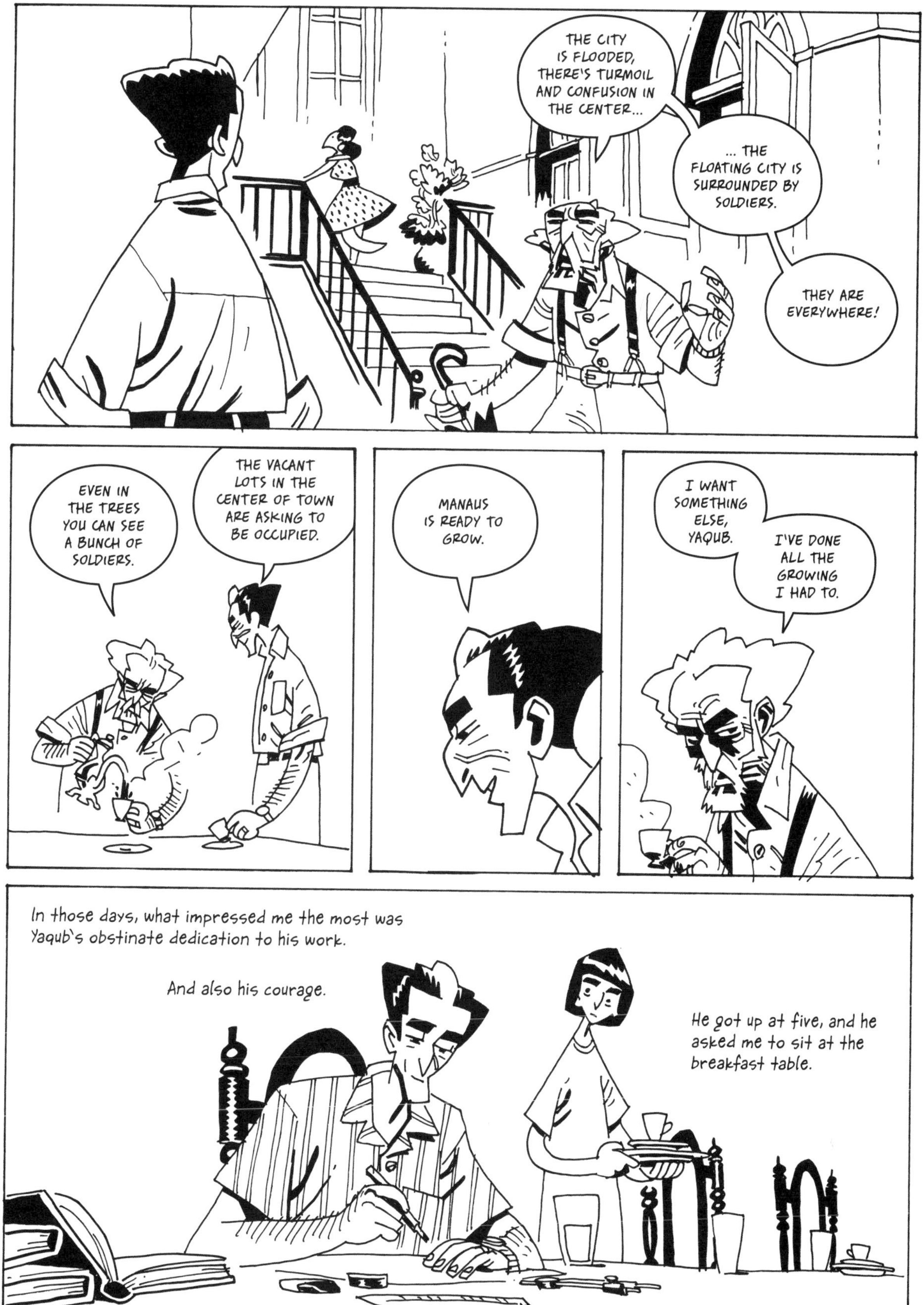
THE CITY IS FLOODED, THERE'S TURMOIL AND CONFUSION IN THE CENTER...
... THE FLOATING CITY IS SURROUNDED BY SOLDIERS.
THEY ARE EVERYWHERE!
EVEN IN THE TREES YOU CAN SEE A BUNCH OF SOLDIERS.
THE VACANT LOTS IN THE CENTER OF TOWN ARE ASKING TO BE OCCUPIED.
MANAUS IS READY TO GROW.
I WANT SOMETHING ELSE, YAQUB.
I'VE DONE ALL THE GROWING I HAD TO.
In those days, what impressed me the most was Yaqub's obstinate dedication to his work.
And also his courage.
He got up at five, and he asked me to sit at the breakfast table.

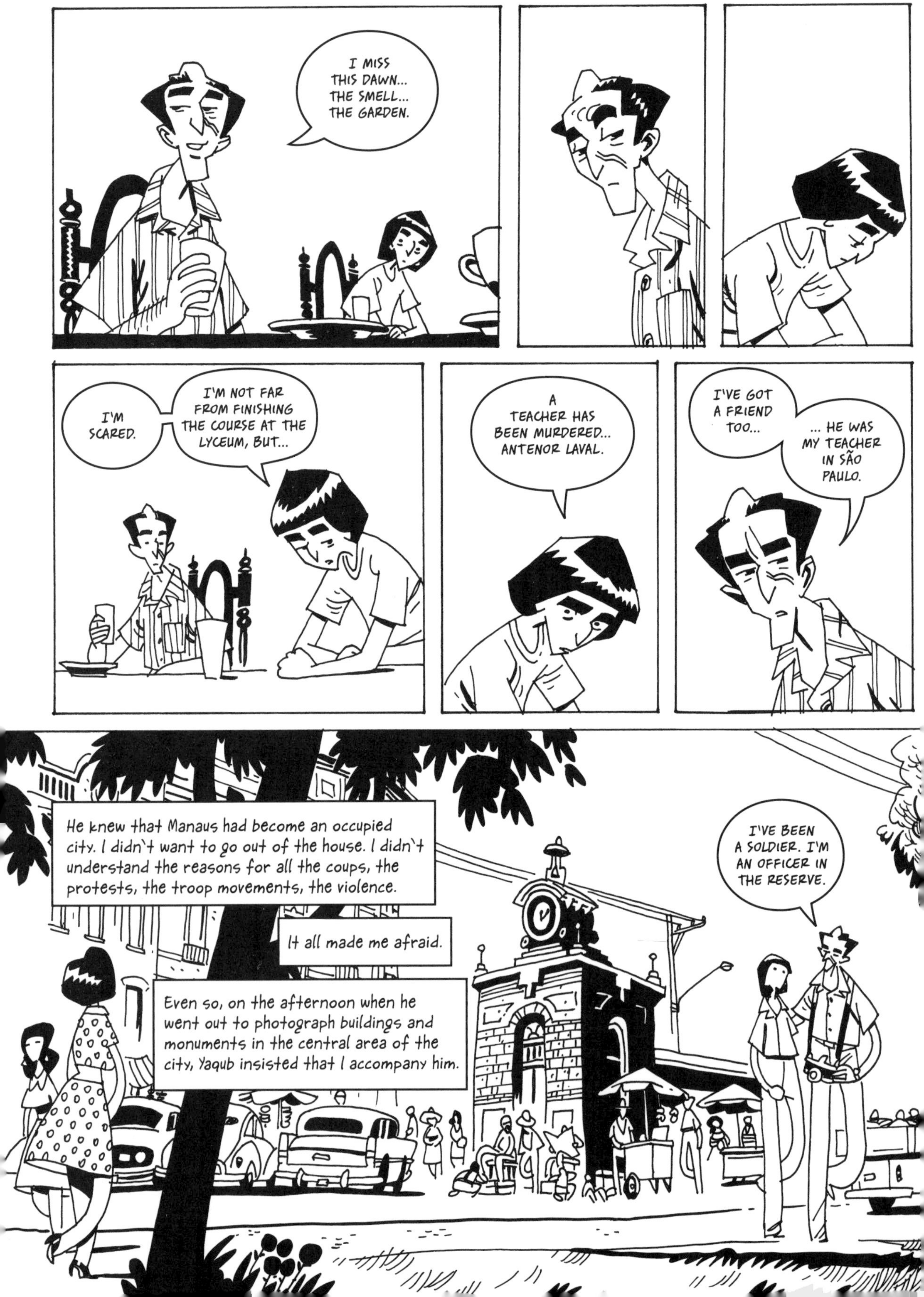
I MISS THIS DAWN... THE SMELL... THE GARDEN.
I'M SCARED.
I'M NOT FAR FROM FINISHING THE COURSE AT THE LYCEUM, BUT...
A TEACHER HAS BEEN MURDERED... ANTENOR LAVAL.
I'VE GOT A FRIEND TOO...
... HE WAS MY TEACHER IN SÃO PAULO.
He knew that Manaus had become an occupied city. I didn't want to go out of the house. I didn't understand the reasons for all the coups, the protests, the troop movements, the violence.
It all made me afraid.
Even so, on the afternoon when he went out to photograph buildings and monuments in the central area of the city, Yaqub insisted that I accompany him.
I'VE BEEN A SOLDIER. I'M AN OFFICER IN THE RESERVE.

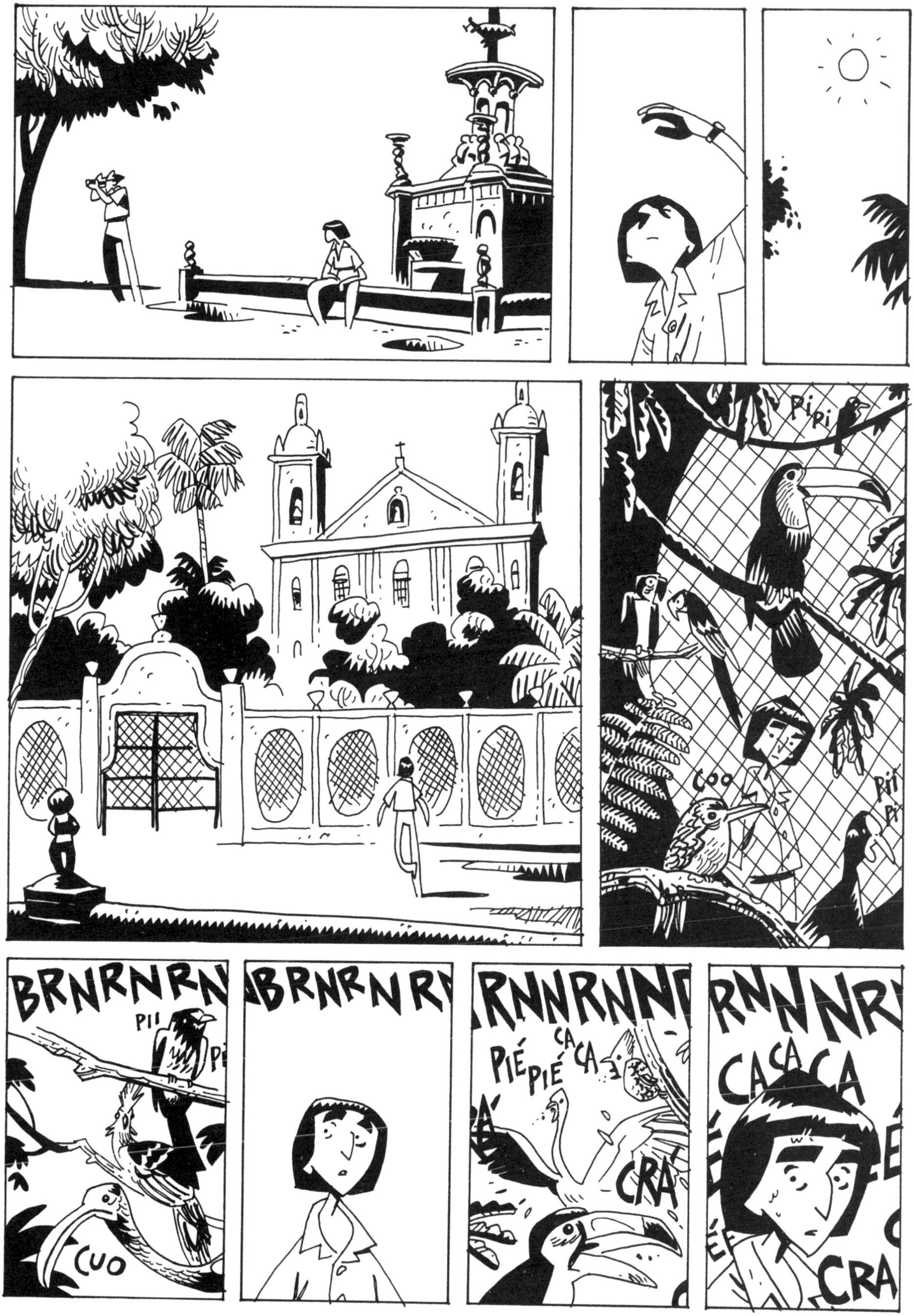
Pipi
COO
Pi
Pi
BRNRNRN
PII
Pi
CUO
BRNRNRNR
RNNRNNN
PIÉ PIÉ
CACA
CRÁ
RNNNR
CACACA
CRA

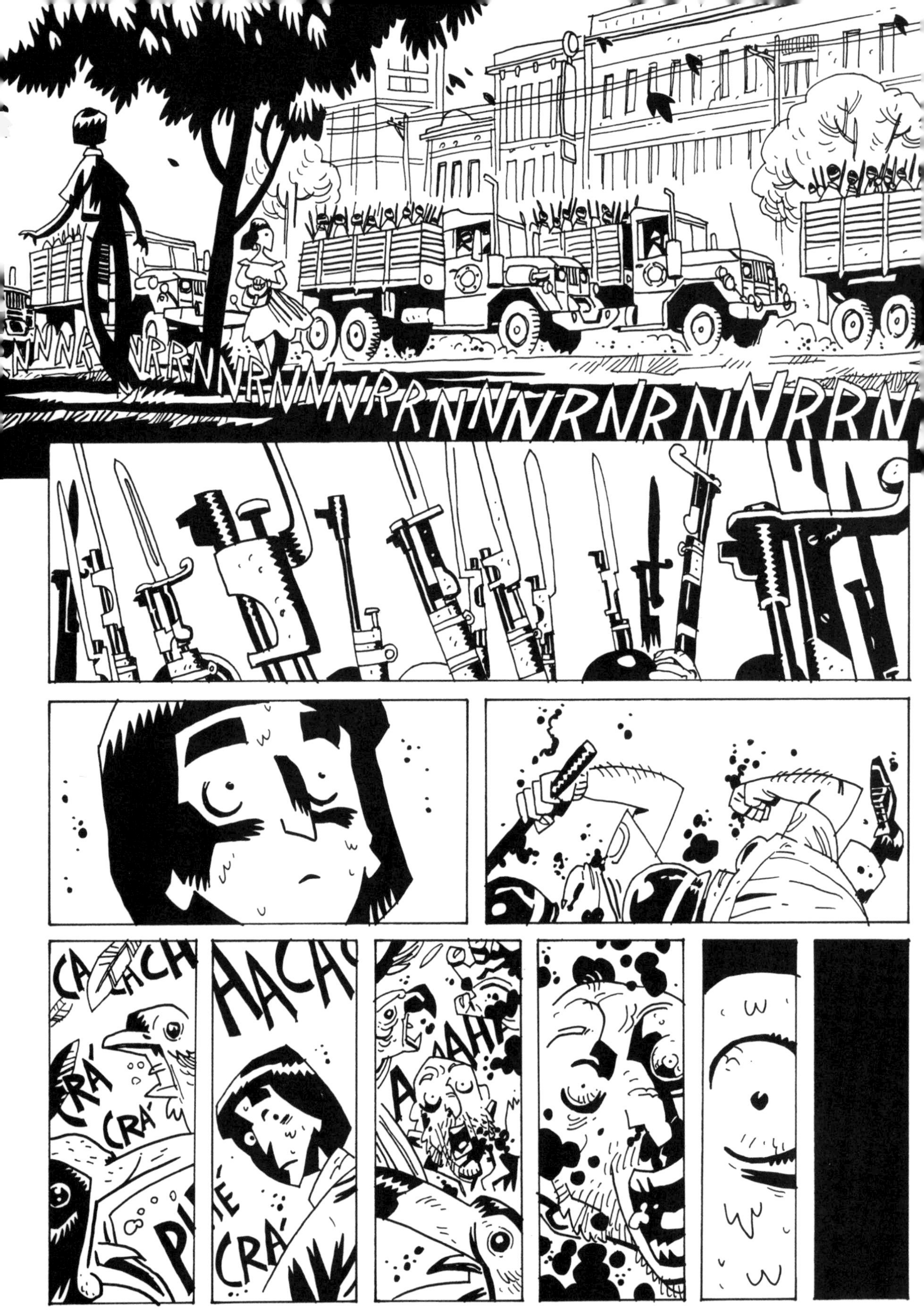
NNNR
NRRNNNRNNNNRRNNNNRNRNNRRN
CRÁ
CRÁ
CRÁ
CRÁ

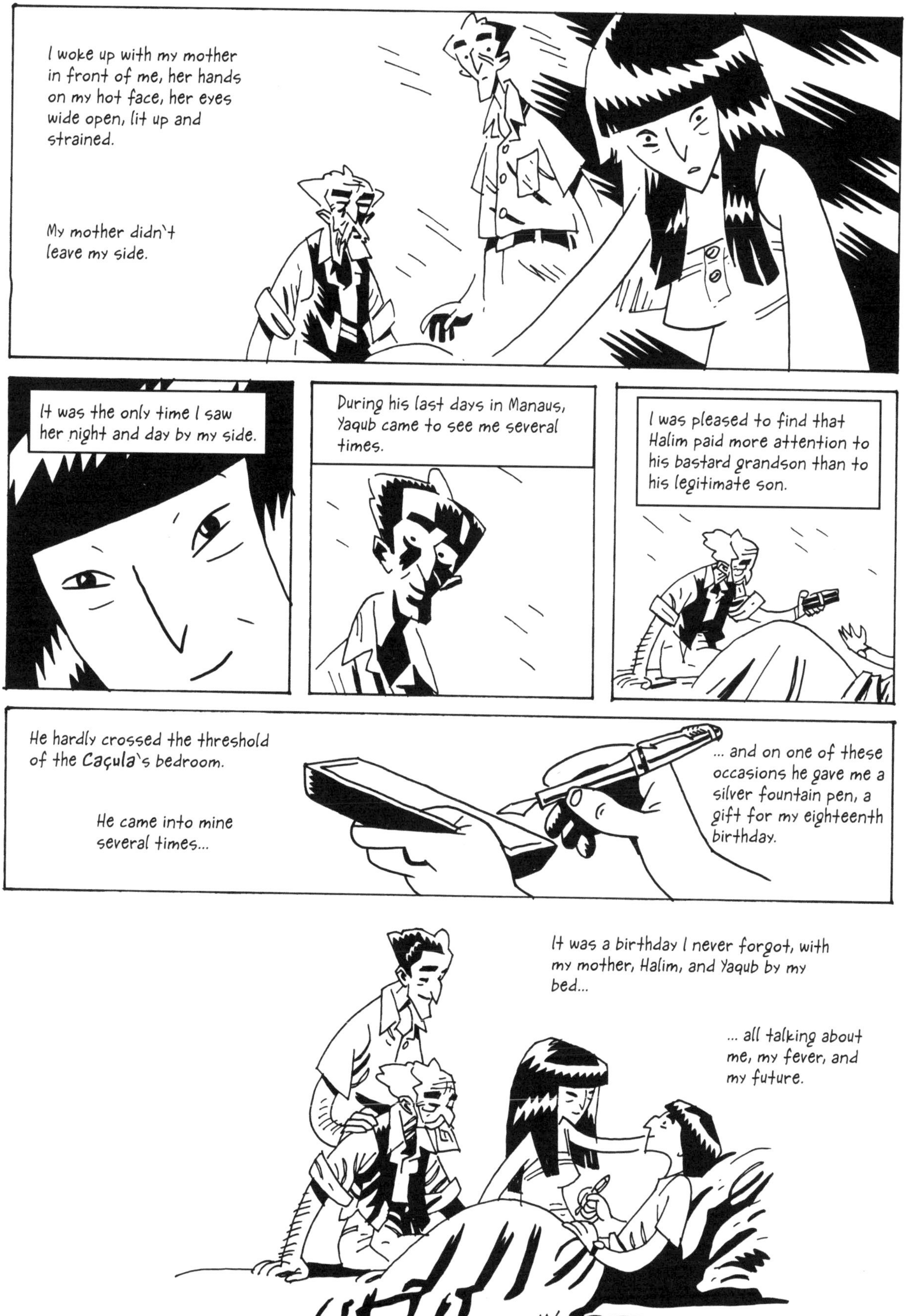

I woke up with my mother in front of me, her hands on my hot face, her eyes wide open, lit up and strained.
My mother didn't leave my side.
It was the only time I saw her night and day by my side.
During his last days in Manaus, Yaqub came to see me several times.
I was pleased to find that Halim paid more attention to his bastard grandson than to his legitimate son.
He hardly crossed the threshold of the Caçula's bedroom.
He came into mine several times...
... and on one of these occasions he gave me a silver fountain pen, a gift for my eighteenth birthday.
It was a birthday I never forgot, with my mother, Halim, and Yaqub by my bed...
... all talking about me, my fever, and my future.

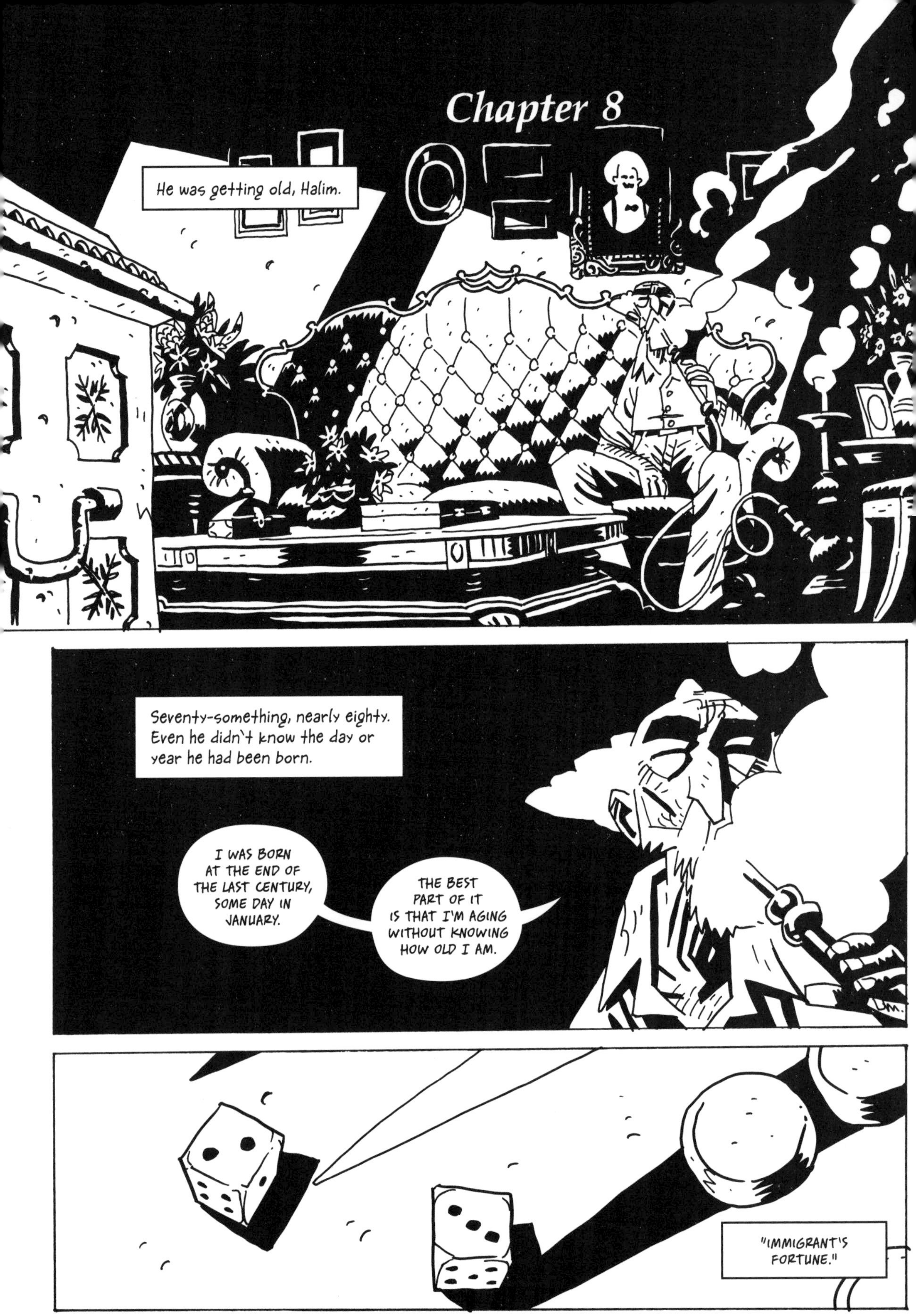
Chapter 8
He was getting old, Halim.
Seventy-something, nearly eighty. Even he didn't know the day or year he had been born.
I WAS BORN AT THE END OF THE LAST CENTURY, SOME DAY IN JANUARY.
THE BEST PART OF IT IS THAT I'M AGING WITHOUT KNOWING HOW OLD I AM.
"IMMIGRANT'S FORTUNE."

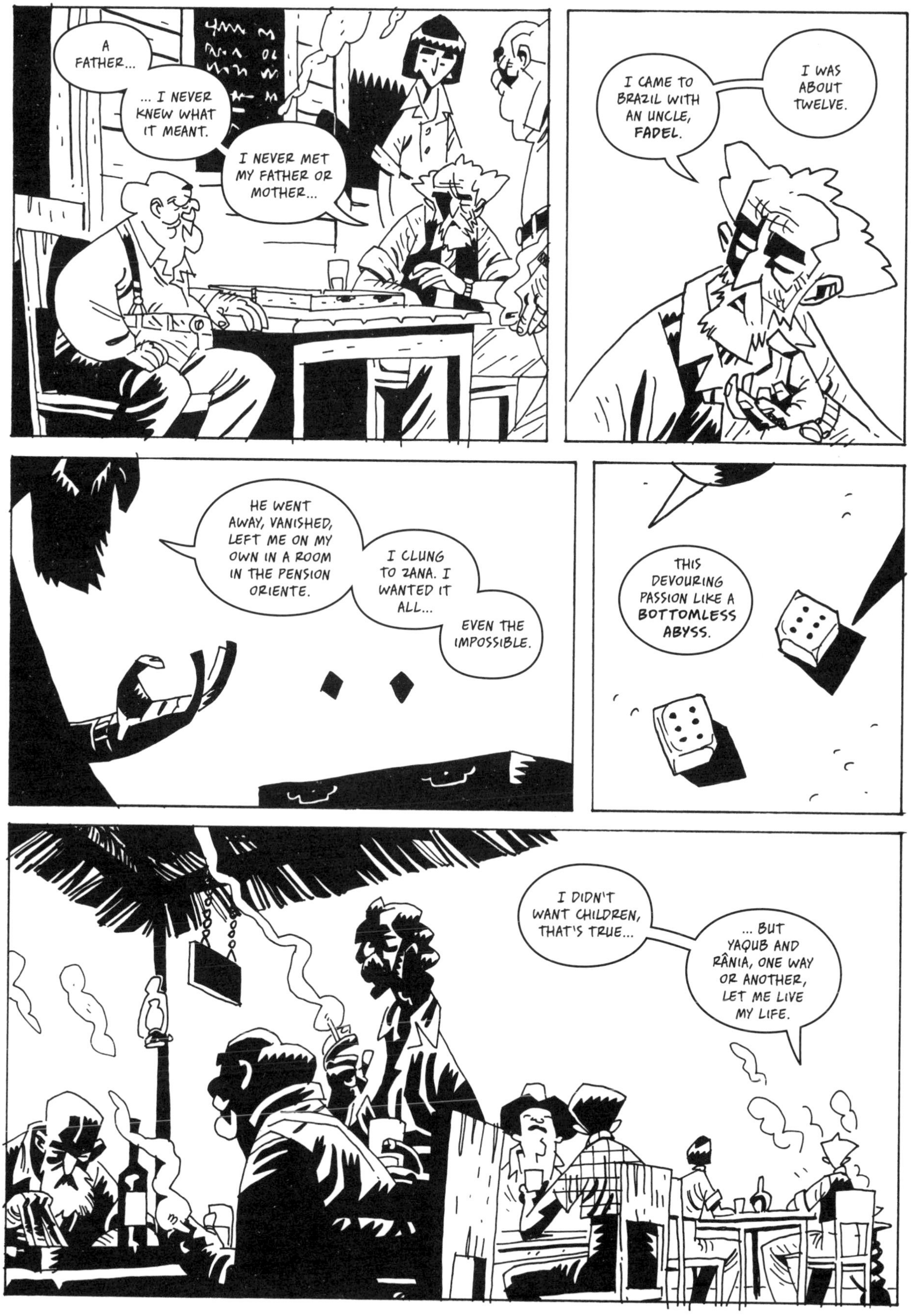
A FATHER...
... I NEVER KNEW WHAT IT MEANT.
I NEVER MET MY FATHER OR MOTHER...
I CAME TO BRAZIL WITH AN UNCLE, FADEL.
I WAS ABOUT TWELVE.
HE WENT AWAY, VANISHED, LEFT ME ON MY OWN IN A ROOM IN THE PENSION ORIENTE.
I CLUNG TO ZANA. I WANTED IT ALL...
EVEN THE IMPOSSIBLE.
THIS DEVOURING PASSION LIKE A BOTTOMLESS ABYSS.
I DIDN'T WANT CHILDREN, THAT'S TRUE...
... BUT YAQUB AND RÂNIA, ONE WAY OR ANOTHER, LET ME LIVE MY LIFE.

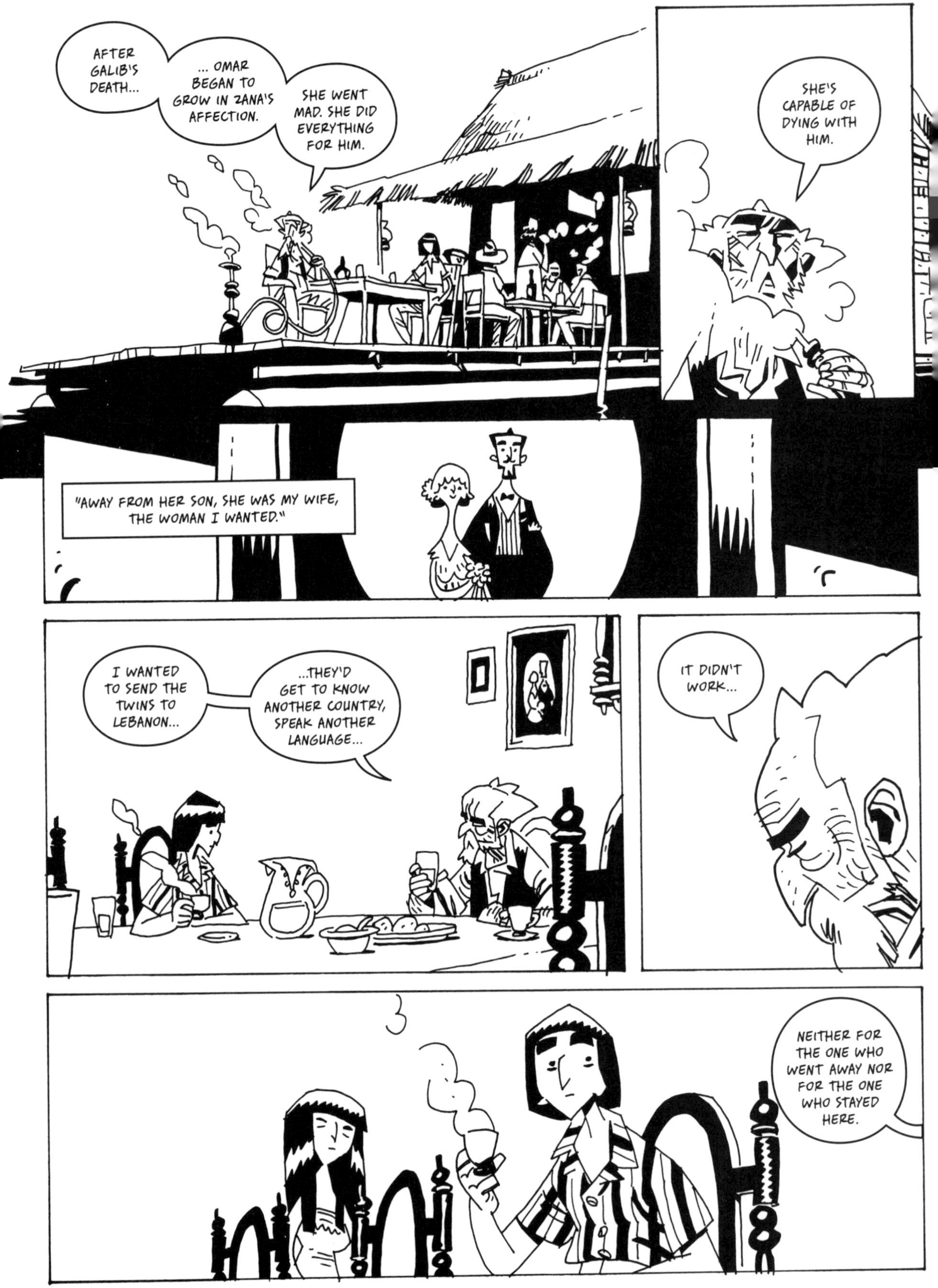
AFTER GALIB'S DEATH...
... OMAR BEGAN TO GROW IN ZANA'S AFFECTION.
SHE WENT MAD. SHE DID EVERYTHING FOR HIM.
SHE'S CAPABLE OF DYING WITH HIM.
"AWAY FROM HER SON, SHE WAS MY WIFE, THE WOMAN I WANTED."
I WANTED TO SEND THE TWINS TO LEBANON...
...THEY'D GET TO KNOW ANOTHER COUNTRY, SPEAK ANOTHER LANGUAGE...
IT DIDN'T WORK...
NEITHER FOR THE ONE WHO WENT AWAY NOR FOR THE ONE WHO STAYED HERE.

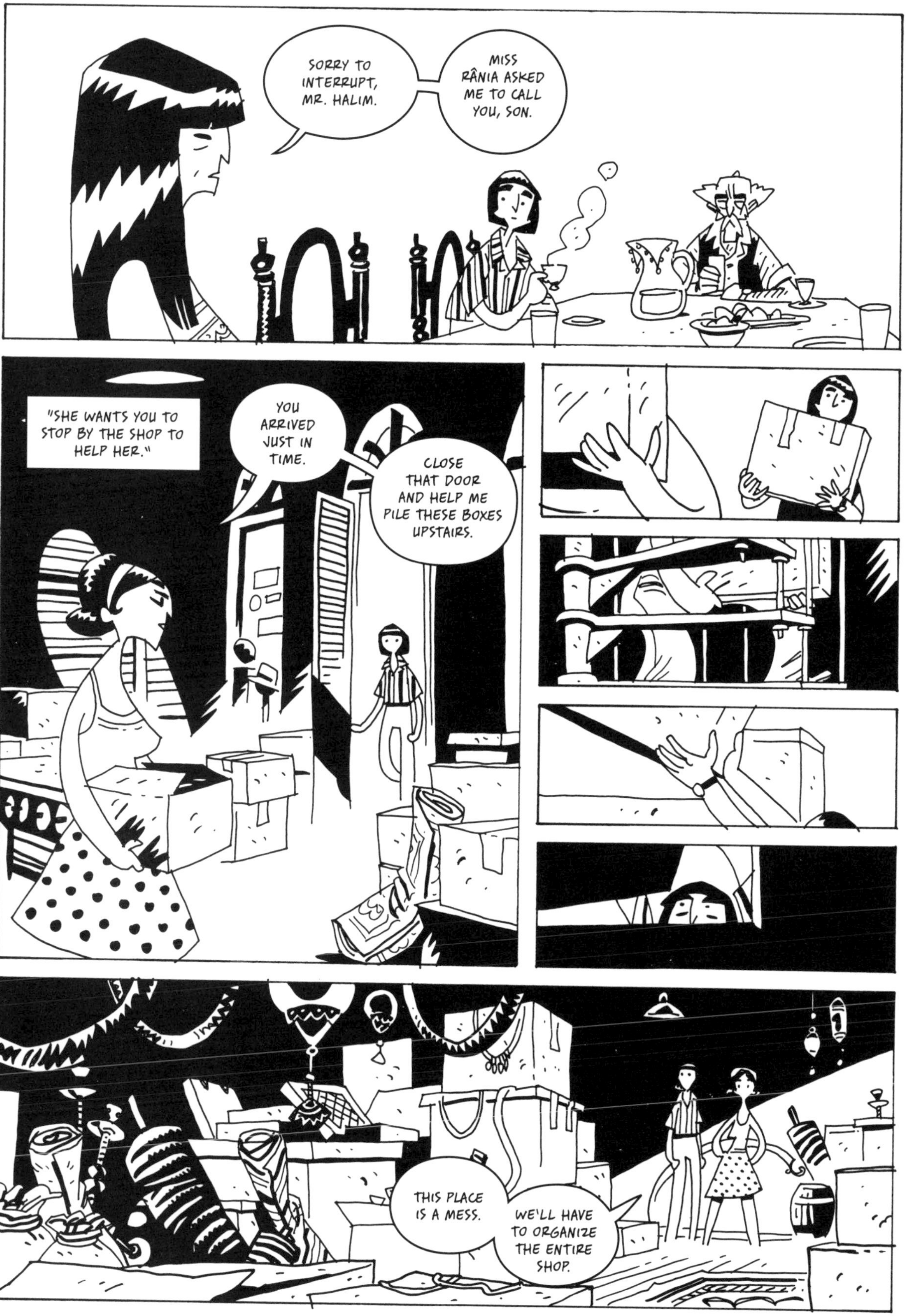
SORRY TO INTERRUPT, MR. HALIM.
MISS RÂNIA ASKED ME TO CALL YOU, SON.
"SHE WANTS YOU TO STOP BY THE SHOP TO HELP HER."
YOU ARRIVED JUST IN TIME.
CLOSE THAT DOOR AND HELP ME PILE THESE BOXES UPSTAIRS.
THIS PLACE IS A MESS.
WE'LL HAVE TO ORGANIZE THE ENTIRE SHOP.

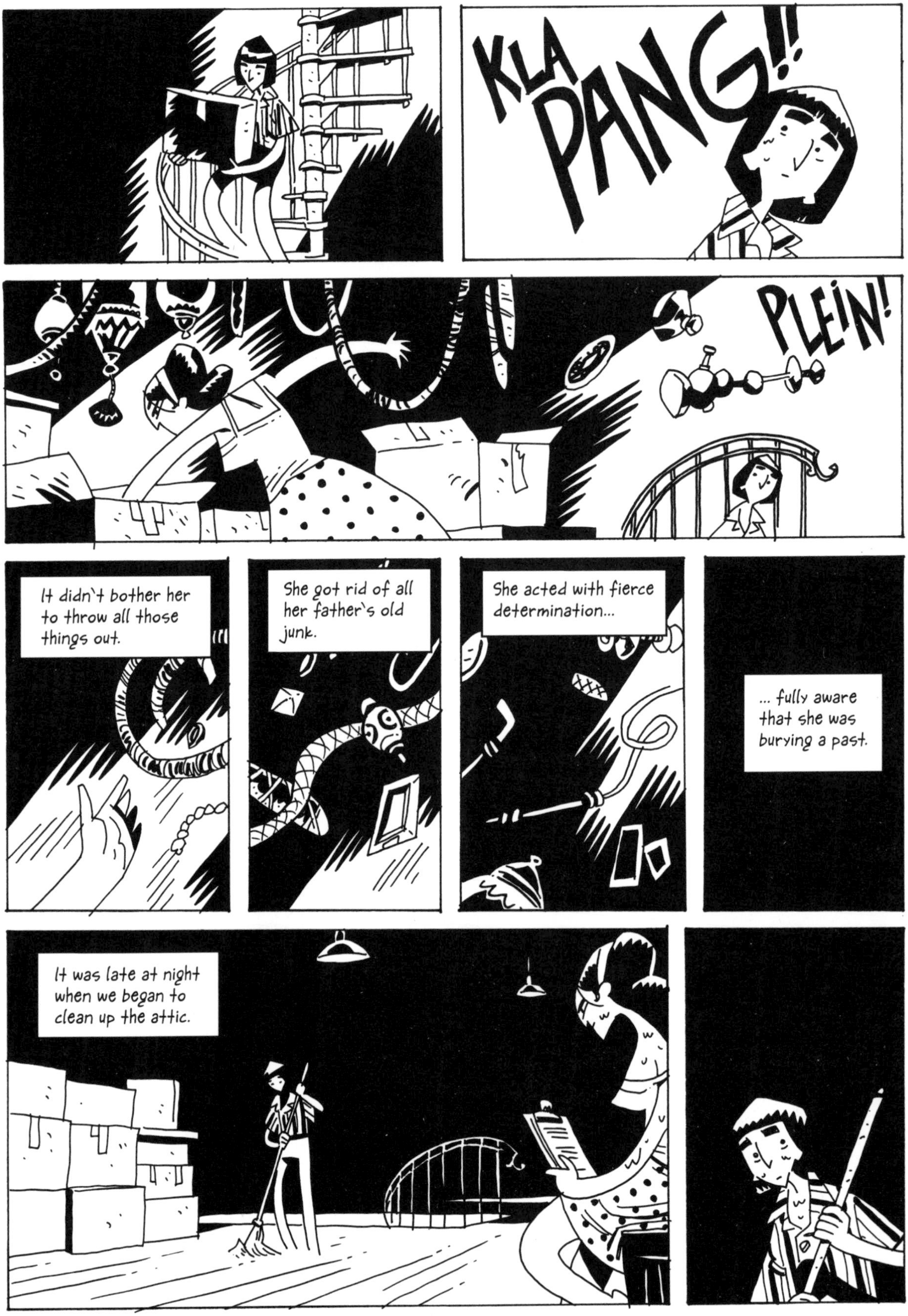
KLA PANG!!
PLEIN!
It didn't bother her to throw all those things out.
She got rid of all her father's old junk.
She acted with fierce determination...
... fully aware that she was burying a past.
It was late at night when we began to clean up the attic.

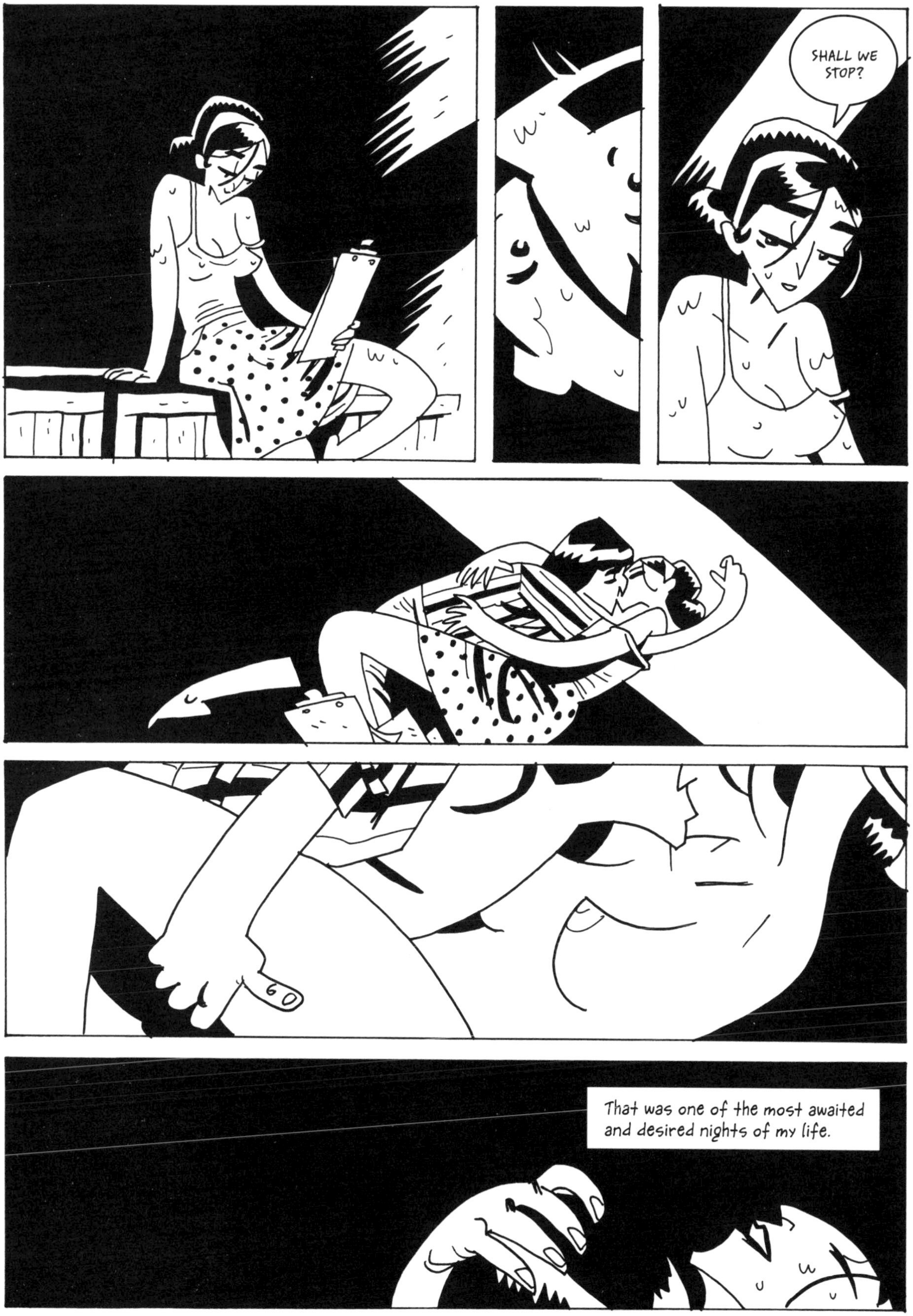
SHALL WE STOP?
60
That was one of the most awaited and desired nights of my life.

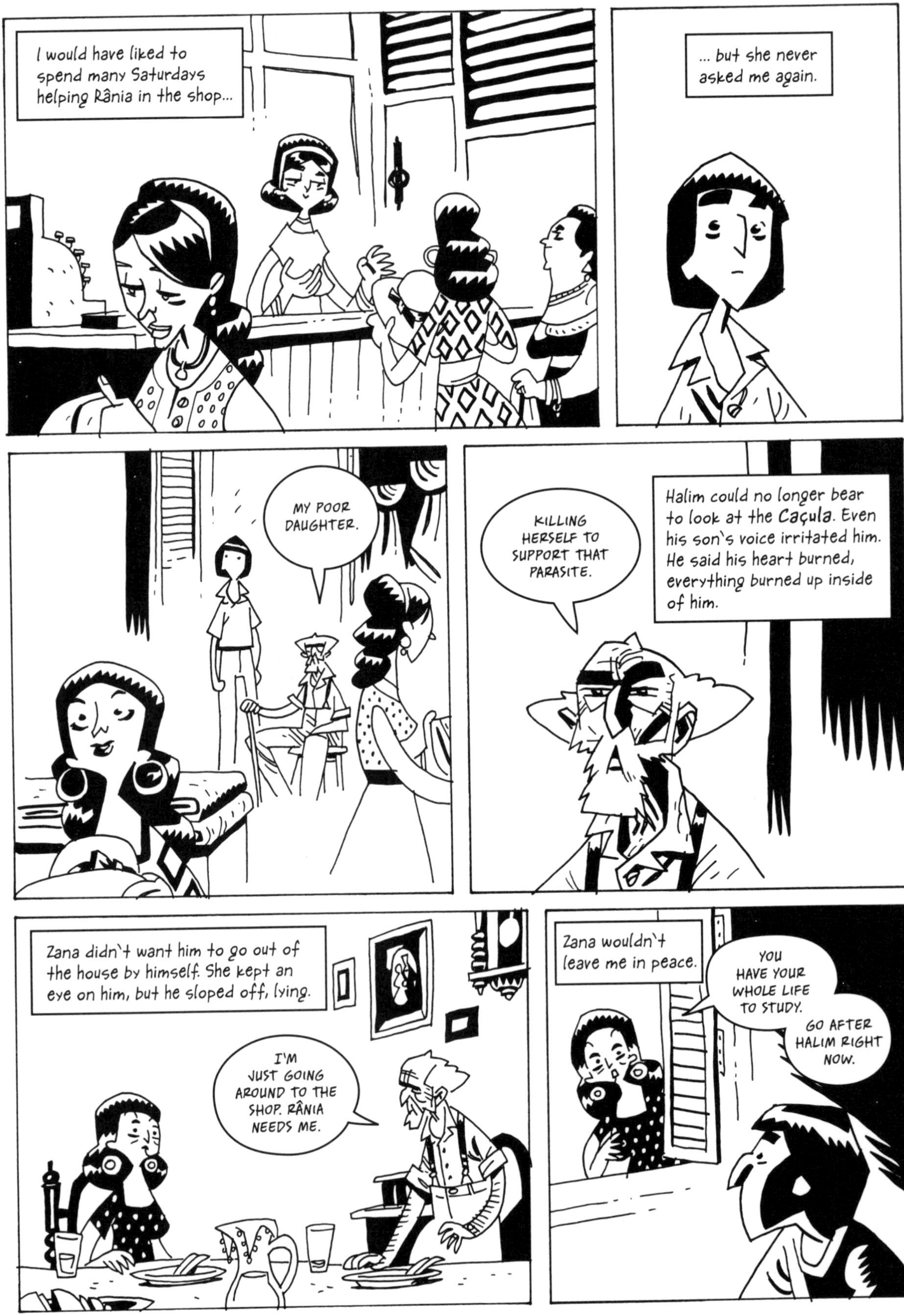
I would have liked to spend many Saturdays helping Rânia in the shop...
... but she never asked me again.
MY POOR DAUGHTER.
KILLING HERSELF TO SUPPORT THAT PARASITE.
Halim could no longer bear to look at the Caçula. Even his son's voice irritated him. He said his heart burned, everything burned up inside of him.
Zana didn't want him to go out of the house by himself. She kept an eye on him, but he sloped off, lying.
I'M JUST GOING AROUND TO THE SHOP. RÂNIA NEEDS ME.
Zana wouldn't leave me in peace.
YOU HAVE YOUR WHOLE LIFE TO STUDY.
GO AFTER HALIM RIGHT NOW.

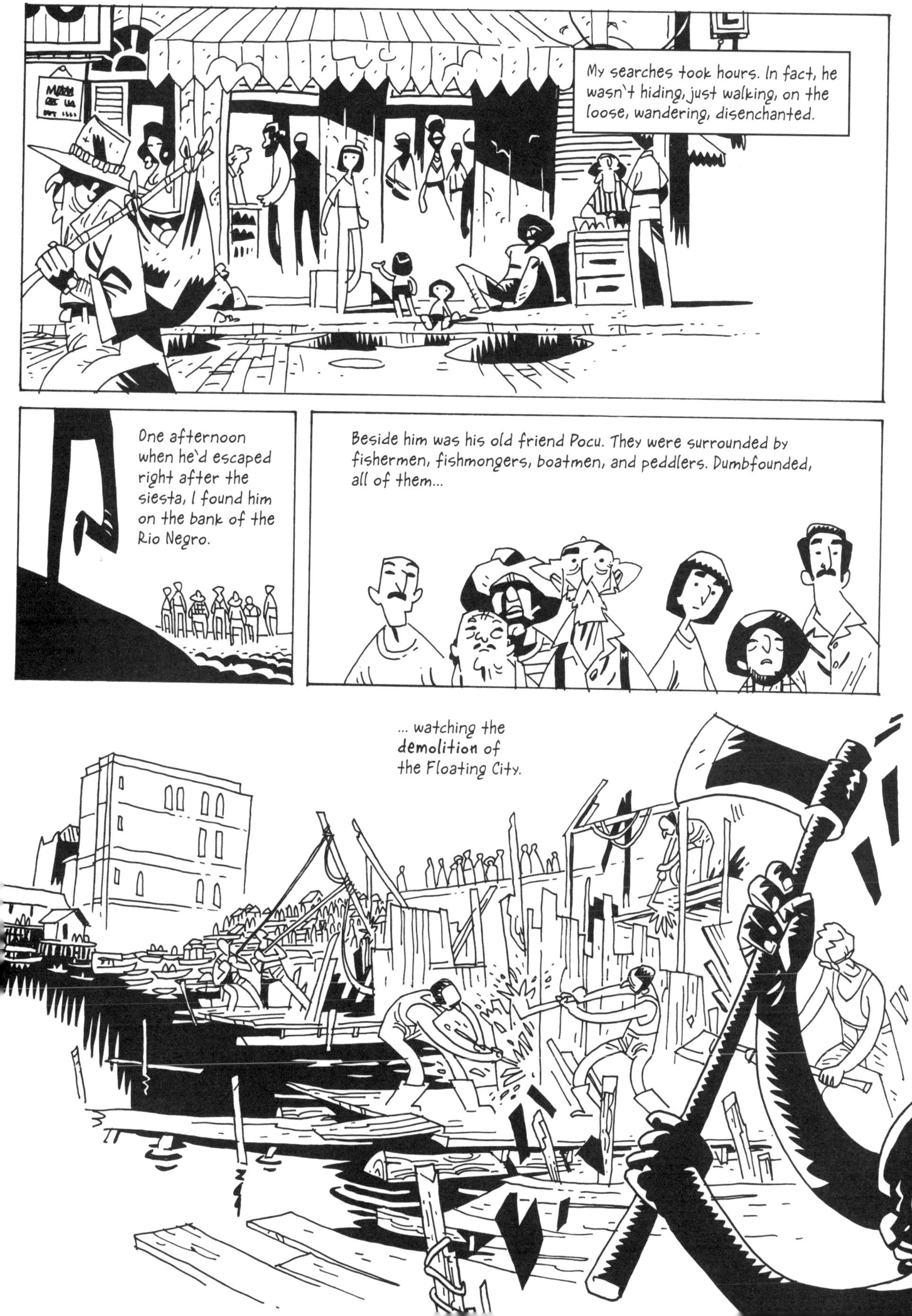
My searches took hours. In fact, he wasn't hiding, just walking, on the loose, wandering, disenchanted.
One afternoon when he'd escaped right after the siesta, I found him on the bank of the Rio Negro.
Beside him was his old friend Pocu. They were surrounded by fishermen, fishmongers, boatmen, and peddlers. Dumbfounded, all of them...
... watching the **demolition** of the Floating City.

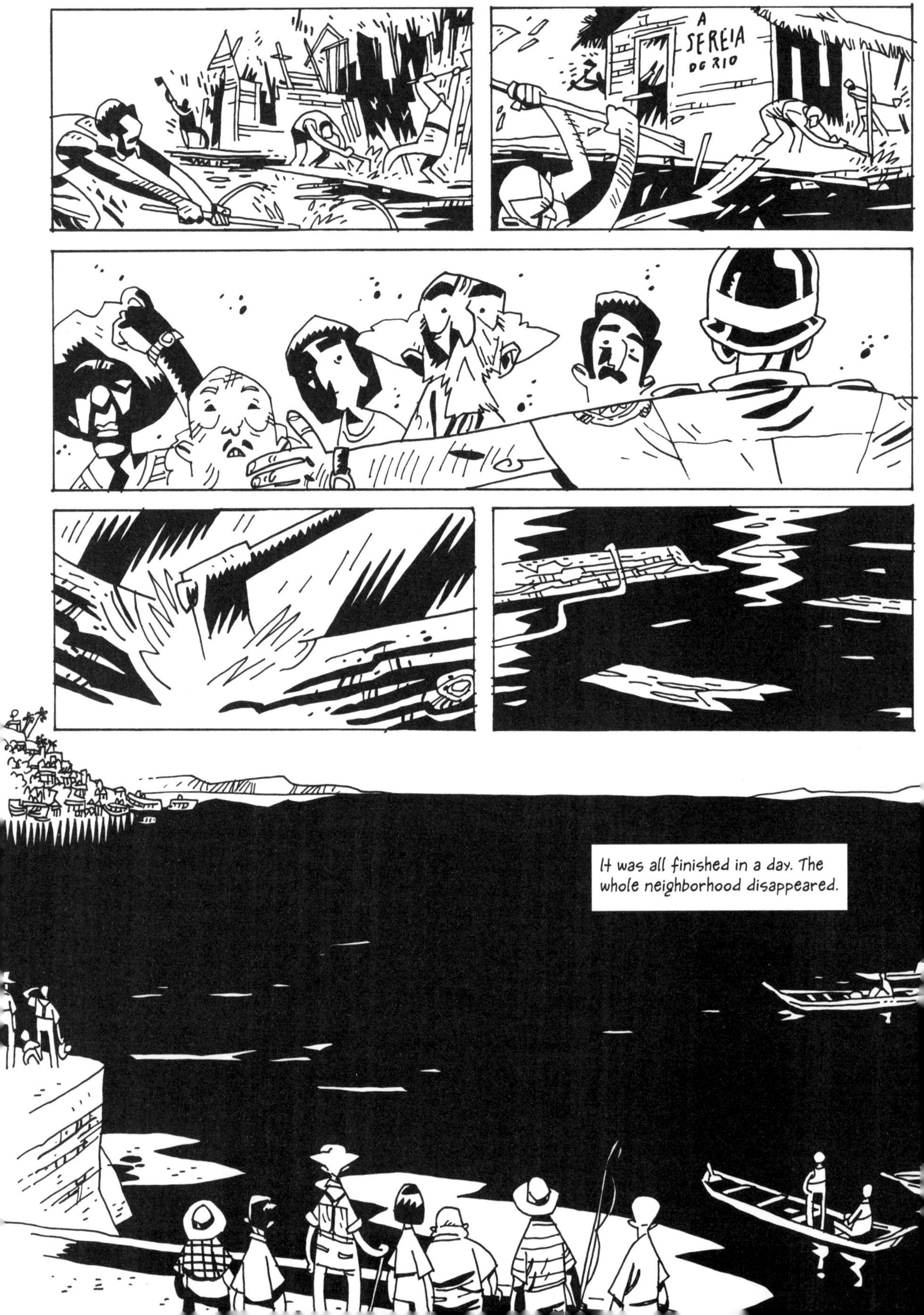
A SEREIA DO RIO
It was all finished in a day. The whole neighborhood disappeared.

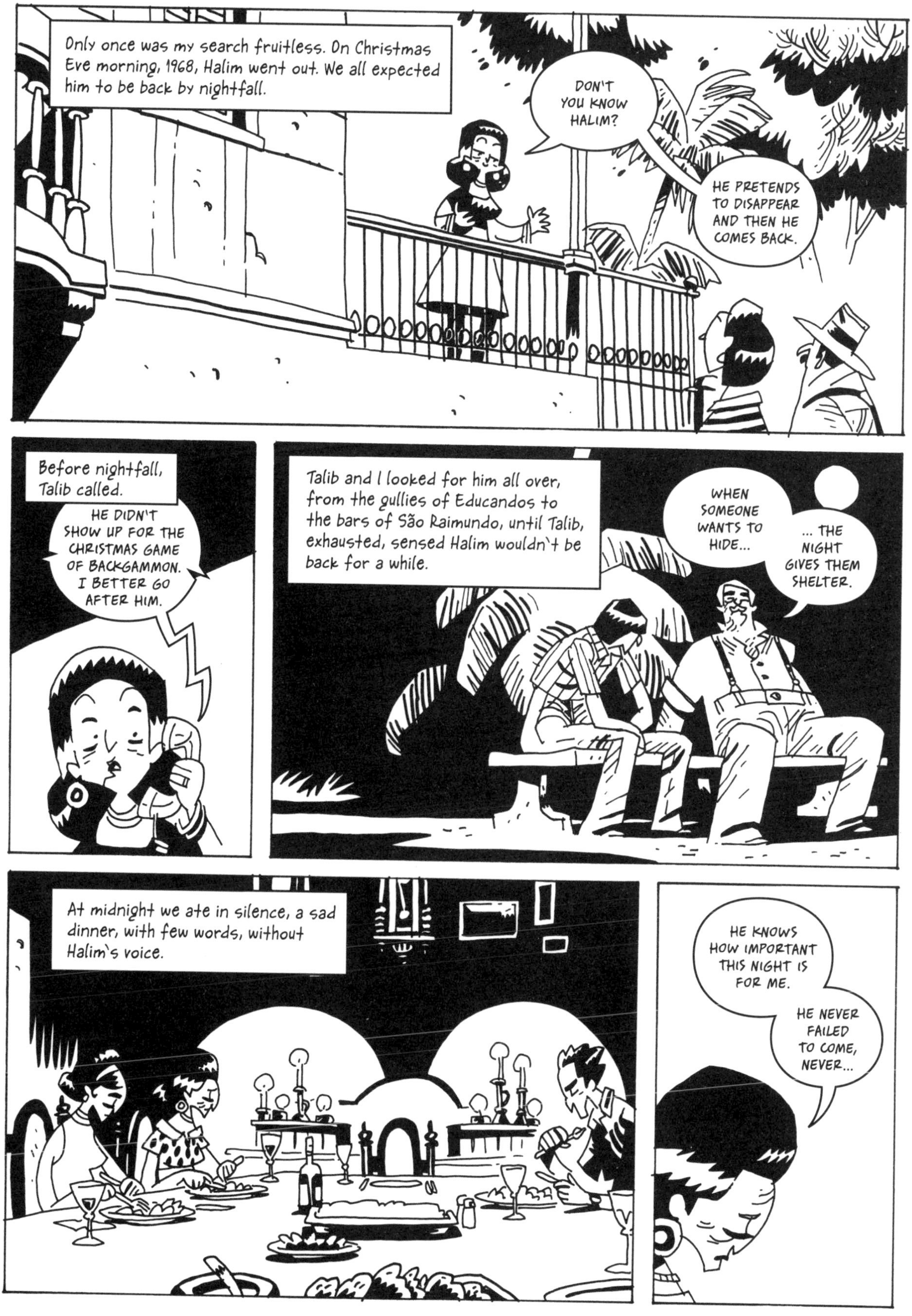

Only once was my search fruitless. On Christmas Eve morning, 1968, Halim went out. We all expected him to be back by nightfall.
DON'T YOU KNOW HALIM?
HE PRETENDS TO DISAPPEAR AND THEN HE COMES BACK.
Before nightfall, Talib called.
HE DIDN'T SHOW UP FOR THE CHRISTMAS GAME OF BACKGAMMON. I BETTER GO AFTER HIM.
Talib and I looked for him all over, from the gullies of Educandos to the bars of São Raimundo, until Talib, exhausted, sensed Halim wouldn't be back for a while.
WHEN SOMEONE WANTS TO HIDE...
... THE NIGHT GIVES THEM SHELTER.
At midnight we ate in silence, a sad dinner, with few words, without Halim's voice.
HE KNOWS HOW IMPORTANT THIS NIGHT IS FOR ME.
HE NEVER FAILED TO COME, NEVER...

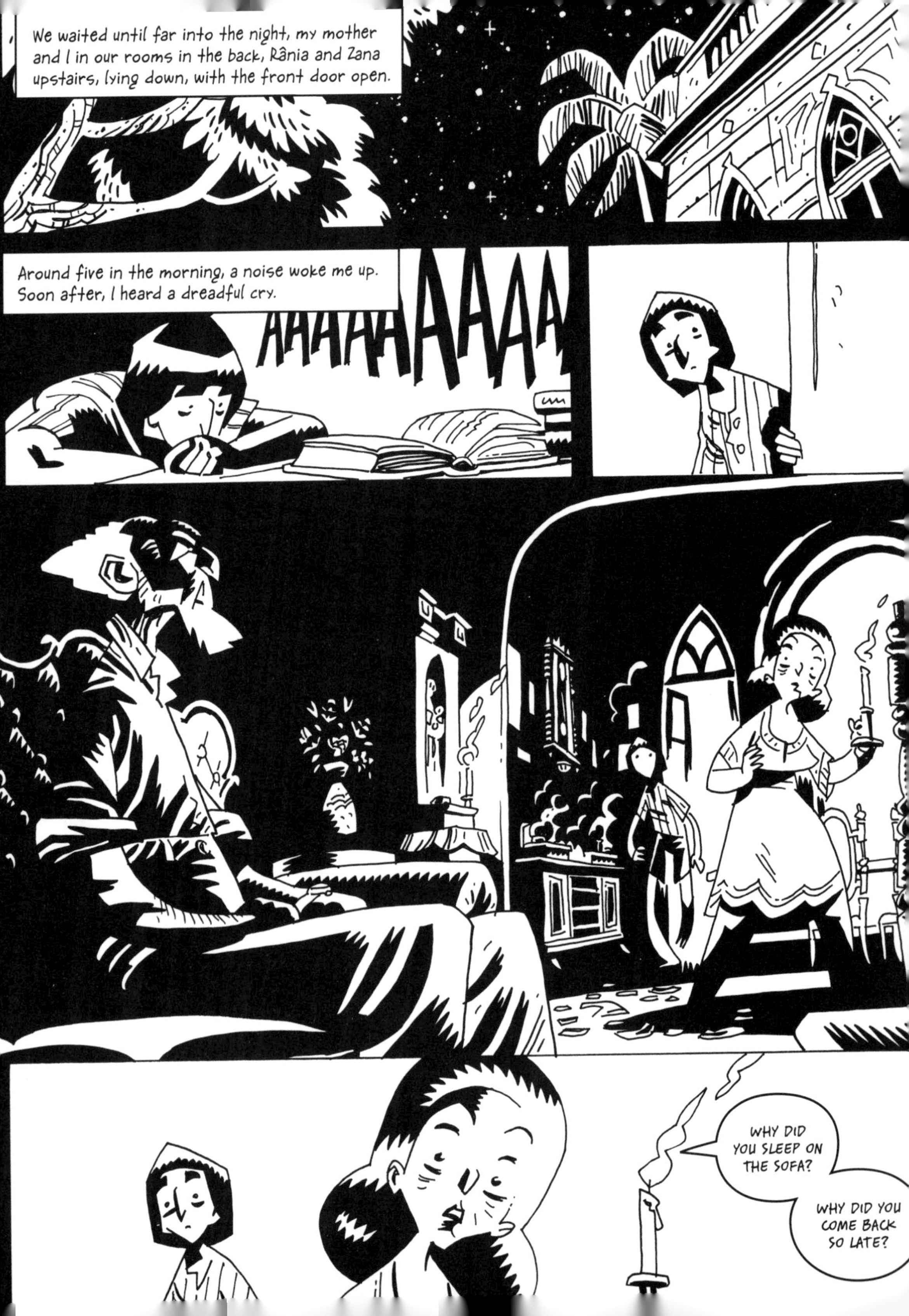
We waited until far into the night, my mother and I in our rooms in the back, Rânia and Zana upstairs, lying down, with the front door open.
Around five in the morning, a noise woke me up. Soon after, I heard a dreadful cry.
AAAAAAAAAAAA
WHY DID YOU SLEEP ON THE SOFA?
WHY DID YOU COME BACK SO LATE?

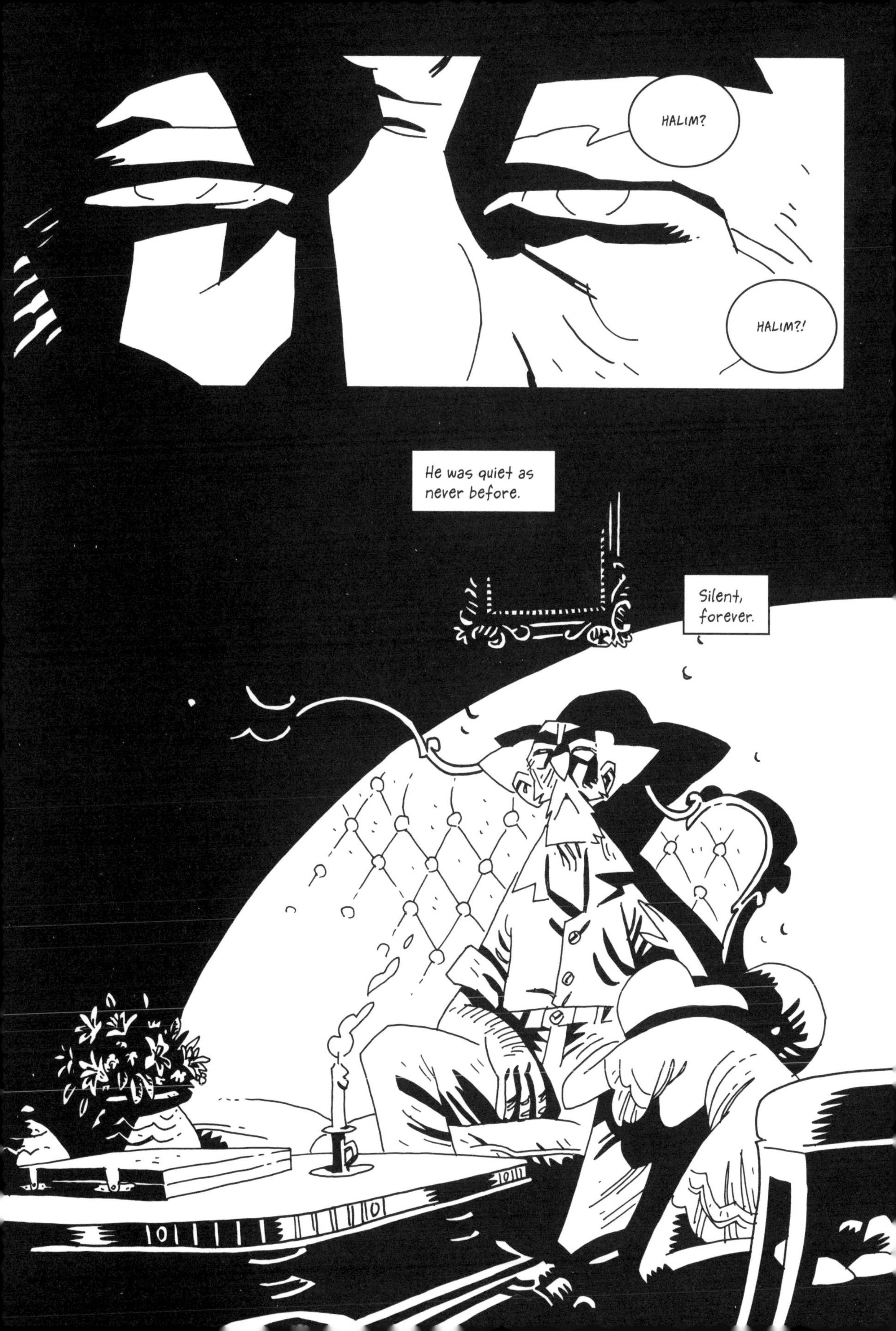
HALIM?
HALIM?!
He was quiet as never before.
Silent, forever.

Chapter 9

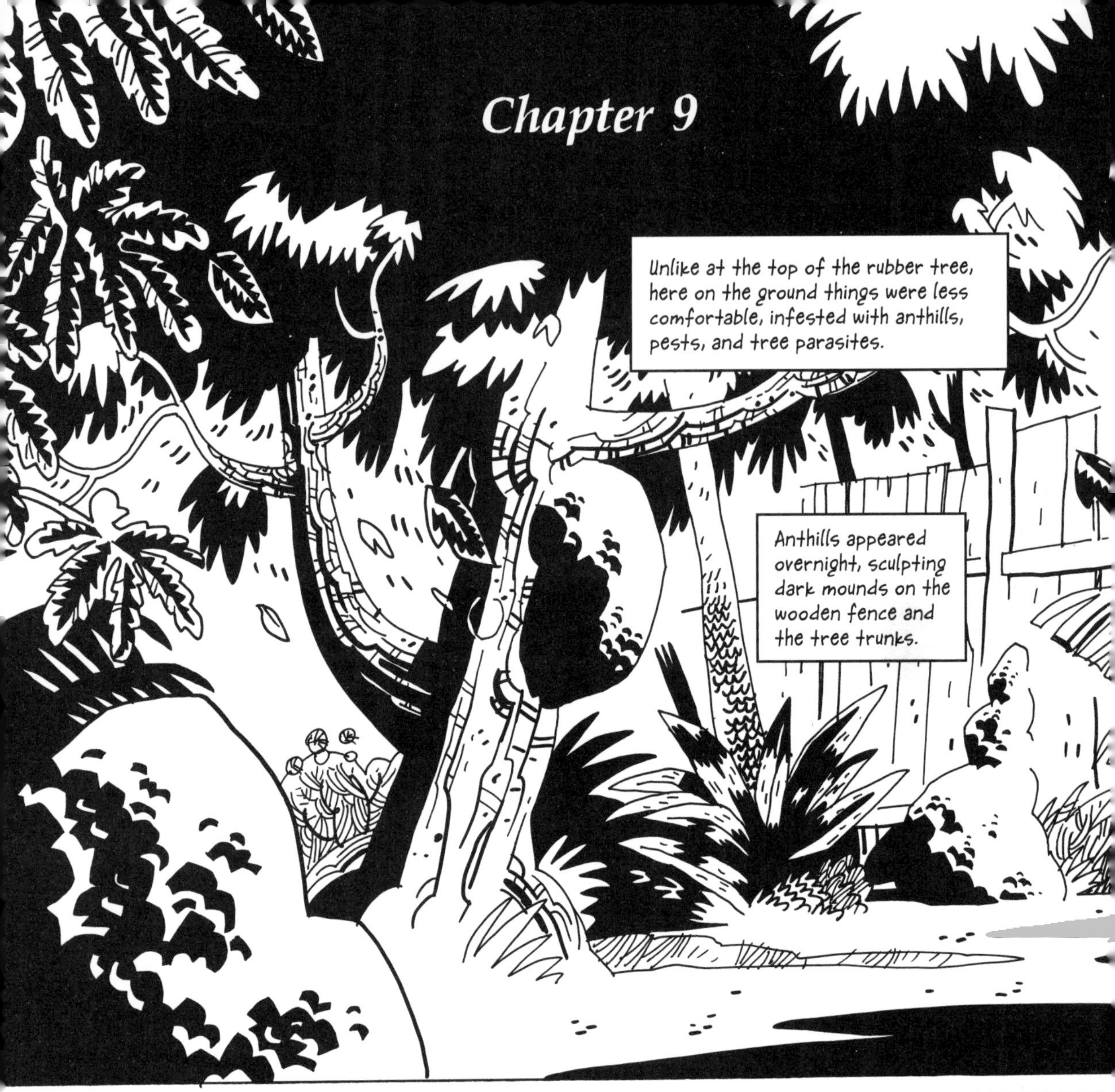
Unlike at the top of the rubber tree, here on the ground things were less comfortable, infested with anthills, pests, and tree parasites.
Anthills appeared overnight, sculpting dark mounds on the wooden fence and the tree trunks.

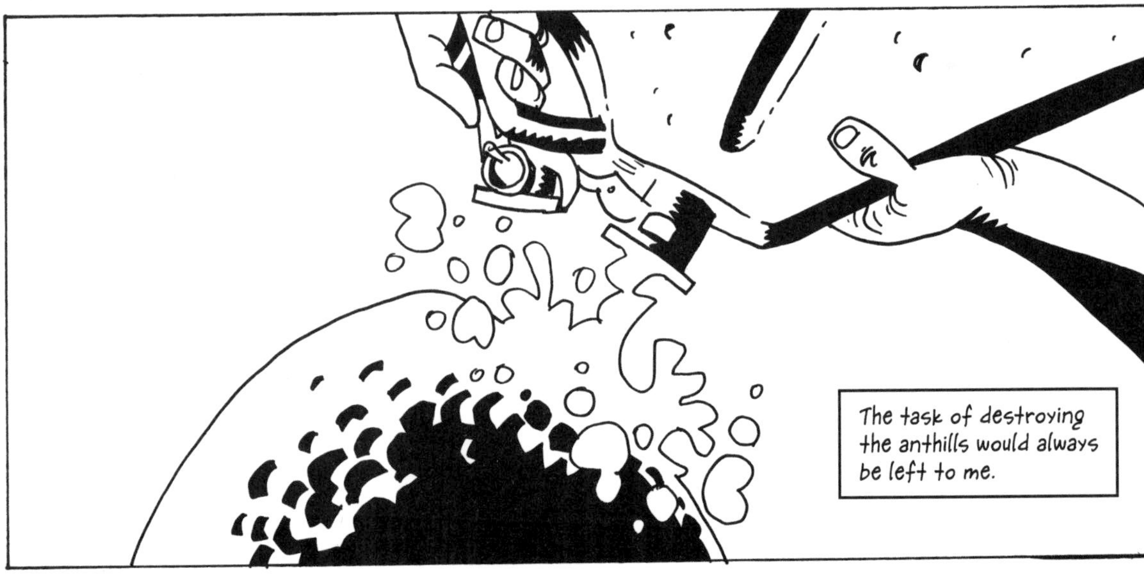
The task of destroying the anthills would always be left to me.

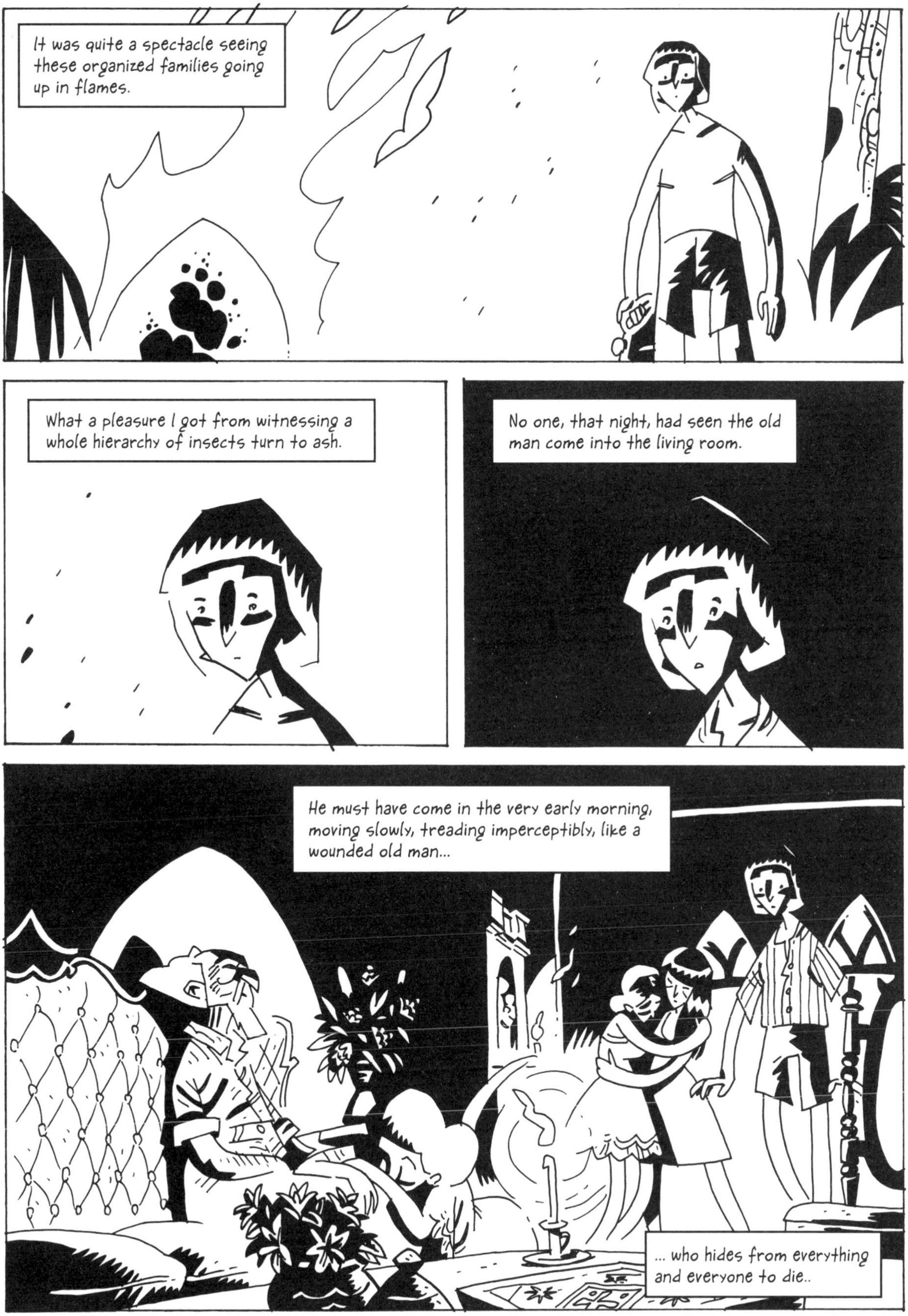
It was quite a spectacle seeing these organized families going up in flames.
What a pleasure I got from witnessing a whole hierarchy of insects turn to ash.
No one, that night, had seen the old man come into the living room.
He must have come in the very early morning, moving slowly, treading imperceptibly, like a wounded old man...
... who hides from everything and everyone to die..

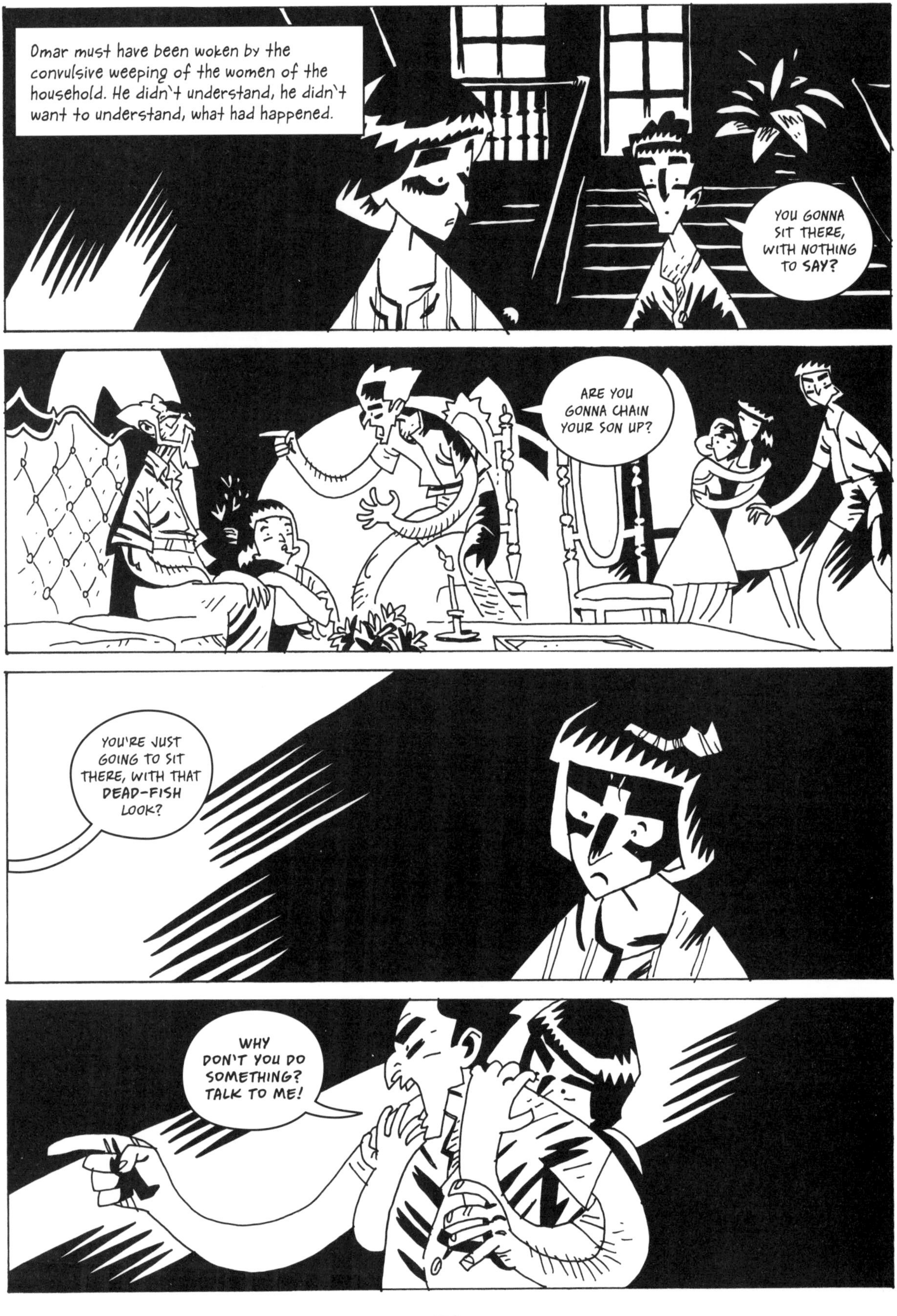

Omar must have been woken by the convulsive weeping of the women of the household. He didn`t understand, he didn`t want to understand, what had happened.
YOU GONNA SIT THERE, WITH NOTHING TO SAY?
ARE YOU GONNA CHAIN YOUR SON UP?
YOU'RE JUST GOING TO SIT THERE, WITH THAT DEAD-FISH LOOK?
WHY DON'T YOU DO SOMETHING? TALK TO ME!

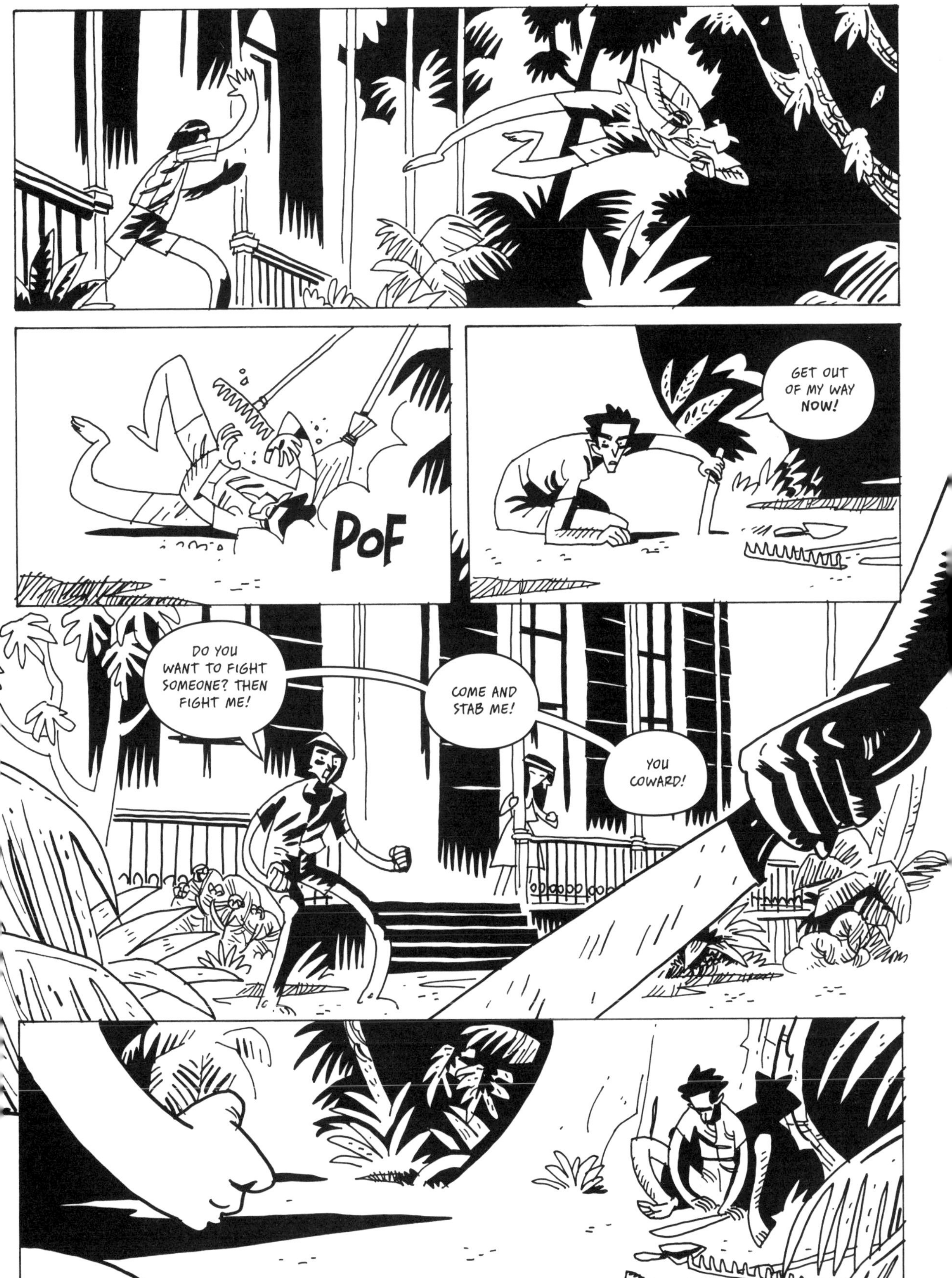
POF
GET OUT OF MY WAY NOW!
DO YOU WANT TO FIGHT SOMEONE? THEN FIGHT ME!
COME AND STAB ME!
YOU COWARD!

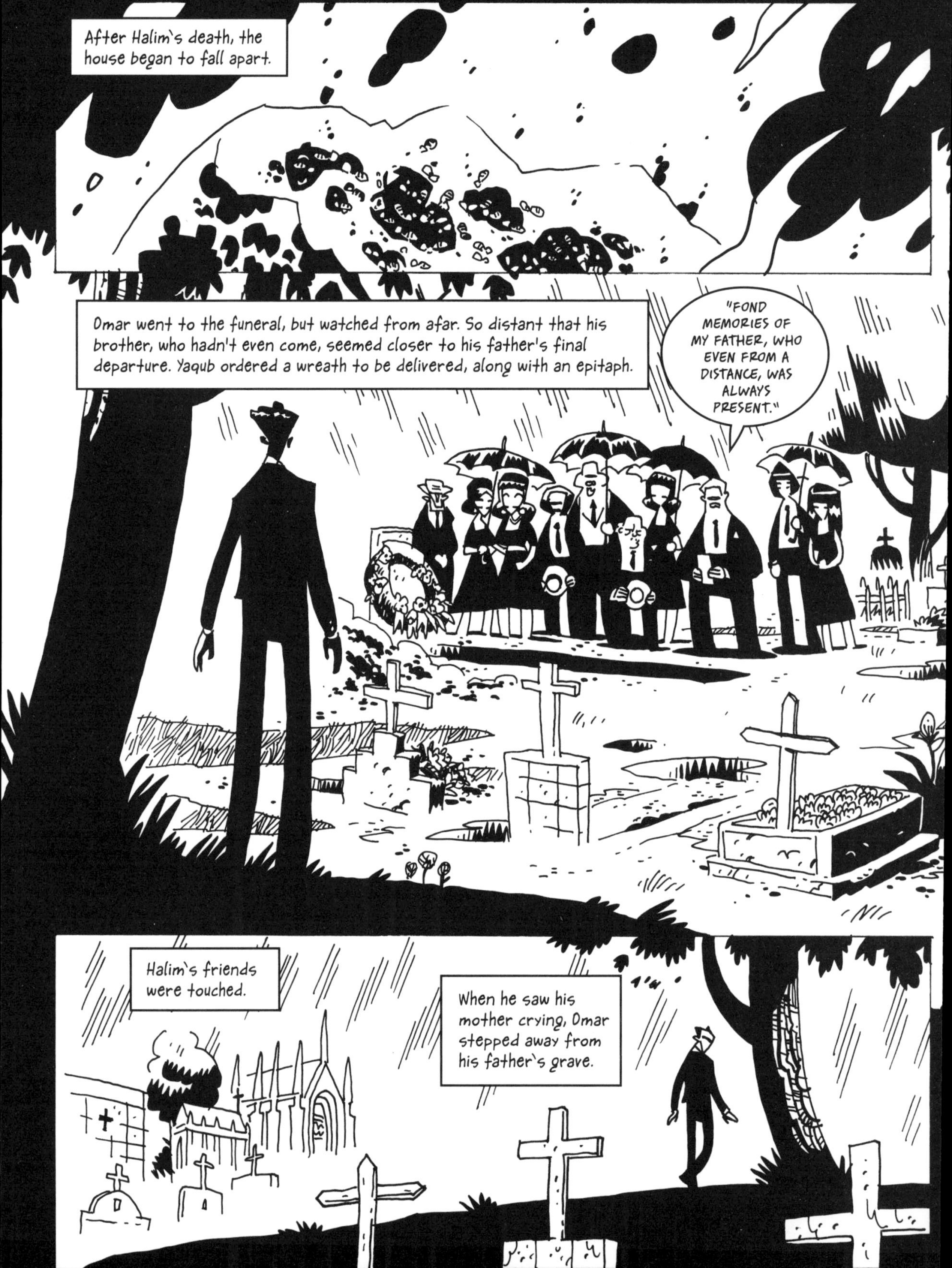
After Halim's death, the house began to fall apart.
Omar went to the funeral, but watched from afar. So distant that his brother, who hadn't even come, seemed closer to his father's final departure. Yaqub ordered a wreath to be delivered, along with an epitaph.
"FOND MEMORIES OF MY FATHER, WHO EVEN FROM A DISTANCE, WAS ALWAYS PRESENT."
Halim's friends were touched.
When he saw his mother crying, Omar stepped away from his father's grave.

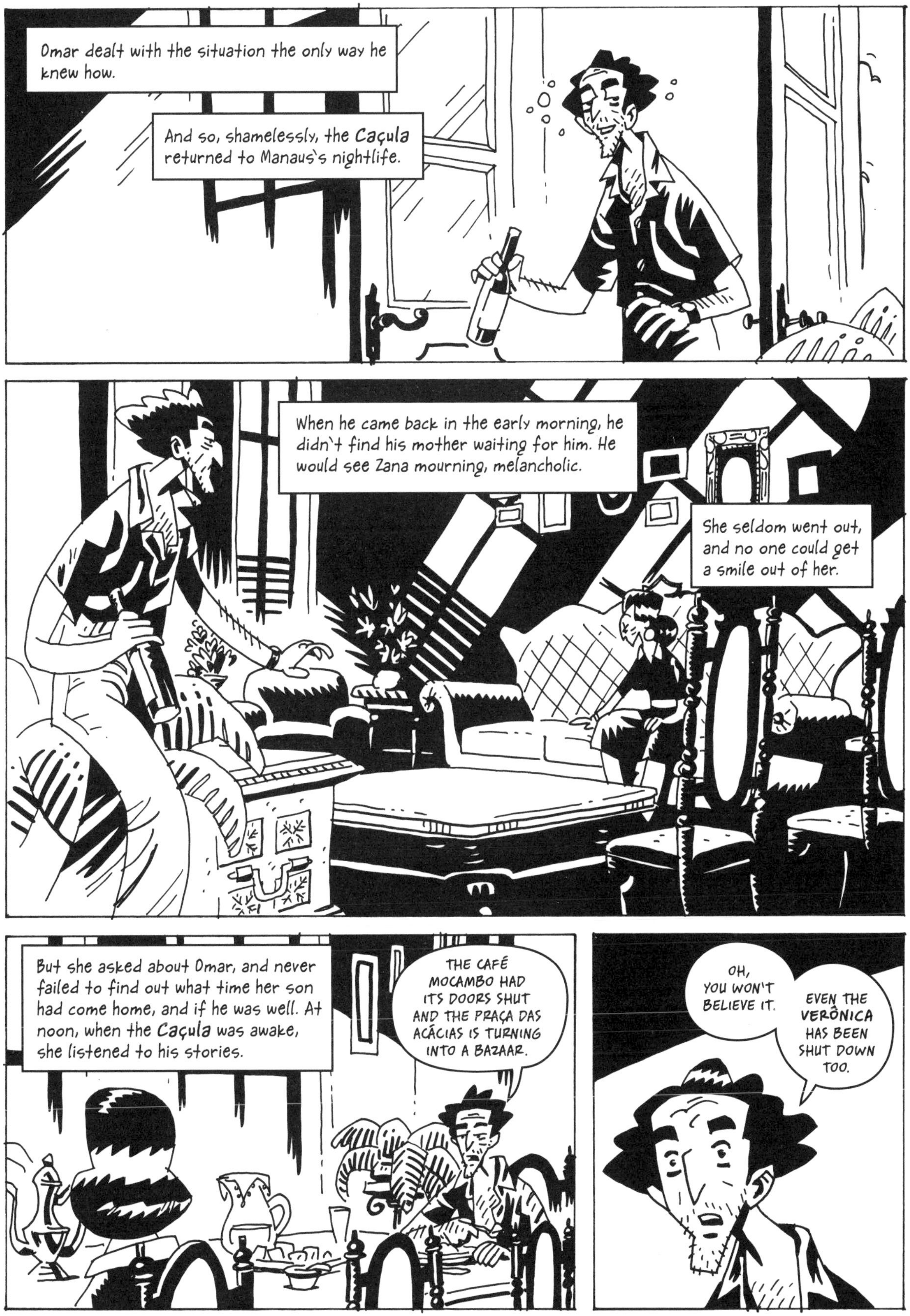
Omar dealt with the situation the only way he knew how.
And so, shamelessly, the Caçula returned to Manaus's nightlife.
When he came back in the early morning, he didn't find his mother waiting for him. He would see Zana mourning, melancholic.
She seldom went out, and no one could get a smile out of her.
But she asked about Omar, and never failed to find out what time her son had come home, and if he was well. At noon, when the Caçula was awake, she listened to his stories.
THE CAFÉ MOCAMBO HAD ITS DOORS SHUT AND THE PRAÇA DAS ACÁCIAS IS TURNING INTO A BAZAAR.
OH, YOU WON'T BELIEVE IT.
EVEN THE **VERÔNICA** HAS BEEN SHUT DOWN TOO.

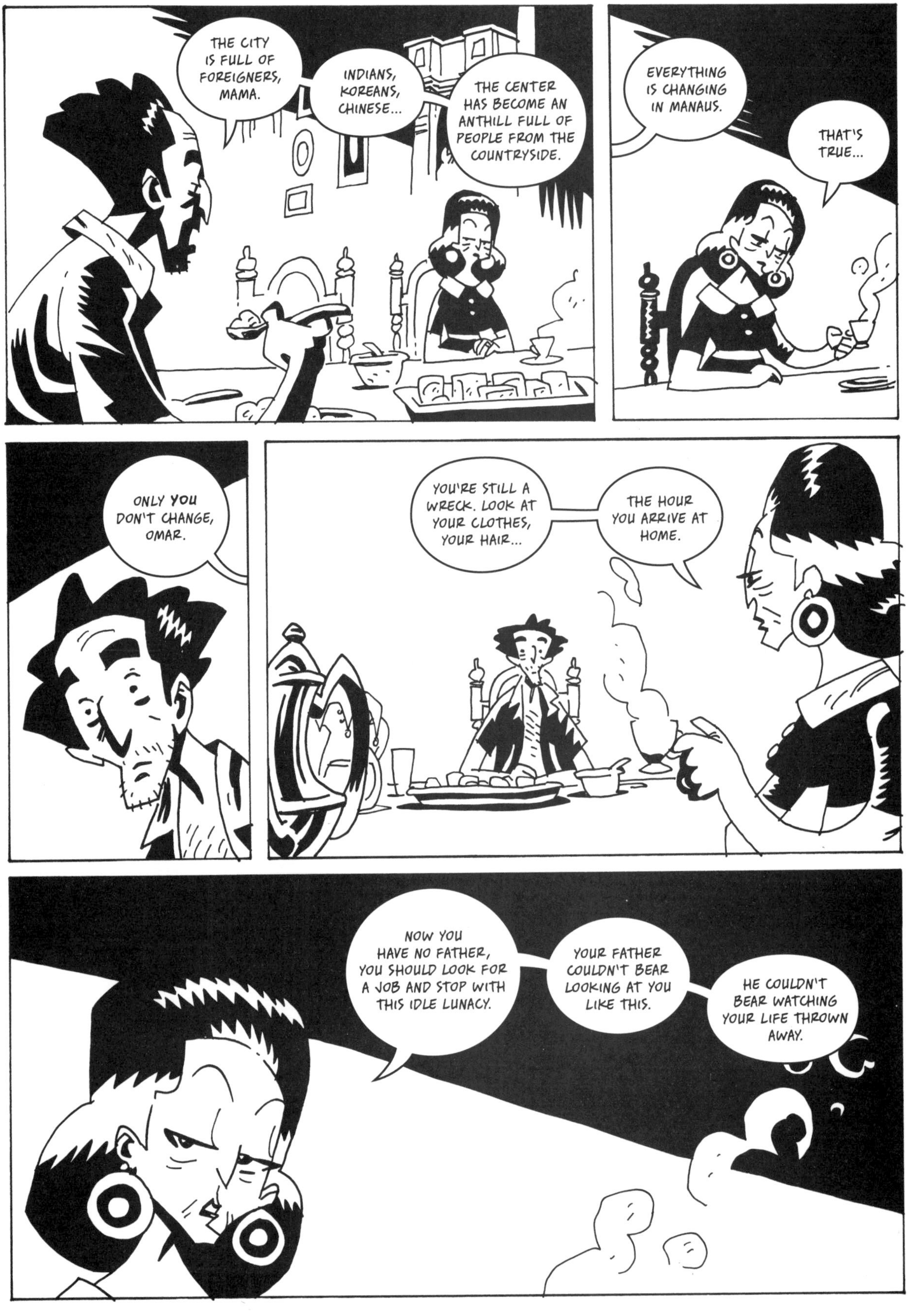
THE CITY IS FULL OF FOREIGNERS, MAMA.
INDIANS, KOREANS, CHINESE...
THE CENTER HAS BECOME AN ANTHILL FULL OF PEOPLE FROM THE COUNTRYSIDE.
EVERYTHING IS CHANGING IN MANAUS.
THAT'S TRUE...
ONLY YOU DON'T CHANGE, OMAR.
YOU'RE STILL A WRECK. LOOK AT YOUR CLOTHES, YOUR HAIR...
THE HOUR YOU ARRIVE AT HOME.
NOW YOU HAVE NO FATHER, YOU SHOULD LOOK FOR A JOB AND STOP WITH THIS IDLE LUNACY.
YOUR FATHER COULDN'T BEAR LOOKING AT YOU LIKE THIS.
HE COULDN'T BEAR WATCHING YOUR LIFE THROWN AWAY.

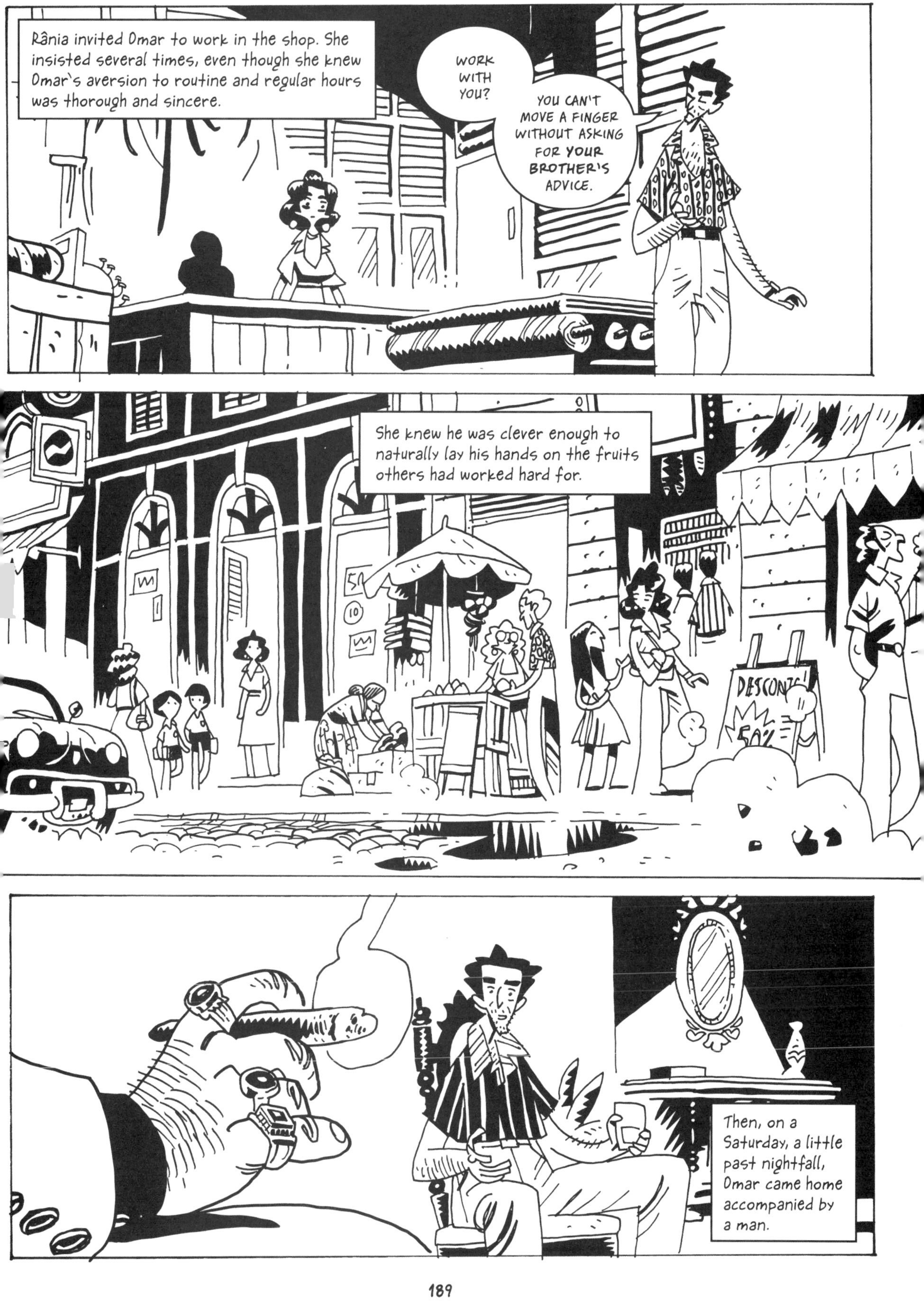
Rânia invited Omar to work in the shop. She insisted several times, even though she knew Omar's aversion to routine and regular hours was thorough and sincere.
WORK WITH YOU?
YOU CAN'T MOVE A FINGER WITHOUT ASKING FOR YOUR BROTHER'S ADVICE.
She knew he was clever enough to naturally lay his hands on the fruits others had worked hard for.
Then, on a Saturday, a little past nightfall, Omar came home accompanied by a man.

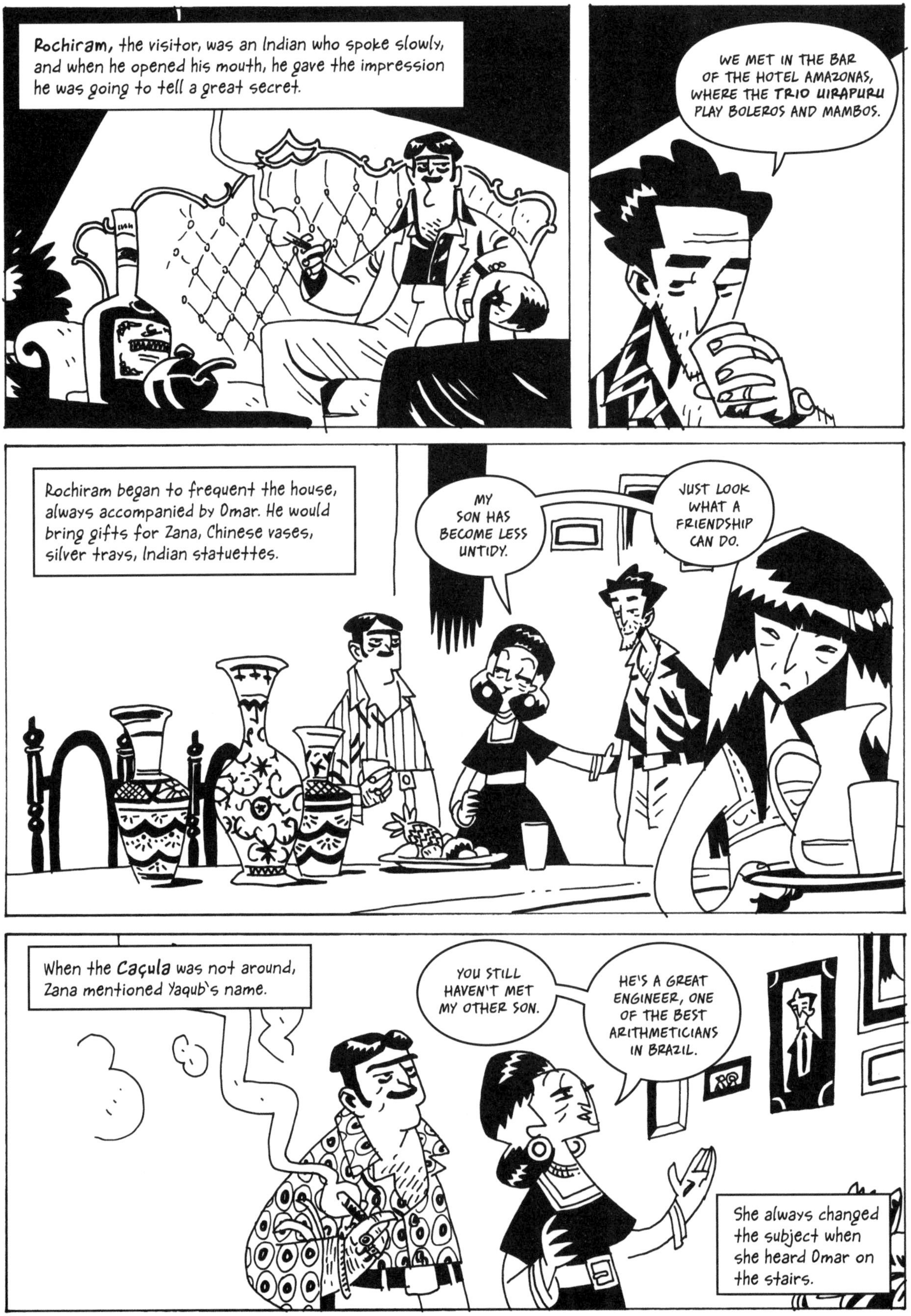
Rochiram, the visitor, was an Indian who spoke slowly, and when he opened his mouth, he gave the impression he was going to tell a great secret.
WE MET IN THE BAR OF THE HOTEL AMAZONAS, WHERE THE TRIO UIRAPURU PLAY BOLEROS AND MAMBOS.
Rochiram began to frequent the house, always accompanied by Omar. He would bring gifts for Zana, Chinese vases, silver trays, Indian statuettes.
MY SON HAS BECOME LESS UNTIDY.
JUST LOOK WHAT A FRIENDSHIP CAN DO.
When the Caçula was not around, Zana mentioned Yaqub's name.
YOU STILL HAVEN'T MET MY OTHER SON.
HE'S A GREAT ENGINEER, ONE OF THE BEST ARITHMETICIANS IN BRAZIL.
She always changed the subject when she heard Omar on the stairs.

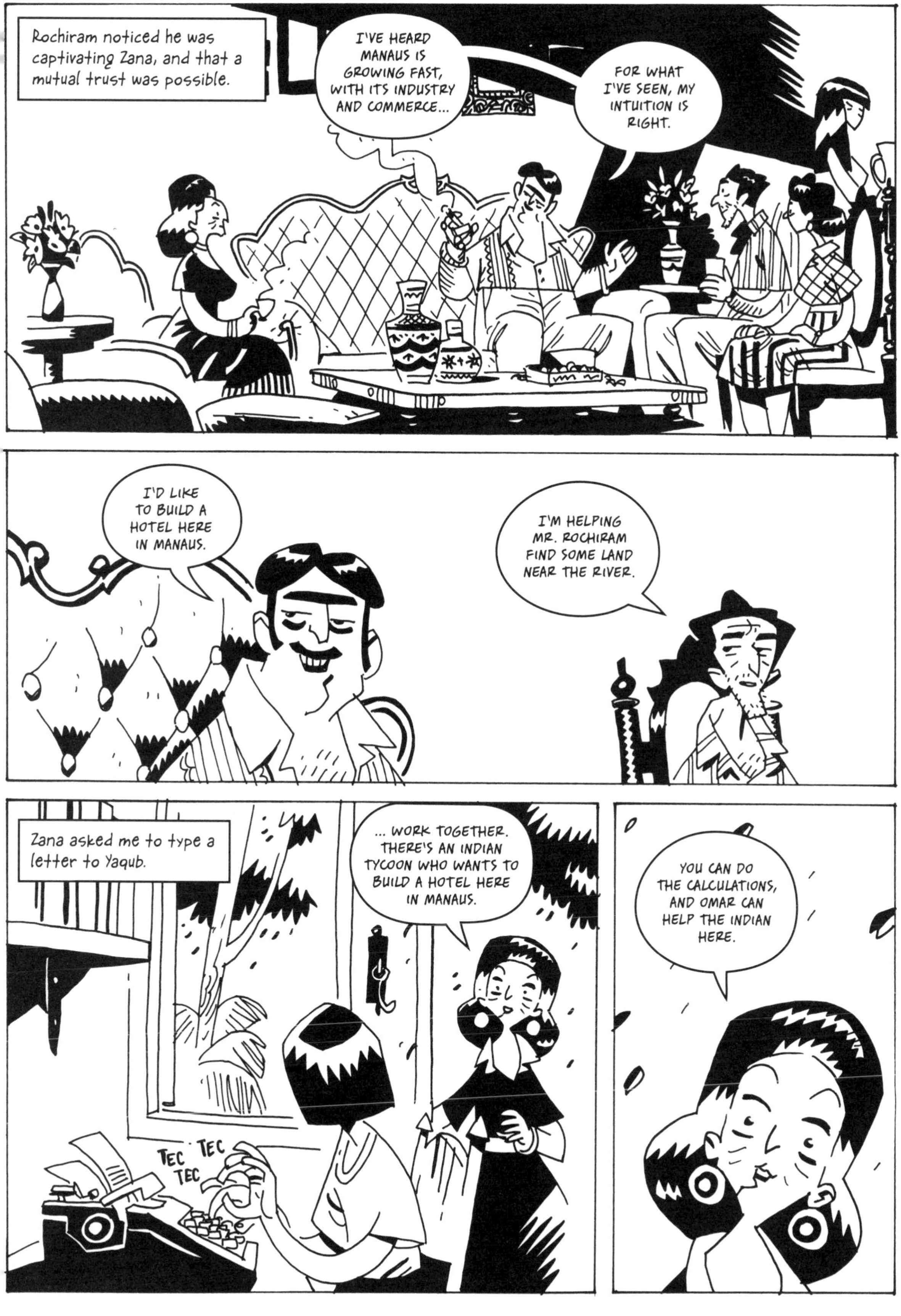
Rochiram noticed he was captivating Zana, and that a mutual trust was possible.
I'VE HEARD MANAUS IS GROWING FAST, WITH ITS INDUSTRY AND COMMERCE...
FOR WHAT I'VE SEEN, MY INTUITION IS RIGHT.
I'D LIKE TO BUILD A HOTEL HERE IN MANAUS.
I'M HELPING MR. ROCHIRAM FIND SOME LAND NEAR THE RIVER.
Zana asked me to type a letter to Yaqub.
... WORK TOGETHER. THERE'S AN INDIAN TYCOON WHO WANTS TO BUILD A HOTEL HERE IN MANAUS.
TEC TEC
TEC
YOU CAN DO THE CALCULATIONS, AND OMAR CAN HELP THE INDIAN HERE.

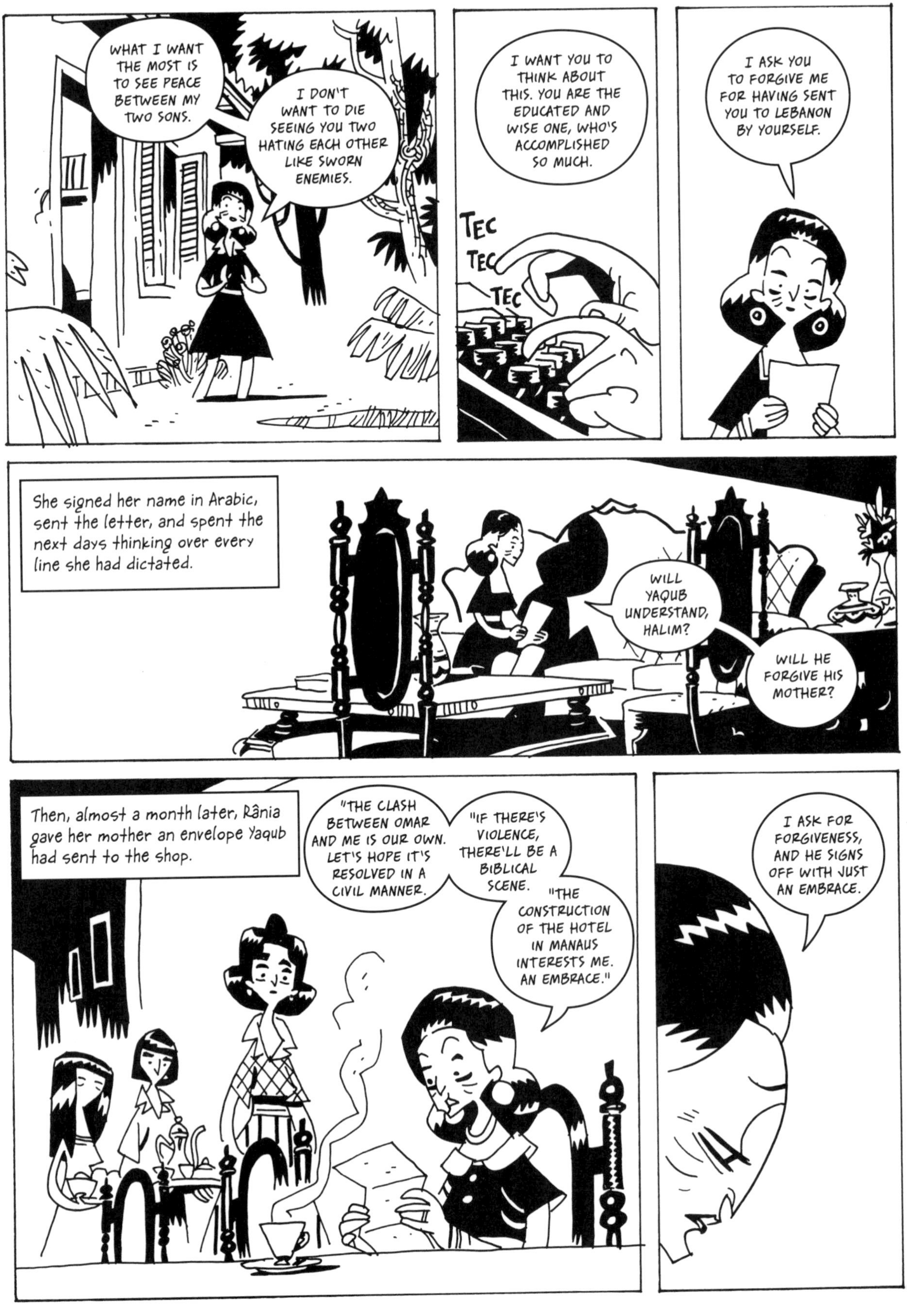
WHAT I WANT THE MOST IS TO SEE PEACE BETWEEN MY TWO SONS.
I DON'T WANT TO DIE SEEING YOU TWO HATING EACH OTHER LIKE SWORN ENEMIES.
I WANT YOU TO THINK ABOUT THIS. YOU ARE THE EDUCATED AND WISE ONE, WHO'S ACCOMPLISHED SO MUCH.
TEC
TEC
TEC
I ASK YOU TO FORGIVE ME FOR HAVING SENT YOU TO LEBANON BY YOURSELF.
She signed her name in Arabic, sent the letter, and spent the next days thinking over every line she had dictated.
WILL YAQUB UNDERSTAND, HALIM?
WILL HE FORGIVE HIS MOTHER?
Then, almost a month later, Rânia gave her mother an envelope Yaqub had sent to the shop.
"THE CLASH BETWEEN OMAR AND ME IS OUR OWN. LET'S HOPE IT'S RESOLVED IN A CIVIL MANNER.
"IF THERE'S VIOLENCE, THERE'LL BE A BIBLICAL SCENE.
"THE CONSTRUCTION OF THE HOTEL IN MANAUS INTERESTS ME. AN EMBRACE."
I ASK FOR FORGIVENESS, AND HE SIGNS OFF WITH JUST AN EMBRACE.

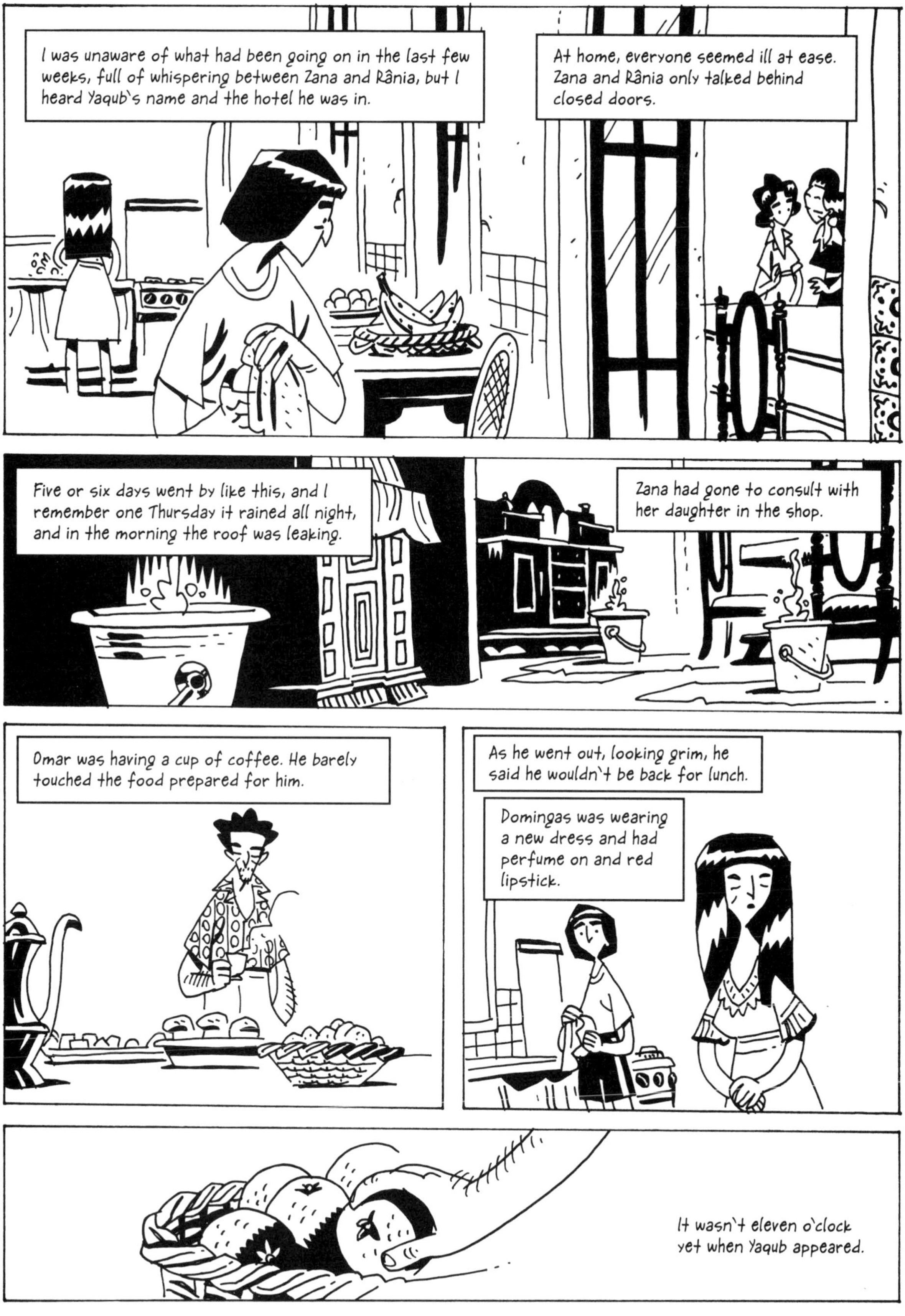
I was unaware of what had been going on in the last few weeks, full of whispering between Zana and Rânia, but I heard Yaqub's name and the hotel he was in.
At home, everyone seemed ill at ease. Zana and Rânia only talked behind closed doors.
Five or six days went by like this, and I remember one Thursday it rained all night, and in the morning the roof was leaking.
Zana had gone to consult with her daughter in the shop.
Omar was having a cup of coffee. He barely touched the food prepared for him.
As he went out, looking grim, he said he wouldn't be back for lunch.
Domingas was wearing a new dress and had perfume on and red lipstick.
It wasn't eleven o'clock yet when Yaqub appeared.

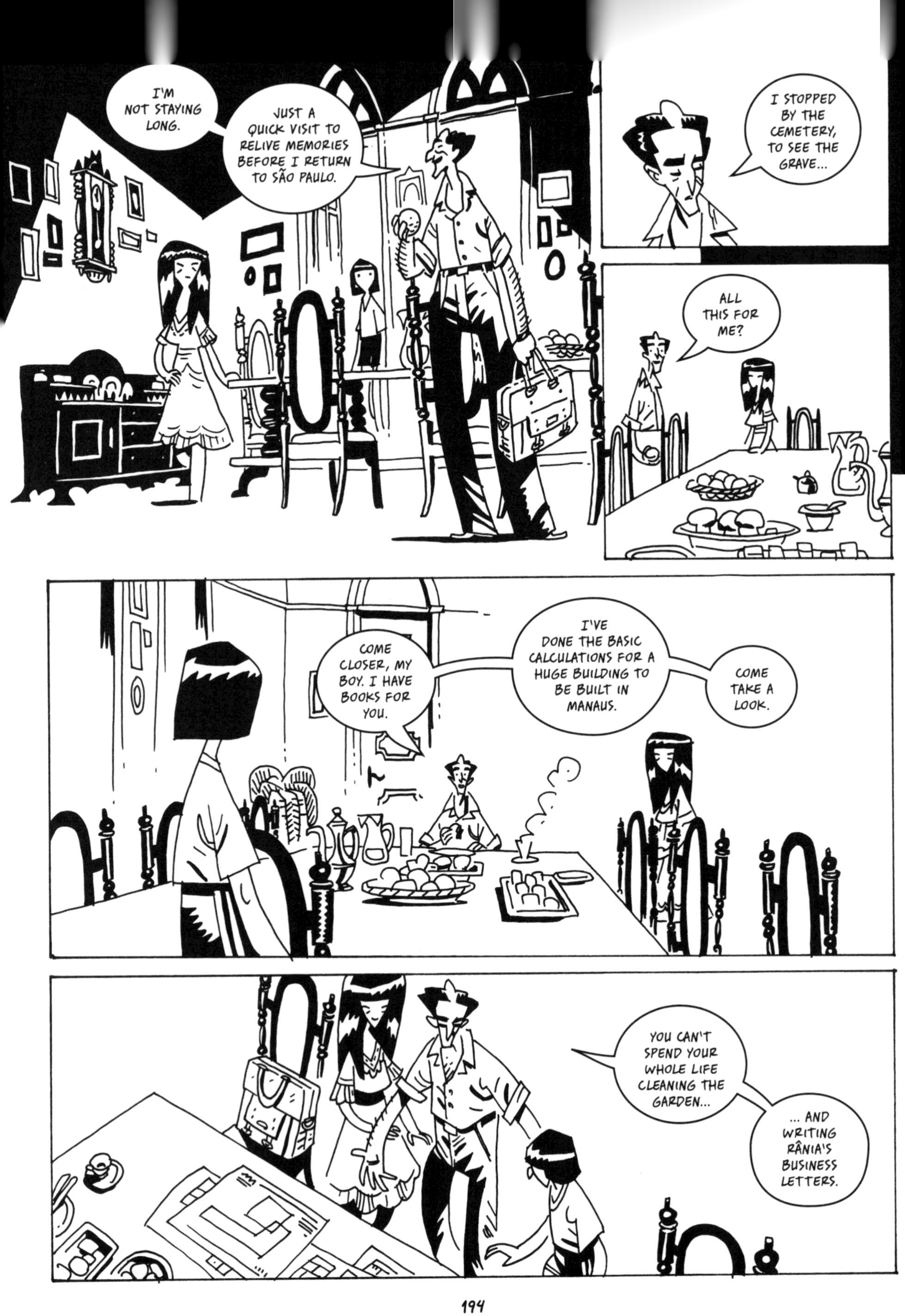
I'M NOT STAYING LONG.
JUST A QUICK VISIT TO RELIVE MEMORIES BEFORE I RETURN TO SÃO PAULO.
I STOPPED BY THE CEMETERY, TO SEE THE GRAVE...
ALL THIS FOR ME?
COME CLOSER, MY BOY. I HAVE BOOKS FOR YOU.
I'VE DONE THE BASIC CALCULATIONS FOR A HUGE BUILDING TO BE BUILT IN MANAUS.
COME TAKE A LOOK.
YOU CAN'T SPEND YOUR WHOLE LIFE CLEANING THE GARDEN...
... AND WRITING RÂNIA'S BUSINESS LETTERS.

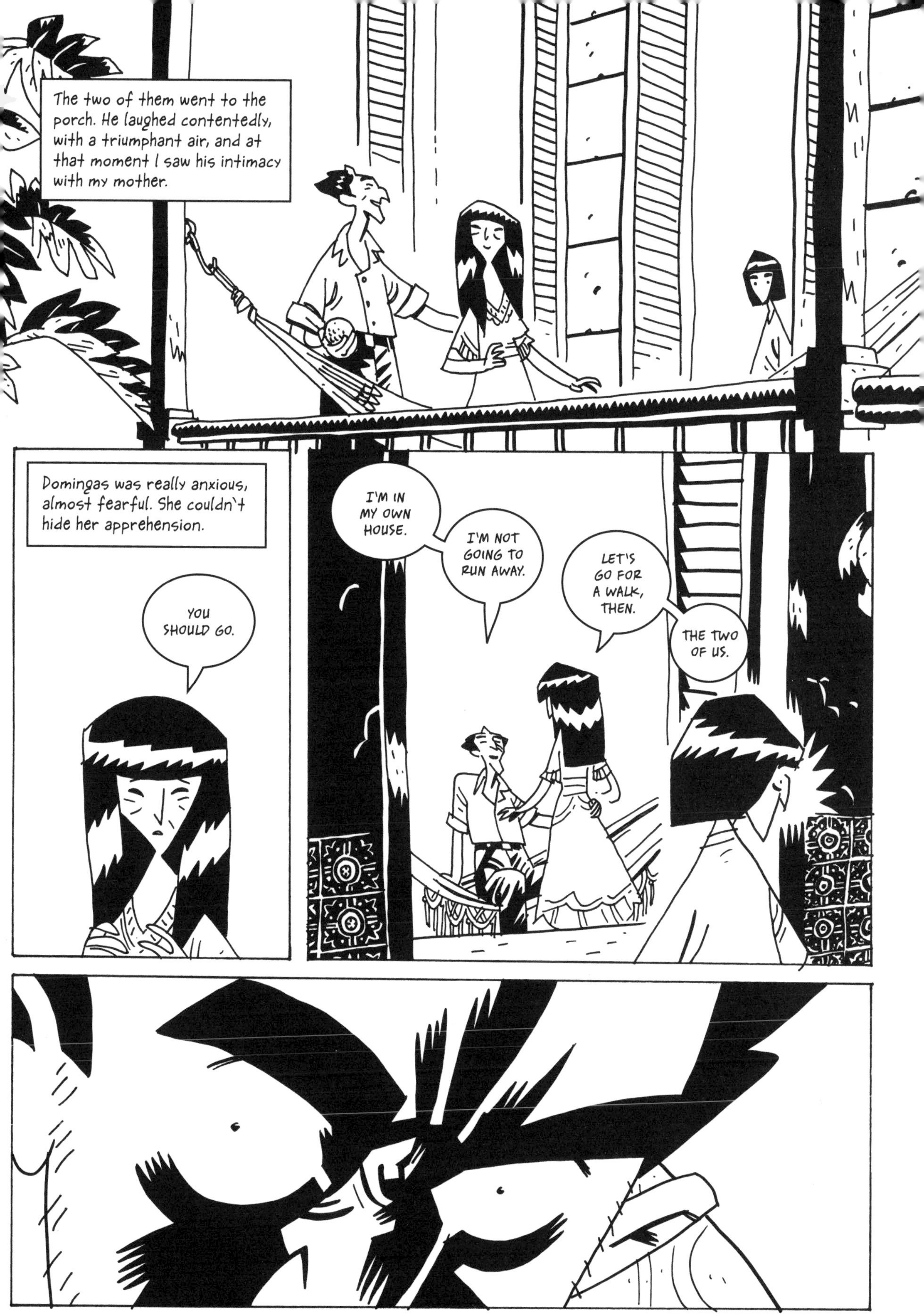
The two of them went to the porch. He laughed contentedly, with a triumphant air, and at that moment I saw his intimacy with my mother.
Domingas was really anxious, almost fearful. She couldn't hide her apprehension.
YOU SHOULD GO.
I'M IN MY OWN HOUSE.
I'M NOT GOING TO RUN AWAY.
LET'S GO FOR A WALK, THEN.
THE TWO OF US.

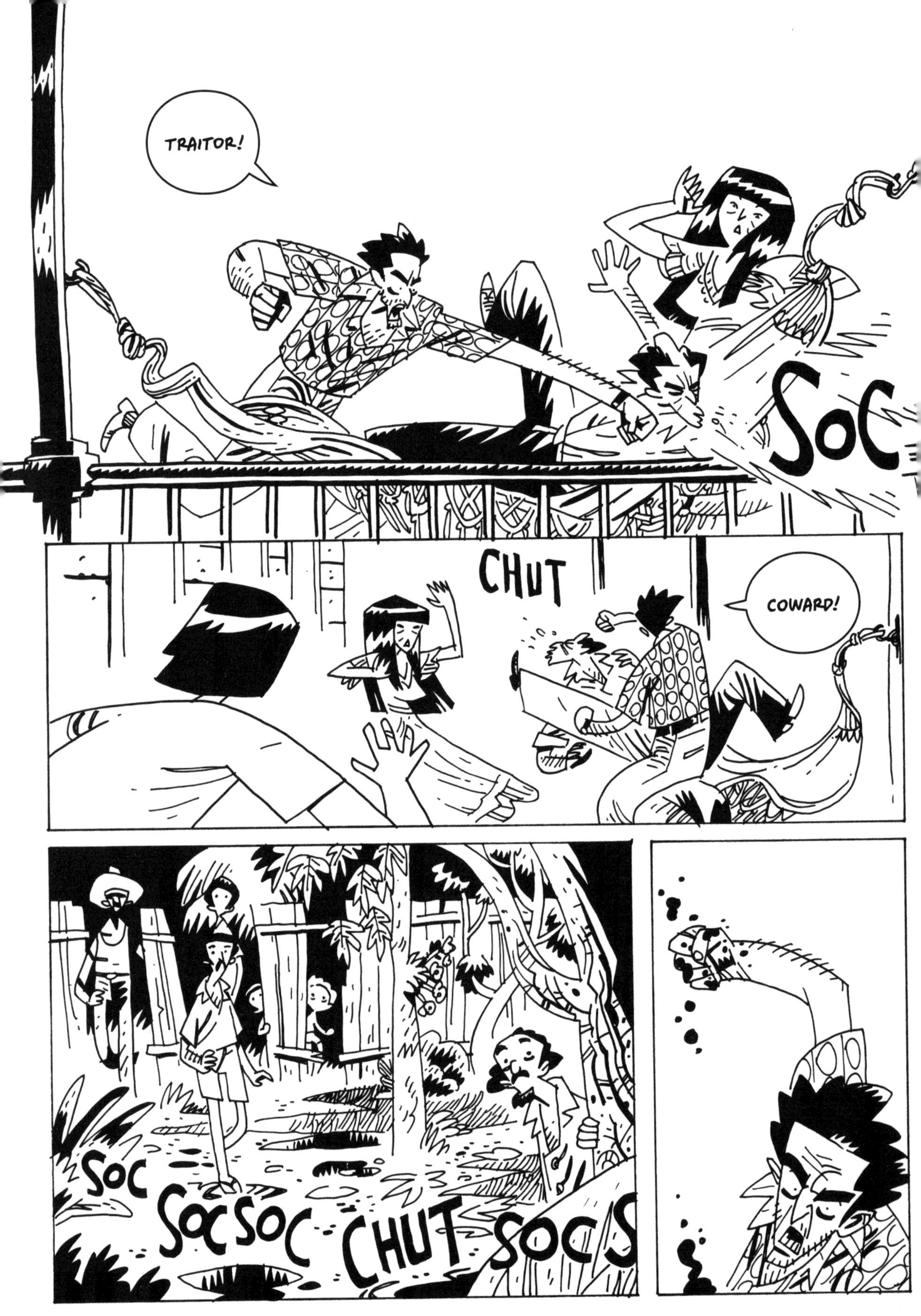
TRAITOR!
SOC
CHUT
COWARD!
SOC
SOC SOC
CHUT
SOC S

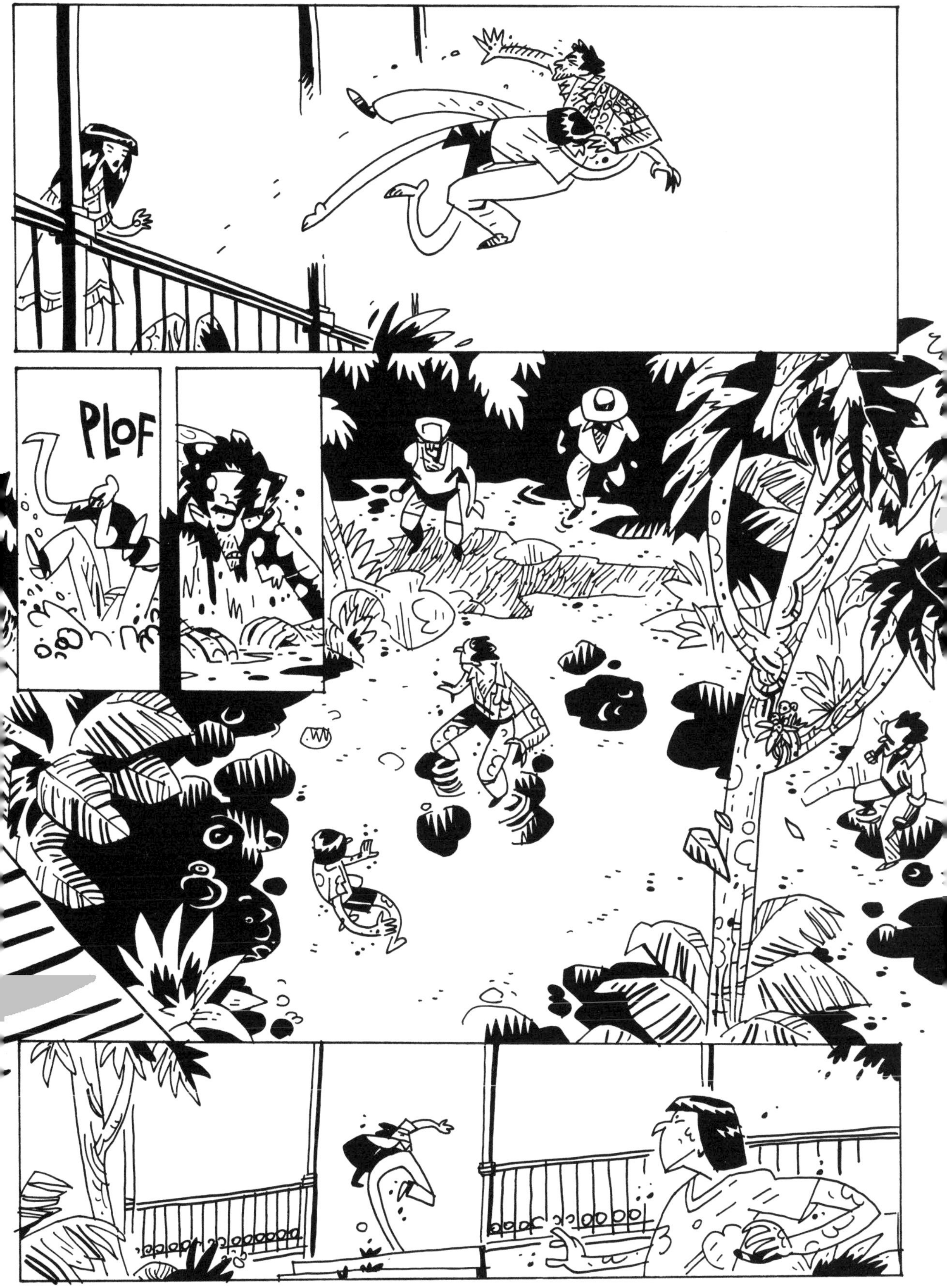
PLOF

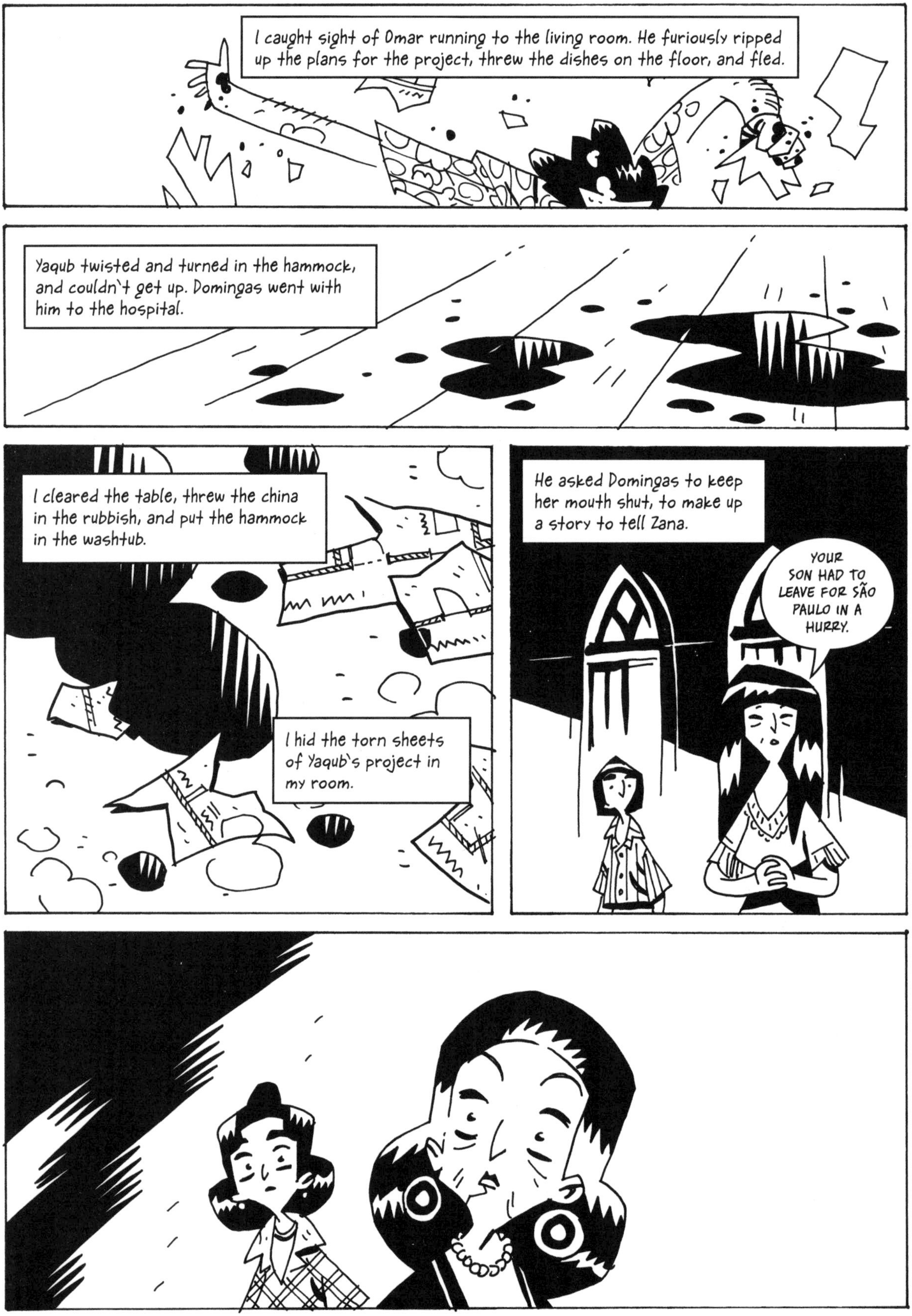
I caught sight of Omar running to the living room. He furiously ripped up the plans for the project, threw the dishes on the floor, and fled.
Yaqub twisted and turned in the hammock, and couldn't get up. Domingas went with him to the hospital.
I cleared the table, threw the china in the rubbish, and put the hammock in the washtub.
I hid the torn sheets of Yaqub's project in my room.
He asked Domingas to keep her mouth shut, to make up a story to tell Zana.
YOUR SON HAD TO LEAVE FOR SÃO PAULO IN A HURRY.

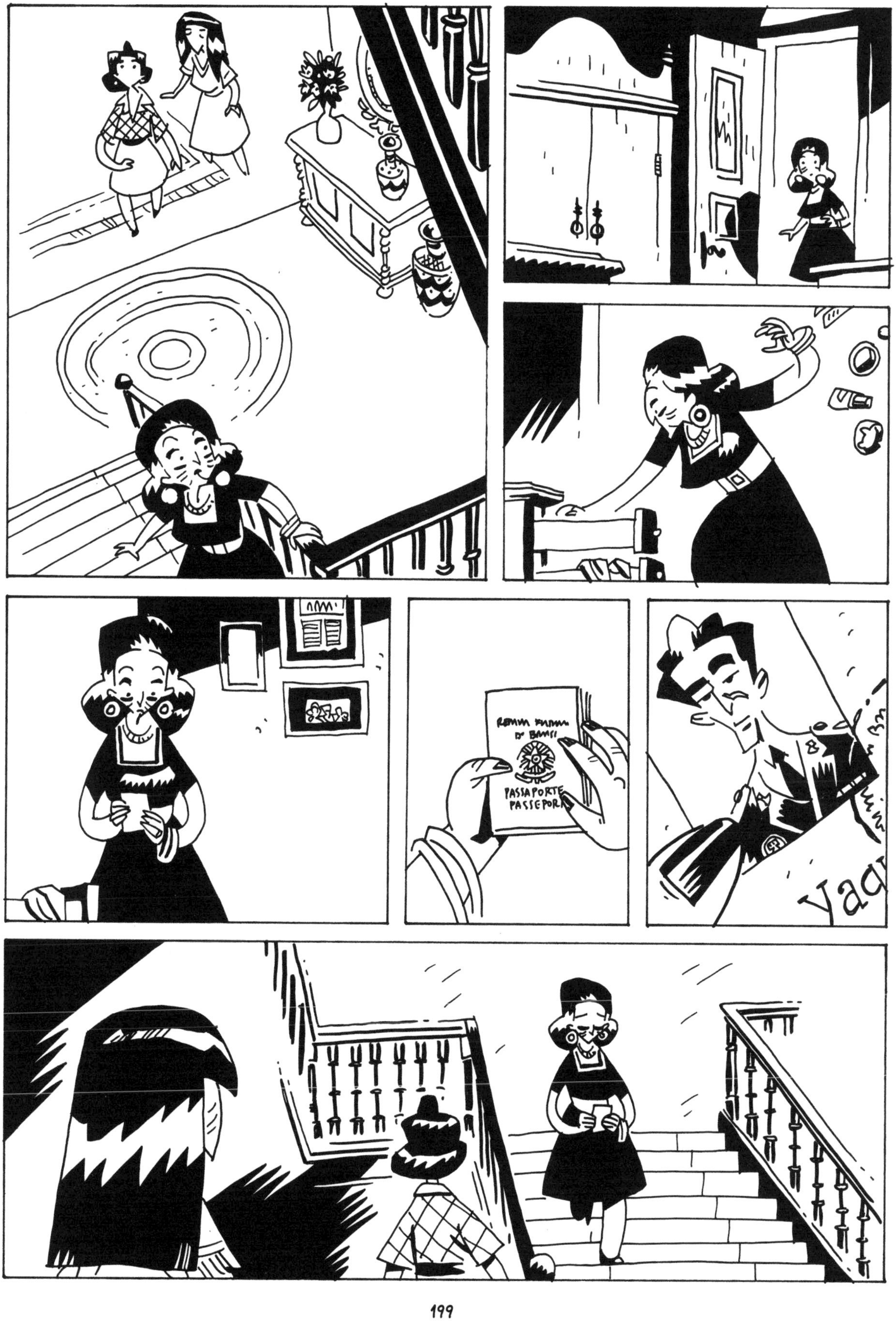
PASSAPORTE

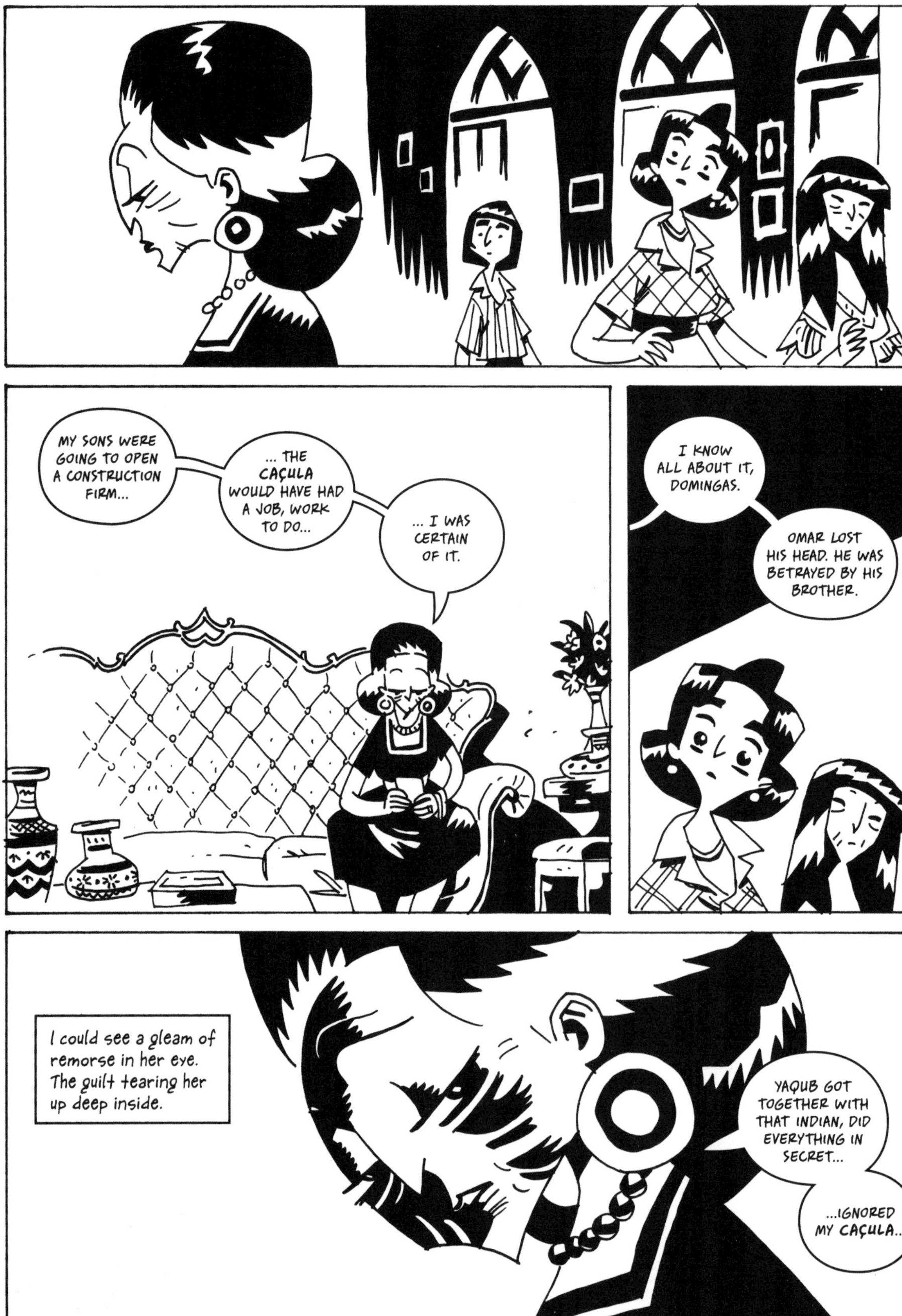
MY SONS WERE GOING TO OPEN A CONSTRUCTION FIRM...
... THE CAÇULA WOULD HAVE HAD A JOB, WORK TO DO...
... I WAS CERTAIN OF IT.
I KNOW ALL ABOUT IT, DOMINGAS.
OMAR LOST HIS HEAD. HE WAS BETRAYED BY HIS BROTHER.
I could see a gleam of remorse in her eye. The guilt tearing her up deep inside.
YAQUB GOT TOGETHER WITH THAT INDIAN, DID EVERYTHING IN SECRET...
...IGNORED MY CAÇULA...

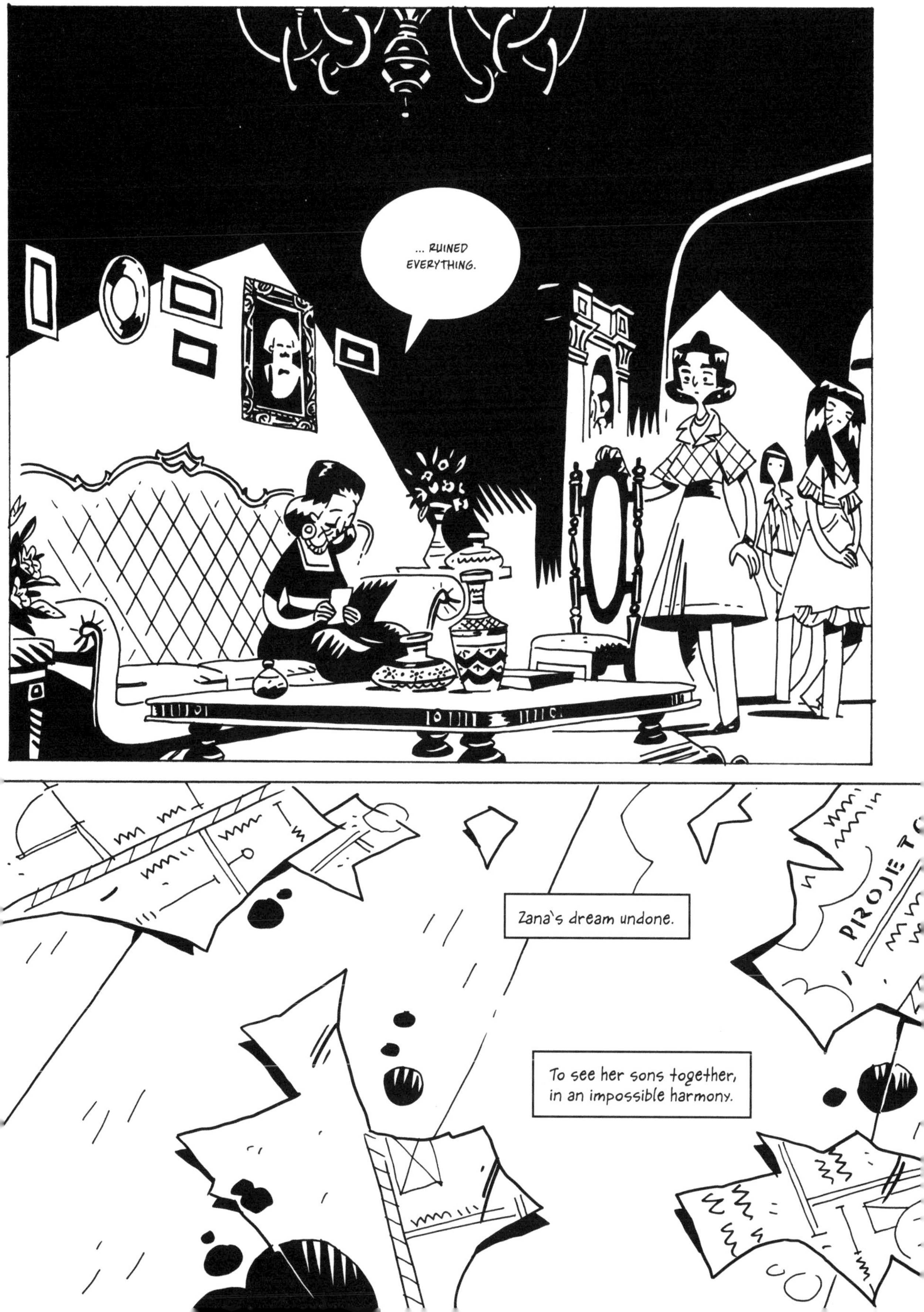
... RUINED EVERYTHING.
Zana's dream undone.
To see her sons together, in an impossible harmony.

Chapter 10

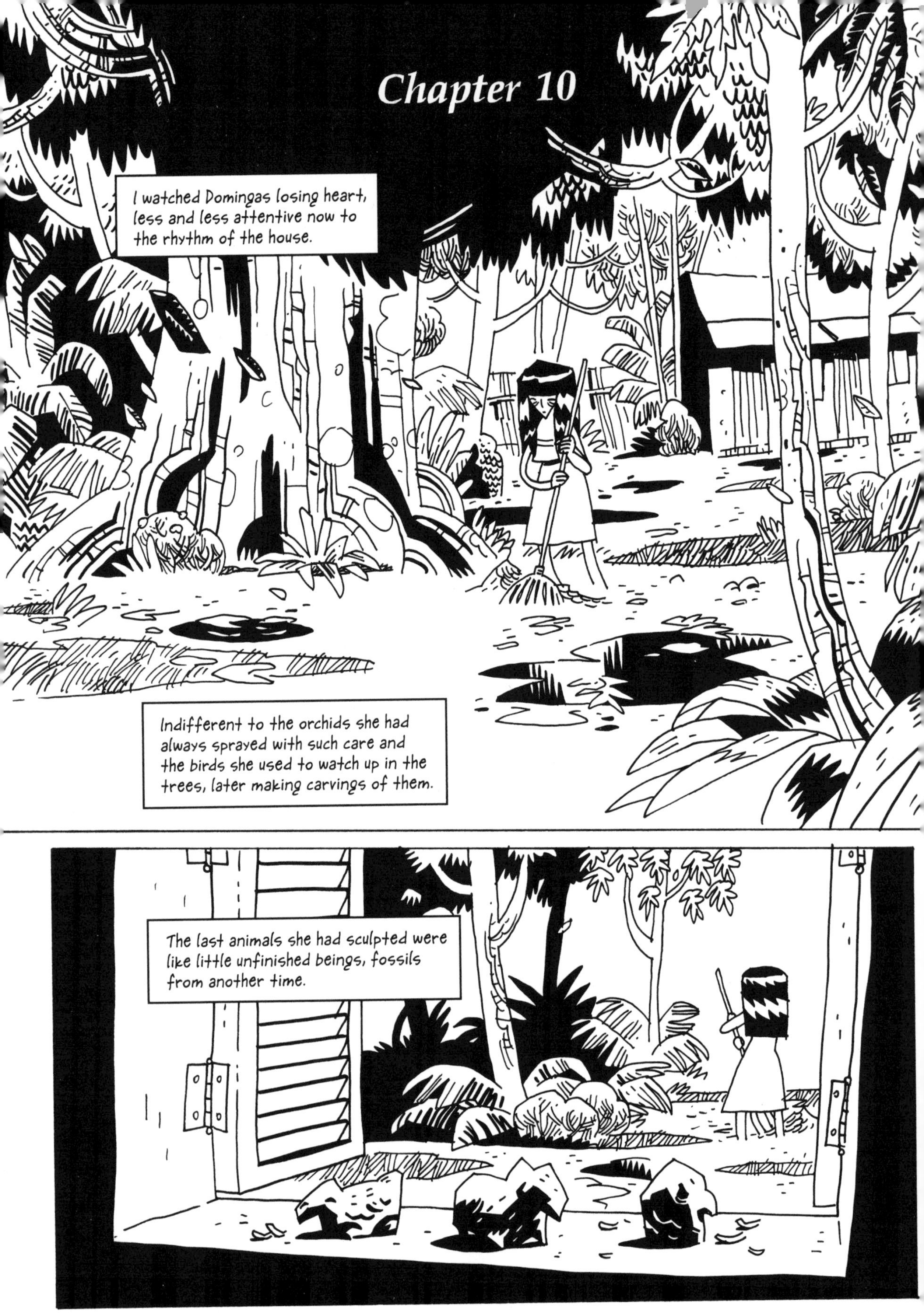
I watched Domingas losing heart, less and less attentive now to the rhythm of the house.
Indifferent to the orchids she had always sprayed with such care and the birds she used to watch up in the trees, later making carvings of them.
The last animals she had sculpted were like little unfinished beings, fossils from another time.

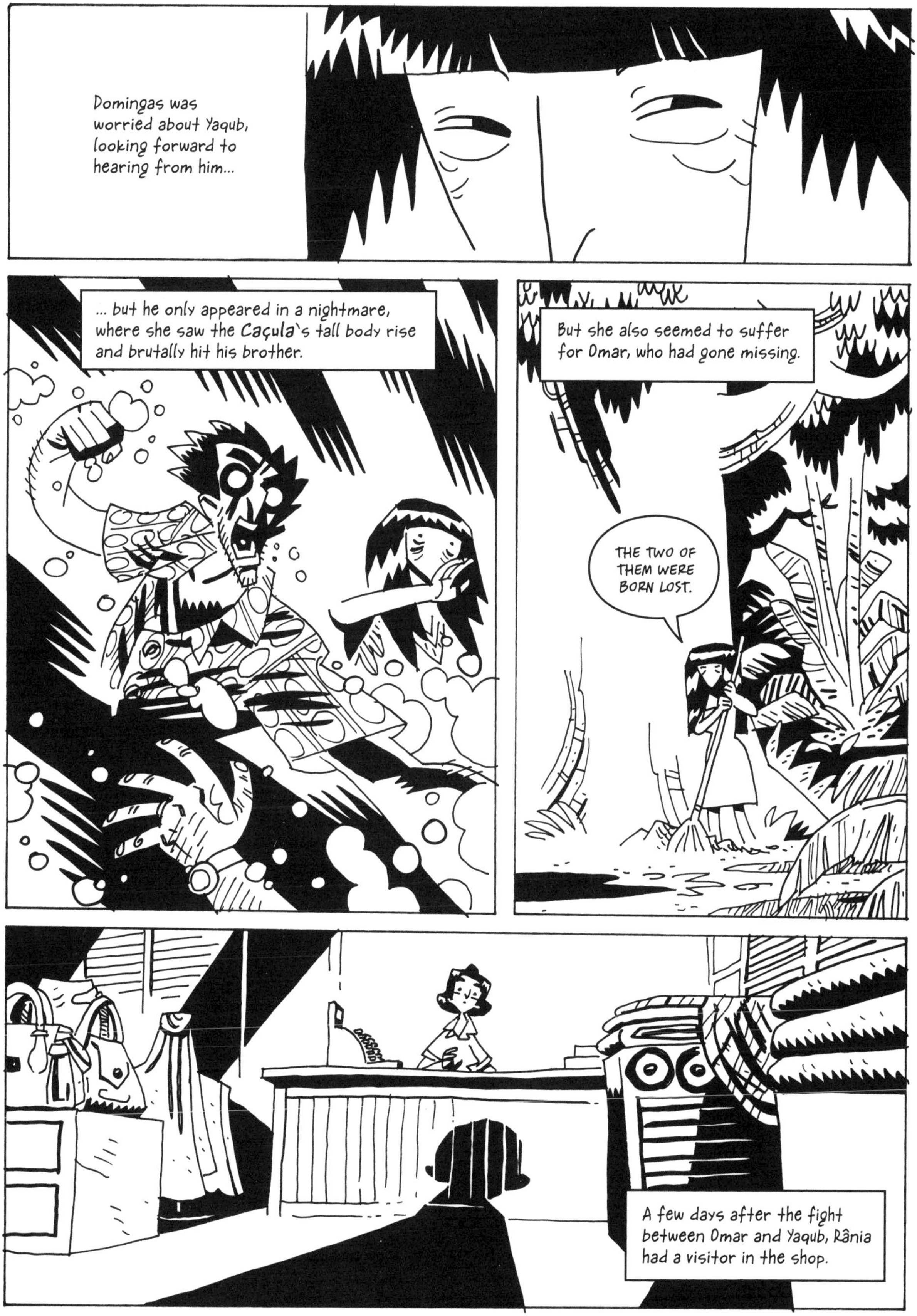
Domingas was worried about Yaqub, looking forward to hearing from him...
... but he only appeared in a nightmare, where she saw the Caçula's tall body rise and brutally hit his brother.
But she also seemed to suffer for Omar, who had gone missing.
THE TWO OF THEM WERE BORN LOST.
A few days after the fight between Omar and Yaqub, Rânia had a visitor in the shop.

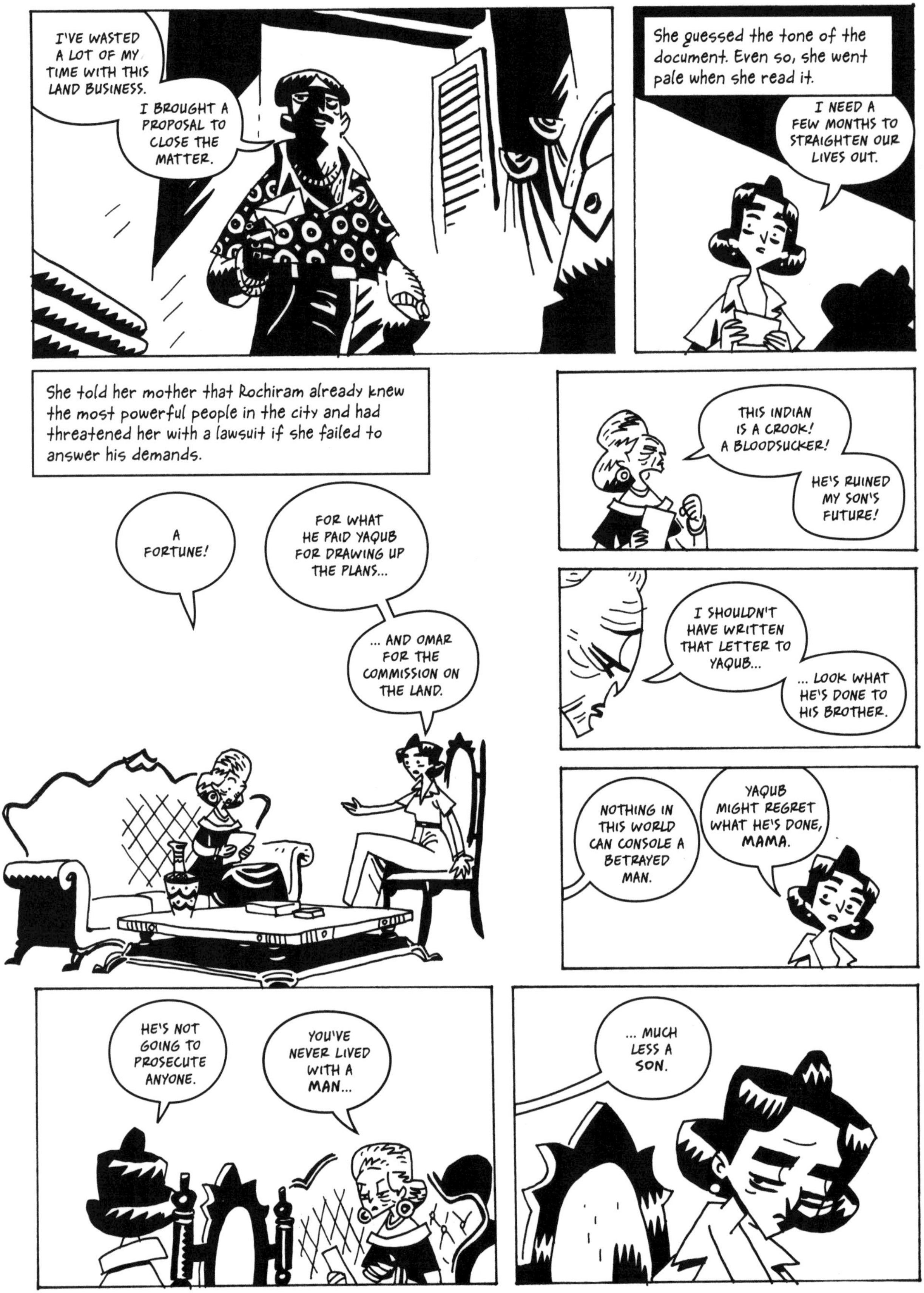
I'VE WASTED A LOT OF MY TIME WITH THIS LAND BUSINESS.
I BROUGHT A PROPOSAL TO CLOSE THE MATTER.
She guessed the tone of the document. Even so, she went pale when she read it.
I NEED A FEW MONTHS TO STRAIGHTEN OUR LIVES OUT.
She told her mother that Rochiram already knew the most powerful people in the city and had threatened her with a lawsuit if she failed to answer his demands.
A FORTUNE!
FOR WHAT HE PAID YAQUB FOR DRAWING UP THE PLANS...
... AND OMAR FOR THE COMMISSION ON THE LAND.
THIS INDIAN IS A CROOK! A BLOODSUCKER!
HE'S RUINED MY SON'S FUTURE!
I SHOULDN'T HAVE WRITTEN THAT LETTER TO YAQUB...
... LOOK WHAT HE'S DONE TO HIS BROTHER.
YAQUB MIGHT REGRET WHAT HE'S DONE, MAMA.
NOTHING IN THIS WORLD CAN CONSOLE A BETRAYED MAN.
HE'S NOT GOING TO PROSECUTE ANYONE.
YOU'VE NEVER LIVED WITH A MAN...
... MUCH LESS A SON.

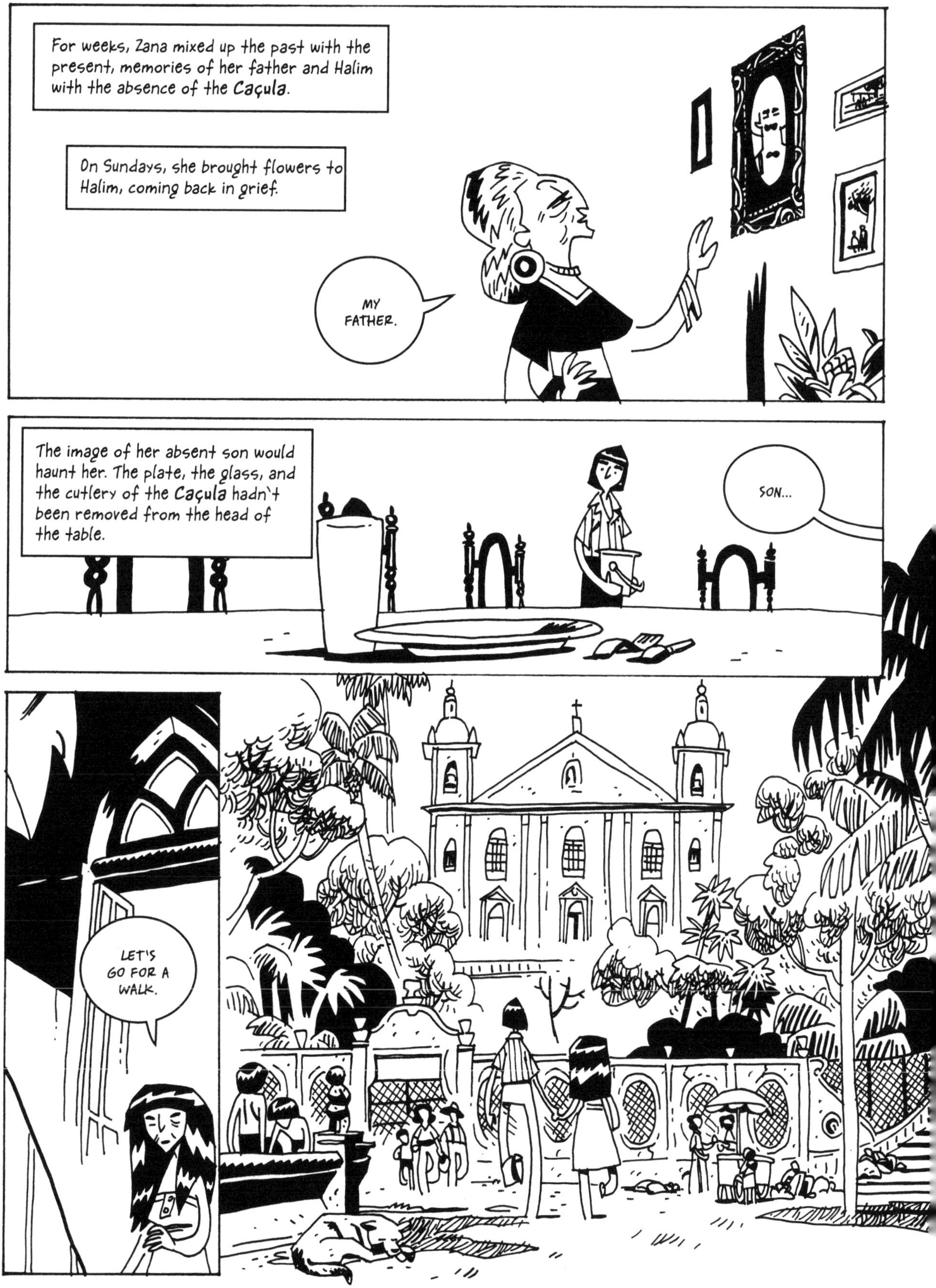
For weeks, Zana mixed up the past with the present, memories of her father and Halim with the absence of the Caçula.
On Sundays, she brought flowers to Halim, coming back in grief.
MY FATHER.
The image of her absent son would haunt her. The plate, the glass, and the cutlery of the Caçula hadn't been removed from the head of the table.
SON...
LET'S GO FOR A WALK.

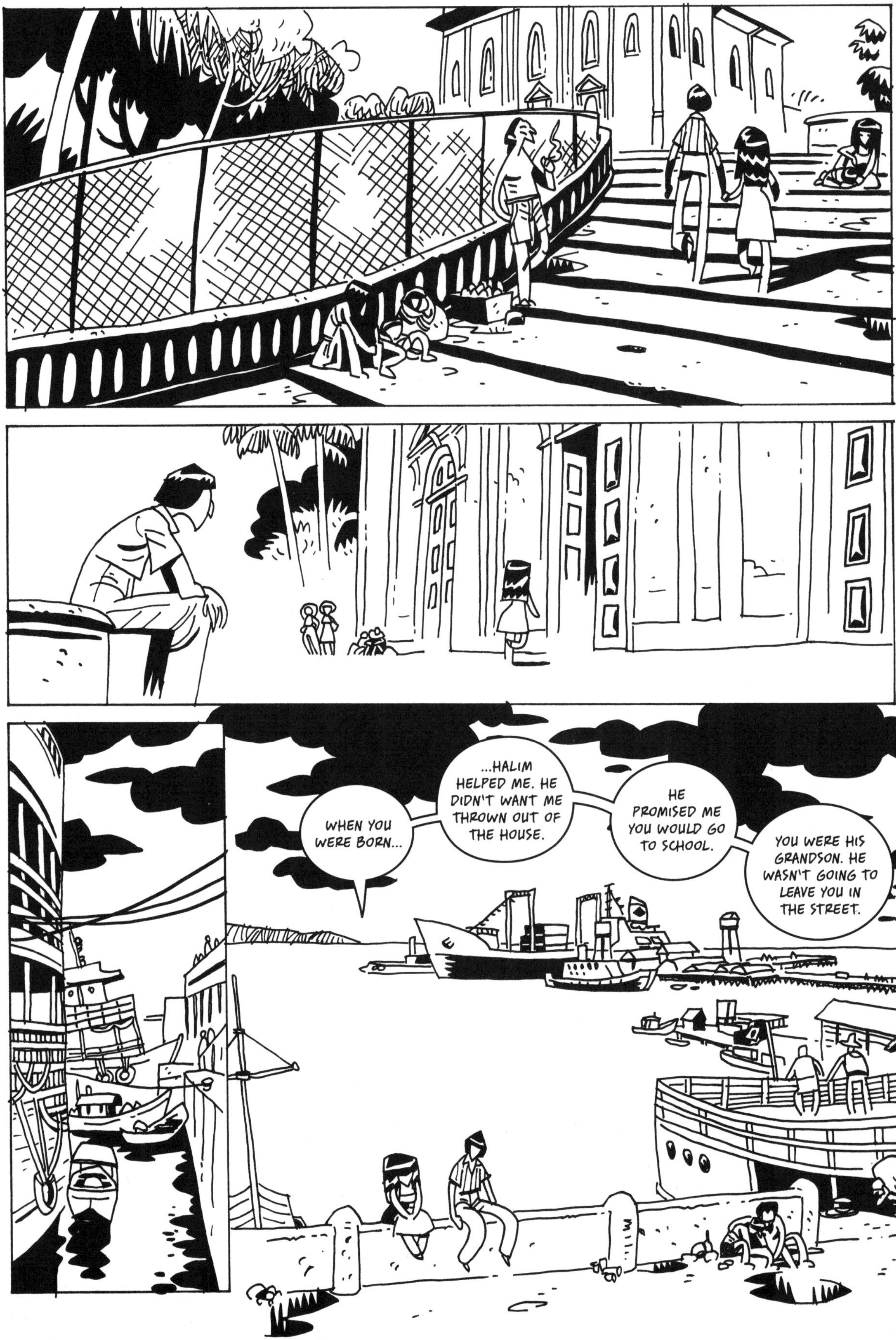
WHEN YOU WERE BORN...
...HALIM HELPED ME. HE DIDN'T WANT ME THROWN OUT OF THE HOUSE.
HE PROMISED ME YOU WOULD GO TO SCHOOL.
YOU WERE HIS GRANDSON. HE WASN'T GOING TO LEAVE YOU IN THE STREET.

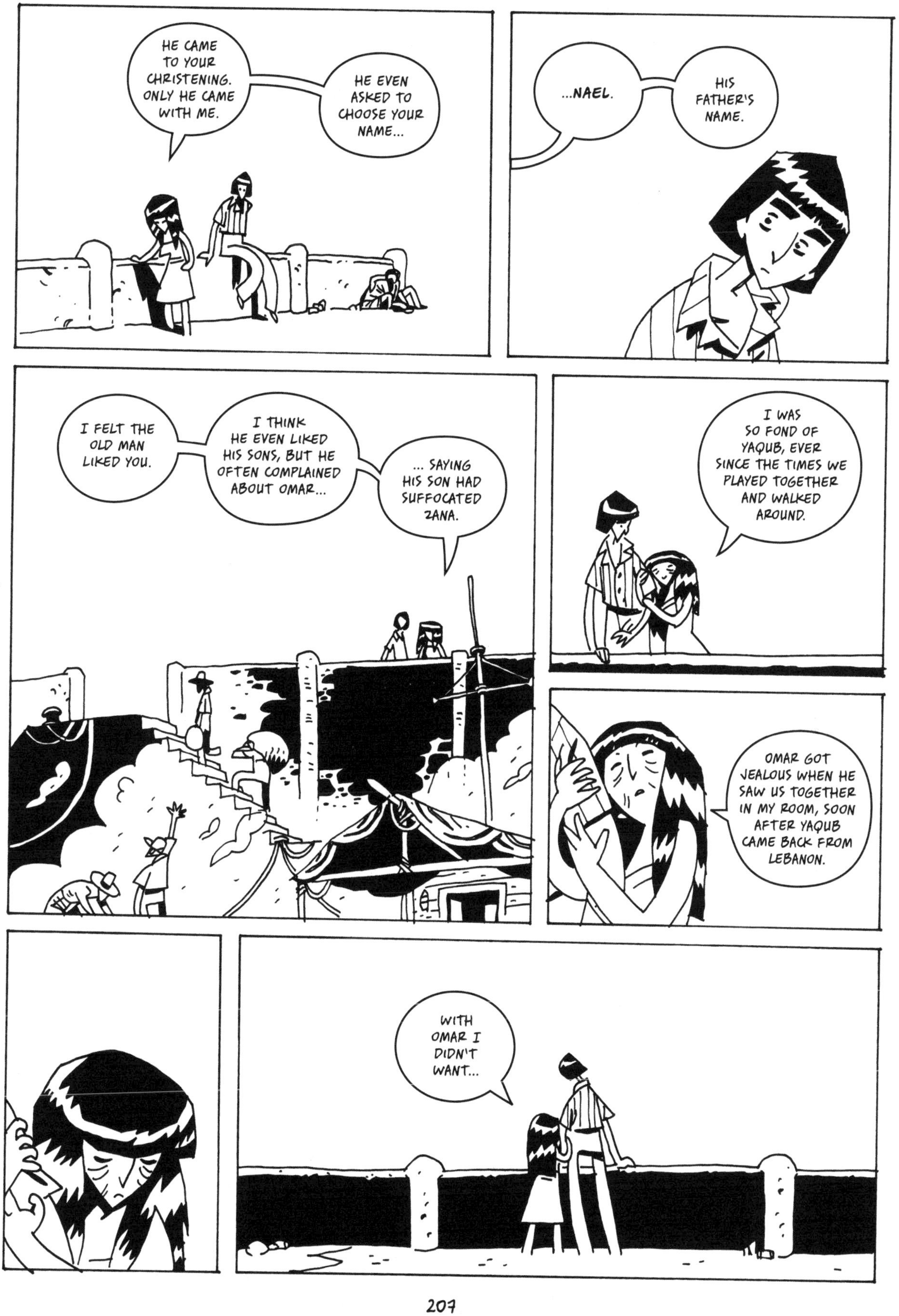
HE CAME TO YOUR CHRISTENING. ONLY HE CAME WITH ME.
HE EVEN ASKED TO CHOOSE YOUR NAME...
...NAEL.
HIS FATHER'S NAME.
I FELT THE OLD MAN LIKED YOU.
I THINK HE EVEN LIKED HIS SONS, BUT HE OFTEN COMPLAINED ABOUT OMAR...
... SAYING HIS SON HAD SUFFOCATED ZANA.
I WAS SO FOND OF YAQUB, EVER SINCE THE TIMES WE PLAYED TOGETHER AND WALKED AROUND.
OMAR GOT JEALOUS WHEN HE SAW US TOGETHER IN MY ROOM, SOON AFTER YAQUB CAME BACK FROM LEBANON.
WITH OMAR I DIDN'T WANT...

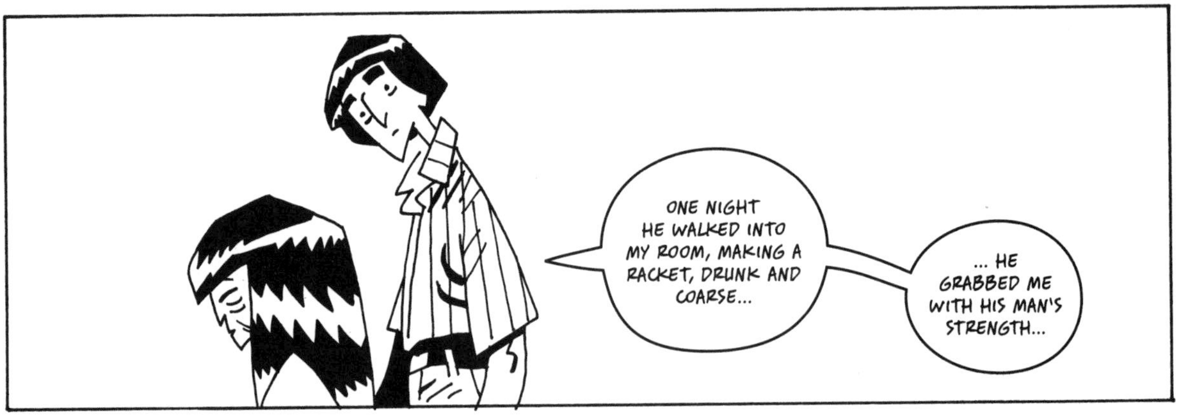
ONE NIGHT HE WALKED INTO MY ROOM, MAKING A RACKET, DRUNK AND COARSE...
... HE GRABBED ME WITH HIS MAN'S STRENGTH...

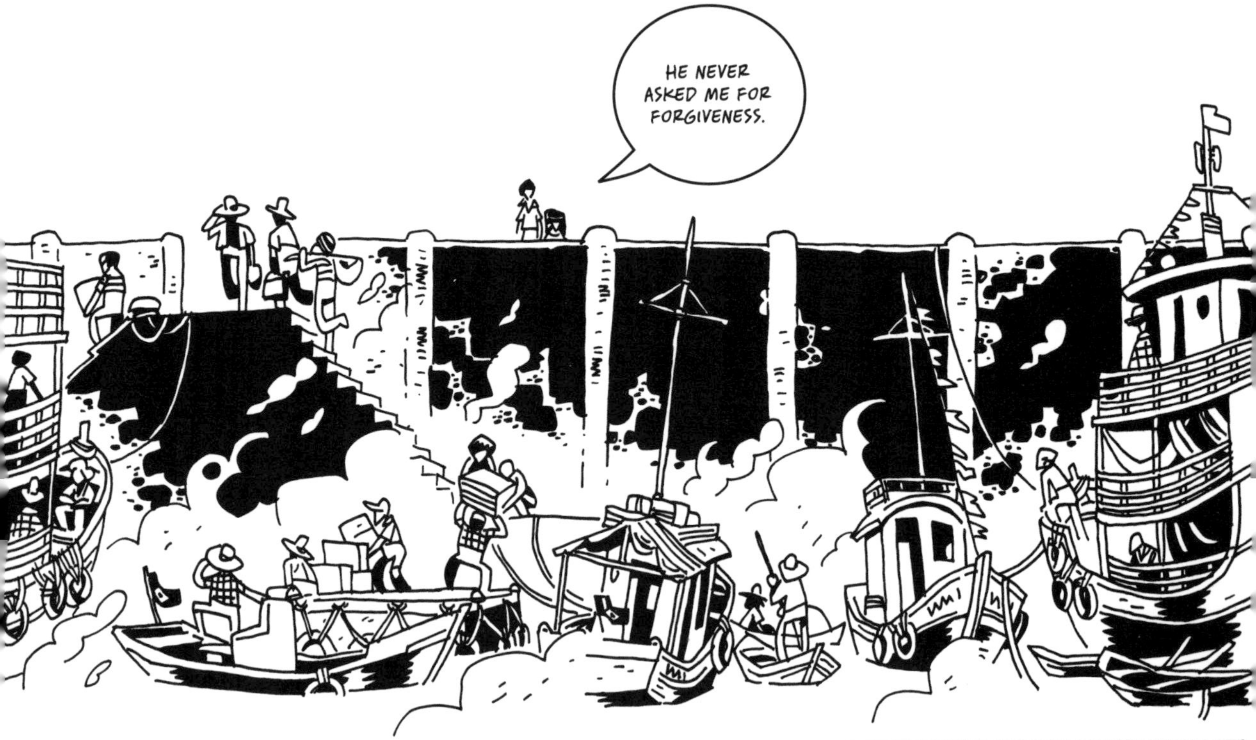
HE NEVER ASKED ME FOR FORGIVENESS.

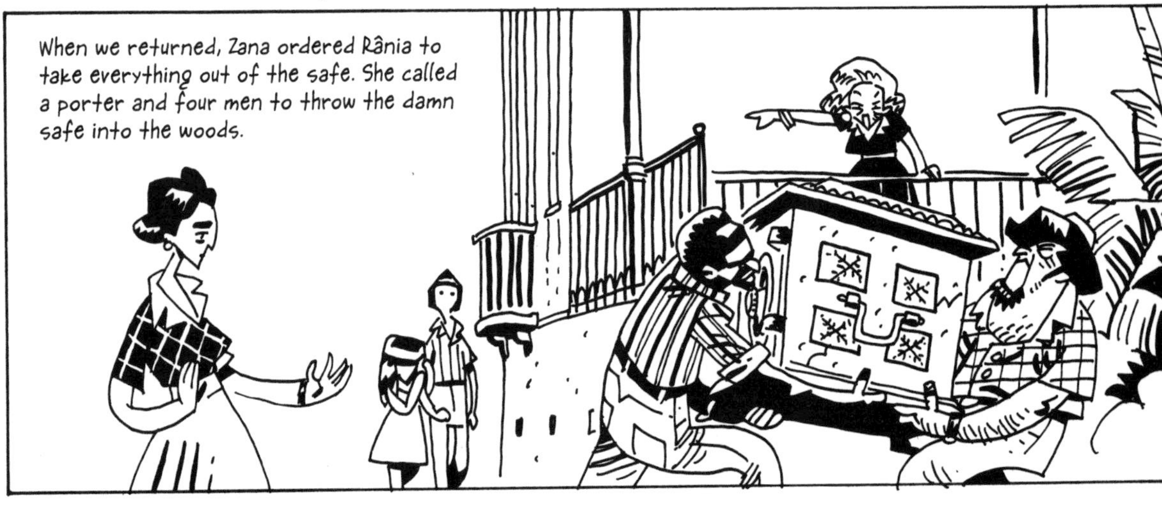
When we returned, Zana ordered Rânia to take everything out of the safe. She called a porter and four men to throw the damn safe into the woods.

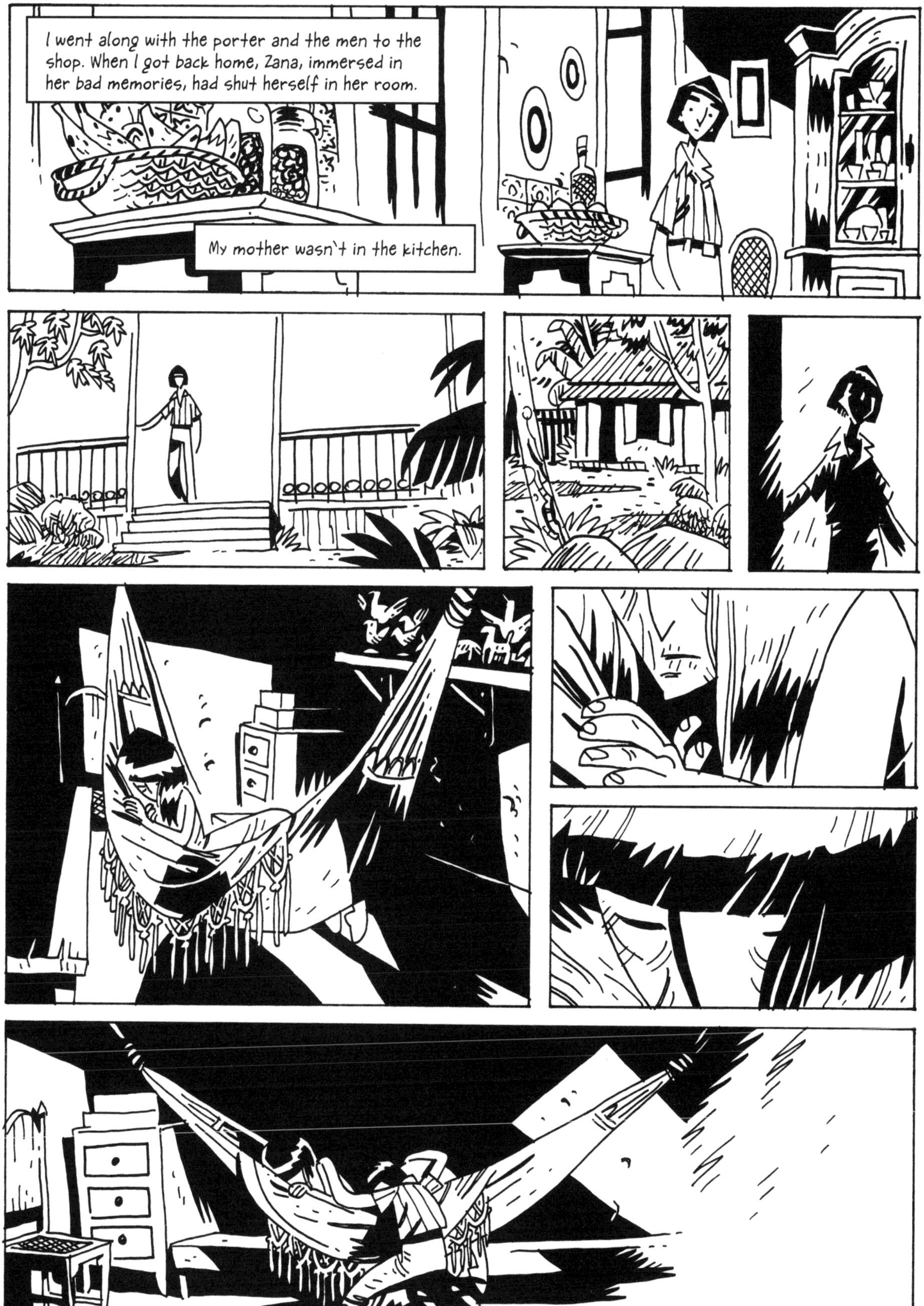
I went along with the porter and the men to the shop. When I got back home, Zana, immersed in her bad memories, had shut herself in her room.
My mother wasn't in the kitchen.

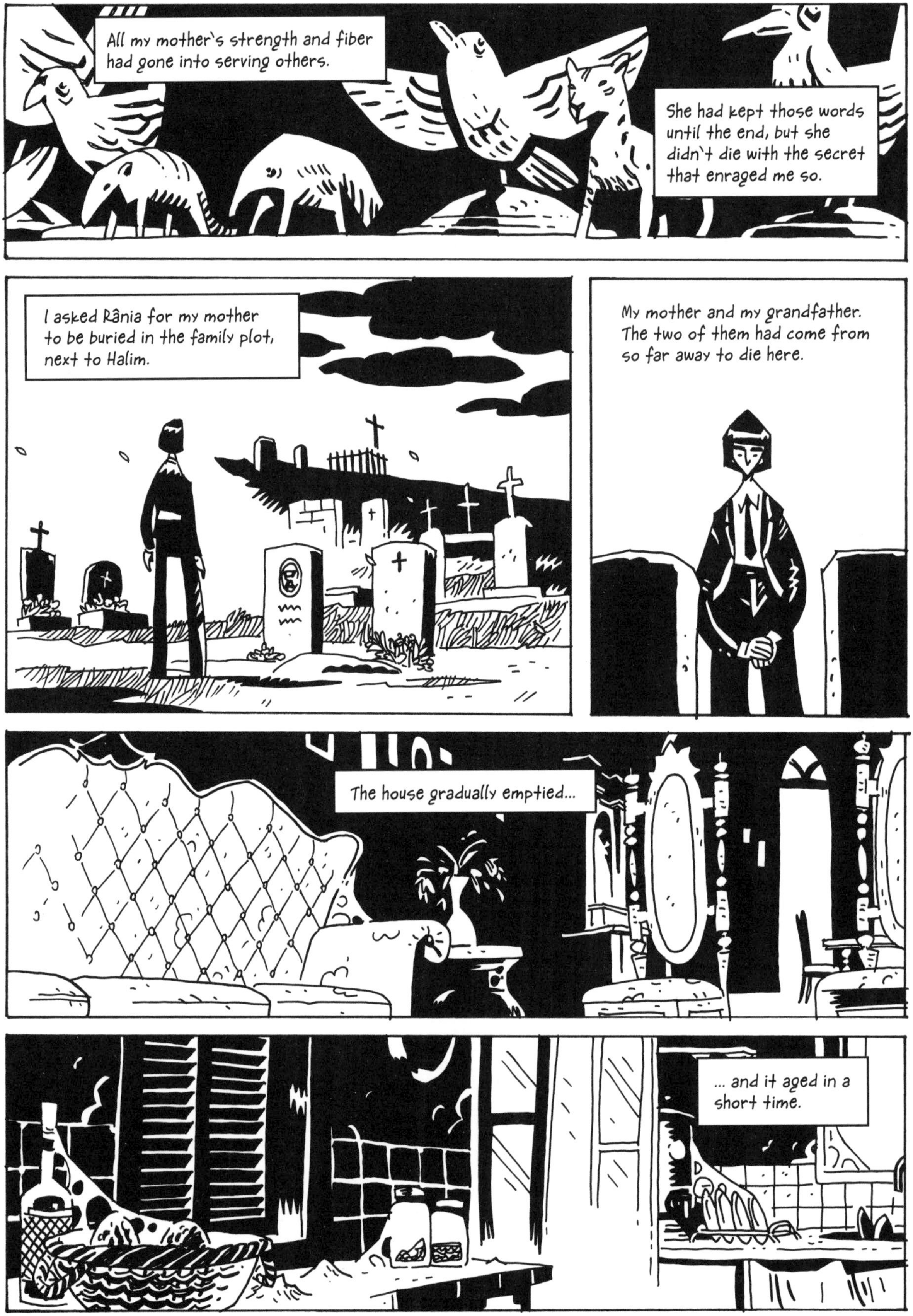
All my mother's strength and fiber had gone into serving others.
She had kept those words until the end, but she didn't die with the secret that enraged me so.
I asked Rânia for my mother to be buried in the family plot, next to Halim.
My mother and my grandfather. The two of them had come from so far away to die here.
The house gradually emptied...
... and it aged in a short time.

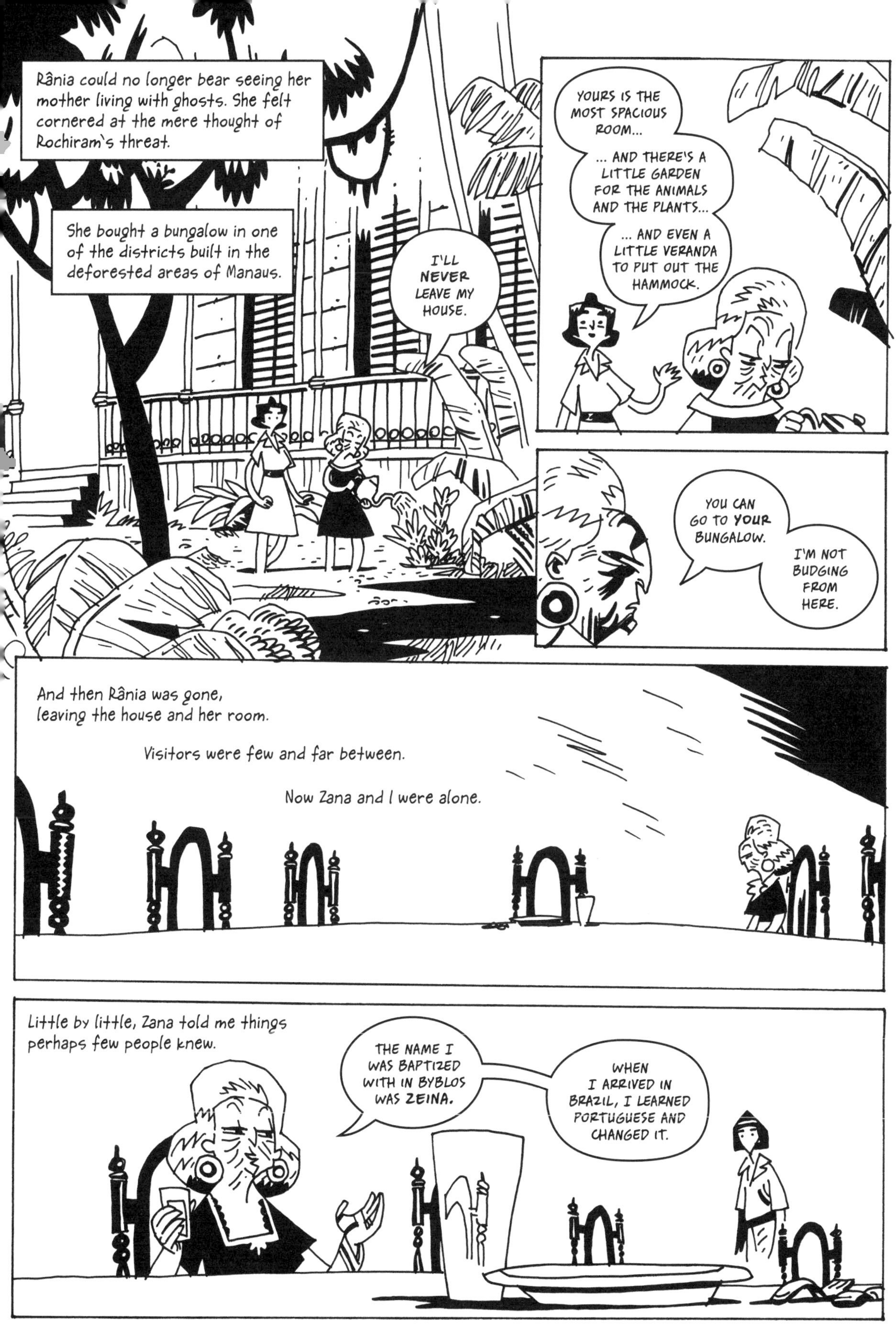
Rânia could no longer bear seeing her mother living with ghosts. She felt cornered at the mere thought of Rochiram's threat.
She bought a bungalow in one of the districts built in the deforested areas of Manaus.
I'LL NEVER LEAVE MY HOUSE.
YOURS IS THE MOST SPACIOUS ROOM...
... AND THERE'S A LITTLE GARDEN FOR THE ANIMALS AND THE PLANTS...
... AND EVEN A LITTLE VERANDA TO PUT OUT THE HAMMOCK.
YOU CAN GO TO YOUR BUNGALOW.
I'M NOT BUDGING FROM HERE.
And then Rânia was gone, leaving the house and her room.
Visitors were few and far between.
Now Zana and I were alone.
Little by little, Zana told me things perhaps few people knew.
THE NAME I WAS BAPTIZED WITH IN BYBLOS WAS ZEINA.
WHEN I ARRIVED IN BRAZIL, I LEARNED PORTUGUESE AND CHANGED IT.

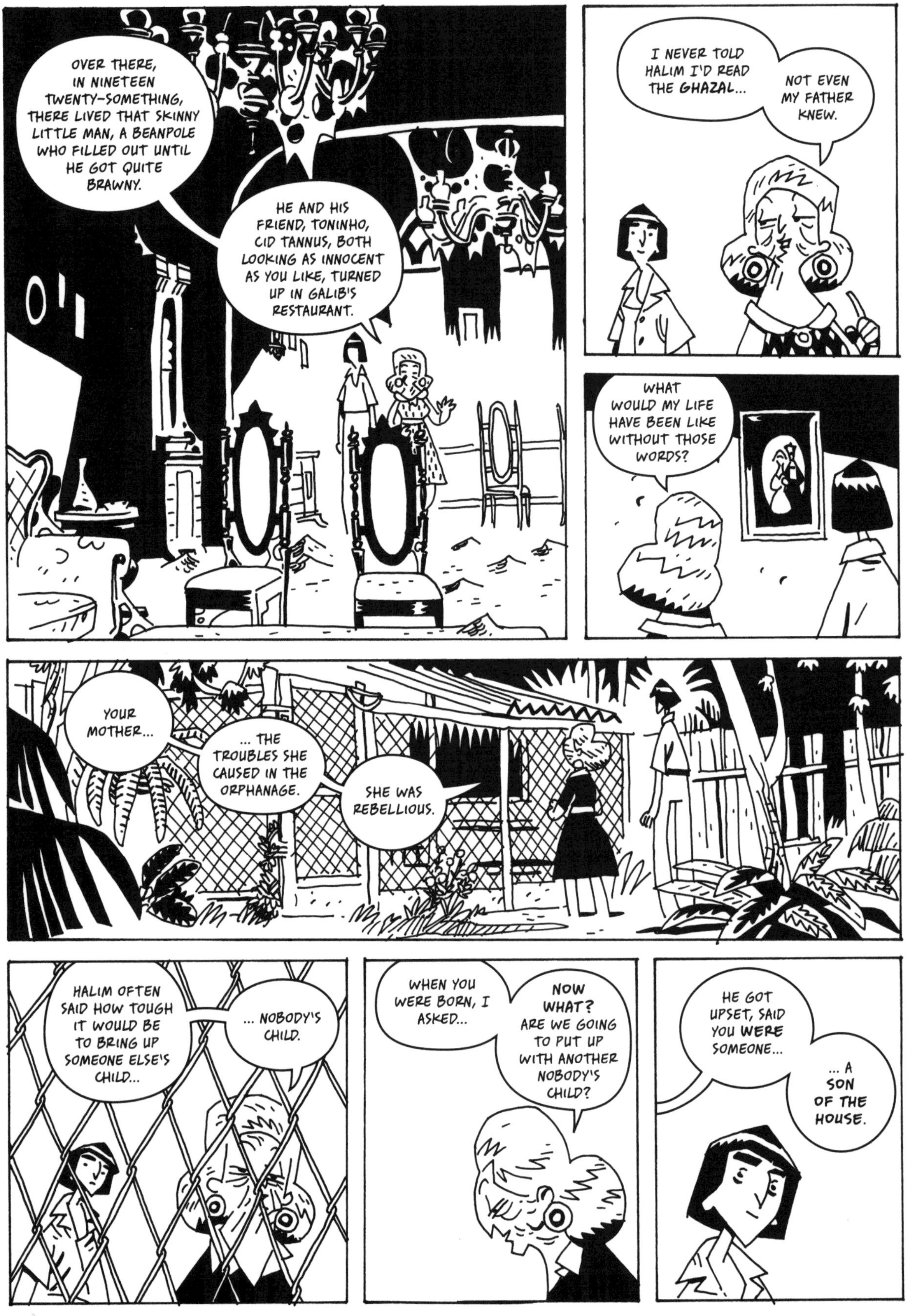
OVER THERE, IN NINETEEN TWENTY-SOMETHING, THERE LIVED THAT SKINNY LITTLE MAN, A BEANPOLE WHO FILLED OUT UNTIL HE GOT QUITE BRAWNY.
HE AND HIS FRIEND, TONINHO, CID TANNUS, BOTH LOOKING AS INNOCENT AS YOU LIKE, TURNED UP IN GALIB'S RESTAURANT.
I NEVER TOLD HALIM I'D READ THE **GHAZAL**...
NOT EVEN MY FATHER KNEW.
WHAT WOULD MY LIFE HAVE BEEN LIKE WITHOUT THOSE WORDS?
YOUR MOTHER...
... THE TROUBLES SHE CAUSED IN THE ORPHANAGE.
SHE WAS REBELLIOUS.
HALIM OFTEN SAID HOW TOUGH IT WOULD BE TO BRING UP SOMEONE ELSE'S CHILD...
... NOBODY'S CHILD.
WHEN YOU WERE BORN, I ASKED...
NOW WHAT? ARE WE GOING TO PUT UP WITH ANOTHER NOBODY'S CHILD?
HE GOT UPSET, SAID YOU **WERE** SOMEONE...
... A **SON OF THE HOUSE.**

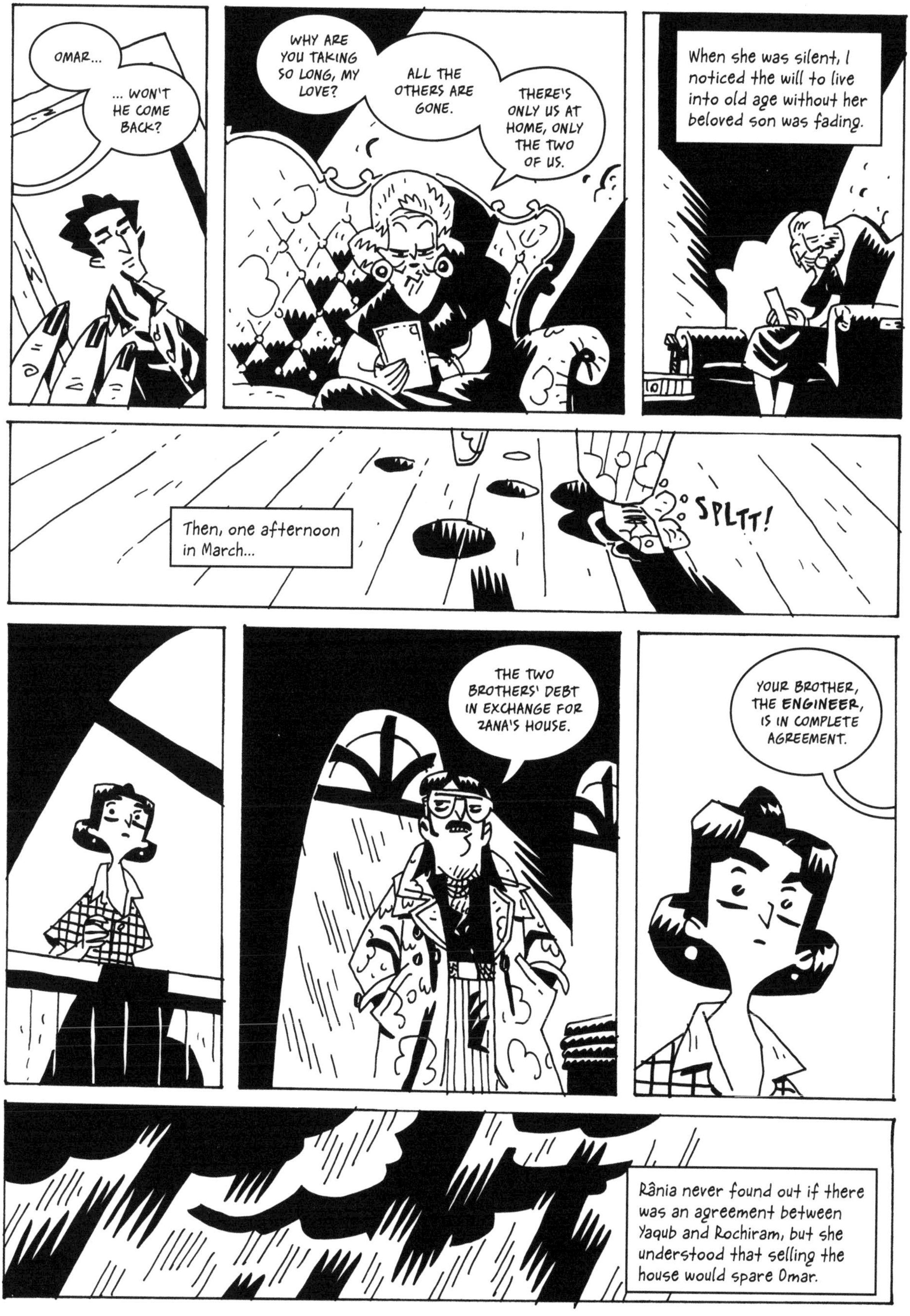
OMAR...
... WON'T HE COME BACK?
WHY ARE YOU TAKING SO LONG, MY LOVE?
ALL THE OTHERS ARE GONE.
THERE'S ONLY US AT HOME, ONLY THE TWO OF US.
When she was silent, I noticed the will to live into old age without her beloved son was fading.
Then, one afternoon in March...
SPLTT!
THE TWO BROTHERS' DEBT IN EXCHANGE FOR ZANA'S HOUSE.
YOUR BROTHER, THE **ENGINEER**, IS IN COMPLETE AGREEMENT.
Rânia never found out if there was an agreement between Yaqub and Rochiram, but she understood that selling the house would spare Omar.

MY HOUSE? ARE YOU MAD?

I DON'T WANT TO LEAVE THIS PLACE, RÂNIA.

I'M NOT GOING TO SELL MY HOUSE, YOU UNGRATEFUL WRETCH.

MY SON WILL COME BACK!

YOU'LL GET USED TO MY HOUSE, MOTHER.

Zana signed the letter of sale a few days later, in a clinic in Rânia's neighborhood. It must have been her last attempt to reconcile her sons.

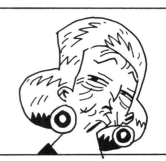

She left before the final act.

I was alone in the house, with the shadows of those who had lived there.

The absolute master, even if only for a short time, of a handsome house in the vicinity of the Manaus harbor.

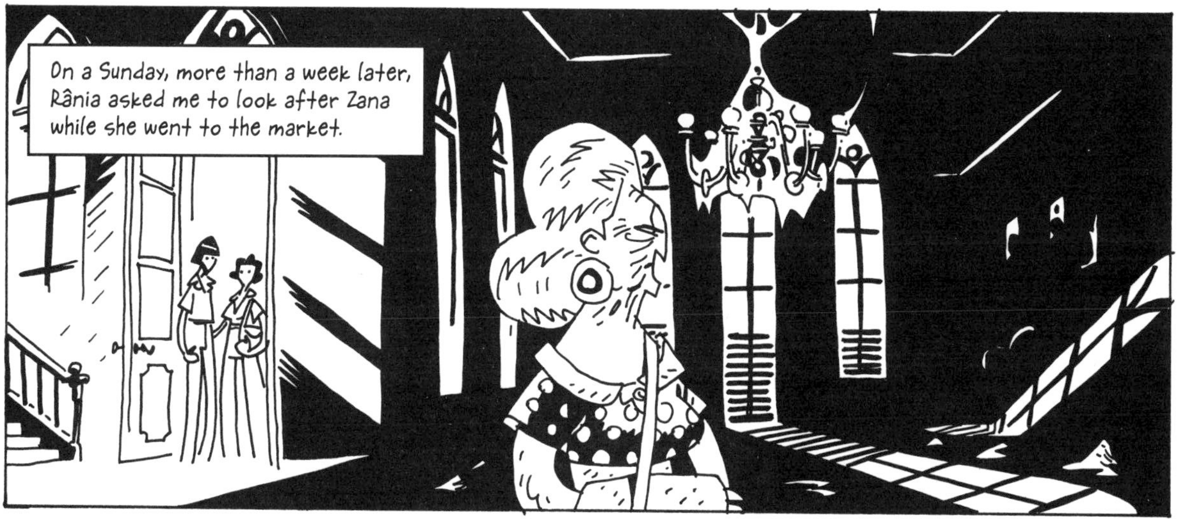
On a Sunday, more than a week later, Rânia asked me to look after Zana while she went to the market.

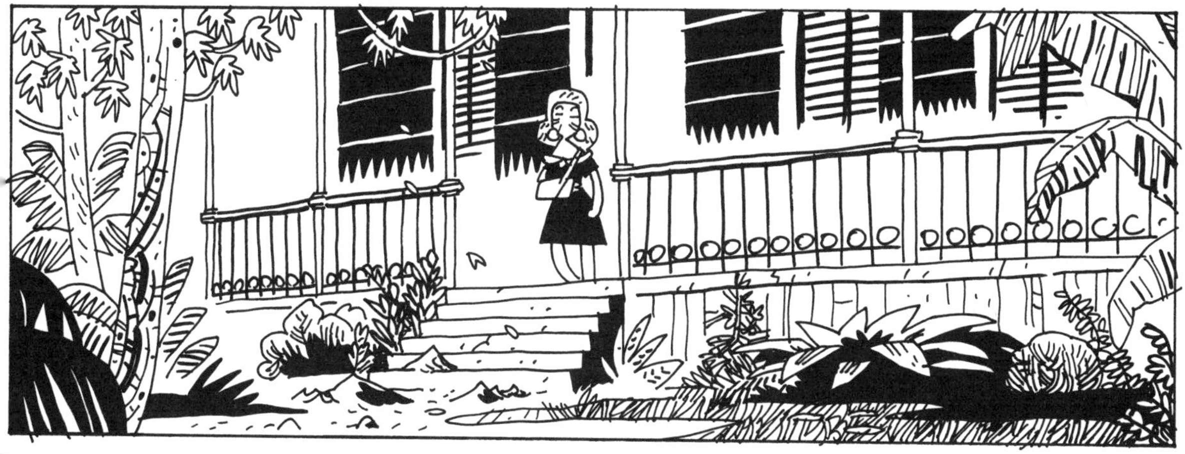

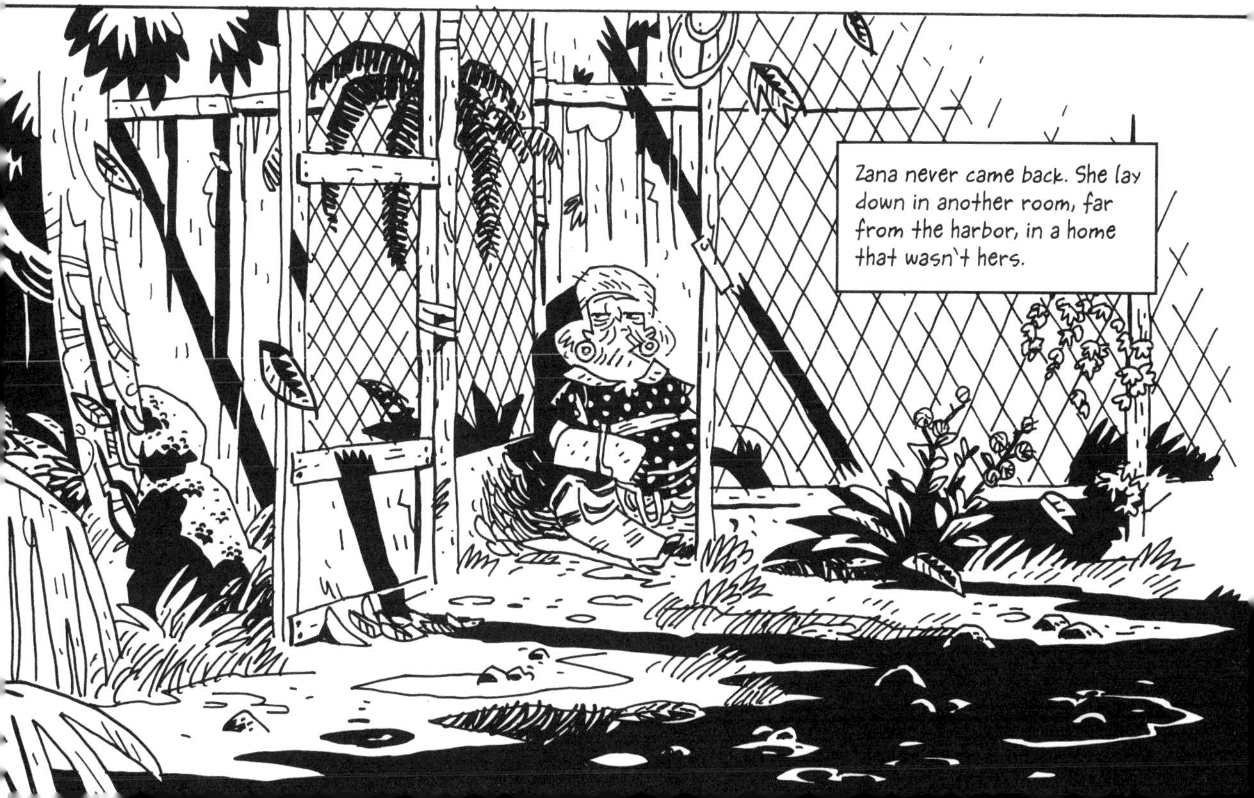
Zana never came back. She lay down in another room, far from the harbor, in a home that wasn't hers.

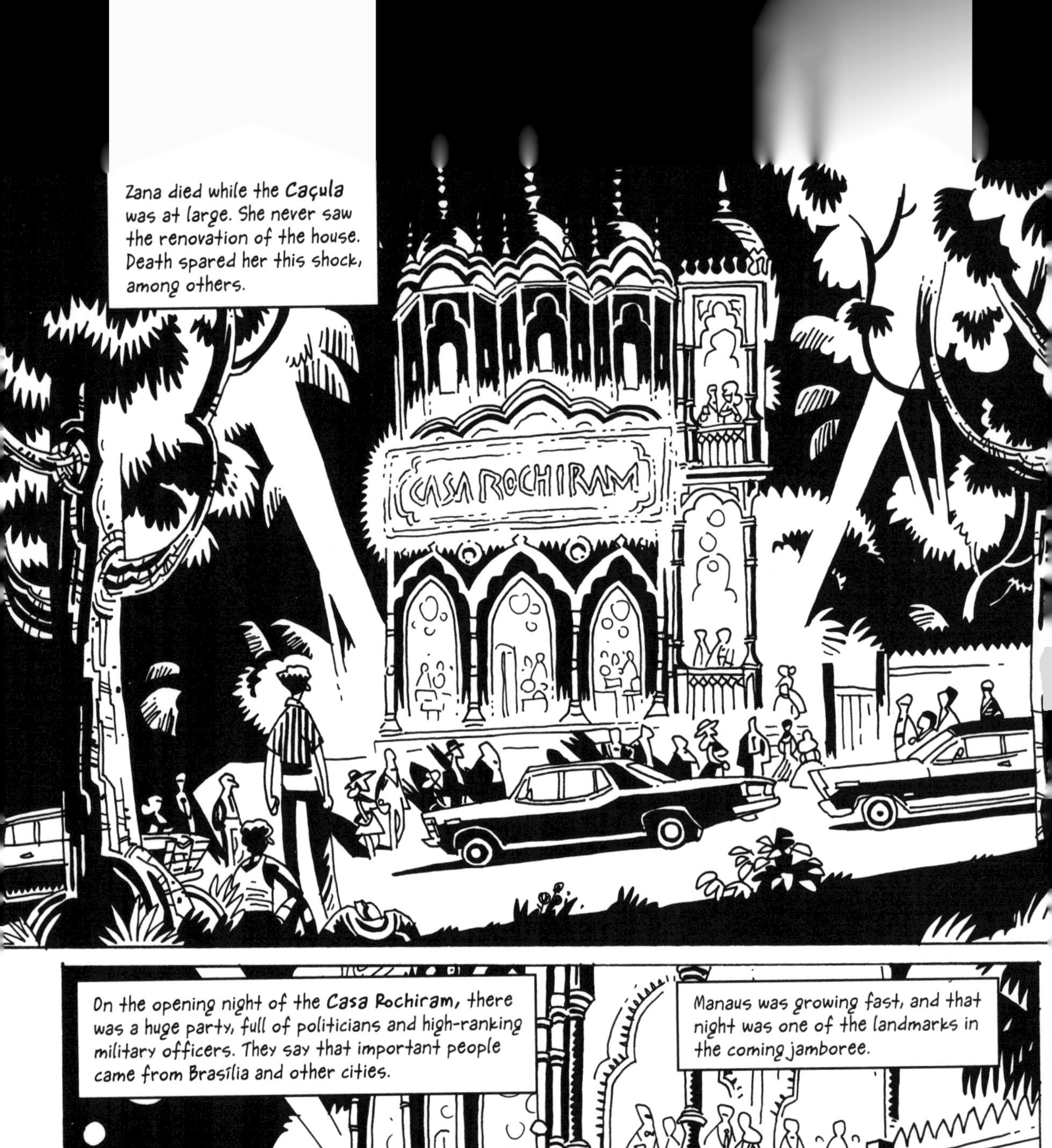
Zana died while the Caçula was at large. She never saw the renovation of the house. Death spared her this shock, among others.
CASA ROCHIRAM

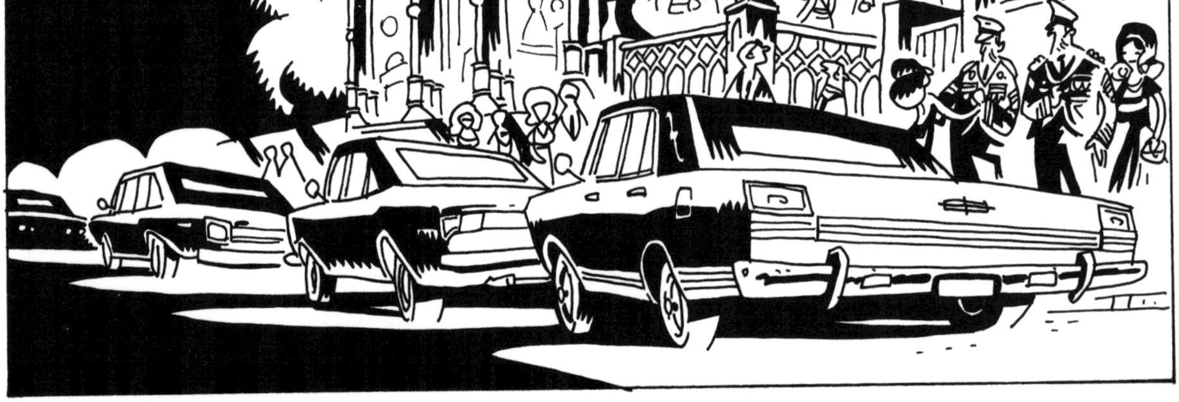
On the opening night of the Casa Rochiram, there was a huge party, full of politicians and high-ranking military officers. They say that important people came from Brasília and other cities.
Manaus was growing fast, and that night was one of the landmarks in the coming jamboree.

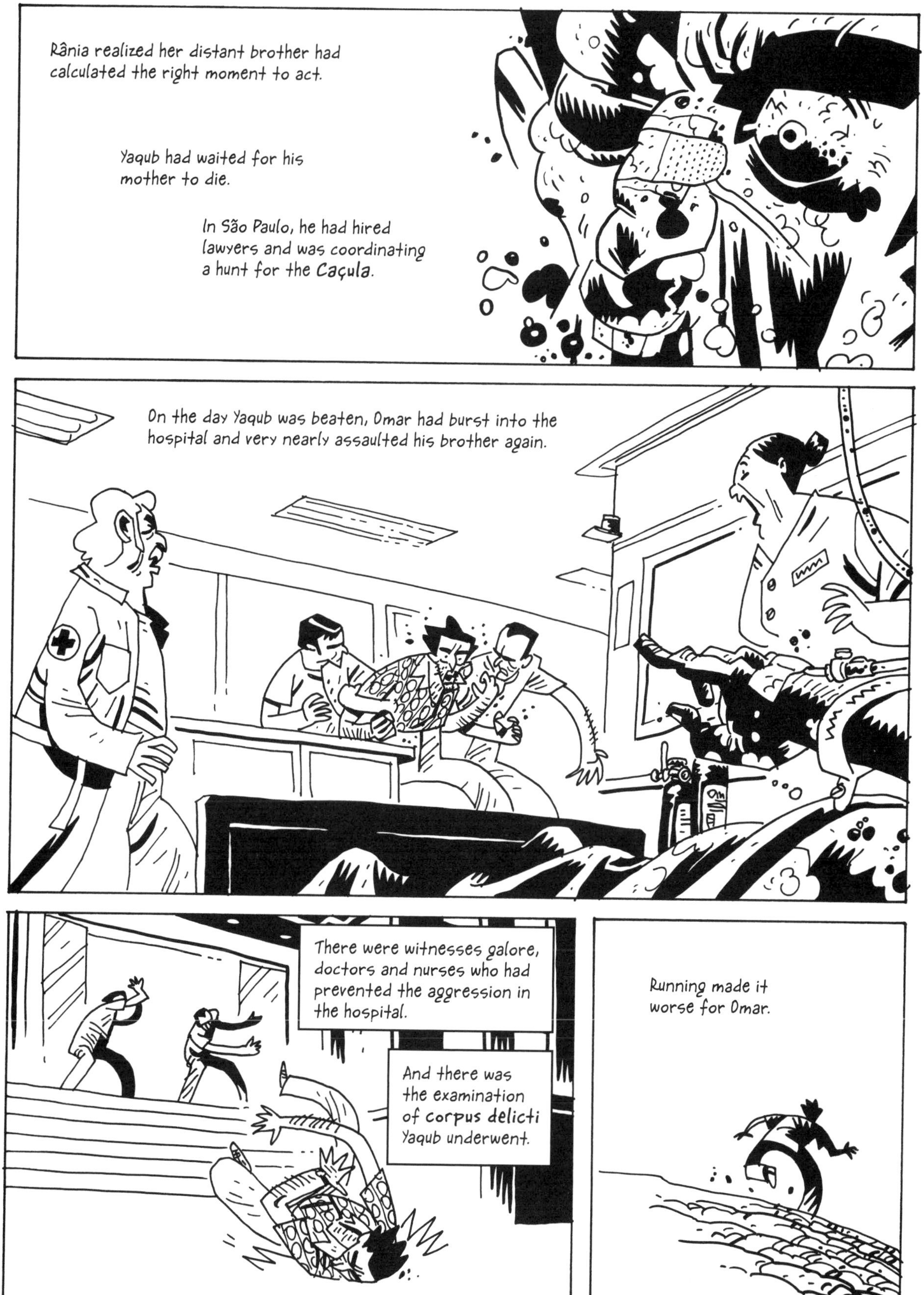
Rânia realized her distant brother had calculated the right moment to act.
Yaqub had waited for his mother to die.
In São Paulo, he had hired lawyers and was coordinating a hunt for the Caçula.
On the day Yaqub was beaten, Omar had burst into the hospital and very nearly assaulted his brother again.
There were witnesses galore, doctors and nurses who had prevented the aggression in the hospital.
And there was the examination of corpus delicti Yaqub underwent.
Running made it worse for Omar.

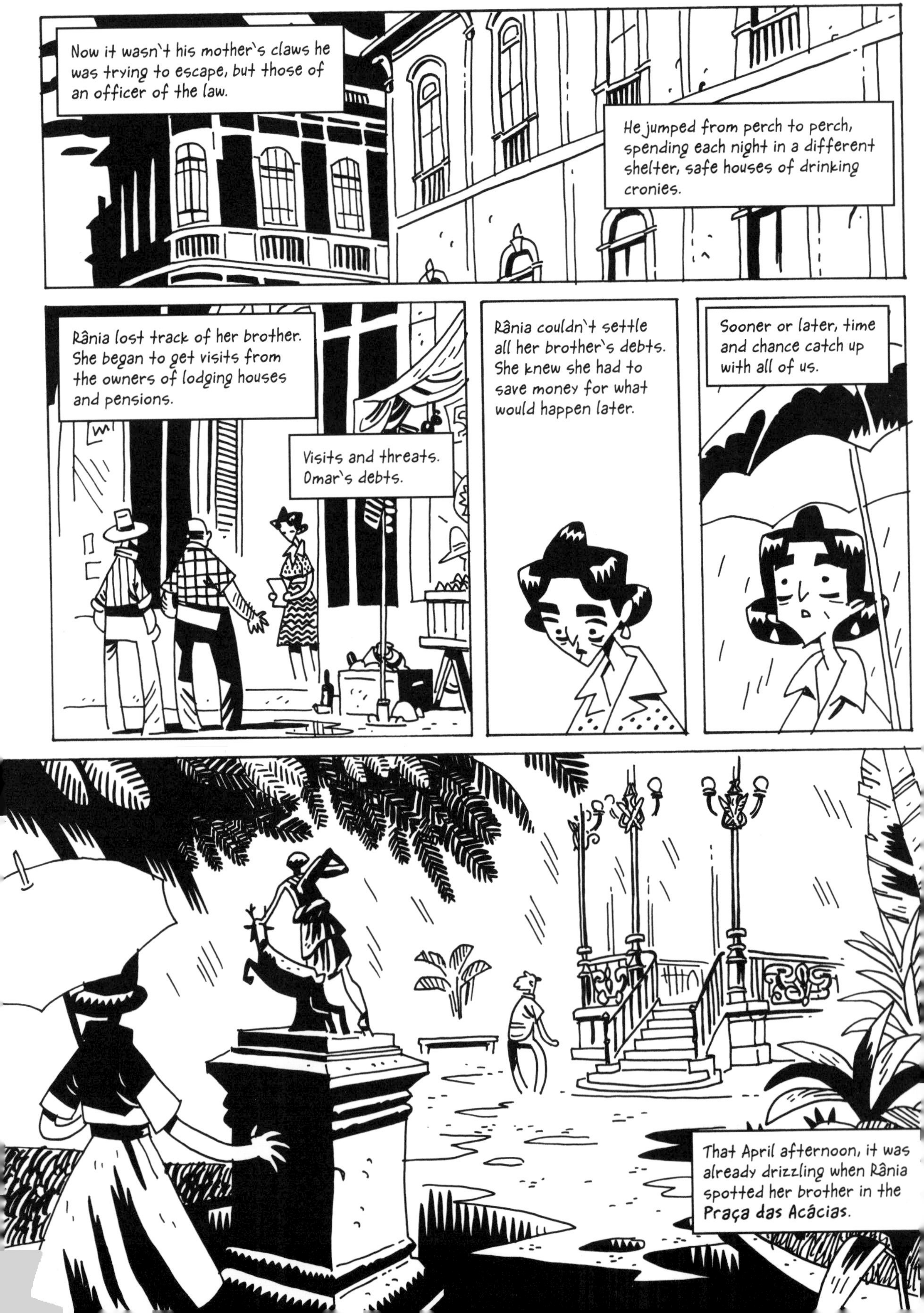
Now it wasn't his mother's claws he was trying to escape, but those of an officer of the law.
He jumped from perch to perch, spending each night in a different shelter, safe houses of drinking cronies.
Rânia lost track of her brother. She began to get visits from the owners of lodging houses and pensions.
Visits and threats. Omar's debts.
Rânia couldn't settle all her brother's debts. She knew she had to save money for what would happen later.
Sooner or later, time and chance catch up with all of us.
That April afternoon, it was already drizzling when Rânia spotted her brother in the Praça das Acácias.

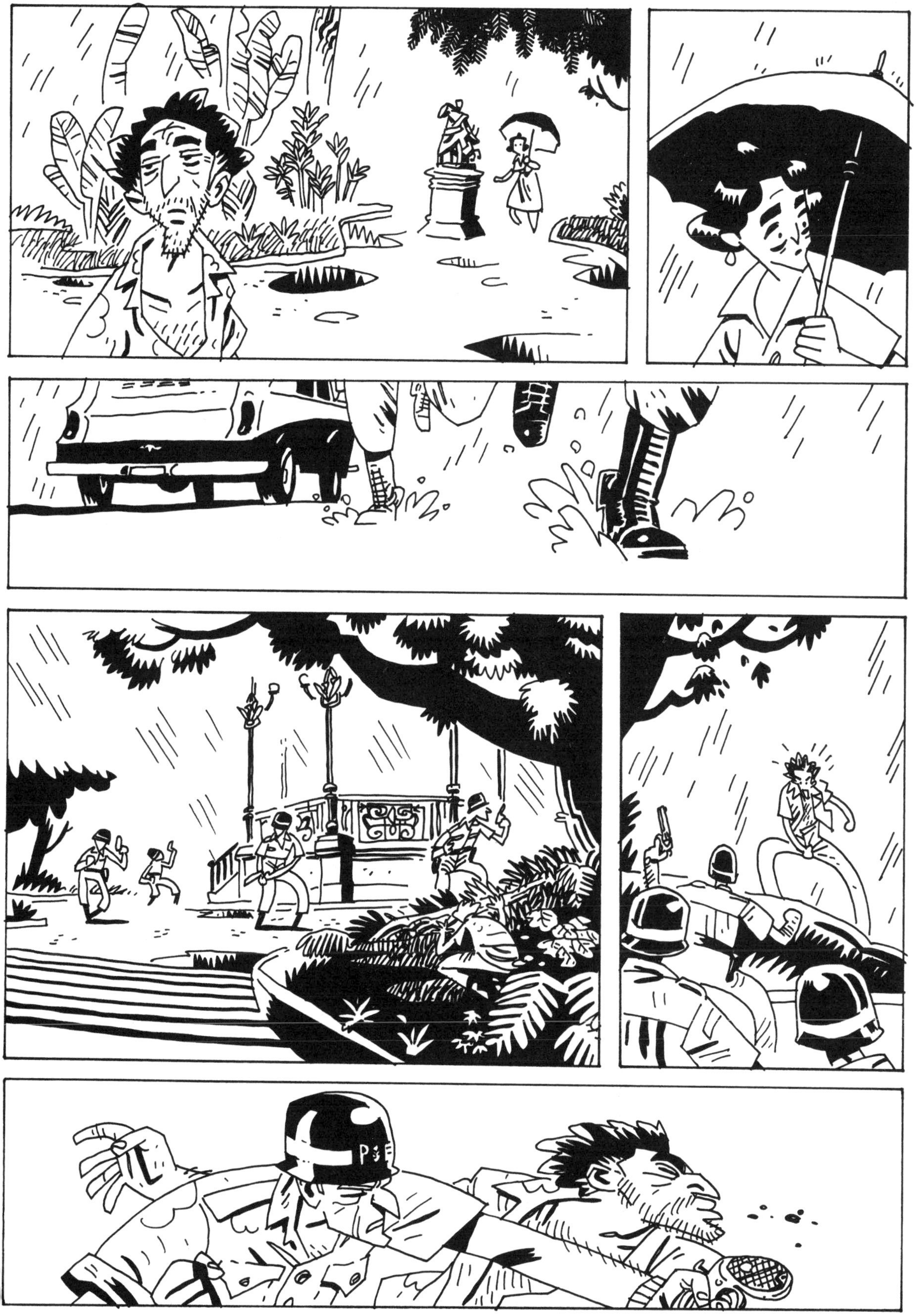

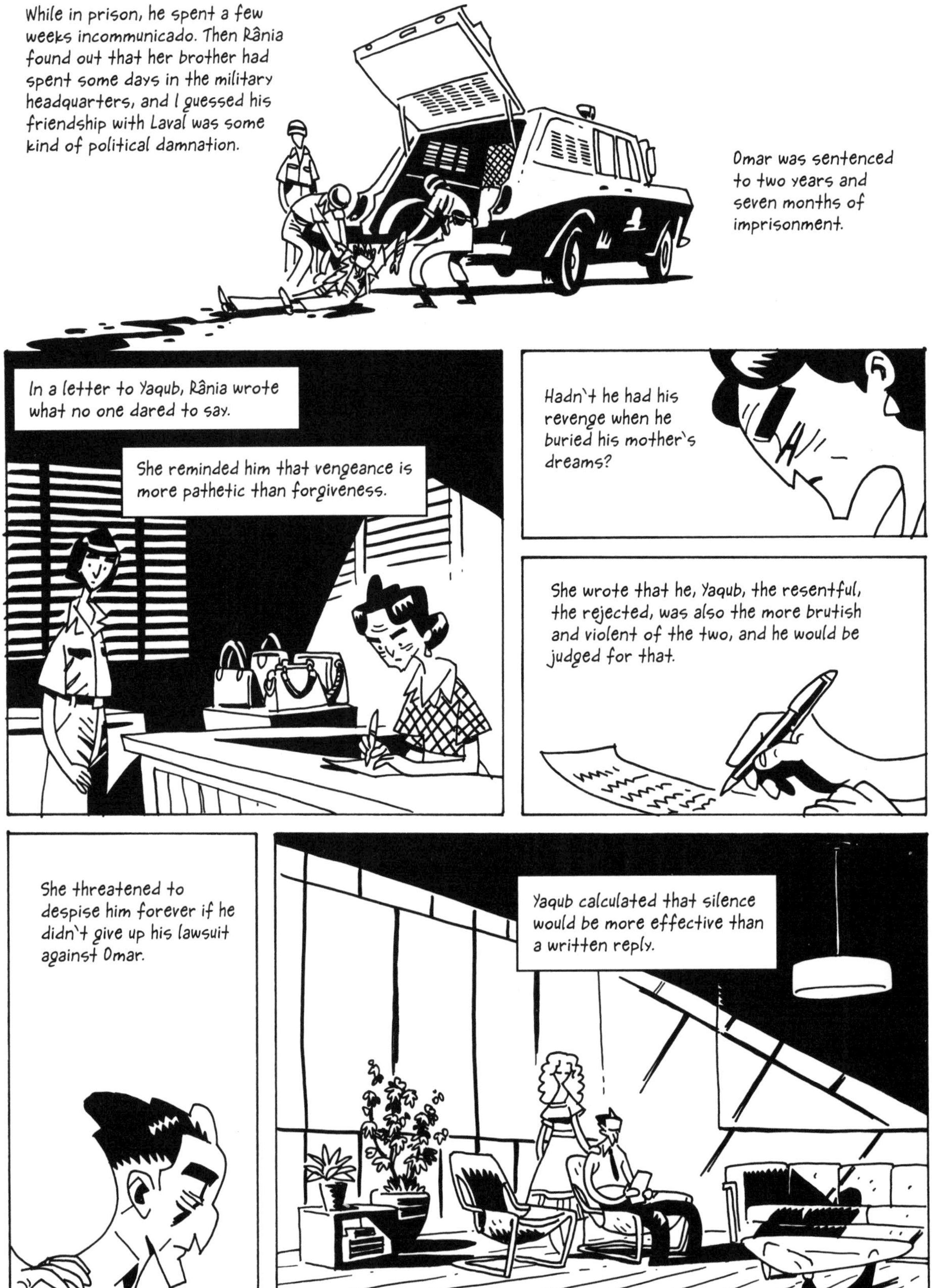
While in prison, he spent a few weeks incommunicado. Then Rânia found out that her brother had spent some days in the military headquarters, and I guessed his friendship with Laval was some kind of political damnation.
Omar was sentenced to two years and seven months of imprisonment.
In a letter to Yaqub, Rânia wrote what no one dared to say.
She reminded him that vengeance is more pathetic than forgiveness.
Hadn't he had his revenge when he buried his mother's dreams?
She wrote that he, Yaqub, the resentful, the rejected, was also the more brutish and violent of the two, and he would be judged for that.
She threatened to despise him forever if he didn't give up his lawsuit against Omar.
Yaqub calculated that silence would be more effective than a written reply.

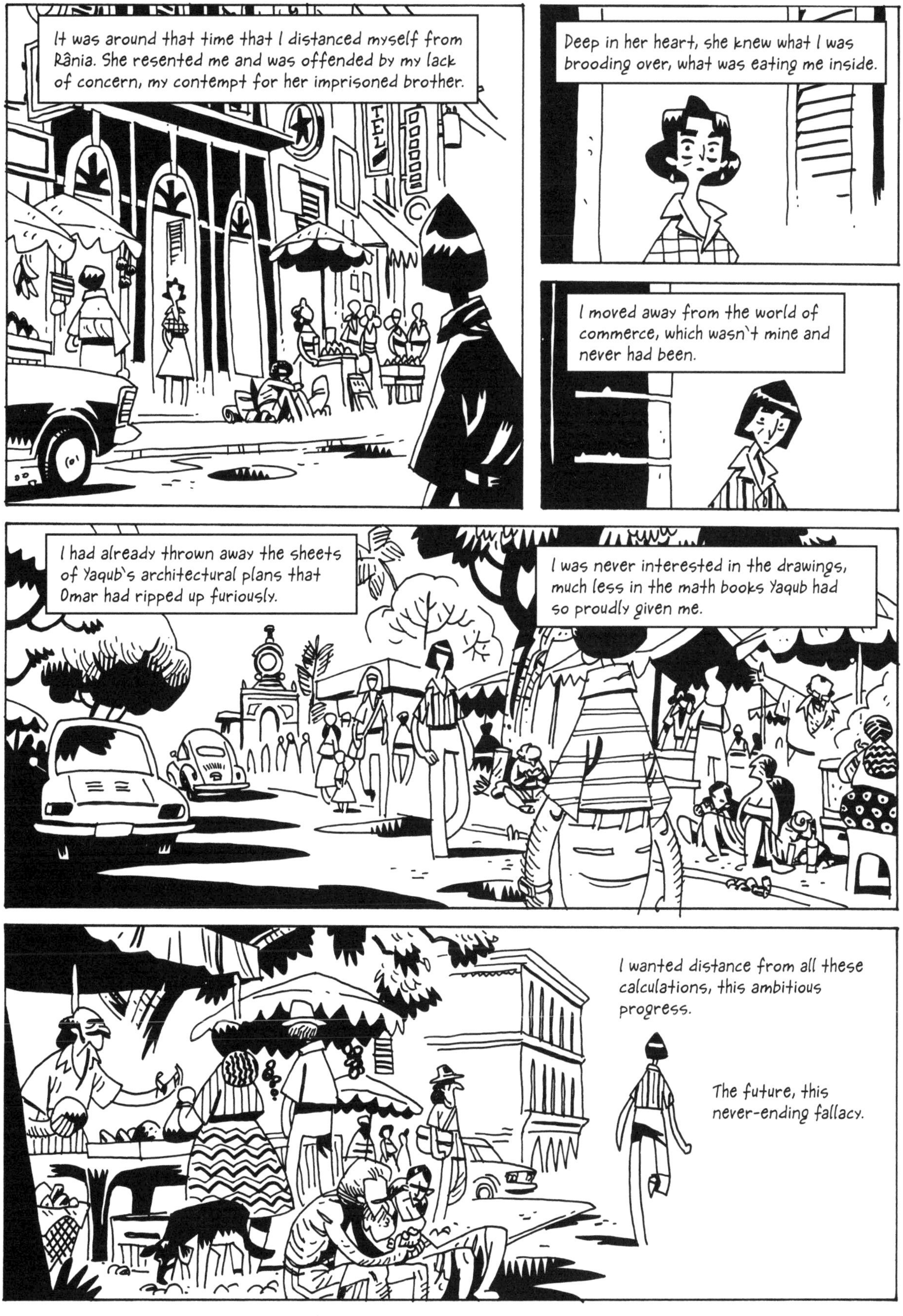
It was around that time that I distanced myself from Rânia. She resented me and was offended by my lack of concern, my contempt for her imprisoned brother.
Deep in her heart, she knew what I was brooding over, what was eating me inside.
I moved away from the world of commerce, which wasn't mine and never had been.
I had already thrown away the sheets of Yaqub's architectural plans that Omar had ripped up furiously.
I was never interested in the drawings, much less in the math books Yaqub had so proudly given me.
I wanted distance from all these calculations, this ambitious progress.
The future, this never-ending fallacy.

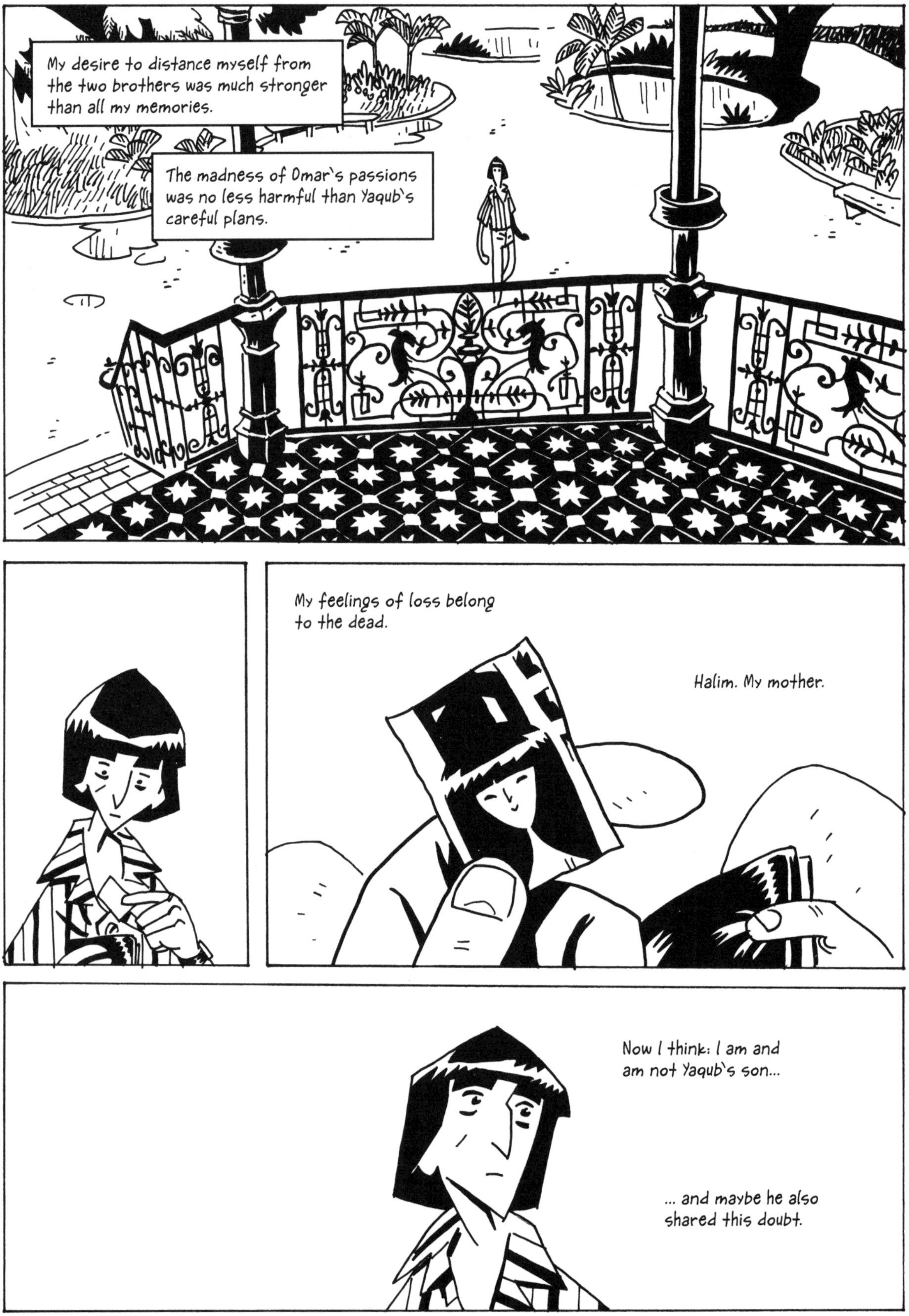
My desire to distance myself from the two brothers was much stronger than all my memories.
The madness of Omar`s passions was no less harmful than Yaqub`s careful plans.
My feelings of loss belong to the dead.
Halim. My mother.
Now I think: I am and am not Yaqub`s son...
... and maybe he also shared this doubt.

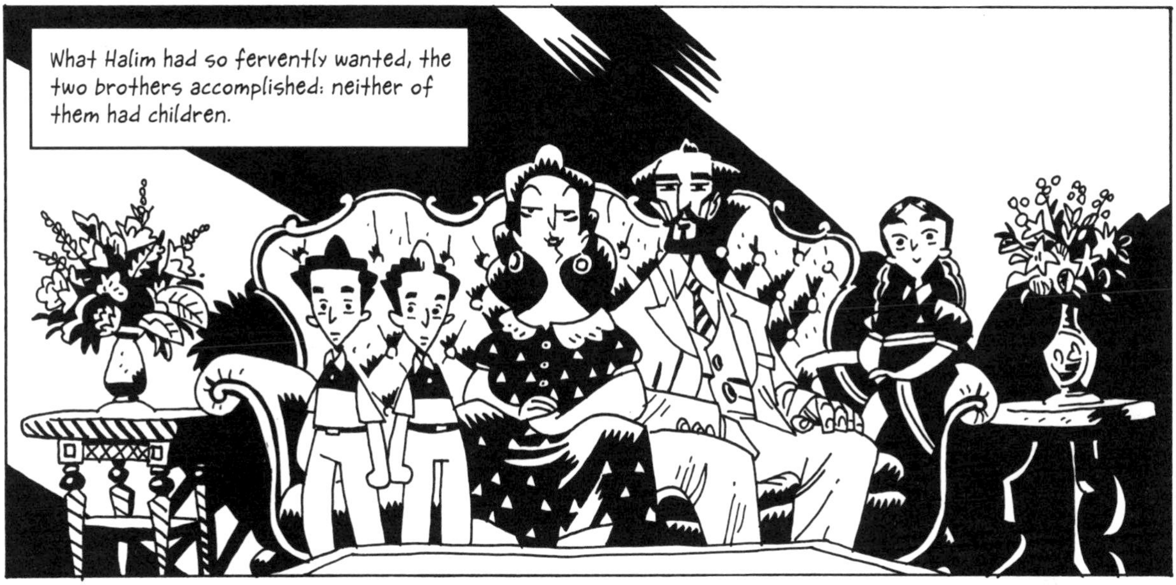
What Halim had so fervently wanted, the two brothers accomplished: neither of them had children.

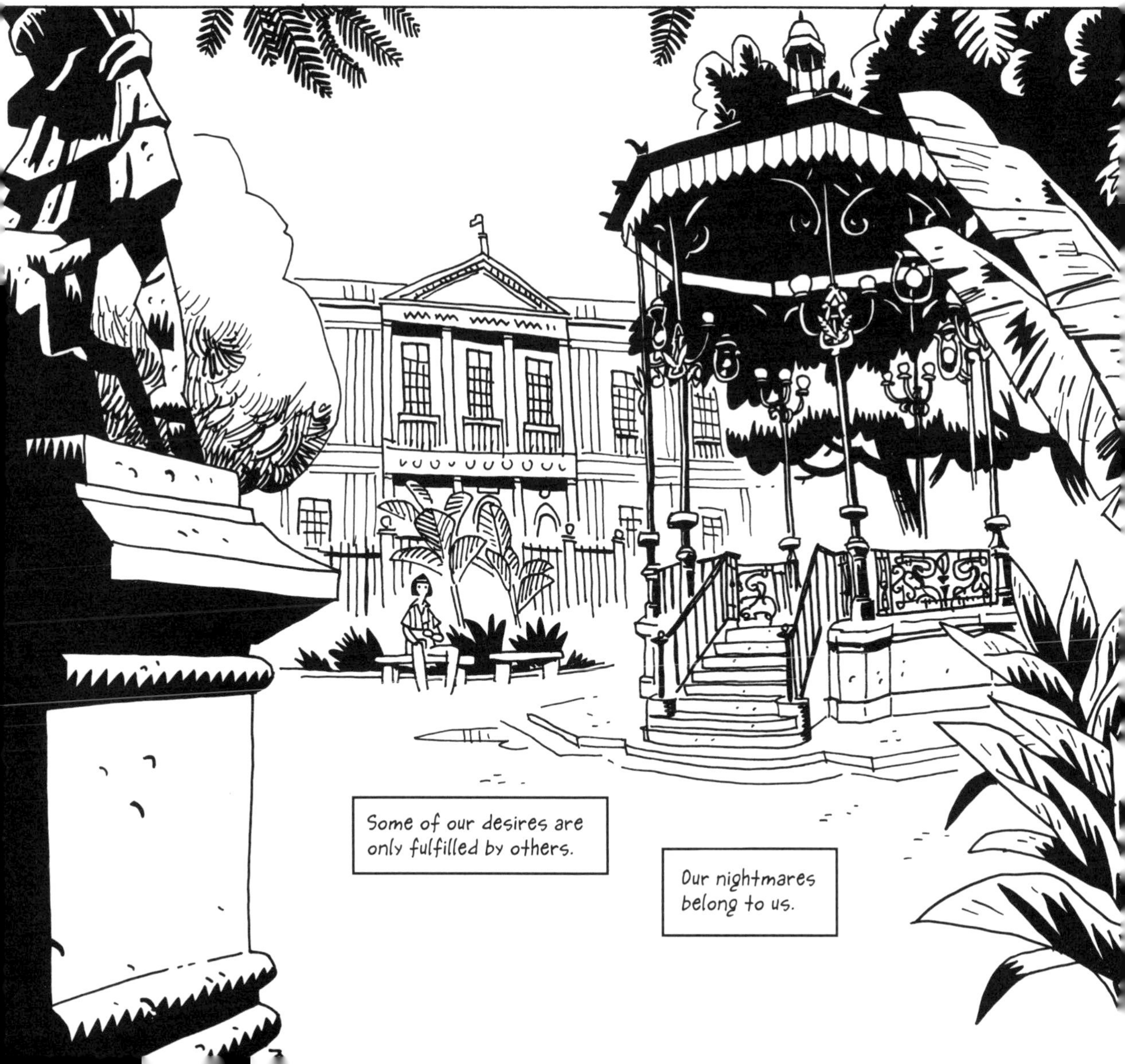
Some of our desires are only fulfilled by others.
Our nightmares belong to us.

Epilogue

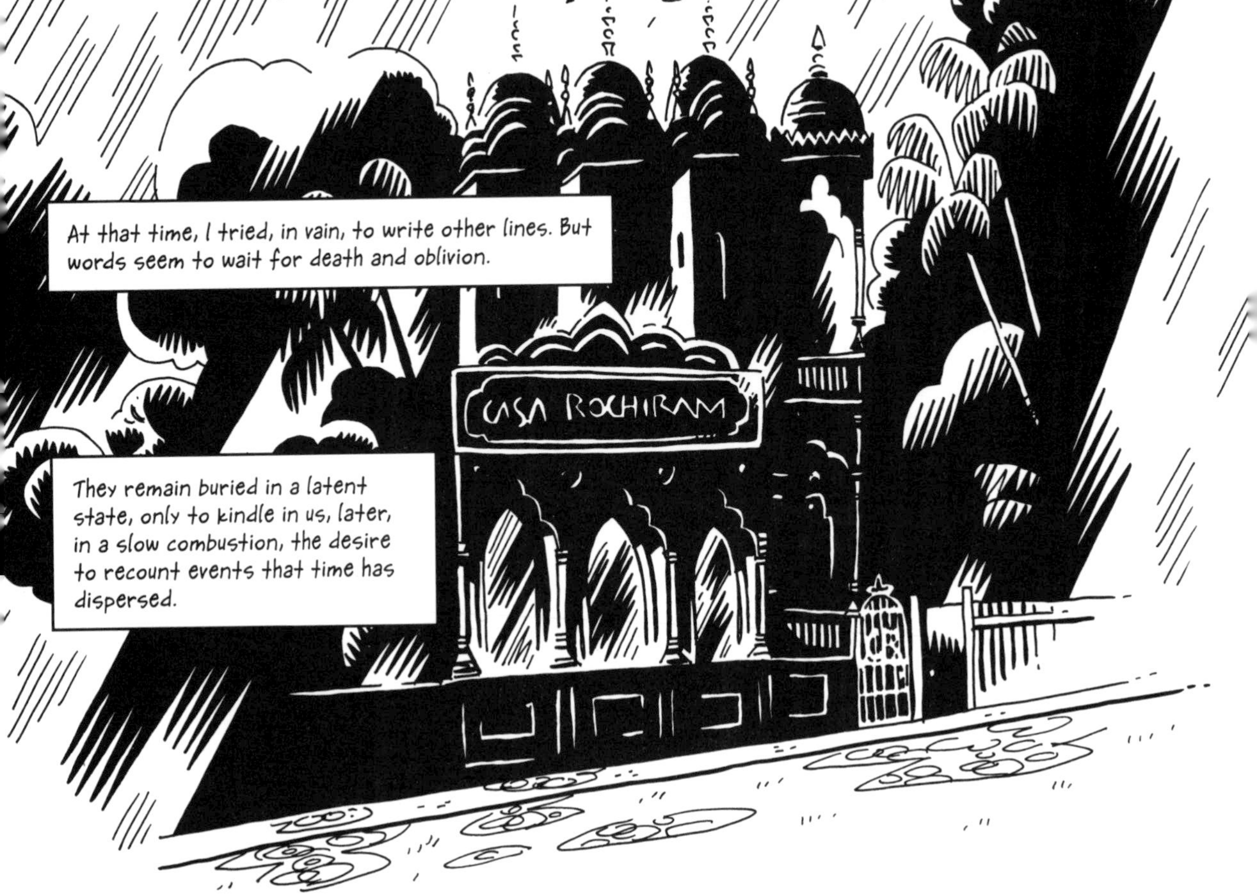
At that time, I tried, in vain, to write other lines. But words seem to wait for death and oblivion.
CASA ROCHIRAM
They remain buried in a latent state, only to kindle in us, later, in a slow combustion, the desire to recount events that time has dispersed.

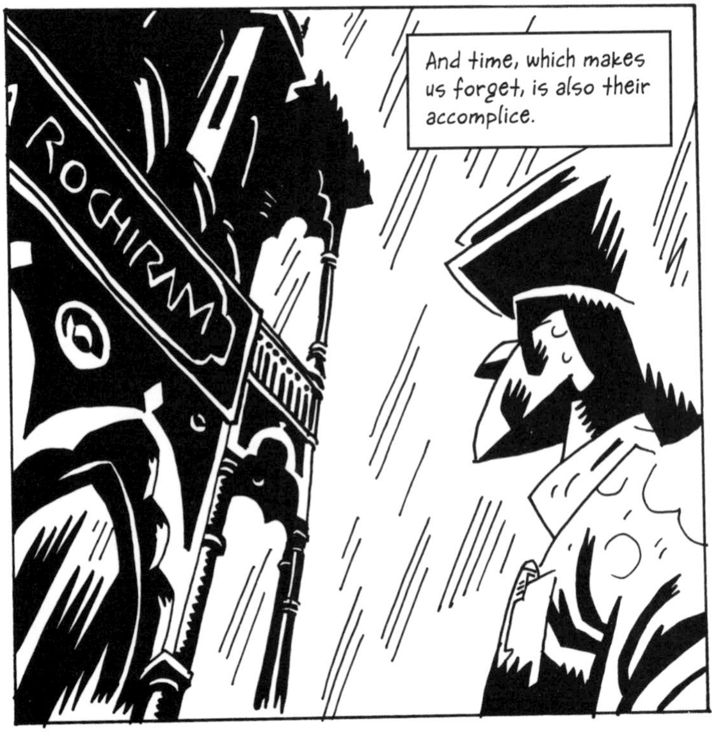
ROCHIRAM
And time, which makes us forget, is also their accomplice.

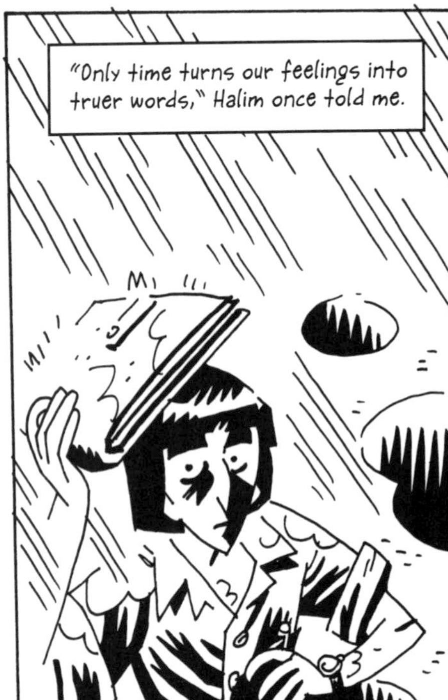
"Only time turns our feelings into truer words," Halim once told me.

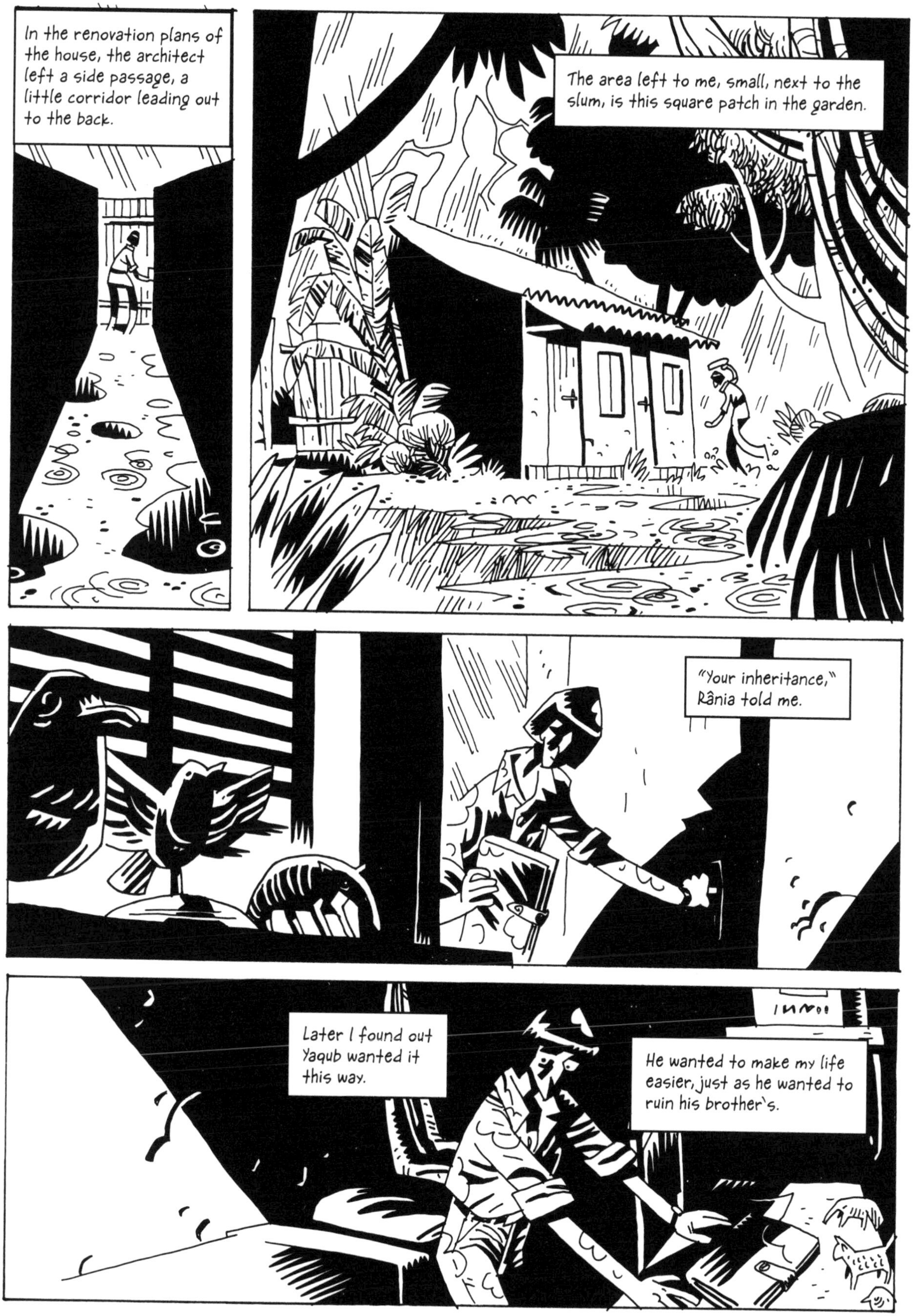
In the renovation plans of the house, the architect left a side passage, a little corridor leading out to the back.
The area left to me, small, next to the slum, is this square patch in the garden.
"Your inheritance," Rânia told me.
Later I found out Yaqub wanted it this way.
He wanted to make my life easier, just as he wanted to ruin his brother's.

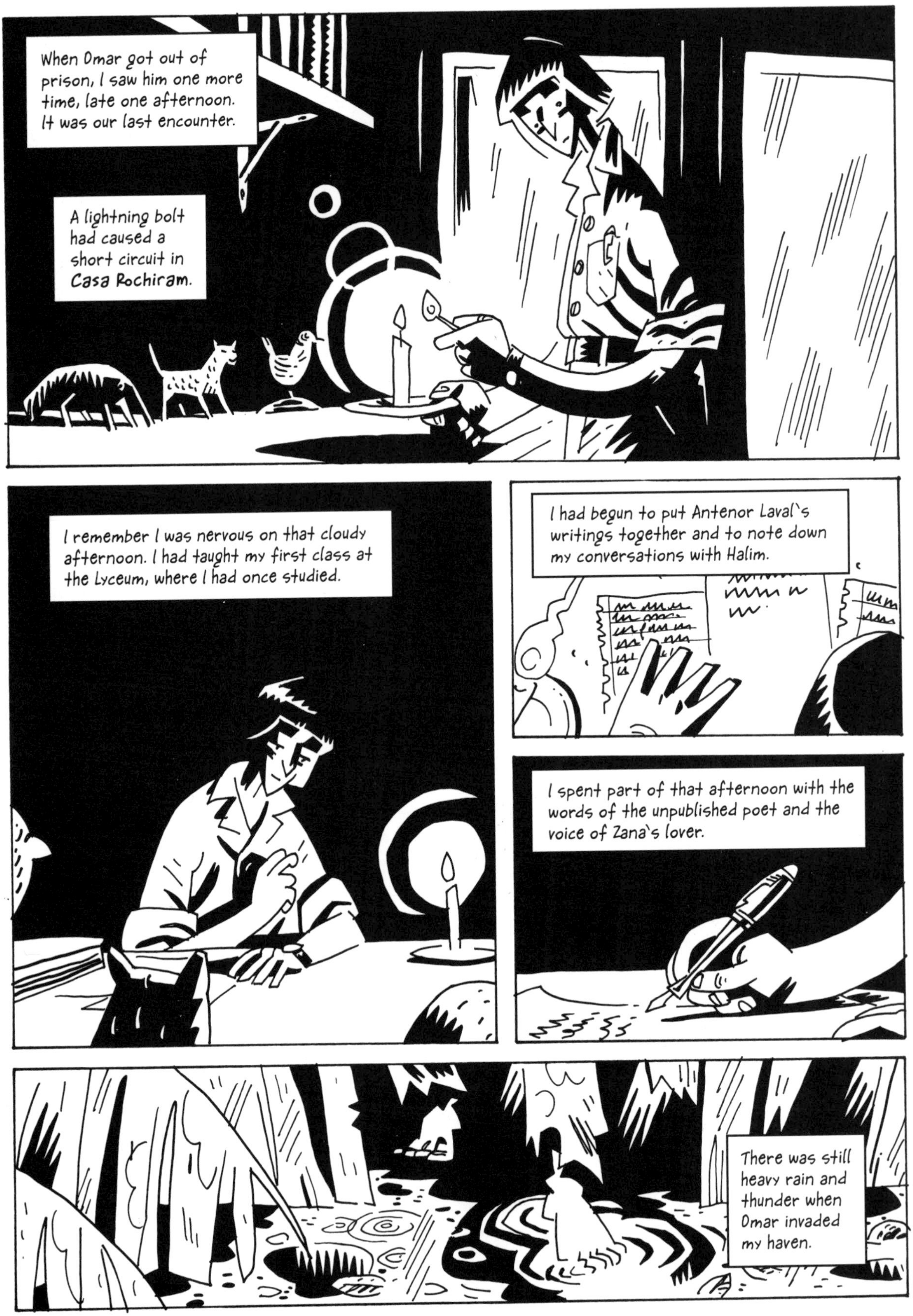
When Omar got out of prison, I saw him one more time, late one afternoon. It was our last encounter.
A lightning bolt had caused a short circuit in Casa Rochiram.
I remember I was nervous on that cloudy afternoon. I had taught my first class at the Lyceum, where I had once studied.
I had begun to put Antenor Laval's writings together and to note down my conversations with Halim.
I spent part of that afternoon with the words of the unpublished poet and the voice of Zana's lover.
There was still heavy rain and thunder when Omar invaded my haven.

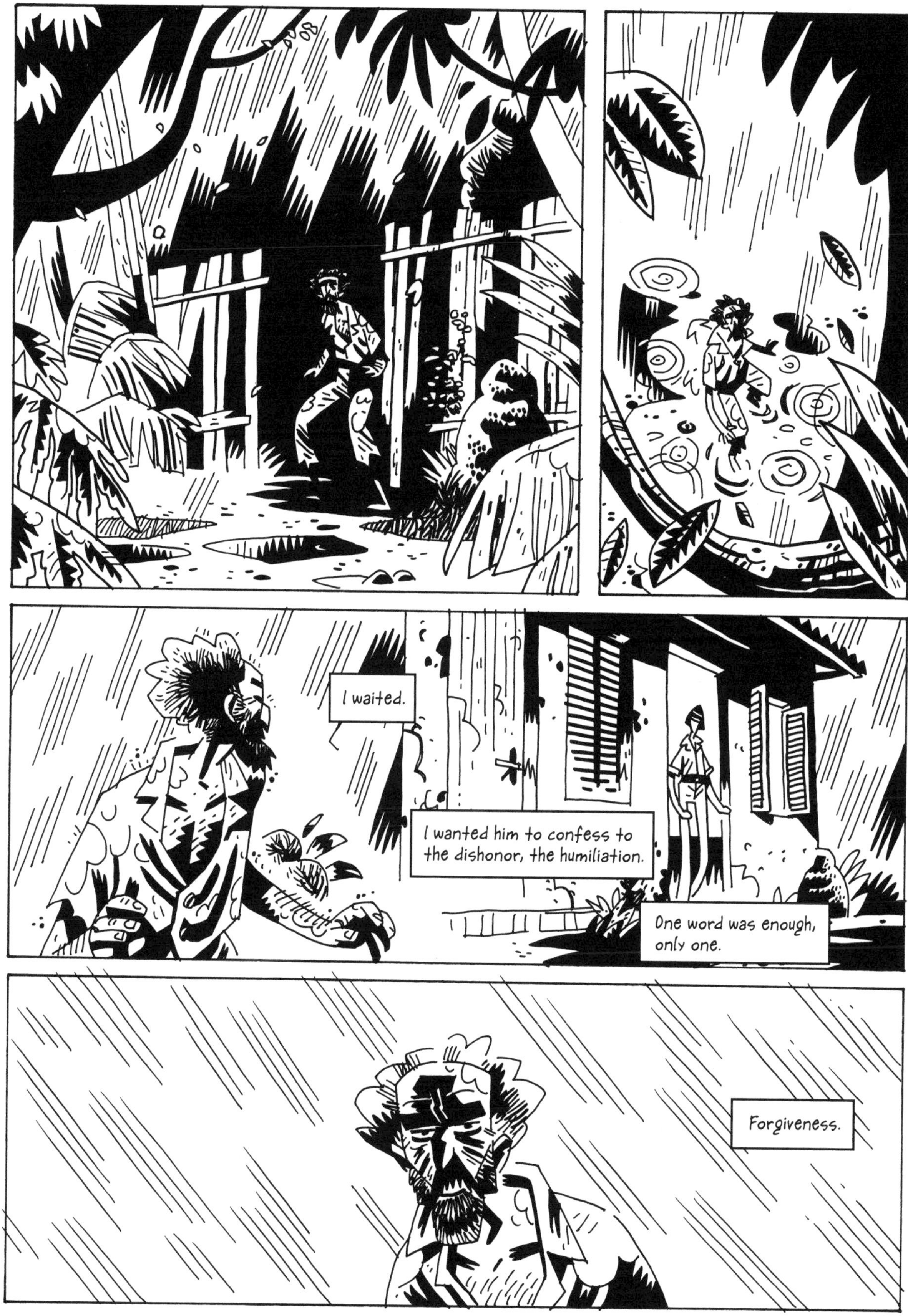
I waited.
I wanted him to confess to the dishonor, the humiliation.
One word was enough, only one.
Forgiveness.

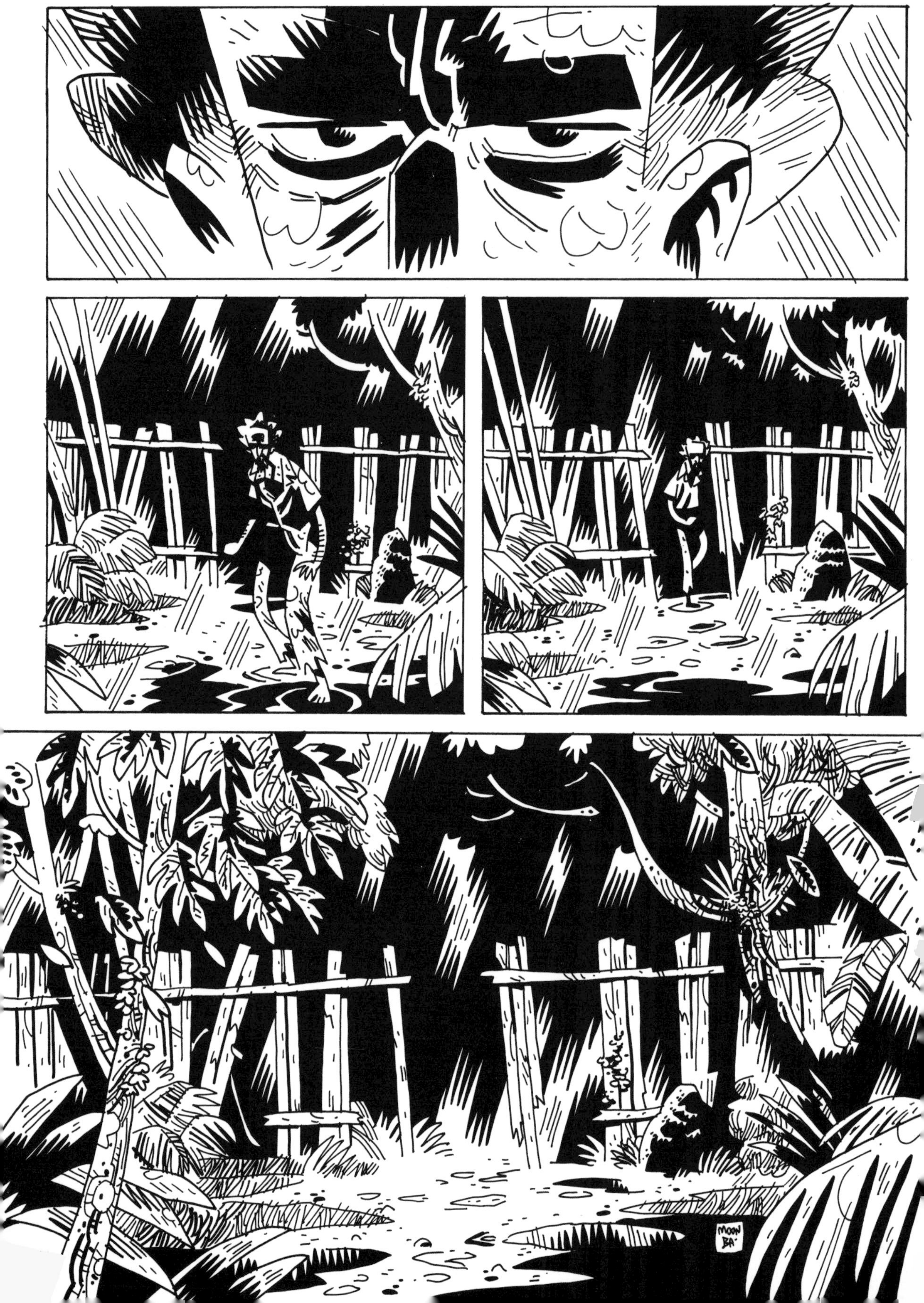
MOON BA